Ius Comparatum - Global Studies in Comparative Law

Volume 56

As globalization proceeds, the significance of the comparative approach in legal scholarship increases. The IACL / AIDC with almost 800 members is the major universal organization promoting comparative research in law and organizing congresses with hundreds of participants in all parts of the world. The results of those congresses should be disseminated and be available for legal scholars in a single book series which would make both the Academy and its contribution to comparative law more visible. The series aims to publish the scholarship emerging from the congresses of IACL / AIDC, including: 1. of the General Congresses of Comparative Law, which take place every 4 years (Brisbane 2002; Utrecht 2006, Washington 2010, Vienna 2014, Fukuoka 2018 etc.) and which generate (a) one volume of General Reports edited by the local organizers of the Congress; (b) up to 30 volumes of selected thematic reports dealing with the topics of the single sections of the congress and containing the General Report as well as the National Reports of that section; these volumes would be edited by the General Reporters of the respective sections; 2. the volumes containing selected contributions to the smaller (2-3 days) thematic congresses which take place between the International Congresses (Mexico 2008; Taipei 2012; Montevideo 2016 etc.); these congresses have a general theme such as "Codification" or "The Enforcement of Law" and will be edited by the local organizers of the respective Congress. All publications may contain contributions in English and French, the official languages of the Academy.

More information about this series at http://www.springer.com/series/11943

Académie Internationale de Droit Comparé
International Academy of Comparative Law

Cecilia Fresnedo de Aguirre
Editor

Legal Aspects of Cruises

Springer

Editor
Cecilia Fresnedo de Aguirre
University of the Republic
Montevideo, Uruguay

ISSN 2214-6881 ISSN 2214-689X (electronic)
Ius Comparatum - Global Studies in Comparative Law
ISBN 978-3-030-83089-2 ISBN 978-3-030-83090-8 (eBook)
https://doi.org/10.1007/978-3-030-83090-8

This Springer imprint is published by the registered company Springer Nature Switzerland AG.
The registered company address is: Gewerbestrasse 11, 6330 Cham, Switzerland

Contents

Part I
General Report

Legal Aspects of Cruises

Cecilia Fresnedo de Aguirre

Abstract This general report conducts a comparative study mainly on the following issues: (1) the importance of cruise business, (2) general and specific rules applicable to cruises, (3) cruise passengers as consumers, (4) package travels, (5) labour rules on cruises' workers, (6) rules on ports that are relevant to cruises, including taxes, costs and rates charged to cruises in different ports, (7) rules on environmental impact of cruises, (8) jurisdiction, arbitration, and choice of law in cruise contracts, and (9) general conditions used by companies offering cruise services, aiming at discovering which the existing sources of law on these matters are and whether they are appropriate and sufficient or not

1 Introduction

Carriage of passengers by sea has been an exceptional activity along history, due to the multiple perils and lack of security it had to face. Only crew members and some few people authorised by the captain travelled by sea. That situation changed dramatically when during the nineteenth century means and techniques of navigation were transformed, and carriage by sea stopped to be limited mainly to cargo and started to move great numbers of passengers from one continent to another. The development of commercial aviation after the Second World War had great impact in carriage of passengers by sea, but during the sixties and the seventies, the cruise industry started to be developed in an increasing manner.[1]

This General Report will be also published, together with the National Reports from each jurisdiction, by Springer Nature Switzerland in a thematic volume.

[1] Estepa Montero (2013), pp. 332–336.

C. Fresnedo de Aguirre (✉)
University of the Republic Uruguay, Montevideo, Uruguay

C. Fresnedo de Aguirre (ed.), *Legal Aspects of Cruises*, Ius Comparatum - Global Studies in Comparative Law 56, https://doi.org/10.1007/978-3-030-83090-8_1

That notorious increase of the cruise business is due to the fact that more and more people have access to different ways of travelling, including cruises and package holidays or package travels that include cruises. This activity generates a great amount of private international law issues regarding different areas of law, such as contracts law, consumer protection law, labour law, port's regulations, and environmental law, among others. Though it can be stated that there is not yet extensive legal research specifically on cruises, there are several general rules that are applicable to cruises and related matters.

This general report conducts a comparative study mainly on the following issues: the importance of cruise business, general and specific rules applicable to cruises, cruise passengers as consumers, package travels, labour rules on cruises' workers, rules on ports that are relevant to cruises, including taxes, costs and rates charged to cruises in different ports, rules environmental impact of cruises, jurisdiction, arbitration, and choice of law in cruise issues, and general conditions used by companies offering cruise services. It is obvious that all these issues require legal regulation, specific and/or general, national, international or supranational. This research aims at discovering which the existing sources of law on these matters are and whether they are adequate and sufficient. It ends up with a non exhaustive list of all those sources of law, without prejudice of their analysis throughout the report.

This general report has greatly benefitted from the thirteen national reports submitted for the Fukuoka Conference[2] by experts on the subject matter from various jurisdictions in Europe, North and South America and Asia.

The aim of this general report is to shed some light on a matter that is neither well known nor enough studied at the universities worldwide.

1.1 *Kinds of Impact That Cruise Tourism Can Originate*

Cruise tourism can originate infrastructure impact because of the construction of dams and passenger terminals, which modify the natural environment, for example, the loss of natural habitat, changes in the local coastal surf and changes in the patterns of sediment.[3]

Cruise tourism can also originate operational impacts derived from the use of energy: operations regarding cruises involve as a result the contamination of the water and the air, since a cruise vessel consumes as an average a volume of gas equivalent to that of 12,000 automobiles. Cruise vessels also produce atmospheric emissions related to toxic ashes and smoke from waste incineration on board, the emission of black and grey waters and other kinds of wastes. There is also an impact

[2] Argentina, Belgium, Brazil, Bulgaria, China (Shanghai), Germany, Japan, Poland, Romania, Spain, Turkey, Uruguay and United States of America.

[3] Ariza Herrerías (2014), p. 24.

originated in the amount of wastes that a cruise produces per person and per day, like oils, sewage water, plastics and dangerous substances, food wastes, glass, etc.[4]

Cruise tourism also produces impacts associated with the trips tourists make, the logistics of supplies to cruise vessels, and the capacity of destinies. They also originate cultural impacts, derived from the mass tourism.[5]

However, since cruise industry is a relatively new and globalised one, and in spite of the studies carried on during the last years, we still have little knowledge regarding its effects, particularly in visited port areas, and the environmental consequences of its activities.[6]

1.2 Maritime Transport of Passengers Throughout History

It is from the nineteenth century that maritime carriage of passengers is developed and maritime transport companies establish regular lines for the carriage of passengers along the oceans.[7]

The origins of cruises can be found in the twentieth century around the fifties or sixties, when several companies like P&O, Holland American Line and Costa Crociere, and afterwards others like Royal Caribbean, Carnival Cruises and Transmediterránea, organize this particular kind of travel for leisure and pleasure. Cruises include accommodation, food, beverage, and several activities and spectacles on board, as well as the possibility of visiting touristic and historic places in each scale along the journey.[8] All these activities are included in what is called combined trip, on an all inclusive basis, and, depending on the travel agency, it can include the air tickets, previous accommodation and transfers. Some kinds of beverages, exclusive services like laundry, hairdresser, special restaurants and some excursions outside the vessel are not generally included.[9]

Over time, cruise ships become true floating cities and the amount of cruise passengers has grown enormously in the last decades, particularly in America and in Europe.[10]

---

[4] Ariza Herrerías (2014), pp. 24–25.

[5] Ariza Herrerías (2014), p. 25.

[6] Vasallo (2015).

[7] Estepa Montero (2012), p. 145.

[8] Estepa Montero (2012), pp. 146–147.

[9] Estepa Montero (2012), p. 147.

[10] Estepa Montero (2012), pp. 148–151; Ariza Herrerías (2014), p. 3.

1.3 Maritime Cabotage

During the transition periods of the EU economic integration cruise services in the Mediterranean, as well as other types of maritime transport services, have been exempted from the application of the Regulation EC/3577/92 on the freedom to provide maritime transport services within E.U. Member States (maritime cabotage). This exemption was first granted for the founding member states and later on also upon the accession of Croatia to the European Union, exemptions were granted to Croatia for cruise services between Croatian ports by ships smaller than 650 gt, by reserving those cruise services for Croatian ships till 31 December 2014. Regulation (EC) N° 3577/92 was declared applicable to cruise services.[11]

Case-law of the EU Court of Justice on the meaning of "maritime cabotage" has been reported. In case C-17/13 it was discussed whether a cruise starting and ending at the same port of a Member State, with the same passengers aboard, was covered by the term "maritime cabotage" within the meaning of the Regulation N° 3577/92. The Court decided that it was, on the grounds of the principle of freedom to provide services of maritime transport within Member States (maritime cabotage).[12] In that case a non-EU (Swiss) river cruise operator claimed that the concept of 'maritime cabotage' applies only to services that involve true sea transport and that the river cruise at issue does not involve such transport. The Court ruled that the term 'sea' referred to by Regulation No 3577/92 is not limited to territorial sea within the meaning of the United Nations Convention on the Law of the Sea,[13] but also covers internal maritime waters which are on the landward side of the baseline of the territorial sea (referring to Case C-323/03, paragraphs 25–27).[14]

1.4 Cruises Travel Through Waters Submitted to Different Legal Regimes

1.4.1 International Waters: Principle of Freedom of Navigation

When cruises sail through international waters, the principle of freedom of navigation enshrined in the United Nations Convention on the Law of the Sea (Montego

[11] Act of 9 December 2011, amending Regulation n° EC/3577/92. See Belgian Report, II.9.7.

[12] See further information on this case and others in the Belgian Report, II.9.7. See also https://curia.europa.eu/jcms/upload/docs/application/pdf/2014-03/cp140041en.pdf.

[13] Signed in Montego Bay (Jamaica) on 10 December 1982, entered into force on 16 November 1994 and approved on behalf of the European Community by Council Decision 98/392/EC of 23 March 1998.

[14] See further information on this case and others in the Belgian Report, II.9.8. See also https://curia.europa.eu/jcms/upload/docs/application/pdf/2014-03/cp140041en.pdf.

Bay, 1982), applies.[15] Under some legal and conventional rules[16] and some case law, a ship on the high seas is considered to be located in the territory of his flag State. On the other hand, it has been stated that the law on shipboard cannot change at every change of waters. In more recent times, legislative and jurisprudential solutions acknowledge that such law is that of the nationality of the ship, which is that of the State that registered it.[17] It has been reported that a ship has the nationality of the State that registered it "only if there is a 'genuine link' between the state and the ship, namely whether the company owning the ship is owned by nationals of the state; whether the officers and crew of the ship are nationals of the state; how often the ship stops in the ports of the state; and how extensive and effective is the control that the state exercises over the ship. Regardless of the theoretical basis, an important factor in what law supplements general maritime law is the ship's nationality".[18]

1.4.2 High Seas

The United Nations Convention on the Law of the Sea (Montego Bay, 1982) provides that "the high seas are open to all States" and that freedom is exercised under the conditions laid down in the Convention. It comprises, among others, freedom of navigation (arts. 87 and 90).

1.4.3 Internal Waters

Internal waters are ruled by the law of the States with adjacent costs to those waters. In principle, foreign vessels cannot enter internal waters, which include ports. The problem of access to ports was solved by customary law and later in time it was ruled by the Convention and Statute on the International Regime of Maritime Ports, Geneva, 9 December 1923. It provides for a simple regime, based on reciprocity for "sea-going vessels" "used for foreign trade" (art. 1).[19]

---

[15]Estepa Montero (2012), p. 135; Ariza Herrerías (2014), p. 9.

[16]For example, Article 27 of the Montevideo Treaty on International Civil Law of 1889 provides that: "Vessels on non-jurisdictional waters are deemed to be located at the place of their registration". If the vessel is on internal or on territorial waters, she is considered to be located in that State where she actually is, the State of the internal or territorial waters (Article 26).

[17]For example, Articles 1–3 of the Montevideo Treaty on International Commercial Navigation Law of 1940.

[18]Felder (2006), p. 26.

[19]Estepa Montero (2012), pp. 135–136. See also the United Nations Convention on the Law of the Sea, Geneva, April 29, 1958.

1.4.4 Territorial Sea

The scope of territorial sea is of 12 nautical miles and is ruled, among other Conventions, by the Convention and Statute on the International Regime of Maritime Ports, Geneva, 9 December 1923. Under Article 2, "…every Contracting State undertakes to grant the vessels of every other Contracting State equality of treatment with its own vessels, or those of any other State whatsoever, in the maritime ports situated under its sovereignty or authority, as regards freedom of access to the port, the use of the port, and the full enjoyment of the benefits as regards navigation and commercial operations which it affords to vessels, their cargoes and passengers". However, the latter is "subject to the principle of reciprocity".

The United Nations Convention on the Law of the Sea (Montego Bay, 1982) provides as a general rule that ships of all States "enjoy the right of innocent passage[20] through the territorial sea" (art. 17), as far as it does not mean a jeopardy or menace to peace or security of the coastal State.[21]

1.5 Final Remarks

Cruise tourism originates impact at different levels affecting not only waters through which they sail but also air, coasts and port areas. It is a relatively new activity that is growing dramatically.

Since cruises travel through waters submitted to different legal regimes, it is important to determine whether they can be ruled by one of them only, for example, that of their flag, or to several national and international laws. In this chapter we have just presented the matter and shown some international substantive rules, and some conflict of laws rules. This topic will be developed hereinafter.

2 The Importance of Cruises in General and in Some Particular Areas and Countries

2.1 General Remarks

It can be asserted that the cruise business has a growing importance almost all over the world, although there are significant differences among regions and countries. Transport of passengers by sea or river is an ancient activity, as old as human kind; however, cruises as a touristic option, have appeared in the late decades, becoming a relatively recent business. The most important developments regarding cruises

[20]Meaning of "innocent passage" is given by Articles 18 and 19.

[21]Ariza Herrerías (2014), p. 9.

appeared in the late fifties not in Europe but in the USA, with a great demand of cruise trips along the Caribbean islands, and then in the Mexican Pacific coast, as well as in Hawaii.[22]

Though there is a popular general idea of what a cruise is, there are several technical distinctions in different legal sources, as will be dealt with throughout this general report. Terms like combined trips, package travels, package tours or package holidays refer to those trips that include not only the cruise but also the airplane trip to and from the port of departure, the land excursions chosen by the tourist when the ship is in port, and eventually some hotel night.[23] There is also a model of cruise that focuses on providing "Onboard Hospitality and Entertainment" (OHE), where the transportation element is servile to entertainment. They may even limit themselves to onboard entertainment and activities rather than destination-based activities, abandoning the multiple-coast-check program and offering long term ocean-only cruises.[24]

There are other specific kinds or categories of cruises like ferry-services, which focus mainly on transportation and mobility with no or "Limited Onboard Involvement" (LOI),[25] in some cases only tax free shops. Many ferries transport the passengers with their vehicles, particularly those that cover short or medium distance trips to residential and touristic destinations, like services across the English Chanel between the United Kingdom and France, or between Cadiz and the Canary Islands. This mode of transport requires new ships with entry and exit ramps for cars[26] and even for bigger vehicles like vans and tourism busses.

"Shore to Shore Floating Services" (SSFS) mobilize conventionally land-based services (events, festivities, casino, etc.) on a floating infrastructure often consisting of immobile ships, and even "Condominium/Residential Model" (CRM) that offers floating residency[27] on condo-cruise ships, floating communities that are increasingly popular. The most famous ocean residence is *The World*, a luxury ocean liner.[28]

This variety of modes of passenger transportation by water[29] makes qualification difficult in some cases,[30] like package travel contract and maritime transport contract, cruise operation and transport operation, among others.[31] Whereas N° 17 of Directive (EU) 2015/2302 explains that only the combination of different types of

---

[22] Estepa Montero (2013), pp. 336–337.

[23] Ariza Herrerías (2014), p. 13.

[24] Belgian Report, II.13.

[25] Mozuni and Jonas (2016), pp. 59–60.

[26] Estepa Montero (2013), p. 334.

[27] Belgian Report, II.13.

[28] http://www.businessinsider.com/what-are-condo-cruise-ships.

[29] See the preamble of the EU Directive 2015/2302 for detailed definitions, whose reproduction in this general report would exceed its appropriate extension.

[30] E.U. Court of Justice, 7 December 2000, cases nr. C-585/08 and C-144/09.

[31] Belgian Report, II.13.

travel services, such as accommodation, carriage of passengers by bus, rail, water or air, as well as rental of motor vehicles or certain motorcycles, should be considered for the purposes of identifying a package or a linked travel arrangement.[32] Thus, in cases where, unlike in the case of a cruise, overnight accommodation is provided as part of passenger transport by road, rail, water or air, accommodation should not be considered as a travel service in its own right if the main component is clearly transport.[33]

Cruise ships have been defined as hotels that are operated on an all-inclusive basis, where owners did not have to pay for the land, and that use for free international space and sometimes privative space of a State, with mobility according to climate and demand, which are significant advantages.[34] From a commercial perspective, the attractive of cruises is due not only to the referred advantages, but also because they offer the facilities of a high level hotel together with the possibility of visiting interesting historic and artistic destinies, beautiful natural landscapes, and everything without moving the luggage from the cabin.[35]

2.2 *Main Cruise Destinies*

There are some traditional destinations for cruises, like for example the USA (Hawaii, Alaska and others), the Caribbean area, Mexico, Northern Europe, the Mediterranean Sea and its coasts, Spain, Italy and Greece, while others are emerging ones, like for example Bulgaria, Romania, Poland.[36] What appears clear is that even those countries which are not main cruise destinies would like to become one.

2.2.1 Europe

General Information

The European Market regarding cruises has grown by 41% over the past 3 years and has more than doubled over the last ten. Over the past 10 years, the cruise industry grew in Europe by more than 10% each year. Fifty four percent of destinations are Mediterranean and Atlantic Islands. Twenty one percent of destinations are Northern Europe. Twenty five percent of destinations are the Caribbean and the rest.[37] The number of EU cruise passengers starting and ending a cruise in the EU amounted to

[32]https://eur-lex.europa.eu/legal-content/EN/TXT/?uri=CELEX%3A32015L2302.

[33]See for further information the Belgian Report, II.13.

[34]Vasallo (2015).

[35]Estepa Montero (2013), p. 336.

[36]In 2013 "Polish ports attended 1,1% of the gross tonnage (GT) of all passenger ships (including cruise ships) entering main European ports". Polish Report, I.1.

[37]See very detailed information of data and sources with statistics in the Belgian Report, I.1–2.

6,113,000 in 2015.[38] In 2016 there were 301 cruise ships by registered flag (ships of 1000 gt[39] and over) worldwide, and 97 out of those 301, i.e. 32% of the total amount of cruise ships in the world were from the EU. In 2014 an estimated 5.85 million passengers embarked on their cruises from a European port,[40] about 27% of the world cruise market.[41]

Some National Jurisdictions

Spain is not only a main cruise destiny but "a landmark in cruise traffic" and "the second European country with the biggest number of cruise passengers, just behind Italy", with an increasing number of cruise passengers arriving in some of the 46 port areas[42] in the country.[43] Figures are amazing and show the important economic impact of cruise market in Spain: 7,662,010 cruise passengers disembarking in Spanish ports from 3700 cruises in 2014, for example, increasing to 8,435,966 cruisers in 2015, meaning 9.4% on the previous year, in spite of some ups and downs.[44]

The main Spanish attractions for cruise tourism are Barcelona—the first European port and the fourth in the world, with 2.68 million cruisers in 2016—Balearic Islands, Málaga, Valencia, Bay of Cadiz, Vigo, A Coruña, and of course the Canary Islands.[45]

On the other hand, Germany, for example, "is more a source market than a destiny for cruises, at least sea cruises".[46] The main ports where cruises start are Hamburg, Rostock, Warnemünde, and Kiel; passengers who book cruises in the Mediterranean Sea usually travel by air to reach the port of embarkation.[47] The figures for embarkation, disembarkation and port visits of the three leading German ports are interesting[48] and reveal a higher percentage of European passengers.[49]

---

[38] EU transport in figures, statistical pocketbook, European Commission, 2017; Belgian Report, I.1.

[39] "Gt" stands for gross tonnage.

[40] GP WILD (International), Business Research and Economic Advisors (BREA) (2015), p. 3.

[41] Belgian Report, I.1.

[42] These 46 ports are comprised in the Spanish port system of state ownership and are "managed by 28 Port Authorities, whose coordination and efficiency control is responsibility of the public body *Puertos del Estado* (State Ports), body attached to the *Ministerio de Fomento* (Ministry of Public Works and Transport), which has been appointed by law for the implementation of government policy on ports". (Spanish Report, 1).

[43] See Spanish Report, 1.

[44] See Spanish Report, 1. See also some figures in Estepa Montero (2013), pp. 339–341.

[45] See Spanish Report, 1.

[46] See German Report, 1.

[47] See German Report, 1.

[48] The German Report, 2, state that: "Hamburg had in 2015 232,000 embarking and 232,000 disembarking passengers and 55,000 port call visits, Warnemünde 132,000 embarking and 131,000 disembarking passengers and 222,000 port call visits, whereas Kiel had 209,000 embarking and 214,000 disembarking passengers and 35,000 port call visits".

[49] See German Report, 2.

Belgium represented 1% of the European market share in 2015, with 245,000 cruise passengers over a total of 6,113,000 in the EU.[50] Its most important passenger port is Bruges-Zeebrugge, due to several reasons, like its maritime accessibility (easy access to open sea) and proximity to Bruges City (just 3 km/2 ml) and it is equipped cruise ship terminal. In terms of cruise traffic in Northern and Atlantic Europe the port of Zeebrugge is half way in the top ten. Also ports of Ostend and Antwerp are important, as well as the ports of Ghent and Brussels for river inland cruises. Regarding the Brussels Sea Port, it is actually an inland port.[51]

The case of Bulgaria is particularly interesting. They have no tradition on cruises; Bulgarians still think that cruises are too expensive for them. In addition, there face some facts that conspire against their success as a cruise destination country, like having Turkey and Greece as neighbours, with their traditional and well developed cruise offers. However, there are cruise companies that include some Bulgarian villages in their itineraries along the Black Sea, like Nessebar, a maritime village protected by the UNESCO. In sum, Bulgaria is not yet a main cruise destination but it has an interesting potential to become one, offering its villages with an ancient and rich history, which enable a cultural tourism and thematic cruises.[52]

Romania is not a main cruise destination either, particularly for maritime passenger ships, due to the current geopolitical situation; it "is a second choice destination for cruise routes in the Mediterranean Sea and the Black Sea".[53] However, the port of Constantza and its new passengers' terminal are relevant for river passenger vessels, since it is a destination for many Danube and maritime cruise routs. This terminal has an important operating capacity and is very well located.[54] Notwithstanding, statistics on the number of cruises and cruise passengers arriving and disembarking on the port of Constantza are very variable and even show a decreasing tendency in the last 3 years.[55]

As for Poland, though it is not a main cruise destiny yet, it shows interesting perspectives. For example, the port of Gdynia expected for 2017 "the largest cruise ship in the history of Polish ports (Norwegian Getaway)", which is an indicator of the growth of Poland's attractiveness as a cruise destiny.[56] In fact, statistics—though

[50]IRN Research, *Cruise Lines International Association Europe (CLIA), Statistics and markets*, 2015, p. 4. See further information in the Belgian Report, I.1.

[51]See further information on EU and Belgian figures regarding cruises, passengers' expenditure on land and passenger nationalities, in the Belgian Report, I.1–2.

[52]See Bulgarian Report, I.1–2.

[53]See Romanian Report I.1.

[54]See Romanian Report. The referred terminal is operated by CN Maritime Port Administration SA Constantza.

[55]The statistics of the port of Constantza are the following: "2013: 69 ships boarded, having 54,616 tourists; 2014: 92 layovers took place, with ships having 70,000 tourists aboard; 2015: 35 layovers took place, with ships having 35,000 tourists aboard; 2016: 14 ship visited with 8,632 tourists aboard; 2017: 21 sea and river ships are scheduled to board at the Constantza Port". Romanian Report, I.2.

[56]See Polish Report, I.1.

variable—are expected to raise its numbers in 2017.[57] The variations in the number of passengers from 1 year to the other are due to some funny reasons, like the possibility of duty free shopping on sea voyages to and from Germany.[58]

2.2.2 Asia

Since 2008, "cruise tourism is booming in Asia", states Professor Li and refers particularly to Shanghai, though China is not a main cruise destiny but departure country.[59] Statistics show an important increase in the number of cruises and cruise passengers from 2012 to 2016: "Till 2016, more than 1010 cruise ships berthed in China, outbound Chinese cruise tourists reached 2.144 million and the inbound foreign cruise tourists reached 128000, Shanghai Wusongkou International Cruise Port became No. 1 in Asia and No. 4 in the world".[60]

Turkey is an important cruise destination and its main ports of embarking and disembarking are Istanbul,[61] Kuşadası,[62] İzmir, Bodrum, Marmaris,[63] Alanya, Antalya and Çanakkale.[64] As for the evolution of the number of cruises and cruise passengers arriving in Turkey, statistics show that: "In 2016, 1296 cruises came to Turkey carrying 1.889.000 passengers.[65] In 2013, 1.572 cruises came to Turkey carrying 2.240.000 tourists whereas the number was 1.587 cruises and 2.095.673 tourists in 2012[66]". Regarding nationalities of cruise passengers, there are mainly German, English, American and Italian; tourists spend approximately US$120–150 daily on cruise ports.[67]

Japan is a main cruise destiny, particularly Hakata Port, Nagasaki Port, and Yokohama Port, among others. Statistics show interesting figures: "The number of cruise ship ports of call at Japanese ports in 2016 was 2,017 times in total, which is the largest number ever (1,443 times for cruise ships operated by foreign shipping companies, 574 times for cruise ships operated by Japanese shipping companies). The number of Japanese cruise passengers in 2016 was 248,000, which is the largest

[57] "The number of cruise ships entering Polish ports equalled 240 in 2010 (5.2 mln GT), 194 in 2011 (3.9 mln GT), 199 in 2012 (4.5 mln GT), 226 in 2013 (3.7 mln GT), 223 in 2014 (3.3 mln GT) and 2015 (4.5 mln GT) and 198 in 2016 (3.8 mln GT)." Polish Report, I.2.

[58] See Polish Report, I.2.

[59] China Report, I.1.

[60] China Report, I.2.

[61] In 2015, 11% of the cruises came to Istanbul while 30% had come in 2013 (Turkish Report, A).

[62] In 2015, 44% of the cruises came to Kuşadası while 26% had come in 2013 (Turkish Report, A).

[63] In 2015, 8% of the cruises came to Marmaris (Turkish Report, A).

[64] See Turkish Report, A.

[65] 2016 Sector Council Report of The Union of Chambers and Commodity Exchanges of Turkey and the statistic received from the Ministry of Transportation, Maritime Affairs and Communications, Directorate of Sea Commerce.

[66] Association of Turkey Travel Agency's (TURSAB) report in 2013 and 2012.

[67] These figures correspond to 2015. See Turkish Report, A.

number ever. The number of foreign passengers who disembarked in Japan was about 1,992,000, which is the largest number ever". There was also an increase in the money cruise passengers spend when they disembark: "For example, the economic effect of cruise ship ports of call (a round-the-world-trip cruise ship of 5,000 gross tons) at Yokohama port led to increased spending of JPY246,000,000 in 2015 from JPY216,200,000 in 2010".[68]

2.2.3 America

From a global point of view, South America is not in the first places as cruise destiny but behind Europe and North America. However, Argentina, for example, has become an important cruise destiny during the last 20 years and figures are increasing, though there is a wide margin to improve them. Argentina offers local maritime routs, like the "*Circuito maritimo de cruceros Australes*", from Buenos Aires to Patagonia, including the ports of Buenos Aires, Mar del Plata, Puerto Madryn and Ushuaia. Secondly, the "*Circuito marítimo de Glaciares*", which goes from the Big Island of Tierra del Fuego with the South American continent—Port of Comodoro Rivadavia or Puerto Deseado—and/or the Antarctic continent and the Islas Malvinas. In 2018 some new itineraries will be added by Alteza Cruises.[69]

At an international level, Argentina also participates in some important South American itineraries, along the Brazilian coast and the southern coast. The demand of cruises to the Antarctic has grown considerably in the last years, both from national and foreign tourists and they use the port of Ushuaia as the departing or scale port.[70]

Brazil is also an important cruise destiny and shows interesting figures: 805,189 passengers embarked in the 2011/2012 season, but only 552,091 in the 2015/2016 season. However, Brazil is still an important cruise market.[71] Statistics on the evolution of the number of cruises and cruise passengers, their nationalities, and the money they spend on land, thorough studies produced by CLIA in partnership with the Fundação Getulio Vargas ("FGV"), a well known research entity in Brazil, may be found online.[72]

Uruguay has also become an important cruise destiny, though its cruise season is limited to the October-April period. The importance of cruises in the country has become relevant, at least since 2006, with an average of around 200 cruises arriving

[68] Japanese Report, I.2.

[69] Argentinean Report, I.1.

[70] Argentinean Report, I.1.

[71] Brazilian Report, I.1.

[72] http://abremar.hospedagemtemporaria.com.br/dados-do-setor/ See Brazilian Report, I.2. See also http://www.abremar.com.br/down/Cruises_2017_English_WEB_v2.pdf, and http://www.abremar.com.br/down/Cruzeiros_2017_Portugues_WEB_FINAL.pdf.

at the ports of Montevideo and Punta del Este each season. Statistics[73] show a growth from 130 cruises arriving at Uruguayan ports in 2006 to a maximum of 237 in the 2013–2014 season. There was a decrease in the following seasons, though larger vessels arrived. The number of cruise passengers arriving in Uruguayan ports grew 113% in the last decade: 149,000 in the 2006–2007 season and 317,000 in the 2015–2016 season. This means an annual average increase of 8% in the number of cruise passengers arriving in Uruguayan ports. However, in the last two seasons there was a fall of 22% in the number of cruise passengers descending in Uruguayan ports.[74]

The USA is a major cruise destiny; it was reported that there are 21 ports service cruise ships in the continental U.S. and three in the territorial/non-continental U.S.[75] The state of Alaska is also a popular global destination for cruises, receiving 4.1 % of the global cruise capacity in 2016 (measured by available lower berth day)[76]. River cruises, are very popular, with 184 ships operating on rivers globally in 2015, and 13 more river cruise ships on order in 2017 to meet increased demand.[77]

2.3 *Importance of Cruise Business*

2.3.1 Statistics

Though cruise business is a small portion of tourism as a whole, there is a clear growth of this sector.[78] There are statistics about the economic impact of cruise business in Europe in several sources, like those published by CLIA Europe, an important cruise industry trade association with offices in Brussels that promotes the interests of cruise ship operators within Europe. It also "promotes cruising to a wider public audience to encourage expansion of the European cruise market and works closely with a range of other stakeholders, including the wider shipping industry, cruise ports and travel agents".[79]

---

[73] Statistics on cruises are published by the Ministry of Tourism: http://mintur.gub.uy/index.php/estadisticas-y-publicaciones/turismo-de-cruceros; see also http://www.turismo.gub.uy/blog/por-que-tantos-cruceros-visitan-uruguay.html?utm_source=programatica&utm_medium=nativa&utm_campaign=cruceros&utm_content=crucero-punta-del-este.

[74] Uruguayan Report, I.1.

[75] All things cruise, *Cruise Departure Ports,* https://allthingscruise.com/cruise-research/cruise-departure-ports/.

[76] Florida-Caribbean Cruise Association, *Cruise Industry Overview, 2017,* http://www.f-cca.com/downloads/2017-Cruise-Industry-Overview-Cruise-Line-Statistics.pdf. *See also* CLIA, *2016 Cruise Industry Outlook,* at 8 https://www.cruising.org/docs/default-source/research/2016_clia_sotci.pdf.

[77] See USA Report, I, and reference to CLIA, *2017 Cruise Industry Outlook* 14, https://www.cruising.org/docs/default-source/research/clia-2017-state-of-the-industry.pdf?sfvrsn=0.

[78] Vasallo (2015).

[79] https://www.cliaeurope.eu.

There are other important sources providing statistics on the importance of the cruise business in Europe, like those reported by some jurisdictions like Belgium,[80] where in "2014 there were 42 cruise lines domiciled in Europe, operating 123 cruise ships with a capacity of around 146.000 lower berths. Another 60 vessels with a capacity of around 89.000 lower berths were deployed in Europe by 18 non--European lines. In 2014 an estimated 6.4 million European residents booked cruises, representing about 30% of all cruise passengers worldwide.[81] In the European Union in 2011 about 570,000 European seafarers were employed in cruise ships".

It has been reported that "in terms of economic value and jobs for Europe, the European cruise industry's total economic output reached €40.2bn in 2014, up 2% from the previous year, including €16.6bn in direct spending by cruise lines, their passengers and crew. In 2014 the cruise industry also accounted for nearly 350,000 European jobs – close to 10,000 more than the previous year – amounting to €10.75bn in employee compensation[82]". Moreover, "in the European Union in 2012 cruise tourism alone generated a direct turnover of €15.5 billion and employed 330,000 people and is expected to grow. European ports had 29.3 million passenger visits, a 75% increase over 2006. Half of European coastal tourism's jobs and value added activities are located in the Mediterranean, but the Atlantic, Baltic and Black Sea regions have significant shares too.[83],[84]

CLIA has also representations in some national markets across Europe. These national chapters provide members with "platforms to work on and solve issues at the local and national levels".[85] However, the studies of this important association include only aggregated figures for Europe as a whole, but no detailed data for countries.[86] Regarding Germany, for example, those statistics show "a decline of 9.4 % in direct cruise spending, which is explained as direct result of a 19.7 % fall in spending at German shipyards. This was partially offset by a 1.2 % increase in passenger and crew expenditures".[87] Spanish statistics on cruise industry show that it has very important economic impact in the country. Spain became the fourth more benefited European market by cruise industry.[88]

In other countries some local and limited statistics are kept. That is the case of Romania, for example, with some statistics at the port level only, which refer to the

[80] Belgian Report, I.3.

[81] GP WILD (International), Business Research and Economic Advisors (BREA) (2015), p. 3.

[82] GP WILD (International), Business Research and Economic Advisors (BREA) (2015), p. 1.

[83] Communication from the Commission to the European Parliament, the Council, the European Economic and Social Committee and the Committee of the Regions a European strategy for more growth and jobs in coastal and maritime tourism, com (2014) 86 final, Brussels, 20.2.2014, p. 2.

[84] See Belgian Report, I.3, which provides further information.

[85] https://www.cliaeurope.eu/.

[86] German National Report, I.3.

[87] German National Report, I.3.

[88] Spanish National Report, I.3.

number of passengers, how many embark and disembark and how many ships dock in the port of Constantza.[89]

CLIA is present not only in Europe but also in North and South America, Asia, and Australasia, representing "the interests of cruise lines, travel agents, port authorities and destinations, and various industry business partners before regulatory and legislative policy makers".[90]

In Argentina, statistics show some ups and downs regarding the cruise activity: the best season of the last years was that of 2012/2013, with 160 arrivals of cruises and 510,815 cruise passengers. During the 2016/2017 season only 82 cruises arrived in Argentine ports with 295,271 passengers. However, it is expected that the activity will increase due to the measures adopted to that purpose.[91]

Uruguay is focused in promoting cruise tourism, which is revealed by the efforts of the Ministry of Tourism and the detailed statistics on cruises and related activities it keeps since 2009.[92]

In the USA it has been reported that during the last decade the global cruise industry has experienced a massive growth; more than 50% of all cruise passengers are from the USA.[93]

2.3.2 Policies Favouring Cruise Business

General Information

There are some countries where governments are developing specific policies to promote and favour cruise business, while others limit themselves to general ones and others do not have policies regarding cruise business at all. Some countries have central general policies at a national scale while others have only local policies to favour cruise business.

Europe

As reported by some European jurisdictions, the EU promotes its cruise business as a part of a broader policy and strategy of sustainable development of the so-called "blue economy". In 2009 the EU Commission presented the main strategic objectives for the European maritime transport up to 2018, identifying key areas, where action by the EU would strengthen the competitiveness of the sector while enhancing its environmental performance.[94] The "Communication from the Commission to the European Parliament, the Council, the European Economic and Social Committee and the Committee of the Regions – Strategic goals and recommendations for the

[89] Romanian National Report, I.2–3.

[90] https://www.cliaeurope.eu/.

[91] Argentine Report, I.3.

[92] Uruguayan Report, Sect. 2. Figures were explained *supra* in Sect. 2.2.3.

[93] See detailed figures in USA Report, I.

[94] Belgian Report, I.4.1; https://ec.europa.eu/transport/themes/strategies/2018_maritime_transport_strategy_en.

EU's maritime transport policy until 2018". The Communication states that for Europe shipping has always been fundamental to its economic growth, that Europe plays a major role in today's shipping world, that a number of measures introduced by Member States, in line with the Community Guidelines for State aids for maritime transport, have contributed to keeping part of the fleet on European registers and generating jobs for European seafarers, among many other things.[95]

In addition, the European Parliament highlighted the importance of cruise tourism for the growth of the tourism sector in Europe; it "called on the Commission, therefore, together with the Member States, to assess the resources required and existing port and nautical infrastructure, and to standardise the sorting of waste and recycling, in order to create innovative planning actions for these areas by developing the concept of the smart port city[96]".[97]

In Spain there are "no legislative or regulatory measures at a national or a regional level for the promotion of the cruise industry". However, there are several governmental "specific policies for the promotion of the cruise industry", like the campaign launched in 2013 by *Puertos del Estado*, named "Blue Carpet: step into Spain on a blue carpet", that aimed at offering a global image of Spain and strengthening the cruise sector in the country by improving the port facilities and the cultural touristic offer.[98]

In Belgium, "the cruise ports of Oostende and Zeebrugge co-operate in the "Belgian Coast Cruise Project" in order to promote cruise tourism in their ports and to reinforce the market position of their ports in the world cruise market.[99] "The strategic policy plan for coastal tourism and recreation (2015–2020)" adopted by the Flemish regional government and the Province of West-Flanders includes the promotion of cruise operations (departure and destination) in Belgian seaports.[100] The building of the cruise terminal infrastructure in Zeebrugge is one of the achievements in this respect[101]".[102]

At a local level, there are some favourable initiatives in Poland, at the Port of Gdańsk, like discounts on port fees for cruising companies visiting the port several times a year, special safety zones for cruise passengers in the port, among others.[103] In Germany, local authorities are competent to adopt this kind of measures, and not

[95] http://eur-lex.europa.eu/legal-content/EN/ALL/?uri=CELEX:52009DC0008.

[96] P8_TA(2015)0391, New challenges and concepts for the promotion of tourism in Europe, European Parliament resolution of 29 October 2015 on new challenges and concepts for the promotion of tourism in Europe (2014/2241(INI)) (2017/C 355/10).

[97] See further information in Belgian Report, I.4.1.

[98] Spanish Report, I.4. See also in this report, the measures taken by the Valencia Port Authority, among others. Estepa Montero (2013), p. 344.

[99] Haven Zeebrugge. (2014). *Belgian Coast Cruise Project*. http://www.poz.be/nl/node/807.

[100] Phlypo and Gheysen (2014), p. 41 (www.toerismevlaanderen.bewww.toerismevlaanderen.be).

[101] Phlypo and Gheysen (2014), pp. 37 and 49 (www.toerismevlaanderen.bewww.toerismevlaanderen.be).

[102] Belgian Report, I.4.2.

[103] Polish Report, I.4.

the federal government. They do not offer any specific promotion for cruise industry, though they have some general economic promotions for shipyards, ports, logistic and tourism.[104]

There are other countries that have no national policies to favour the development of cruise tourism and cruise business, but where there are some voices claiming for the development of such business. That is the case of Bulgaria, for example, where though there are no national policies, some tourism companies are trying to develop effective products to develop cruise tourism, on the basis that there is a non-developed niche in the tourism national level. It has been suggested that the measures to be adopted in order to develop cruise tourism are a strategy of active publicity to popularize cruise tourism in the country, to establish long term relations with cruise companies for them to include Bulgarian ports in cruise itineraries and to establish itineraries departing from Bulgarian ports.[105]

America

The Ministry of Tourism in Uruguay has designed some general policies to stimulate tourism, though there are not public specific policies regarding cruise activity. However, it can be stated that in recent years Uruguayan authorities have taken some measures to encourage the arrival of cruise ships. For example, a meeting was held in 1916 in Buenos Aires, Argentina, between Uruguayan and Argentine authorities for the purpose of planning bilateral cooperation to promote the arrival of cruise ships on both sides of the Río de la Plata.[106]

Argentina has committed itself to a policy in favour of the cruise business. Its authorities have designated specific policies in that sense, like for example the Federal Strategic Plan on Sustainable Tourism elaborated in 2014 and projected up to 2025, which is included in the "Cruise Maritime Circuit". Other measures to encourage cruise business are the improvement of port terminals, like the cruise specific terminal of "Benito Quintela Martín", in Buenos Aires, and the addition of the Mar del Plata port as a cruise destiny. It is also remarkable the project to encourage and promote of river cruises, particularly in the Hidrovía Paraguay-Paraná, consisting of the construction of five fluvial terminals in Corrientes, Entre Ríos, Misiones and Santa Fe. It is also worth mentioning that there are also some important measures already in force in Argentina, like reduction in taxes and simplification of paperwork among many others.[107]

On the other hand, Brazil does not have specific policies to favour the cruise business; on the contrary, according to CLIA/FGV cruise companies mention high taxes and operational costs as the most significant difficulties to be overcome in Brazil.[108]

---

[104] German Report, I.4.

[105] Bulgarian Report, I.4. See the analysis of the strong and weak aspects regarding the development of the cruise product at a national level, included in the referred Report, I.4.

[106] Uruguayan Report, I.4.

[107] See Argentine Report, I.4.

[108] Brazilian Report, I.4.

In the USA, president Grover Cleveland signed the Passenger Vessel Services Act of 1886 (PVSA),[109] which was aimed at protecting the American shipping industry and American jobs. The Act restricts the coastwise transportation of people between U.S. points, reserving it for U.S. built, owned, and documented vessels.[110]

Asia

Japan has some measures at a national level, like the provision of an information desk at the service of foreign cruise ships regarding their Japanese ports of call. That desk centrally provides information on port facilities and sightseeing information among others. The authorities grant subsidies for the costs incurred by local governments or private businesses in setting mobile boarding bridges or roofed passages. But perhaps the most important measure to encourage cruise business is the establishment of "an interest-free loan system for companies who maintain passenger terminal facilities for cruise ships".[111]

2.3.3 Port Services Offered to Cruises

The main and modern cruise ports generally provide good services to cruises. That is the case, for example, in South America, of Argentina, Brazil and Uruguay. In Argentina, the Buenos Aires port, where the cruise terminal "Benito Quintela Martín" was inaugurated in March 2011, offers good quality services not only through administrative authorities but also through third parties. The referred terminal is one of the biggest and most modern in South America. The services provided to cruises are of good quality at all the Argentine ports included in the national cruise circuit, like for example, in Puerto Madryn.[112]

In Brazil the situation varies depending on the port. There were important investments recently in some ports as Santos, Rio de Janeiro and Salvador, which present good infrastructure for passengers. Other ports do not have special terminals for cruises or even divisions between cargo and passenger terminals. Curiously, some relevant cruise destinations, such as Buzios (RJ), do not have ports at all. In those cases, private docks are used.[113]

Uruguayan ports provide the necessary services required by cruises. These services are more complete at the Montevideo Port and are provided by the National Ports Administration (*Administración Nacional de Puertos*). They include docks for docking cruises, waste treatment, sewage and black waters discharge, re-provisioning and tourist services for passengers, among others. In Punta del Este port cruises must be anchored in Maldonado Bay and that is the reason why

[109] Passenger Vessel Services Act, 46 U.S.C. § 55103(b).

[110] See further information in the USA Report, II.

[111] Japanese Report, I.4.

[112] See Argentine Report, I.5 for more details.

[113] Brazilian Report, I.5.

port services are more limited; they include berths for cruise ships, tenders and tourist services for passengers.[114]

Something similar occurs in Europe. Services offered to cruises are good in most important cruise destiny ports. In Spain, for example, according to the data base of *Puertos del Estado* services provided to cruises are of good quality.[115] Poland also offers good quality services for cruise and ferry shipping in its ports, including full spectrum of port services, like pilotage, towage, mooring, supply of fresh water, among many others. The cost of those services is partly included in tonnage and tariff fees paid to port administrator.[116] In Belgium, particularly in the port of Zeebrugge, shuttle bus, parking area for private cars, busses and taxis, a terminal building that houses all kinds of facilities are provided for. There are reception facilities for the removal of the ship-generated waste and vessel waste treatment services (collection and processing), medical support and many other services. There are also ship services on request provided by private suppliers, like general maintenance and repairs and cleaning, as well as ship supplies services.[117]

In Romania services offered to cruises are considered of medium to good quality, though there are no complaints from tourists on this matter. Some services are provided by port administration, like waste removal and power and water supply, while others are performed by private authorized companies, like ship chandlering and bunker supply.[118]

In Asia there are also good quality services offered to cruises.[119]

2.3.4 Ship Management Industry

Ship management includes crew, technical and commercial management.[120] The services that a ship management company is entitled to provide are the following:[121]

1. The ship management company should do the supervision of the maintenance of machinery on board the ship. The process should also include different surveys and repair work of the ship.
2. The ship management company should provide adequate crew for manning the ship.
3. The company should arrange for loading and unloading of the cargo.
4. The ship management company can hire the ship on behalf of the ship owner.

---

[114] Uruguayan Report, I.5.

[115] See Spanish Report, I.5 for more details.

[116] See Polish Report, I.5 for more details.

[117] Belgian Report, I.5.

[118] Romanian Report, I.5.

[119] National Reports from China and Japan, I.5.

[120] Polish Report, I.7.

[121] https://www.marineinsight.com/maritime-law/what-is-ship-management.

5. The company should negotiate the contracts for bunker and lube oil.
6. The ship management company pays the expenses on behalf of the owner.
7. The ship management company should make an arrangement for the entry of the ship in the P&I (Protection and Indemnity) association.
8. The company also deals with various claims related to insurance, salvage, etc.
9. The ship management company should arrange for the insurance in relation to the ship.
10. The ship management company's services also include arrangement for providing victualling and stores for the crew of the ship.

In America, for example in Argentina, ship management industry generally considered and not limited to cruises is of great importance. It is mainly based on foreign trade; however, the activity is increasing regarding cruise activity and becomes a powerful economic engine for the involved regions.[122] Something similar occurs in Brazil, where the management companies are mainly involved in cargo shipping, oil and gas, supply vessels and port support. There are no Brazilian ship management companies in the cruise business.[123] There are not published statistics on the economic importance of ship management industry in Uruguay, where there is only a cabotage fleet, consisting mainly of fishing vessels, passenger traffic of minor and medium sized and some medium-sized tanks and cargo ships.[124]

In Europe, it can be stated, in the light of the jurisdictions considered in this report, that the situation varies from one country to the other. For example in Germany there are German based cruise lines. The biggest three are AIDA Cruises in Rostock, a branch of Costa Crociere in Genoa (Italy), part of the Carnival Group, TUI Cruises in Hamburg, a joint venture of TUI (Hanover) and Royal Caribbean Cruises, and Hapag Lloyd in Hamburg, part of the TUI group.[125]

In Romania the ship management industry is relevant for the country and particularly for the port of Constantza,[126] while in Bulgaria there is no ship management industry.[127] In Belgium there are several ship management firms.[128]

Although after 1989 the Polish navy has lost its significance in the world shipping market, the ship management industry has been developing effectively in Poland. Moreover, since 2008 it has become "one of the driving engines of the Polish maritime economy. As Poland provides high quality services while still being a reasonably priced country it is possible to attract foreign investment into ship management activities conducted from Poland". Though there are no statistics reported regarding the size of the ship management in Poland, it can be assumed

[122] Argentine Report, I.7.

[123] Brazilian Report, I.7.

[124] Uruguayan Report, I.7.

[125] German Report, I.7.

[126] Romanian Report, I.7.

[127] Bulgarian Report, I.7.

[128] Like for example Exmar, Diamond, Maritec, Euronav, among others. Cfr. https://directories.lloydslist.com/services-browse/ss/3123/country/Belgium. See Belgian Report I.7.

that the volume of operations is quite large.[129] It is interesting to notice that the Polish Ship Managers' Association experience "indicates continuing transition from traditional (or "in-house") ship management model in which the owner is fully responsible for operation of the ship and employs personnel under his authority, to outsourcing ship management model, where management of the ship is contracted out to a third-party organisation or a company, which runs day to day operations of the ships: technical, crewing, commercial, accounting and financing etc. Currently in Poland a hybrid ship management model exists which is an interim stage between above two models".[130] In Poland there has been a transformation of crewing agencies into management companies, offering all types of management activities.[131]

If we look to Asia, it has been reported that in China, ship management industry is important,[132] while in Japan the ship management business is not a major industry.[133]

2.3.5 Shipyards and Cruises

The construction and also the repairmen of cruise vessels is an activity which requires high specialisation. It has been reported that in 2014 the cruise business generated 16,600 millions of Euros in Europe, and that the mayor part of that amount was due to the construction of cruise vessels, mainly in Italy, France, Germany and Finland.[134] However, there are some attempts from the Asian competitors, mainly Japanese, Korean and Chinese, to enter the cruise shipbuilding market and it seems they are being successful: AIDA, a German operator, hired the construction of two

[129] The Polish national reporters inform us that "members of the Polish Ship Managers' Association (PSMA) manage (both in full or partial aspect) approximately 200 ships of different types with a combined of 2.3 million deadweight tonnage (DWT). The average tonnage of a vessel managed by a PSMA member is between 9-11.000 DWT with the most dominant types being reefers, LPG carriers and bulk carriers" (I.7).

[130] Polish Report, I.7.

[131] See Polish Report, I.7 where the Polish national reporters explain that: "The reasons for the current role of ship managers in the Polish maritime economy are manifold. First one is compliance with leading international legal standards. Moreover, despite the downfall of major shipowners, Poland still possesses a highly qualified and experienced management, as well as technical and maritime personnel. Polish seafarers are known for their high standards of training and diligence. Statistics show that over 35 000 Polish seafarers living in Poland work on ships of foreign shipowners or ship operators. Additionally approximately 10 000 people work ashore as marine superintendents or managers. Both these groups constitute approximately 1.5% of total number of Poles working abroad responsible for 37–38% percent of the total number of yearly money transfers to the country. Furthermore, Poland is conveniently located in the heart of Europe, usually within one hour of flight from major shipping centers".

[132] Chinese Report, I.7.

[133] Japanese Report, I.7.

[134] Vasallo (2015).

new vessels to the Japanese builder Mitsubishi for a better price than in former opportunities.[135]

In America and considering the jurisdictions dealt with in this report, there are a large number of shipyards able to serve cruise vessels of different sizes, for example in Argentina,[136] in Brazil throughout the country though they do not have tradition with cruise vessels,[137] and in Uruguay, where the dike with greater capacity of the country is the TSAKOS floating dock, located in the harbour of Montevideo.[138]

Looking again towards Europe, Spain is the fourth major centre for cruise ship construction and maintenance and the business is increasing.[139] In Germany there is one of the leading shipyards for cruise ships in the world, which is the Meyer Werft in Papenburg. There are other important shipyards located at the Baltic Sea.[140] In Romania there are several construction and repair yards for sea and river vessels.[141] Poland has managed to maintain ship repair yards in spite of the period of large crisis in the shipyard industry. The national reporters inform that they "continue to offer shipping industry with wide range of services, from minor to class repairs and ships' conversions. In particular, Gdańsk has become a renowned centre with shipyards specializing in passenger ships and ferries. There are limits however relating to the size of ships attended in Polish shipyards due to restrictions on the size of ships entering and depth of the docks".[142] Also in Belgium, though several shipyards have disappeared by the end of last century due to the crisis in the shipping business and the competition distortion by low-wage countries, there are still many shipyards where ships can be repaired, especially in Antwerp.[143] On the other hand, in countries like Bulgaria there are no good shipyards to provide services to cruises.[144]

Regarding Asia, in Japan, "Mitsubishi Heavy Industries builds cargo-passenger ships and small or medium-sized passenger ships. Tsuneishi Shipbuilding has also

[135] Estepa Montero (2013), p. 338.

[136] See more information in the Argentine Report, I.8.

[137] See the very illustrative map included in the Brazilian Report, I.8 (Mapa dos Estaleiros no Brasil).

[138] Uruguayan Report, I.8, where the authors specify that the characteristics of the referred dike are: length 200 m, inner breath of 31.5 m, a lifting capacity of 15,000 tons and two cranes of 10 and 15 tons. See: http://www.tsakosmonte.com.uy/.

[139] See more information in the Spanish Report, I.8.

[140] See more information in the German Report, I.8.

[141] See more information in the Romanian Report, I.8.

[142] Polish Report, I.8.

[143] Belgian Report, I.8, mentions, for example: Antwerp Ship Repair, Engine Deck Repair Belgium (dry dock maximum capacity 180,000 dwt), Longueville Shiprepairs, etc. Also "in the Baudouin Canal (Zeebrugge), there is a recycling terminal (operated by Denolf Recycling) and a drydock shipyard (operated by Flanders Ship Repair/Longueville). The shipyard offers 24-hour services (mechanical repairs, welding, piping, propulsion and engines works, diving, high-pressure cleaning, painting, sandblasting). The shipyard has a drydock (Berth 413) with length 106 m (348 ft) and lifting capacity of 4500 tons".

[144] Bulgarian Report, I.8.

expanded their business to building of cruise ships".[145] In China the existence of several shipyards has been reported.

2.3.6 Relevance of Cruise Business in Labour Market

There is no much information and statistics reported on this topic. However, and shedding some light on the matter, it can be said that in some countries like Argentina, Brazil, Spain, Germany, China and Japan, cruise business is relevant regarding labour market, but in others like Romania, Bulgaria and Poland it is null or not significant yet.

Since 2016 the cruise industry in Argentina has been recovering and consequently the creation of related jobs. The impact is bigger in cruise destiny regions.[146] In Brazil the cruise business is a relevant labour market.[147] In Uruguay there are no specific statistics on the relevance of cruises regarding the labour market, but only general ones on the impact of tourism in general on the national labour market.[148]

In Spain the cruise business is relevant regarding the labour market, generating 25,483 jobs in 2014 with an increase of 12.1% in 2015.[149] The generation of jobs in Germany[150] is also important, as well as in China[151] and Japan.[152]

On the other hand, in countries like Bulgaria, there is no impact at all of the cruise business on the labour market.[153] In Romania and in Poland that impact is not significant yet.[154]

2.3.7 Flags of Convenience

Flying flags of convenience instead of the natural ones, which are those of the ship and her owners' nationality, became a necessity during some war conflicts occurred during the twentieth century, when it was inevitable to fly neutral flags to avoid

[145] Japanese Report, I.8.

[146] Argentine Report, I.6.

[147] In the Brazilian Report, I.6, for example, the national reporter informs that "According to CLIA/FGV, the 2015/2016 cruise season created 30.884 jobs: 2.497 crewmembers and 28.387 direct and indirect jobs".

[148] See more information in the Uruguayan Report, I.6.

[149] Spanish Report, I.6.

[150] See more information in the German Report, I.6.

[151] Chinese Report, I.6.

[152] Japanese Report, I.6.

[153] See more information in the Bulgarian Report, I.6.

[154] See more information in the Romanian Report, I.6 and in the Polish Report, I.6.

being attacked. However, once the war conflicts where over, many ship-owners kept on using flags of convenience since they discovered it was a very good business.[155]

Nowadays it is a common worldwide practice to sail under flags of convenience which consists of registering ships—cruise ships and cargo ships—not in the ship-owner's country but in another with less safety and labour requirements, fewer taxes and other advantages. This practice has even been referred to as "a fundamental principle of maritime law", but at the same time recognized to be "the crux of the most difficult challenges in this industry", at least for those governments that attempt to regulate personal and environmental safety and raise due tax revenues. It has been reported that only one big cruise ship built in the last 50 years—Pride of America, which is operated by Norwegian Cruise Lines and was launched in 2005—is currently registered in the U.S. and thus is U.S. flagged.[156] The most popular flags of convenience are those of Panama, Liberia and Bahamas, in that order, being the latter the most popular registry for cruise ships.[157] However, there are many other flags that are used as flags of convenience.[158]

The right of the States to register ships under their flags is recognized by the International Maritime Organization (IMO) and the United Nations Convention on the Law of the Sea, Montego Bay, 1982 (Article 90).[159] There is some case law reported by some jurisdictions considered in this general report, like *Lauritzen v. Larsen,*[160] where the United States Supreme Court stated the U.S. position on the law of the flag.[161]

Under Article 92 of the Montego Bay Convention ships shall be subject to its exclusive jurisdiction on the high seas. Article 94 provides that: "Every State shall effectively exercise its jurisdiction and control in administrative, technical and social matters over ships flying its flag. (. . .)". As a consequence of the common practice of using flags of convenience, passengers or other claimants are often under the jurisdiction of countries with very poor legal systems and no real connection to the case.

[155] Beltrán Montiel (1981), p. 99; Aguirre Ramírez and Fresnedo de Aguirre (2016), pp. 120–121.

[156] USA Report, I, which refers to *How the cruise ship industry sails under the radar*, Jan. 24, 2012, reuters.com/article/uk-italy-ship-regulation/how-the-cruise-ship-industry-sails-under-the-radar-idUSLINEBON02M0120124. See also https://www.ncl.com/cruise-ship/pride-of-america.

[157] See detailed information in the USA Report. I.

[158] Romero Basaldúa (1996), p. 247, mentions as countries offering flags of convenience: Antigua and Barbuda, Netherlands Antilles, Bahamas, Bermuda, Cayman Islands, Cook Islands, Cyprus, Gibraltar, Honduras, Lebanon, Malta, Marshall Islands, Mauritius Islands, Panama, Saint Vincent, Sri Lanka, Tuvalu, and Vanuatu.

[159] http://www.un.org/depts/los/convention_agreements/texts/unclos/unclos_e.pdf See also Articles 91 on nationality of ships, 92 on status of ship, providing that ships shall sail under the flag of one State only, and 94 on duties of the flag State.

[160] *Lauritzen v. Larsen*, 345 U.S. 571 (1953).

[161] USA Report. I.

In spite of the efforts of the international community to obtain the proper flagging of ships, the results are not too encouraging.[162]

2.4 *Final Remarks*

Statistics demonstrate that the cruise business has a growing importance almost all over the world, and that it has a great economic impact, particularly in some regions and countries.

Port services offered to cruises are generally good or very good, or at least acceptable in most cruise destinies.

Ship management industry is generally not limited to cruises and is increasing in several jurisdictions.

Cruise building and repairmen market is relevant in Europe and also in Asia; in America there are also many shipyards able to serve cruise vessels appropriately.

Though there is no much information and statistics on the matter, it can be stated that cruise business is relevant in labour market of several countries, while in others is null.

It is a common worldwide practice to sail under flags of convenience, which has been referred to as "a fundamental principle of maritime law", but at the same time recognized to be "the crux of the most difficult challenges in this industry", at least for those governments that attempt to regulate personal and environmental safety and raise due tax revenues. It seems we are far from overcoming problems derived from such extended practice.

3 General and Specific Rules Applicable to Cruises

3.1 *Cruises as an Issue To Be Approached by Several Law Matters*

It is obviously difficult to reach an adequate legal regulation regarding a complex matter like the touristic phenomenon, including of course cruise services.[163] At present a variety of norms coexist at the global level: substantive international conventions, international and national conflict of laws rules and substantive national rules, both of legal and administrative nature, together with sources of self-regulation, soft law and lex mercatoria, most of which will be analysed or at least mentioned hereinafter. Those rules refer to different areas of the law that are all relevant to cruises, most of them with a general scope of application, though some of

[162] Aguirre Ramírez and Fresnedo de Aguirre (2016), p. 121.

[163] Barreiro (2008), p. 322.

them refer specifically to carriage of passengers by sea and some of them even more specifically to cruises. Let as have a look to that diverse legal scenery.

In most countries, like for example, Argentina,[164] Bulgaria,[165] Canada,[166] Japan,[167] Poland,[168] Romania[169] and Uruguay[170] there are no specific rules addressed to cruises but more general provisions on several areas of the law which include in their scope of application different activities related to the cruise business. That is the case, for example, of Maritime Law, Commercial Law, Criminal Law, Civil Law, Environmental Law, Tax Law and others,[171] as we will analyse throughout this general report. However, some specific rules on cruises can be found in some countries or regions like for example in China,[172] Belgium,[173] and Brazil.[174] As those specific rules are very few,[175] rules applicable to broader categories of maritime activities are also applicable to cruises.[176]

3.2 *General Rules Applicable in the Absence or Insufficiency of Specific Rules*

It is generally recognised that if there are no specific rules on a certain topic in a certain legal system, general rules on that topic will be applicable. In our case, general rules on carriage of passengers by sea—both of a national or international origin—are applicable to cruise passengers, since cruises are considered a speciality of maritime transport.[177] This can be observed throughout various jurisdictions, like Argentina, Brazil, Belgium, Bulgaria, China, Japan, Poland, Romania, Turkey, and Uruguay. In the absence or insufficiency of rules on carriage of passengers by sea,

[164] Argentine Report, II.9.

[165] Bulgarian Report, II.9.

[166] Chircop et al. (2016), pp. 658–666.

[167] Japanese Report, II.9.

[168] Polish Report, II.9.

[169] See more details in Romanian Report, II.9.

[170] Uruguayan Report, II.9.

[171] For example, information on the cruise market and competition law is provided for in the Belgian Report, II.9.13.

[172] Chinese Report, II.

[173] Belgian Report, II.9.

[174] Brazilian Report, II.9–10.

[175] The USA reports to have "a robust legislative framework regulating major aspects of cruises, including vessel design requirements, safety requirements, civil and criminal liability regimes, labor regulations, and environmental protection. Most of the legislative measures that apply to cruises are maritime laws applying to maritime vessels in general, although a few U.S. laws specifically apply to cruise vessels".

[176] Belgian Report, II.9 and III.14.

[177] Spanish Report, III.14.

general rules on international contracts should apply to cruise contracts, as it is reported, for example, from Bulgaria,[178] China,[179] Romania,[180] and Uruguay.[181] Together with the aforementioned general rule, it must be taken into account the prevailing application of rules on consumer protection, when applicable.[182] In Brazil general rules on international contracts may be seldom applicable to cruises, because Consumer Code regulations are applied in most cases.[183]

3.3 *Sources of Law Relevant to Cruises*

This chapter will deal only with the sources of law relevant to cruises in some jurisdictions that are considered in this general report. Most of the subjects mentioned in this epigraph are developed hereinafter in further specific epigraphs and chapters.

3.3.1 In Europe

In Bulgaria

In Bulgaria the national Act on Consumers' Protection is applicable to cruise passengers since they are consumers of the "cruise touristic product". That product is a service under the referred Act. Besides, Bulgaria is a member of the European Union and therefore the Union's Acts regarding consumers' protection are part of the Bulgarian national legislation. These Acts prevail if the national rules are in contradiction with the European Acts, particularly with Regulation N° 593/2008 of the European Parliament and of the Council of June 17, 2008 (Rome I). However, Bulgarian national rules are harmonized with the European Union's Acts.[184] When there is no direct conventional rules applicable, conflict-of-laws rules indicating the national rules applicable apply. The *lex loci contractus* rules the legal formalities of the contract and its proof. Regarding the content of the contract, there are several possible formulas, among which the main ones are the *lex patriae* of the carrier applies, the law of the flag and the law of the place of performance.[185]

[178] Bulgarian national Report, III.16 and VIII.41 with detailed information.

[179] Chinese Report, III.14–17.

[180] Romanian Report, III.16.

[181] Uruguayan Report, III.16.

[182] Romanian Report, III.18.

[183] Brazilian Report, III.16.

[184] Bulgarian National Report, III.18.

[185] See further details in the Bulgarian National Report, III.14.

In Germany

In Germany the Directive 90/314/EEC of 13 June 1990 on package travel, package holidays and package tours (the Package Travel Directive of 1990) currently superseded by the Directive 2015/2302 has been transposed to ss. 651a et seq. of the Civil Code (BGB).[186]

The German legislator adapted the rules for carriage by sea to the Athens Convention by the review of the sea carriage provisions of the Handelsgesetzbuch (Commercial Code). These provisions are also applicable to internal waterways and therefore they play a certain role for river cruises, as neither the Athens Convention nor Reg. (EU) 392/2009 apply to river cruises.[187]

The Directive 90/314/EEC (Package Travel Directive) was implemented by Germany in 1995. The German legislator amended the contract law sections of the Civil Code (Bürgerliches Gesetzbuch) by a special chapter about package travel (originally §§ 651a to 651k BGB).

In Poland

In Poland, consumer protection law is that of the European law and are in general applicable to cruises, particularly those on unfair contract terms.[188] Consumer protection rules regarding "contracts negotiated away from business premises and distance contracts which are implemented into the Polish law in the Consumer Rights Act of 2014[189] are not applicable to the contracts on package as defined in the Directive 90/314/EEC of 13 June 1990 on package travel, package holidays and package tours[190] (the Package Travel Directive of 1990) currently superseded by the directive 2015/2302[191]". As a cruise tour often fulfils the prerequisites of a package, a consumer in such contracts may not benefit from the protection afforded in the Consumer Rights Act.[192]

The Polish Maritime Code of 2001[193] applies to cruises.

The Directive 2009/45/EC of the European Parliament and of the Council of 6 May 2009 on safety rules and standards for passenger ships[194] which have been implemented in Poland by the Maritime Safety Act of 2011[195] are rules of public law character.[196]

186 German national Report, III.14, 18.
187 German national Report, III.14.
188 Polish Report, III.18.
189 Consolidated text in Journal of Laws 2017 item 683.
190 OJ L 158, 23.6.1990, pp. 59–64.
191 OJ L 326, 11.12.2015, pp. 1–33.
192 See more detailed information in Polish Report, III.18.
193 Consolidated text in Journal of Laws 2016, item 66.
194 OJ L 163, 25.6.2009, pp. 1–140.
195 Consolidated text in Journal of Laws 2016 item 281.
196 See more detailed information in Polish Report, III.15.

In Spain

In Spain, the Royal Decree-Legislative 1/2007 of 16 November approving the Recast text of the General Law on Consumer Protection and other supplementary laws (*Real Decreto Legislativo 1/2007, de 16 de noviembre, por el que se aprueba el texto Refundido de la Ley General para la Defensa de los Consumidores y Usuarios y otras leyes complementarias*, B.O.E. 30 November 2007) is applicable to cruise passengers.[197] Also the Royal Decree 357/2015, 8 May 2015, on compliance and enforcement of the 2006 Maritime Labour Convention, applies to cruises.[198]

The Travel Packages Act (*Ley 21/1995, de 6 de Julio reguladora de los viajes combinados*), which is the transposition of the European Council Directive 90/314/EEC of 13 June 1990 on package travel, package holidays and package tours. This directive was replaced by the new Directive (EU) 2015/2302 of the European Parliament and of the Council of 25 November 2015 on package travel and linked travel arrangements, which had to be transposed by the Member States before 1st January 2018.[199]

The Spanish Law on Shipping (*Ley 14/2014 de 24 de julio, Ley de Navegación Maritima*) regulates in Articles 287–300 the passage contract and is therefore applicable to cruises. Article 298 regulates carrier's liability and Article 299 its limitation. It follows the solutions in the Athens Convention and its 2002 London Protocol. Chapter III of Title III of this Law deals with able seafarers on board Spanish ships.[200]

The law governing the employment contracts in Spain is determined by Article 8 of the Regulation (EC) 593/2008 of the European Parliament and of the Council of 17 June 2008 on the law applicable to contractual obligations (Rome I).[201] There are also some specific collective agreements.[202]

The main regulation on ports, including cruise ships, is the Real Legislative Decree 2/2011, 5 September and its annexes, and some ministerial rank regulations.[203]

Rules on jurisdiction regarding cruise matters are in the Spanish Law on Judiciary (*Ley Orgánica del Poder Judicial*) amended by Act 7/2015 of July 7, and in the Spanish Law on Shipping (*Ley 14/2014, 24 de Julio, de Navegación maritima*).

Regulation CEE 4.055/86, 22/12/86 rules the application of the principle of free provision of services in maritime transport among member States (communitarian coastal navigation or intra-communitarian transport) and among member States and third countries of the continental shelf. Regulation CEE 3.572/92, 7/12/92 rules the application of the principle of free provision of services to maritime transports at the

---

[197] Spanish Report, II.12.

[198] Spanish Report, IV.22.

[199] Spanish Report, II.9.

[200] See further information in Spanish Report, IV.22.

[201] Spanish Report, IV.22.

[202] Spanish Report, IV. 21.

[203] Spanish Report, V. 28.

interior of the member States. As a consequence, a system of full freedom to perform maritime traffic of cruises exists in Spain. That traffic is mainly seasonal and may be exercised regularly, repeating routes and duration of cruises, or occasionally with specially designed trips.[204]

3.3.2 In the Americas

In Argentina

In Argentina,[205] cruises are not specifically ruled. Rules on passage contract—which is an adhesion contract—are applicable (Articles 317–346 of the Navigation Act—Ley de Navegación—and Athens Convention 1974). It is a mixed contract since it includes obligations that belong to the transport (the trip) together with other obligations, like providing entertainment, obligation of navigability (Article 317 of the Navigation Act), which imply to put and maintain the vessel in navigability conditions: to exercise due diligence to guarantee the security and integrity of the passenger, by maintaining generic navigability (floatability, govern, propulsion, provision of trained crew) and concrete navigability (food, lodging, entertainment, swimming pool, sports, casino, gym).

Act N° 24.240 on Consumer Defence excludes air carriage from its scope of application, but says nothing on carriage by sea. Therefore, it applies to carriage by sea, as has been recognised by commentators and courts.[206]

The Navigation Act N° 20.094, the REGINAVE Decree N° 4.516/73, the Travel Agents' Act N° 18.829 and its Regulatory Decree 2182/72 are applicable to cruises.

In Brazil

In Brazil the Federal Act N° 8.078/90, known as Consumer Code, is applicable to cruises.[207]

The Presidential Decree N° 7.381/2010 provides legal definitions for cabotage, international, long haul and hybrid cruises as well as defines scales, embarks, disembarks and transit.[208]

In Uruguay

In Uruguay, Act 17.250 on consumer relations applies to cruise passengers. The passenger is a "final recipient" of the service and the passenger contract is an adhesion contract that refers to "general contracting conditions" imposed unilaterally by the carrier. Article 31 prohibits abusive clauses in adhesion contracts and exemplifies mentioning clauses of limitation and exemption of liability unless a rule of law allows it, the waiver of consumer rights, the authorization to the supplier

---

[204] Estepa Montero (2012), pp. 139–140; Ariza Herrerías (2014), p. 10.

[205] See: Estepa Montero (2012), pp. 142–144; Ariza Herrerías (2014), pp. 13 y ss.

[206] See Argentine Report, II.18 and case law mentioned there.

[207] Brazilian Report, III.16, 18.

[208] Brazilian Report, II.9–10.

to unilaterally modify the terms of the contract, those that reverse the burden of proof to the detriment of the consumer, among others.[209] The carrier's obligation to transport the passengers implies to do it safely up to destination. This obligation is of public order and cannot be repealed by clauses of irresponsibility. Act 17.250 on consumer relations is very clear in this regard.

In Uruguay general rules on carriage of passengers are in the Commercial Code (Articles 1282–1289), Act N° 19.246 of August 15, 2015 on Maritime Commercial Law.[210] Under Articles 1282–1289 of the Commercial Code, the main obligation of the carrier is to transport the passenger from one place to another, and as accessory obligations, he must provide accommodation and food to the passenger as well as take care of his safety and health. On the other hand, the main obligation of the passenger is to pay the price; travelling without paying is a criminal misconduct provided for in the Penal Code (Article 366) and the captain has the privilege over the baggage (Article 1289 Commercial Code). Obviously there are other accessory obligations: the day and time designated for the departure the passenger must get on board (Article 1283 *ejusdem*).

The omission of compliance with this obligation is sanctioned with the obligation to pay the price, even if he misses the vessel and cannot travel. If the voyage is cancelled because of the fault of the carrier, he owes damages according to the general rules on breach of contract. Under Article 1285.1 *ejusdem* if the voyage is terminated by force majeure at the port of departure the contract is terminated, without any right to compensation. The passenger has also the obligation to obey the captain (Article 1286 *ejusdem*) who has disciplinary power to keep order on board and even criminal investigation powers in case of crime (Article 1075 *ejusdem*), including the power of arresting a passenger and handing it over to the authorities of the first port of arrival.[211]

USA

The USA sources of law regarding cruises are mainly the U.S. Const., art. III, § 2, cl. 1; 28 U.S.C. § 3033(1); Passenger Vessel Services Act, 46 U.S.C. § 55103(b); Merchant Marine Act, also known as the Jones Act, 1920, and further amendments: Jones Act, 46 U.S.C. §30104; Death on the High Seas Act 46 U.S.C. app. §§ 761–768 (1920) (DOHSA), codified at 46 U.S.C. 303, et seq., US House of Representatives, Office of the Law Revision Council, *United States Code. Chapter 303 Death on the High Seas*;[212] Cruise Vessel Security and Safety Act of 2010, Pub. L. 111-207, 124 Stat. 2243, et seq., Jul. 27, 2010, enacted at

[209] For further information please see Aguirre Ramírez and Fresnedo de Aguirre (2011). See Uruguayan Report, III.15 and 18.

[210] Uruguayan Report, III.14.

[211] Uruguayan Report, III.15.

[212] http://uscode.house.gov/view.xhtml?path=/prelim@title46/subtitle3/chapter303&edition=prelim.

46 U.S.C. §3507;[213] and Marine Protection, Research, and Sanctuaries Act (16 U.S. C. § 1431 and 33 U.S.C. § 1401).[214]

The General Maritime Law (GML) governs many maritime relationships, while the Constitution "grants the federal courts the judicial power to hear all cases of admiralty and maritime jurisdiction. From this grant of power, the federal courts have developed the substantive law applicable to these cases. GML is a result of the federal court's decisions, including the body of judicial principles that have been adopted by the federal courts in resolving maritime disputes". (...) "State law can supplement GML provided it does not conflict with GML precedent, federal law, or the need for uniformity – namely that there is not a rule that is different from state to state". (...) "In addition to the judicially created body of GML, Congress has enacted a number of statutes that control issues concerning..." for example, the rights of marine employees. Such federal statutes control over the GML. "...treaties that the United States has ratified have the same force as a statute, and likewise control areas governed by their terms".[215]

3.3.3 In Asia

In Japan

In Japan provisions on carriage of passengers by sea in Part III "Maritime Commerce" of the Commercial Code apply to cruise passengers. It is to be noted that there is a revised proposal of the Commercial Code which may be enacted during 2018 that provide that "any special clauses to exclude or reduce carrier's liability for damages caused by death or bodily injury of passengers during carriage of passengers are prohibited irrespective of whether the passenger is a consumer or not, while some exceptions are allowed".[216]

In Turkey

In Turkey, general rules on carriage of passengers and their baggage by sea are those in the Turkish Commercial Code's Fifth Book Maritime Law, Fifth Chapter Contract of Carriage of Passengers by Sea, Articles 1247–1271. These rules are mostly enactment of the 2002 Athens Convention, though Turkey is not yet party to this Convention. There are also several provisions in Tourism Law, Port Law and others that refer to cruises.[217]

[213] See USA Report, IV; https://www.gpo.gov/fdsys/pkg/BILLS-111hr3360enr/pdf/BILLS-111hr3360enr.pdf [hereinafter CVSSA].

[214] USA National Report.

[215] Felder (2006), pp. 25–27.

[216] Japanese Report, III.18.

[217] See Turkish Report, B.

3.4 Sources of Self-regulation, Soft-Law, Lex Mercatoria

Current practices and usages developed through the years regarding maritime activities are relevant for cruise business. There are also some specific soft law instruments on cruise business issued by private organizations like CLIA:[218] Guidelines on cruise ship medical facilities,[219] cruise industry standard on waste management practices and procedures (2006),[220] Cruise Industry Influenza Protocol (2009),[221] and Ten Points Cruise Passenger Bill of Rights (2013),[222] among others.[223]

3.4.1 Medical Facilities

Regarding medical facilities, many cruise ship physicians are members of the American College of Emergency Physicians (ACEP) and serve on that organization's Cruise Ship and Maritime Medicine Section. ACEP has also issued Health Care Guidelines for Cruise Ship Medical Facilities (2014)[224] regarding facilities, staffing, equipment and procedures for medical infirmaries on cruise ships travelling outside territorial waters of the coastal state. Patients requiring more comprehensive facilities or treatment are typically referred to a shore side medical facility. CLIA cruise lines travelling regularly on itineraries beyond the territorial waters of the coastal state, have agreed to meet or exceed the requirements of the referred ACEP Guidelines.[225]

3.4.2 Cruise Industry Influenza Protocol (2009)

In April 2009 a new strain of the H1N1 flu virus, commonly known as 'swine flu', broke out in several countries and panic spread. The World Health Organisation raising its pandemic alert to phase six representing 'widespread human infection'.

---

[218] As explained *supra* in Sect. 2.3.1, CLIA (Cruise Lines International Association) Europe is an important cruise industry trade association with offices in Brussels that promotes the interests of cruise ship operators within Europe. CLIA has also representations in some national markets across Europe (national chapters) and is also present in North and South America, Asia, and Australasia.

[219] https://www.cruising.org/about-the-industry/regulatory/industry-policies/health/medical-facilities.

[220] https://www.cruising.org/about-the-industry/regulatory/industry-policies/environmental-protection/waste-management.

[221] https://www.vallettawaterfront.com/DetailPage.aspx?id=156262.

[222] https://www.cruising.org/about-the-industry/regulatory/industry-policies/other/pbor.

[223] See Belgian Report, II.9.

[224] http://www.acep.org/cruiseship/.

[225] https://www.cruising.org/about-the-industry/regulatory/industry-policies/health/medical-facilities.

By end of April 2009, CLIA developed a special questionnaire that was implemented and given out to all guests and crew prior to embarkation. The aim of that tool was to provide the ship's medical staff with an important early risk evaluation. Any arrival with influenza-like symptoms is required to undergo a quayside medical examination that includes a quick, accurate test to determine the presence or absence of an influenza that could be H1N1.[226]

3.4.3 Ten Points Cruise Passenger Bill of Rights (2013)

As reported in CLIA's website, CLIA member lines have voluntarily adopted the *Cruise Industry Passenger Bill of Rights*, which is effective for all passengers that book an oceangoing cruise on a CLIA member cruise line worldwide.[227]

3.5 *Liability Issues*

3.5.1 Applicable Rules: General or Specific?

In most countries there are no specific rules on liability regarding cruises. Therefore, general rules on liability apply, unless specific rules on consumer protection are applicable. In the latter case, consumer protection rules prevail over civil codes' general rules.[228] There is some case-law showing the application of the Consumer Code only or the application of both the Civil and the Consumer Codes.[229]

3.5.2 International Rules: The Athens Convention Relating to the Carriage of Passengers and Their Luggage by Sea of 1974 and Protocols

Scopes of Application and Definitions

The Athens Convention relating to the Carriage of Passengers and their Luggage by Sea[230] as amended by the relevant Protocols has been ratified by several countries from Europe and from other regions. In fact, the 1974 Athens Convention is in force in several countries like Argentina, Bahamas, Barbados, China, Congo, Dominica,

---

[226] https://www.vallettawaterfront.com/DetailPage.aspx?id=156262.

[227] See the full text of the *Cruise Industry Passenger Bill of Rights* in https://www.cruising.org/about-the-industry/regulatory/industry-policies/other/pbor.

[228] This is the case, for example, of Brazil (National Report IX.45).

[229] See Brazilian National Report IX.46.

[230] See text, complete list of signatures, ratifications, acceptances, approvals, accessions, Declarations, Reservations and other information at https://treaties.un.org/doc/Publication/UNTS/Volume%201463/volume-1463-I-24817-English.pdf.

Egypt, Equatorial Guinea, Estonia, Georgia, Guyana, Ireland, Jordan, Liberia, Libya, Luxembourg, Malawi, Nigeria, Poland, Russian Federation, Saint Kitts and Nevis, Switzerland, Tonga, Ukraine, Vanuatu and Yemen.[231]

Article 1 of the Convention provides for a definition of several terms, like "carrier", "performing carrier", "contract of carriage", "ship", "passenger", "luggage", among others.

Under Article 2, the scope of application of the Athens Convention includes "...any international carriage if: (a) The ship is flying the flag of or is registered in a State Party to this Convention, or (b) The contract of carriage has been made in a State Party to this Convention, or (c) The place of departure or destination, according to the contract of carriage, is in a State Party to this Convention. 2. Notwithstanding paragraph 1 of this Article, this Convention shall not apply when the carriage is subject, under any other international convention concerning the carriage of passengers or luggage by another mode of transport, to a civil liability regime under the provisions of such convention, in so far as those provisions have mandatory application to carriage by sea". Article 21 states that: "This Convention shall apply to commercial carriage undertaken by States or Public Authorities under contracts of carriage within the meaning of Article 1."

Parties' Liability

Several Articles in the Convention rule the parties' liability. Article 3 deals with the carrier's liability for the damage suffered as a result of the death of or personal injury to a passenger and the loss of or damage to luggage. His responsibility is limited to two cumulative hypotheses: (1) that the incident which caused the damage occurred in the course of the carriage, and (2) that the incident "was due to the fault or neglect of the carrier or of his servants or agents acting within the scope of their employment" (Article 3.1). The burden of the proof is of the claimant (Article 3.2). Article 3.3 establishes some presumptions on when the incident is due to the fault or neglect of the carrier or of his servants or agents. In principle the carrier shall not be liable for the loss of or damage to valuables, except if they were deposited with the carrier for the agreed purpose of safe-keeping, and even in the latter case, limits are applicable (Article 5). Article 6 deals with contributory fault cases.

Article 4 states rules on how liability is distributed in those cases where the carrier entrusts the carriage or part of it to a performing carrier and the requirements that a special agreement entered into by the carrier and the performing carrier must fulfil to be validated.

Limits of Liability

Limits of liability are dealt with in Articles 7–13. Article 7 refers specifically to the limitation of liability of the carrier for the death of or personal injury to a passenger (700,000 francs per carriage) but admits that "the national law of any State Party to

[231] http://www.imo.org/en/About/Conventions/StatusOfConventions/Documents/Status%20-%202018.pdf and national reports. It is worth noting that several countries have denounced the Convention, like for example, Albania, Belgium. Croatia, Greece and Spain, among other countries.

this Convention may fix, as far as carriers who are nationals of such State are concerned, a higher per capita limit of liability". The carrier and the passenger may also agree, expressly and in writing, to higher limits of liability than those prescribed in Articles 7 and 8 (Article 10.1). Article 8 states the limit of liability of the carrier for the loss of or damage to cabin luggage (12,500 francs per passenger, per carriage) and vehicles (50,000 francs per vehicle, per carriage) and admits some restricted agreements between the carrier and the passenger.

Article 9 is a key point in the Convention since it deals with monetary unit and conversion. It states that "the franc mentioned in this Convention shall be deemed to refer to a unit consisting of 65.5 milligrams of gold of millesimal fineness 900", and then "converted into the national currency of the State of the court seized of the case...". Under Article 10.2, "Interest on damages and legal costs shall not be included in the limits of liability prescribed in Articles 7 and 8".

Under Article 11, defences and limits established in the Convention for carriers are applicable to carriers' servants and agents. Article 12 refers to limits of liability in case of aggregation of claims.

Article 19 provides for a compatibility clause, which states that "This Convention shall not modify the rights or duties of the carrier, the performing carrier, and their servants or agents provided for in international conventions relating to the limitation of liability of owners of seagoing ships".

The carrier and his servants or agents lose their benefit of the limits of liability if it is proved that the damage resulted from an act or omission of the carrier or his servants or agents "done with the intent to cause such damage, or recklessly and with knowledge that such damage would probably result" (Article 13).

Article 15 rules how the passenger shall give notice to the carrier or his agent in case of loss or damage to his luggage and the consequences for not doing so.

Invalidity of Some Contractual Provisions

Article 18 refers to the invalidity of some contractual provision concluded before the occurrence of the incident which has caused the death of or personal injury to a passenger or the loss of or damage to his luggage, particularly those purporting to relieve the carrier of his liability towards the passenger or to prescribe a lower limit of liability than that fixed in this Convention or to shift the burden of proof which rests on the carrier, among others. The nullity of that provision shall not render void the contract of carriage which shall remain subject to the provisions of this Convention.

The 1990 Protocol to Amend the Athens Convention Relating to Carriage of Passengers and Their Luggage by Sea

This Protocol of 1990 was intended to raise the limits set out in the Athens Convention but it did not enter into force and was superseded by the 2002 Protocol. Therefore, it will not be analyzed here.

The 2002 Protocol or "Athens Convention Relating to the Carriage of Passengers and Their Luggage by Sea, 2002"

The Protocol was adopted on November 1, 2002 and entered into force on April 23, 2014, 12 months after being accepted by 10 States. The European Union became a party to the Protocol through the Council Decision 2012/22/EU of 12 December 2011 concerning the accession of the European Union to the Protocol of 2002 to the Athens Convention relating to the Carriage of Passengers and their Luggage by Sea, 1974, with the exception of Articles 10 and 11 thereof.[232]

The Protocol main improvements are those related with the strict liability of the carrier, including compulsory insurance or other financial security, such as the guarantee of a bank or similar financial institution, to (Article 4bis), with a right of direct action against insurers up to specified limits, and for rules on jurisdiction and the recognition and enforcement of judgments. The Protocol also introduces other mechanisms to assist passengers in obtaining compensation. Regarding liability, it includes "an "opt-out" clause, enabling State Parties to retain or introduce higher limits of liability (or unlimited liability) in the case of carriers who are subject to the jurisdiction of their courts".[233]

Decision 2012/22/EU states that the Protocol and its raising the limits of liability, among other improvements, are "in accordance with the Union's objective of improving the legal regime relating to carriers' liability".[234]

It is important to point out that the 2002 Protocol amends the 1974 Athens Convention fixing liability limits in **Units of Account**, and that under Article 9, the Unit of Account is the **Special Drawing Right** (SDR) as defined by the International Monetary Fund.[235] The 1974 Athens Convention fixed the limits of liability in francs that referred "to a unit consisting of 65.5 milligrams of gold of millesimal fineness 900". It must be noticed that the Protocol "allows a State Party to regulate by specific provisions of national law the limit of liability for personal injury and death, provided that the national limit of liability, if any, is not lower than that prescribed in the Protocol. A State Party, which makes use of this option is obliged to inform the IMO Secretary-General of the limit of liability adopted or of the fact that there is none" ("opt-out" clause).[236]

The 2002 Protocol supposedly intended an improvement since "any future raises in limits can be achieved more readily. Under the 1974 Convention, limits can only be raised by adopting amendments to the Convention which require a specified number of States' acceptances to bring the amendments into force". It introduces "a

---

[232] https://eur-lex.europa.eu/legal-content/EN/TXT/?uri=celex%3A32012D0022.

[233] http://www.imo.org/en/About/Conventions/ListOfConventions/Pages/Athens-Convention-relating-to-the-Carriage-of-Passengers-and-their-Luggage-by-Sea-(PAL).aspx.

[234] Whereas (1) of the Decision 2012/22/EU.

[235] See detailed text of Article 9 in https://eur-lex.europa.eu/legal-content/EN/TXT/?uri=celex%3A32012D0022.

[236] http://www.imo.org/en/About/Conventions/ListOfConventions/Pages/Athens-Convention-relating-to-the-Carriage-of-Passengers-and-their-Luggage-by-Sea-(PAL).aspx.

tacit acceptance procedure for raising the limits of liability. A proposal to amend the limits, as requested by at least one-half of the Parties to the Protocol, would be circulated to all IMO Member States and all States Parties and would then be discussed in the IMO Legal Committee. Amendments would be adopted by a two-thirds majority of the States Parties to the Convention as amended by the Protocol present and voting in the Legal Committee, and amendments would enter into force 18 months after its deemed acceptance date. The deemed acceptance date would be 18 months after adoption, unless within that period not less than one fourth of the States that were States Parties at the time of the adoption of the amendment have communicated to the IMO Secretary-General that they do not accept the amendment".[237]

The limit of the compulsory insurance or other financial security shall not be less than 250,000 Special Drawing Rights (SDR) per passenger on each distinct occasion and the liability of the carrier for the death of or personal injury to a passenger is limited to 250,000 SDR per passenger on each distinct occasion. Ships are to be issued with a certificate attesting that insurance or other financial security is in force.[238]

If the loss exceeds the limit, the carrier is further liable—up to a limit of 400,000 SDR per passenger on each distinct occasion—unless the carrier proves that the incident which caused the loss occurred without the fault or neglect of the carrier (Article 7.1).[239]

The 2002 Protocol replaces Article 3 of the Athens Convention, which deals with the carrier's liability, for the following text:

1. For the loss suffered as a result of the death of or personal injury to a passenger caused by a shipping incident, the carrier shall be liable to the extent that such loss in respect of that passenger on each distinct occasion does not exceed 250,000 units of account, unless the carrier proves that the incident:

   (a) resulted from an act of war, hostilities, civil war, insurrection or a natural phenomenon of an exceptional, inevitable and irresistible character; or
   (b) was wholly caused by an act or omission done with the intent to cause the incident by a third party.

   If and to the extent that the loss exceeds the above limit, the carrier shall be further liable unless the carrier proves that the incident which caused the loss occurred without the fault or neglect of the carrier.

2. For the loss suffered as a result of the death of or personal injury to a passenger not caused by a shipping incident, the carrier shall be liable if the incident which caused the loss was due to the fault or neglect of the carrier. The burden of proving fault or neglect shall lie with the claimant.

[237] http://www.imo.org/en/About/Conventions/ListOfConventions/Pages/Athens-Convention-relating-to-the-Carriage-of-Passengers-and-their-Luggage-by-Sea-(PAL).aspx.

[238] http://www.imo.org/en/About/Conventions/ListOfConventions/Pages/Athens-Convention-relating-to-the-Carriage-of-Passengers-and-their-Luggage-by-Sea-(PAL).aspx.

[239] http://www.imo.org/en/About/Conventions/ListOfConventions/Pages/Athens-Convention-relating-to-the-Carriage-of-Passengers-and-their-Luggage-by-Sea-(PAL).aspx.

3. For the loss suffered as a result of the loss of or damage to cabin luggage, the carrier shall be liable if the incident which caused the loss was due to the fault or neglect of the carrier. The fault or neglect of the carrier shall be presumed for loss caused by a shipping incident.
4. For the loss suffered as a result of the loss of or damage to luggage other than cabin luggage, the carrier shall be liable unless the carrier proves that the incident which caused the loss occurred without the fault or neglect of the carrier.
5. For the purposes of this Article:
   (a) "shipping incident" means shipwreck, capsizing, collision or stranding of the ship, explosion or fire in the ship, or defect in the ship;
   (b) "fault or neglect of the carrier" includes the fault or neglect of the servants of the carrier, acting within the scope of their employment;
   (c) 'defect in the ship' means any malfunction, failure or non-compliance with applicable safety regulations in respect of any part of the ship or its equipment when used for the escape, evacuation, embarkation and disembarkation of passengers; or when used for the propulsion, steering, safe navigation, mooring, anchoring, arriving at or leaving berth or anchorage, or damage control after flooding; or when used for the launching of life saving appliances; and
   (d) 'loss' shall not include punitive or exemplary damages.
6. The liability of the carrier under this Article only relates to loss arising from incidents that occurred in the course of the carriage. The burden of proving that the incident which caused the loss occurred in the course of the carriage, and the extent of the loss, shall lie with the claimant.
7. Nothing in this Convention shall prejudice any right of recourse of the carrier against any third party, or the defence of contributory negligence under Article 6 of this Convention. Nothing in this Article shall prejudice any right of limitation under Articles 7 or 8 of this Convention.
8. Presumptions of fault or neglect of a party or the allocation of the burden of proof to a party shall not prevent evidence in favour of that party from being considered.

Regarding the interpretation and application of both the 1974 Convention and the 2002 Protocol, Article 15 states that:

1. The Convention and this Protocol shall, as between the Parties to this Protocol, be read and interpreted together as one single instrument.
2. The Convention as revised by this Protocol shall apply only to claims arising out of occurrences which take place after the entry into force for each State of this Protocol.
3. Articles 1 to 22 of the Convention, as revised by this Protocol, together with Articles 17 to 25 of this Protocol and the annex thereto, shall constitute and be called the Athens Convention relating to the Carriage of Passengers and their Luggage by Sea, 2002.

3.5.3 Law Applicable in Some Countries and Regions

In Argentina, while on board, the liability regime of carriage of passengers by sea applies. The characteristics of that liability are: it is contractual, mandatory (art. 339 LN), limited and it must be insured.[240] The carrier's liability starts from the

[240] Chami and Adragna (2013) Regarding limitation of liability, see also Chami n.d.

moment the passenger steps on the landing stage he must use to get on board, or when he gets on board of the smaller boat that will carry him to the bigger vessel. However, opinions on this point are not unanimous.[241] The period of liability on board is from embarkation until landing of the passenger, and on land, since landing until re-embarkation of the passenger.[242]

Argentinean Courts have stated that in a cruise trip and regarding the carrier's obligation, ports of embarkment and disembarkment have the same importance as the intermediate ports, and that the fulfilment of the whole planned itinerary is essential; if it is not fulfilled, the carrier is responsible, unless the breach of contract is due to *force majeur* (Act of God). In that case, under Article 327 of the Navigation Act, the passenger must pay only in proportion of the itinerary performed.[243]

In the USA, the Jones Act gives a cause of action to injured sailors to seek damages from their employers for the negligence of the ship owner. The Death on the High Seas Act (DOHSA)[244] is a U.S. admiralty law that established a cause of action for damages against the "person or vessel" responsible for a wrongful death in international waters—beyond 3 nautical miles from the shore of the United States—resulting from negligence. Under U.S. law, liability of a cruise ship for personal injury or death is clearly defined.[245] A special duty of care owed to passengers by cruise lines was set out in the Shipping Act of 1984, which deems cruise ships as common carriers.[246] Thus, the cruise lines have a duty to protect passengers from physical harm, including from negligence, and also attacks and other criminal behaviour on board. Generally, it is prohibited for a ship transporting passengers within the United States or between the U.S. and a foreign country to limit in the passenger's ticket or contract the liability of the owner, master, or agent for personal injury or death caused by the negligence or fault of the owner or the owner's employees or agents; or the right of a claimant for personal injury or death to a trial by court of competent jurisdiction.[247]

In Canada, there is a substantive regime governing carrier liability to passengers: the Marine Liability Act, SC 2001 (MLA),[248] which applies whether a contractual choice of law clause exists or not, and where the carriage of passengers is "from one place of Canada to the same or another place in Canada, either directly or by way of a

---

[241] Ray (2002), p. 8.

[242] Chami and Adragna (2013).

[243] CN Civ. y Com. Fed., Sala II, 8-3-85, ED, 114-648, quoted in Vázquez Ferreyra and Fiscella (1997), pp. 333–334.

[244] Death on the High Seas Act 46 U.S.C. app. §§ 761–768 (1920) (DOHSA), codified at 46 U.S.C. 303, et seq., US House of Representatives, Office of the Law Revision Council, *United States Code. Chapter 303 Death on the High Seas* http://uscode.house.gov/view.xhtml?path=/prelim@title46/subtitle3/chapter303&edition=prelim.

[245] 46 U.S.C.A. § 30509 (Oct 6, 2006).

[246] Shipping Act of 1984, 46 U.S.C. §1702.

[247] See further information in USA Report, II, including case-law.

[248] See full text in http://laws-lois.justice.gc.ca/PDF/M-0.7.pdf.

place outside Canada", and applies also, subject to some exceptions,[249] to the carriage by water of persons "otherwise than under a contract of carriage". Although some contractual modifications of that regime are allowed, "the essential elements of the regime are unalterable to the advantage of the carrier (usually the author of the contract. . .)".[250]

At the European level, the European Union has issued Regulation (EC) N° 392/2009 of the European Parliament and of the Council of 23 April 2009 on the liability of carriers of passengers by sea in the event of accidents,[251] which is the relevant rule in Spain—and in other European countries—when it comes to the liability regime and the insurance for the carriage of passengers at sea as set out in the relevant provisions of the Athens Convention as amended by the Protocol of 2002 and the IMO Reservation and Guidelines for the Implementation of the Athens Convention adopted by the Legal Committee of the IMO on 19 October 2006.[252]

The relevance of this Regulation is that though identical to the Athens Convention 2002, it extends its scope of application to all carriages by sea within the EU. Consequently, under Article 2 of the Regulation (EC) N° 392/2009 a cruise which, for example, calls only on ports of one member state of the EU and therefore is not under the scope of the Athens Conventions, will be governed by the rules on liability in the Regulation, that are identical to those in the Convention. Therefore, in some countries this Regulation applies to national sea carriage of passengers by internal waters and by river cruises.[253]

In Europe, the carrier's liability in passenger carriage contracts is often governed by a supranational or international instrument; therefore, the question of the interrelationship between the package travel[254] contract liability regime and the passenger carriage liability regime arises. For maritime cruises, carrier's liability is ruled basically by the Athens Convention relating to the Carriage of Passengers and their Luggage by Sea (1974 as amended by Protocols.[255]

In Belgium, the EU Directive 2015/2302 (Recital 35 and art. 14, 4 and 5) was implemented/transposed by Belgian Act of 21 November 2017 (art. 51 and 52).[256]

In Bulgaria there are no specific rules on liability regarding cruises and they do not apply those included in the Athens Convention and its 2002 Protocol since they

[249] MLA, ss 37(2)(b)(i),(ii), (iii), (iv); 37.1(1), (2).

[250] Chircop et al. (2016), pp. 662–664. See further analysis the Canadian Maritime Liability Act in pp. 664–675.

[251] https://eur-lex.europa.eu/legal-content/EN/TXT/PDF/?uri=CELEX:32009R0392&from=EN.

[252] Spanish Report, II.12.

[253] German Report, III.15.

[254] See hereinafter in this general report, Sect. 5, on combined trips, package travels and alike.

[255] See hereinafter in this general report, Sect. 12.3 on sources of law applicable to cruises and particularly on the Athens Convention.

[256] See further information in Belgian Report, II.9.16.

consider that the Convention does not include any indication that its rules on liability can be applied to cruise cases.[257]

In France the carrier is responsible in case of damage occurred to the passenger, but the carrier is not necessarily obliged to provide full compensation. His liability is based on proved negligence, due to the freedom of movement of the passenger on board, with some exceptions.[258]

3.6 Insurance for Carriage of Passengers by Sea and Particularly for Cruises

Though cruises have been considered one of the safest ways of travelling and recreation in the world,[259] when an accident occurs, damages use to be important. Therefore, insurance is vital, but not always enough, due to limits of liability that are usually incorporated into maritime law. In the *Costa Concordia* case, 4200 persons were on board when the accident occurred, 30 of whom died or disappeared and 60 were injured. Several agreements were reached and indemnities paid, but the case showed that these tragic events produce immense damages and require incalculable amounts of money to indemnify them. Carriage of passengers by sea is covered by pools due to the high value of the interests assured, through insurance companies, re-assurance companies and Protection and Indemnity Clubs (P&I Clubs). The insufficiency of the limited amounts of liability to compensate damages to passengers in many cases may probably lead to a revision of limits of liability.[260]

3.7 Final Remarks

Cruise business is a complex activity dealt with by different areas of the law, including sources of self-regulation, soft-law and lex mercatoria.

General rules on liability apply to cruises aspects together with consumer protection law, which prevail over the former.

Though cruises have been considered one of the safest ways of travelling and recreation in the world, when an accident occurs, damages use to be important. Therefore, insurance is vital, but not always enough, due to limits of liability that are usually incorporated into maritime law.

[257] Bulgarian National Report, IX.45.

[258] Delebecque (2001), p. 68.

[259] Haiek (2012), p. 201. The author mentions, in page 208, that the insurer company Allianz Global Corporate & Specialty (AGCS) reaffirms the idea that maritime transport is one of the safer means, with the lowest death accident rate, comparing with land vehicles and even walking.

[260] Haiek (2012), pp. 209–213.

4 Cruise Passengers as Consumers

4.1 The Importance of Consumer Law in the Protection of the Tourist, Including the Cruise Passenger

The protection of the tourist, including the cruise passenger, requires both the legal protection provided by the State when the tourist faces unfortunate situations and the assurance of the possibility to claim from the tourist's place of residence. That protection includes security, respect for the tourist's rights, including those derived from the different contracts of touristic services he entered into, and the necessary guarantees that he will obtain compensation for lack of performance, among others. Consumer Law has had a decisive influence in this complex system of protection of tourists.[261] It generally applies horizontally cross-sector wise, save specific exceptions, which is relevant since cruise passengers are normally qualified as consumers.[262]

If we analyze consumer protection rules we find out that they are applicable to cruise passengers, since cruise passengers are included in the legal definitions of consumers. That is the case, for example, of Argentina,[263] Brazil,[264] Canada,[265] Romania,[266] Bulgaria,[267] Uruguay[268] and Japan.[269] Moreover, in some general conditions used by cruise operators in their cruise contracts refer to the passenger as "consumer".[270] Therefore, cruise passengers are protected both by general provisions on carriage of passengers and their luggage by sea, like the Athens Convention on the topic, which are not exclusively addressed to cruise passengers but to passengers by sea in general, and also by rules on consumers.

---

[261] Barreiro (2008), pp. 322–323.

[262] Belgian Report, III.18.

[263] Cappagli (2016), p. 14, N° 112–113. The author quotes the opinion of Radovich (2012), in similar sense.

[264] Brazilian Report, II.12.

[265] Chircop et al. (2016), p. 659.

[266] Romanian Report, II.12.

[267] Bulgaria Report, VIII.41.

[268] The cruise passenger is a consumer under Uruguayan Act N° 17.250, particularly Articles 2, 4. See complete text in http://www.impo.com.uy/bases/leyes/17250-2000.

[269] Japanese Report, III.18.

[270] See, for example, Section 11, entitled "Obligations of the Consumer", in the General Conditions of *Goldium Cruises*: http://www.goldiumcruceros.com/informacion-legal.php?id=3; those in *Viajes El Corte Inglés*: https://www.viajeselcorteingles.es/documento/condiciones/pdf_condiciones_cruceros.pdf; those in *Pullmantur*: https://www.pullmantur.travel/general/condiciones-generales.html.

4.2 National and Regional Rules on Tourists' Protection

It can be asserted, with doctrinal support, that most part of tourists' protection is provided by Acts on Consumer Defence. That is the case, among others, of Argentina, Brazil, Chile, Spain, United States of America, Nicaragua, Mexico, Peru, Dominican Republic and Uruguay. Moreover, it is to be noted that all those Acts on consumer's defence are remarkably uniform in their main guidelines, like those referring to the right to information, the duty to comply with the conditions agreed, the prohibition of misleading advertising and of abusive clauses, and even the objective liability of travel agencies and those providing different kinds of touristic service.[271]

In Argentina, Consumer Law is applicable to tourism contracts though at the beginning there were some resistance to accept it. However, nowadays it is fully accepted both by scholars and jurisprudence because of two main reasons: the first one is the constitutional basis of Consumer Law (Articles 42–43 of the Argentinean National Constitution). The second reason is that tourism contracts are clearly included in the definition of consumer contracts. In Brazil there is also a constitutional basis of Consumer Law; in the Constitutions of Nicaragua (Article 66) and Peru (Article 65) there are only some references to the right to information. The Spanish Constitution also incorporated the consumer protection (Article 51).[272]

In Argentina, Capaggli states that lately through case law and afterwards under Act 24.240 on Consumer Defence and amendments, and at present also applying Articles 1092–1122 of the Civil and Commercial Code, the issue of the pre-eminence of the law of consumer protection over those ruling different areas of the law, like maritime law is at stake. He concludes that under Article 1 of Act 24.240 on Consumer Defence, which coincides with Article 1092 of the Civil and Commercial Code, passengers are consumers but as the Navigation Act is a specific law, it applies to contracts of carriage of passengers by sea, and Act on consumer Defence, as a general law, applies in case the specific Navigation Act contains no specific provision. He points out that the Navigation Act aims at protecting users of transport by sea and in many aspects coincide with the rules in the Consumer Defence Act (for ex.: Article 37 of the latter with Article 280 of the former).[273]

In Brazil it has been recommended to harmonise the specific rules in tourism law with the general ones in the Consumer Code[274] to guide tourism service providers on how to comply with them without affecting the touristic activity. Articles 29–44 of the Consumer Code include rules on offer, publicity and abusive practices. In brief, the provider must give specific, clear, concrete and visible information on the characteristics of the service and that information must be included in the contract, being the offer and the contract linked. The consumer may require the fulfilment of

[271] Barreiro (2008), p. 324.

[272] Barreiro (2008), pp. 31–32.

[273] Cappagli (2016), pp. 14–15, N° 111–121.

[274] Act N° 8078 in force since March 11, 1991.

the services offered, accept an equivalent service or even terminate the contract and obtain compensation for damages. That is the case, for example, when the relationship between price and cabin was not correctly explained. The Consumer Code pre-establish as null those clauses that are considered abusive, like those reducing the liability of the provider of the service, those that eliminate the option of the consumer to reimbursement, those that transfer liability to a third party, those that put on the consumer the charge of the proof, those that permit the provider to alter the price or to alter the contract unilaterally, among other.[275]

In Uruguay, Consumer Law is applicable to tourists and tourist services since tourists are considered consumers.[276] Act N° 17.250 on Consumer Relations, Consumer Defence (*Ley de Relaciones de Consumo, Defensa del Consumidor*), August 11, 2000[277] defines in Articles 30 which clauses are considered to be abusive in adhesion contracts and exemplifies in Article 31.

Other countries, like Mexico approved Federal Act on Consumer Protection in 1976, and Dominican Republic approved Act N° 358-05 on General Protection of the Consumer of User in 2005.[278]

There are some countries where there are specific rules on consumer protection applicable to cruise passengers, like China, where a model contract of cruise tourism was implemented in Shanghai in 2015 and some national rules at the national level stipulating the national service standards in cruise terminals.[279]

In the U.S.A. there are some consumer protection laws in place for cruise passengers, but strong regulations or laws for most aspects of cruises are still to be enacted. The Commission's Office of Consumer Affairs & Dispute Resolution Services reviews any problems and inquiries from passengers and will contact a cruise line on the passenger's behalf.[280]

In Europe, the Directive 90/314/EEC was repealed by Directive (EU) 2015/2302 of the European Parliament and of the Council of 25 November 2015 on package travel and linked travel arrangements. Whereas N° 2 of Directive 2015/2302 points out that the market of package travel, package holiday and package tours had undergone considerable changes since the adoption of Directive 90/314/EEC, among other reasons, because of internet, which has become an increasingly important medium through which travel services are offered or sold and enables packages

[275] Schüter and Winter (2000), pp. 154 and 158–160.

[276] Facal and Pezzutti (2008), p. 301.

[277] https://www.impo.com.uy/bases/leyes/17250-2000.

[278] Barreiro (2008), p. 323.

[279] Chinese Report, II.

[280] See further information in USA Report, II. It has been reported that: "The office's role is to ensure a quick and fair consideration of the issues involved, but the final resolution of such complaints or inquiries remains between the cruise line and the individual: the consumer has to initiate action on her/his own behalf against the cruise line. It should be noted, further, that most forum selection clauses in cruise ticket agreements do not allow cruise passengers to utilize this service and hence the process is not very effective."

to be combined in a customised way. Directive (EU) 2015/2302 aims at updating Directive 90/314/EEC, taking into account those developments.[281]

Directive (EU) 2015/2302 addresses its interrelationship with consumer protection legislation. Among its objectives it is that of achieving a right balance between a high level of consumer protection and the competitiveness of businesses.[282] It recognises that the majority of travellers buying packages or linked travel arrangements are consumers within the meaning of Union consumer law.[283] It adapted certain EU consumer protection legislative acts, like Regulation (EC) No 2006/2004 on cooperation between national authorities responsible for the enforcement of consumer protection laws.[284]

EU Directive 2015/2302 defines in Article 3 (6) the "traveller" (as protected by its regime) also as the person who is entitled to travel on the basis of a contract concluded within the scope of the Directive. That means that the traveller-consumer should have the benefit of the protection of the Directive irrespective of whether he is a direct contracting party, a transferee or a member of a group on whose behalf another person has concluded a contract in respect of a package. However, Directive 2015/2302 excludes from its field of application the package travel that is bought by a general agreement for the arrangement of business travel between a travel organiser and another professional (art. 2,2,c). Consequently a framework contract between an employer of travellers and a cruise company is outside the scope of the EU Directive.[285]

Directive (EU) 2015/2302 is applicable to combined trips involving cruises and "seeks to cover not only traditional package holidays organized by tour operators, but also to those consumers that book in the end combined trips by booking themselves a combination of transport plus hotel or a car rental via a website. This may include a cabotage service plus a car rental".[286] According to a decision of the Court of Justice of the European Union (CJEU)[287] the EU Package Travel Directive (2015/2302) was applicable to cruises. Moreover, it was "the most important legislative instrument for complaints of cruise passengers against the cruise line".[288]

The information requirements laid down in Directive (EU) 2015/2302 are without prejudice to the information requirements laid down in other applicable European Union legislation, such as Directive 2000/31/EC on certain legal aspects of

[281] https://eur-lex.europa.eu/legal-content/EN/TXT/?uri=CELEX%3A32015L2302.

[282] Whereas N° 5.

[283] Whereas N° 7. However, "it is not always easy to distinguish between consumers and representatives of small businesses or professionals who book trips related to their business or profession through the same booking channels as consumers".

[284] Belgian Report, II.12.

[285] Belgian Report, II.13.

[286] Spanish Report, IV.25.

[287] CJEU 7.12.2010, combined cases C-585/98 and C-144/09—Pammer and Hotel Alpenhof.

[288] German Report, III.18. *OJ L 326, 11.12.2015, pp. 1–33.* See https://eur-lex.europa.eu/search.html?qid=1526244939663&whOJ=NO_OJ%3D326,YEAR_OJ%3D2015&type=advanced&lang=en&SUBDOM_INIT=ALL_ALL&DB_COLL_OJ=oj-l.

information society services, in particular electronic commerce, in the Internal Market (Directive on electronic commerce), Directive 2006/123/EC on services in the internal market, and Regulation (EU) No 1177/2010 concerning the rights of passengers when travelling by sea and inland waterway.[289]

The EU Sea Passengers' Rights Regulation No 1177/2010[290] expressly declares in its Article 2 (1) (c), that it is applicable to cruises.[291] It aims at ensuring passengers the basic protection when travelling by sea and inland waterway in case of transport disruption (delayed or cancelled departures), by imposing duties on the service provider. These duties are mainly to provide information, assistance (supply of food and beverage, accommodation, communication, transport), rerouting, compensation and reimbursement. It also imposes special duties on the operator vis-à-vis disabled passengers/customers or passengers with reduced mobility.[292]

It is worth mentioning that the Regulation (EU) N° 1177/2010 distinguishes between "commercial passenger services" and "cruise services" and reflects their different characteristics in the different scope of the rights that it grants to passengers. Commercial passenger services are passenger transport services operated between ports according to a published schedule. Cruises are defined as waterborne (by sea or inland waterway) services operated exclusively for the purpose of pleasure or recreation, supplemented by accommodation and other facilities, exceeding two overnight stays on board (art. 3 (t) Regulation No 1177/2010).[293]

Directive 2011/83/EU on consumer rights[294] was amended to ensure that certain consumer rights laid down in that Directive also apply to package travel. It applies without prejudice to rules on the protection of personal data laid down in Directive 95/46/EC on the protection of individuals with regard to the processing of personal data and on the free movement of such data, to be replaced by the General Data Protection Regulation (GDPR) 2016/679,[295] and to the EU rules on

[289] Belgian Report, II.12.

[290] Regulation (EU) No 1177/2010 of the European Parliament and of the Council of 24 November 2010 concerning the rights of passengers when travelling by sea and inland waterway and amending Regulation (EC) No 2006/2004 (EU Sea Passengers' Rights Regulation), OJ No. L 334 of 17.12.2010, p. 1.

[291] German Report, II.12; Spanish Report, II.9; Polish Report II.9; Japanese Report, II.9.

[292] See further information in Belgian Report, II.9.8.

[293] See further information in Belgian Report, II.9.8.

[294] Directive 2011/83/EU of the European Parliament and of the Council of 25 October 2011 on consumer rights, amending Council Directive 93/13/EEC and Directive 1999/44/EC of the European Parliament and of the Council and repealing Council Directive 85/577/EEC and Directive 97/7/EC of the European Parliament and of the Council. http://eur-lex.europa.eu/legal-content/EN/TXT/?uri=celex:32011L0083.

[295] Regulation (EU) 2016/679 on the protection of natural persons with regard to the processing of personal data and on the free movement of such data, and repealing Directive 95/46/EC (General Data Protection Regulation).

private international law, including Regulation (EC) No 593/2008[296] and Regulation (EU) No 1215/2012.[297]

In some countries there are specific rules that aim at dealing with unfair terms not individually negotiated, such as Article 80 et seq. of the Royal Decree-Legislative 1/2007 of 16 November approving the Recast text of the General Law on Consumer Protection and other supplementary laws (*Real Decreto Legislativo 1/2007, de 16 de noviembre, por el que se aprueba el texto Refundido de la Ley General para la Defensa de los Consumidores y Usuarios y otras leyes complementarias*, B.O.E. 30 November 2007), in Spain.

4.3 *Final Remarks*

Consumer Law is of the utmost importance in the protection of the tourist, including the cruise passengers. Consumer law is mandatory in most jurisdictions and therefore prevails over other sources of law.

5 Combined Trips, Package Travels, Package Tours or Package Holidays

5.1 *Concept of Combined Trips, Package Travels or Package Holidays*

Combined trips, package travels, package tours or package holidays are those that include not only the cruise but also the airplane trip to and from the port of departure, the land excursions chosen by the tourist when the ship is in port, and eventually some hotel night.[298] Package holiday and package tour are defined as synonymous: "a completely planned holiday arranged by a company at a fixed price, which includes travel, hotels, meals, etc."[299] "Package travel is understood as travel for more than twenty-four hours or which includes an overnight stay and that combines, at least, two travel services (transport, accommodation, meals or guided visits) as a significant part of the journey, and which is sold at an inclusive price".[300]

[296] Regulation (EC) No 593/2008 on the law applicable to contractual obligations (Rome I).

[297] Regulation (EU) No 1215/2012 on jurisdiction and the recognition and enforcement of judgments in civil and commercial matters.

[298] Ariza Herrerías (2014), p. 13.

[299] Longman Dictionary of Contemporary English, Third Edition, p. 1017.

[300] http://www.cec-msssi.es/en/CEC/web/secciones/viajes_combinados.htm.

However, under the wording of the Directive 90/314/EEC (Package Travel Directive)[301] it was not clear whether a cruise is a package, as a package consists of at least two travel services, usually carriage and accommodation. But in the already mentioned case *Pammer and Hotel Alpenhof* (2010)[302] the CJEU declared that a cruise—in this case a voyage by freighter—is a package, because transport and accommodation are involved. In 2012, the German Supreme Court (Bundesgerichtshof, BGH) also declared that a cruise is a package.[303] According to these decisions a cruise is a package notwithstanding whether it is combined with carriage to and from the embarkation and disembarkation port, or with other services as land excursions or special entertainment aboard. This is relevant regarding liability issues.[304] Whereas N° 10 of Directive (EU) 2015/2302 warns that "In the light of market developments, it is appropriate to further define packages on the basis of alternative objective criteria which predominantly relate to the way in which the travel services are presented or purchased and where travellers may reasonably expect to be protected by this Directive". It deals with the different types of travel services and terms used to designate them.[305]

In the case C-585/08 the question of whether the services offered by a freighter (cargo carriage vessel) on board are comparable to those in a cruise, and the EU Court of Justice held that a contract concerning a voyage by freighter is a contract of transport which, for an inclusive price, provides for a combination of travel and accommodation that corresponds to the concept of 'package' within the meaning of Article 15(3) of Council Regulation (EC) No 44/2001 of 22 December 2000 on jurisdiction and the recognition and enforcement of judgments in civil and commercial matters, in the sense of art. 2(1) of Directive 90/314.[306]

5.2 *Retailers, Travel Agents, Tour Operators and Their Liability*

A travel agent is a person who owns, operates or works for a travel agency,[307] while a tour operator is a person or company that provides package holidays.[308] These distinctions might become relevant when it comes to determining liabilities. For

[301] And also under the German transposition norm (§ 651a BGB).

[302] CJEU 7.12.2010, combined cases C-585/98 and C-144/09—Pammer and Hotel Alpenhof.

[303] BGH 18.12.2012, X ZR 2/12.

[304] See further information in German Report, III.18, 24.

[305] See also Whereas N° 11–12 and subsequent ones.

[306] See further information in Belgian Report, II.9.15. See also http://freecases.eu/Doc/CourtAct/3611261 and https://www.eui.eu/Projects/CentreForJudicialCooperation/Documents/2012-05-25-26/C-585OpinionAGTrstenjak.pdf.

[307] http://www.dictionary.com/browse/travel-agent?s=t.

[308] http://www.dictionary.com/browse/tour-operator?s=t.

example, it has been reported from Germany that the Bundesgerichtshof originally decided that the travel agent is not liable, while the tour operator that sells a package including a cruise and the carriage to and from the port of embarkment and disembarkment is liable under the package travel law.[309] Another case reported was that where the flight to the port of embarkment had to be cancelled due to volcano ash and the consumer could not reach the ship. The Bundesgerichtshof said that this was a case of *force majeure*, so that the consumer could ask for repayment of the money paid for the cruise.[310]

In Argentina, travel agents have a special legal regime, provided for in Act 18.829 and Decree 2182/72, which expressly include cruises. Travel Agencies need to have a licence issued by the Agencies Registry and they are controlled by the National Direction of Tourism. Services to be provided must be agreed in a signed contract and agencies are liable for any service committed by them, their branch offices or correspondents, though with some exceptions.[311] In "*Martinotti, Adalberto A. v. Marsans Internacional Argentina S.A. y otro*" the operating agency responsible for touristic services and the intermediary agency were condemned to compensate damages for non performance of the travel contract.[312]

If the cruise line sells the cruise and the carriage to and from the port, it is a package which includes the carriage and in the case the carriage is late and the passenger misses the ship, it is the responsibility of the cruise line either to bring him to the next port or to compensate him. But if the traveller books the carriage to the port separately, it is his own risk that the carriage is in time.[313] Under the new Package Travel Directive adopted in November 2015[314] a travel agent who sells the cruise and the carriage as a package and not separately may become liable as if being a tour operator for carriage and cruise.[315]

The obligations of the retailer or where applicable the organiser, are generally established and published. Let us see, for example, those published by the European Consumer's Centre in Spain (*Centro Europeo del Consumidor en España*): the retailer or organiser must provide the traveller with a clear, precise and written programme or informative brochure, containing details of the package offered, and information like travel destination(s) and means of transport, including characteristics and categories, duration, itinerary and travel programme, list of accommodation indicating location, category and main features, and tourist category in countries

---

[309] The German Report mentions in III.18 the case BGH 30.9.2010, Xa ZR 130/08, NJW 2011, 599.

[310] The German Report mentions in III.18 the case BGH 18.12.2012, X ZR 2/12, NJW 2013, 1674.

[311] Correa (2005), p. 7, IV.

[312] Judgment of June 25, 2007, "Sala A de la C. Nac. Com.", and comments in: Hocsman and Buccheri (2008).

[313] German Report, III.18.

[314] Directive EU/2302/2015 of the European Parliament and of the Council of 25 November 2015 on package travel, linked travel arrangements, amending regulation (EC) 2006/2004 and Directive 2011/83/EU of the European Parliament and of the Council and repealing Council Directive 90/314/EEC, OJ No. L 326 of 11.12.2015, p. 1.

[315] German Report, III.18.

where official rating exists, number of meals to be served and whether or not refreshments are included in the menu, documentation required for travel (passports, visas and heal formalities required), total price of the package, and indication of costs of optional excursions, amount or percentage of the total that is to be paid as a down payment, and the timetable for payment of the balance and financing conditions, where available. Also the minimum number of persons required for the package to take place, and where applicable, the time-limit for advising the traveller of the cancellation if that number is not reached, causes and consequences of the cancellation of the package, name and address of the travel organiser, and, where applicable, their legal representative in Spain, any additional and appropriate information regarding the nature of the package offered.[316]

It is highlighted in the referred web page that the information contained in the brochure is binding for the organiser or the retailer of the package travel, except in any of the following circumstances: that, in the event of modifications, the customer is notified in writing before signing the contract and this condition appears in the brochure in order to be accepted, or that modifications are made subsequently, provided that his condition has been previously agreed in writing between the contracting parties.[317]

5.3 *Price Reductions for Lack of Conformity*

It has been reported[318] that price reductions for lack of conformity are important in German travel law, including cruises, and that there are several examples in lower courts case law. Some examples of lack of conformity alleged by cruise passengers are that there was no water in the swimming pool, even when the sea was calm,[319] that the temperature in the cabin was sometimes too cold and sometimes too hot,[320] that there was no information about a non smoking policy before departure,[321] that a sofa was not long enough to sleep on it,[322] among others.[323] Another cause of lack of conformity is the replacement of the ship, which gives the consumer the right to cancel the trip before departure. Also the shortfall of land excursions, which is often the result of political unrests,[324] enables the cruise line and the passenger to cancel

[316] http://www.cec-msssi.es/en/CEC/web/secciones/viajes_combinados.htm.

[317] http://www.cec-msssi.es/en/CEC/web/secciones/viajes_combinados.htm.

[318] German Report, III.18.

[319] AG München 27.4.2001, 274 C 23427/00, RRa 2002, 25.

[320] OLG Koblenz, 13.6.2012, 5 U 1501/11, NJW-RR 2012, 1082.

[321] OLG Rostock 27.10. 2008, 1 U 183/08, NJW 2009, 302.

[322] AG Offenbach 31.1.2001, 31 C 6017/00, RRa 2001, 97.

[323] The so called Würzburger Tabelle (Würzburg list) includes a comprehensive list of court decisions, http://würzburger-tabelle.de.

[324] LG Leipzig 27.4.2005, 1 S 4/05, NJW-RR 2005, 995 (two Egyptian ports).

the whole cruise for that reason before departure, but after departure it is the risk of the cruise line whether they are able to call at the ports which are promised. German courts have considered that it depends on the relevance of a port for the whole trip, whether the cruise line has to compensate the consumer if a port is missed, even if the reasons are political unrest or bad weather conditions.[325]

5.4 *Service Fees Charged Aboard*

It is quite frequent that cruise lines charge some service fees aboard.

In some countries, like Germany, it was disputed whether the cruise line could charge aboard a service fee in addition to the price for the cruise, "because this might not be in line with the principle of indicating the total price, which is part of German and European law". In a recent judgment, the Bundesgerichtshof said that a compulsory service fee has to be included into the total price.[326]

5.5 *Supranational, International and National Rules on Package Travels*

Most legal systems do not contain specific rules on combined trips, package travels or similar or equivalent denominations. That is the case, for example, of Argentina, Brazil, Bulgaria,[327] China, Romania,[328] and Uruguay. However, more general rules are applicable to this spreading phenomenon.

In Argentina the Travel Agents' Act N° 18.829 applies to the travel agent's liability in case there was one. The rules applicable to the carrier's liability will depend on whether the damage occurred in the aquatic, aerial or terrestrial medium. If the damage occurred at sea, the Navigation Act N° 20.094, the 1940 Montevideo Treaty on International Commercial Navigation Law, and the Athens Convention will apply. If the damage occurs during the aerial section of the trip, the Aeronautic Code and the 1999 Montreal Convention will apply, depending on the case. If the damage occurs on land, several national rules[329] or the 1940 Montevideo Treaty on International Terrestrial Commercial law,[330] depending on the case, apply.

---

[325] BGH 14.5.2013, X ZR 15/11, NJW 2013, 3170—Greenland.

[326] BGH 7.5.2015, I ZR 158/14, MDR 2015, 1433—Der Zauber des Nordens. See German Report, III.18.

[327] Bulgarian national Report, IV.24.

[328] See further information in Romanian Report, IV.24–25.

[329] See Argentine Report, IV.24.

[330] Particularly Articles 17 and 18.

In Argentina, combined trips are those where the previous combination of at least two of the following elements is offered in exchange of a global price, by a travel agency, including a night-stay or the provision of services for more than 24 hours: (1) carriage, (2) accommodation, and (3) other touristic services that are not accessory to the carriage or accommodation and accounting for a significant proportion of the package.[331]

Publicity made by the travel agency in relation to the cruise is binding (art. 61 LGDCU). The offer-program handled to the passenger is binding (art. 156 LGDCU), and any clause included in the contract stating that publicity of the offer-program is not binding is considered abusive. Different kinds of insurances are required to the passenger.

Argentinean courts heard a case where a family entered into a contract called "tour package" with a tourism corporation, which included a cruise along different points of the Caribbean Sea. They planned to visit Puerto Rico, but they could not enter that state because they lacked the required visa. They claimed against the tourism corporation for damages. The defendant stated that there was a clause in the general conditions that freed the corporation from liability. The court accepted the claimant's position, considering that it was an adhesion contract, in a printed form and with the letterhead of the corporation, and that in case of darkness, doubt or silence, it had to be construed against the party issuing the general conditions. The court stated that the clause freeing the corporation from liability was subordinated to the principal obligations of the corporation, which included the duty of controlling that the passengers had the needed documentation.[332]

The judgment reaches the right solution but on insufficient legal grounds, since it does not even mention the applicable legislation on consumer protection.[333] Art. 37 of Act N° 24.240 provides that the clauses that denature obligations or limit liability for damages and those that import waiver or restriction of consumer rights or expand the rights of the other party will be deemed as inexistent. Other argument that should have been considered by the court are that the corporation assumed an obligation related to the ends desired (the trip), and therefore it cannot exempt itself for the non-performance arguing that it tried to perform the contract but was not able to.[334]

In Uruguay the regulation of different issues regarding combined trips can be found mainly in two areas of law: contract law[335] and consumer protection law.[336]

---

[331] Art. 151 of the *Texto refundido de la Ley General de Defensa de los Consumidores y Usuarios* (LGDCU).

[332] Borda (2003).

[333] In Argentina, Act N° 24.240—Adla, LIII-D, 4125.

[334] Borda (2003).

[335] Sconfienza Pérez (2003), pp. 81–89, in http://revista.fder.edu.uy/index.php/rfd/article/view/199, refers to the regulation of the "tourist agency contract", under contractual obligations rules in the Civil Code, Act N° 16.603.

[336] Act No. 17.250 on Consumer Protection.

There are also some administrative law rules that apply to one of the contracting parties: the travel agency.[337] The 1940 Montevideo Treaty on International Terrestrial Commercial law[338] also applies, depending on the case.

In Brazil all the general labour rules are, in principle, applicable to this category of trips.[339]

In the EU, Directive 90/314/EEC of 13 June 1990 on package travel, package holidays and package tours[340] (the Package Travel Directive of 1990) currently superseded by the Directive 2015/2302 is applicable to combined trips involving cruises and "seeks to cover not only traditional package holidays organized by tour operators, but also to those consumers that book in the end combined trips by booking themselves a combination of transport plus hotel or a car rental via a website. This may include a cabotage service plus a car rental".[341]

There are some countries, like Poland, that include specific rules on package (travel) which may be considered a combined trip, and is defined as "not less than two touristic services forming uniform program for an inclusive price and when those services include overnight accommodation, cover a period of more than twenty-four hours or change of place of domicile (Art. 3, Act on touristic services of 1997)".[342] The notion of package travel has been introduced into the Polish national legal system by the Act on touristic services of 1997, that implement the European Union Directive 90/314/EEC of 13 June 1990 on package travel, package holidays and package tours, currently superseded by the directive 2015/2302 which so far has not been implemented into the Polish legal system.[343]

Directive 93/13/EEC of 5 April 1993 on unfair terms in consumer contracts and Directive 2005/29/EC concerning unfair business-to-consumer commercial practices in the internal market ('Unfair Commercial Practices Directive') do not exclude package travel contracts from its scope of application.

Directive 2011/83/EU of the European Parliament and of the Council of 25 October 2011 on consumer rights, amending Council Directive 93/13/EEC and Directive 1999/44/EC of the European Parliament and of the Council and repealing Council Directive 85/577/EEC and Directive 97/7/EC of the European Parliament and of the Council, does neither apply to contracts that fall within the scope of Directive 90/314/EEC on package travel, package holidays and package tours (Article 3.3.g) nor to contracts for passenger transport services, with the exception of article 8(2) (information requirements for distance contracts) and articles 19 (cost of the payment transaction) and 22 (express consumer consent with extra payment) (Article 3.3.k).

[337] See, for example, Decree N° 268/2015 and Law No. 19.253. Uruguayan Report, IV.24.

[338] Particularly Articles 17 and 18.

[339] Brazilian Report, III.24.

[340] OJ L 158, 23.6.1990, p. 59–64.

[341] Spanish Report, IV.25.

[342] Polish Report, IV.24.

[343] Polish Report, IV.25.

In Spain package travels are regulated specifically in Articles 150–165 of the "*Real Decreto Legislativo 1/2007 de 16 de noviembre, por el que se aprueba el texto refundido de la Ley General para la Defensa de los Consumidores y Usuarios*". These provisions deal with precontractual information and contract formation, specific consumer rights, contract modification, contract termination and liability, noncompliance, liability and guarantees.[344]

The Directive 90/314/EEC (Package Travel Directive) was implemented by Germany in 1995. The German legislator amended the contract law sections of the Civil Code (Bürgerliches Gesetzbuch) by a special chapter about package travel (originally §§ 651a–651k BGB). As the original Package Travel Directive was a minimum standard Directive, the German legislator could maintain some rules which are more in favour for the consumer than the Directive, in particular rules about a non fault liability for lacks of conformity which gives the consumer a right for a price reduction in many cases.[345]

In Belgium, Act of 21 November 2017 on the sale of package travel, linked travel arrangements and travel services has transposed the Directive (EU) 2015/2302 into Belgian law.[346]

5.6 *Final Remarks*

Cruises are frequently a part of package travels and even considered a package itself, since it provides not only the carriage but also accommodation, meals, entertainment, land excursions and others for a fixed price. Package travels are ruled by general and specific rules, and involve several actors like travel agents and tour operators, each of which has its particularities and liabilities.

6 Labour Rules on Cruises' Workers

The labour legal regime of workers on board of cruises depends on the flag of the vessel. The flag determines also civil and criminal jurisdiction (arts. 27, 28 and 94.3. b) of the Montego Bay Convention of 1982).[347]

Their working regime is mainly temporal. However, there are some companies that employ cruise workers and then provide staff globally to big cruise companies, located in countries with minimal legal rules on the matter.[348]

[344] Spanish Report, III.14 and IV.24.

[345] German national Report, III.18.

[346] Belgian Report, II.9.15.

[347] http://www.un.org/depts/los/convention_agreements/texts/unclos/unclos_e.pdf.

[348] Estepa Montero (2012), pp. 140–141.

6.1 Specific Labour Rules on Cruises' Workers

In most jurisdictions considered in this general report it has been reported that there are no specific labour rules on cruises' workers, but that general labour rules on maritime or seafarer workers apply.

6.2 General Labour Rules That Are Applicable to Cruises' Workers in the Absence of Specific Rules on the Matter

At the international level, the Maritime Labour Convention (ILO, 2006, as amended)[349] has 86 Member States all over the world.[350] It was incorporated into the EU law by means of Council Directive 2009/13/EC of 16 February 2009.

Regionally, the Montevideo Treaty on International Commercial Navigation of 1940,[351] ratified by Argentina, Paraguay and Uruguay states that the seafarers' employment contract (*contrato de ajuste*) is ruled by the law of the nationality of the vessel where the seafarers provide their services, as well as everything concerning the internal order of the ship, the rights and duties of the captain, officials and seafarers, and that the courts of the State of the flag have jurisdiction on the matter (Articles 20–24).[352]

In many countries there are rules on maritime workers, seamen's contracts or employment contracts for ship's crew, though not specific on cruises' workers. In the absence of those rules, general labour rules on maritime workers are applicable to cruises' workers. That is the case of Argentina, Brazil, China, Japan, Turkey, and Uruguay, among others.

In Argentina, Navigation Act N° 20.094[353] rules seamen's contracts in Articles 631–674. As Argentina is a party to the 1940 Montevideo Treaty on International Commercial Navigation, as well as Paraguay and Uruguay, the Treaty is applicable when the case falls within its scope of application. In Brazil, which is not a party of the referred Treaty, the labour rules applicable to cruises' workers are contained in the Normative Resolution no. 71/2006 of the National Immigration Council concerns the granting of visas to foreign seafarers and other regulations.[354] The Decree

[349] http://www.ilo.org/global/standards/maritime-labour-convention/lang%2D%2Den/index.htm Adopted by the International Labour Conference at its 94th (Maritime) Session (2006) and entered into force 20 August 2013.

[350] http://www.ilo.org/dyn/normlex/en/f?p=NORMLEXPUB:11300:0::NO::P11300_INSTRUMENT_ID:312331.

[351] http://www.audm.com.uy/pdf/leyes/tratado-de-derecho-de-navegacion-comercial-internacional-1940.pdf.

[352] See also Articles 22–24.

[353] http://servicios.infoleg.gob.ar/infolegInternet/verNorma.do?id=43550.

[354] Brazilian Report, III.10, 20.

N° 5.452/43 (Labour Act, or "CLT"), which is the main general regulation in this matter, is applicable to the work contracts signed in Brazil. Some of the cruise companies that operate in Brazil signed "Termos de Ajustamento de Conduta – TACs" with the Public Labour Prosecutor's Office, which are public agreements in which these companies committed to obey certain rules.[355] Brazilian labour courts tend to be very protective in their interpretations towards workers, applying the CLT in most cases.[356]

In Uruguay, general rules included in the Constitution, Acts, and Decrees, are applicable in the absence of specific rules. Collective agreements reached between workers and employers within the different activity sectors that are reached through the Salary Councils (created by Act No. 10.499) are applicable to merchant ships (including passenger ships) flying Uruguayan flag. Issues like workers' salaries and licenses are regulated by the negotiations carried out in the Group N°13 of Wages Council called "Transport and storage" Subgroup N ° 09 "Maritime transport".[357]

When the case is not within the scope of application of the 1940 Montevideo Treaty on International Commercial Navigation, the seafarers' employment contract is ruled in Uruguay by Act N° 19.246 on Maritime Commercial Law (2014), particularly Article 7, which sends up to the 1940 Montevideo Treaty on International Commercial Navigation regarding all maritime law issues, including specifically seafarers' employment contract. Therefore, those contracts are ruled by the law of the nationality of the vessel where the seafarers provide their services, as well as everything concerning the internal order of the ship, the rights and duties of the captain, officials and seafarers, and the courts of the State of the flag have jurisdiction on the matter.[358]

In Europe, Article 8 of Regulation (EC) 593/2008 of the European Parliament and of the Council of 17 June 2008 on the law applicable to contractual obligations (Rome I), deals with individual employment contracts without paying specific regard to seafarers' employment contracts. This conflict of laws rule poses the problem of which is the habitual place of work when services are provided on high seas, or on different jurisdictions and non-sovereignty areas through which the ship navigates.[359]

In Germany the Seearbeitsgesetz (SeeArbG, Sea Labour Act)[360] was adopted in 2013 and supersedes general labour law. It is applicable for German ships, i.e., ships under German flag of all kinds: cargo ships and passenger ships.[361] Notice that this national law is a transposition of the 2006 Maritime Labour Convention (MLC),

---

[355] Brazilian Report, III.22.

[356] Brazilian Report, III.26.

[357] https://www.mtss.gub.uy/web/mtss/9-transporte-maritimo See: Uruguayan Report, IV.22.

[358] See on this matter: Fresnedo de Aguirre (2015), pp. 127–168, particularly pp. 154 et seq.

[359] Spanish Report, IV.22.

[360] For details of the SeeArbG cf. *Bubenzer*, Transportrecht 2014, 393, and *Zimmer*, Zeitschrift für Europäisches Arbeitsrecht 2015, 297.

[361] See further information in German Report, IV.20.

which came into force on 20 August 2013, and for Germany on 14 August 2014.[362] The Belgian Act of 3 June 2007 on the seafarers' employment contract has harmonized Belgian law to the international conventions on the matter.[363]

The port state control has its legal basis not only in the MLC, but also in European law. There is a Directive on port State control of 2009,[364] amended in 2013.[365] The purpose of these Directives is not only to enforce labour law, but also environmental law.

In the USA, "seafarers have no common law right to sue their employer for negligence. Rather, they were entitled to maintenance (reasonable expenses of room and board while ashore and unfit for duty), cure (reasonable medical expenses incurred for curative care), and unearned wages (wages that would have been received had the seafarer not become sick or injured, until the end of the voyage). A seafarer assigned to a vessel could also sue for unseaworthiness, meaning that if a sea man suffered injury or death that was caused by the vessel that was not fit for its intended purposes, he would be entitled to damages". The Jones Act of 1920 "granted seafarers a right of action against their employers for damages caused by negligence", and also to other employees "permanently assigned to the vessel in aid of its mission — such as cooks, bartenders, musicians and beauticians". Regarding the Jones Act, courts have also determined that "the statute can apply to foreign-flagged vessels, although Congress made no specific mention that the law should apply extraterritorially".[366]

"More recently, general maritime law has applied these choice-of-law principles to extend to all maritime tort cases, not just those between employer and employee. While they will use a balancing of factors in identifying the contacts of the parties in resolving what law may supplement GML in tort matters, U.S. courts will also recognize the parties' contractual choice of law with respect to maritime contracts".[367]

In Japan the Seamen Act, which is a domestic law, was amended on 1 March 2013 since Japan ratified the Maritime Labour Convention 2006 which was adopted by ILO in February 2006.[368]

In Turkey there are no specific labour rules on cruises' workers. However there is a Maritime Labour Code that is applicable to cruises, though only to the crewmembers of the Turkish flagged vessels (Article 1 of the Maritime Labour

[362] German Report, IV.21.

[363] Belgian Report, IV.22.

[364] Directive 2009/16/EC of the European Parliament and of the Council of 23 April 2009 on port state control, OJ no. L 131, p. 57 of 28.5.2009.

[365] Directive 2013/38/EU of the European Parliament and the Council of 12. August 2013, amending Directive 2009/16/EC on port State control, OJ no. L 218, p. 1 of 14.8.2013.

[366] Felder (2006), pp. 27–29.

[367] Felder (2006), p. 29.

[368] Japanese Report, IV.23.

Code). Turkey is planning to become a party to 2006 Maritime Labour Convention.[369]

In other countries there are neither special provisions on cruise workers nor on maritime workers or seafarers, and general labour rules apply. That is the case, for example, of Bulgaria,[370] Poland[371] and Romania.[372] In Poland, for example, those general rules include Maritime Labour Convention 2006 and European directives, as well as national acts: Maritime Labour Act of 2015 and Labour Code from 1974.[373]

It has been reported by some jurisdictions to be quite frequent that cruises' workers are not enough protected by the labour law "once the ship leaves the port", and there is some case-law on that matter.[374] Perhaps that is the reason why the cruise sector activities often raise conflicts involving labour and social security law.[375]

6.3 *The 2006 Maritime Labour Convention*[376]

A complete analysis of this Convention would exceed the scope of this general report, but anyway, it is worth making some references to its solutions. It must be noted that under Article II.8, "unless expressly provided otherwise, a reference to this Convention constitutes at the same time a reference to the Regulations and the Code".

The personal scope of application is widely determined in Article II: it applies to all seafarers and to all ships, except expressly provided otherwise. Any doubt shall be clarified by the competent authority in each Member after consultation with the ship owners' and seafarers' organizations concerned with the question at stake. Therefore, seafarers working in cruise ships are included, in principle, within the personal scope of application of this Convention.

The Convention provides for substantive rules on seafarers right to a safe and secure workplace, to fair terms of employment, to decent working and living conditions on board ship, which must be implemented through national laws or regulations, through applicable collective bargaining agreements (Articles IV and V).

---

[369] Turkish Report, 3.

[370] Bulgarian national Report, IV.22–23. In Bulgaria, the Labour Code is applicable to every individual working contract. It is a national Code though it is harmonized with the European Rules.

[371] Polish Report, IV.22.

[372] Romanian Report, IV.20–23.

[373] Polish Report, IV.23.

[374] Romanian Report, IV.26.

[375] For further information on this topic see Belgian Report, IV.26. Case-law is also reported there.

[376] http://www.ilo.org/global/standards/maritime-labour-convention/lang%2D%2Den/index.htm See Spanish Report IV.26 and Belgian Report, IV.20.

The 2006 Maritime Labour Convention has been implemented in the European Union by Council Directive 2009/13/EC of 16 February 2009 implementing the Agreement concluded by the European Community Ship-owners' Associations (ECSA) and the European Transport Workers' Federation (ETF) on the Maritime Labour Convention, 2006, and amending Directive 1999/63/EC.[377]

6.4 Final Remarks

In general, the labour legal regime of workers on board of cruises depends on the flag of the vessel. In most jurisdictions, general labour rules, or those on seafarer workers apply. In State Parties and when the issue is within the scope of application of the 2006 Maritime Labour Convention, its substantive rules on seafarers apply.

7 Rules on Ports That Are Relevant Regarding Cruises

7.1 General and Specific Rules

7.1.1 In Europe

In Europe, the Council Decision 87/594/EEC of 30 November 1987 accepting, on behalf of the European Community, Annex F.3 to the International Convention on the simplification and harmonization of customs procedures,[378] refers to the location of customs offices, customs formalities, among other issues, and specifies that in some instances, such as cruise ships, it may be possible for travellers to accomplish all the necessary customs formalities on board.[379]

There are several instruments like the Commission Communication to the Council and the European Parliament entitled "Towards integrated management of the external borders of the Member States of the European Union",[380] the Code of Practice on security in ports (Geneva, 2003),[381] which is the product of the cooperation between the International Labour Organization (ILO) and the International Maritime Organization (IMO). Also the amendment of the International Convention for the Safety of Life at Sea, 1974 (SOLAS)[382] created a new Chapter XI-2 on

---

377 Spanish Report, IV.20, 22; Belgian Report, IV.20.

378 https://eur-lex.europa.eu/legal-content/EN/TXT/?uri=CELEX:31987D0594.

379 Belgian Report, II.9.3.

380 https://eur-lex.europa.eu/legal-content/EN/TXT/?uri=LEGISSUM:l33205.

381 http://www.imo.org/en/OurWork/Security/Guide_to_Maritime_Security/Documents/ILOIMOCodeOfPracticeEnglish.pdf.

382 http://www.imo.org/en/About/Conventions/ListOfConventions/Pages/International-Convention-for-the-Safety-of-Life-at-Sea-(SOLAS),-1974.aspx.

special measures to enhance maritime security, which is supplemented by the International Ship and Port Facility Security (ISPS) Code,[383] which contains, inter alia, requirements that relate to the security of the ship and to the immediate ship/port interface. The overall security of port areas was left to further joint work between ILO and IMO.[384]

SOLAS was first adopted before the First World War in 1914, after the 1912 Titanic disaster resulted in the deaths of more than 1500 passengers. In its most recent form it came into force in 1980, and currently has 162 member states.[385]

This Convention, as amended, contains internationally agreed safety standards for passenger ships engaged on international voyages. Resolutions adopted by the IMO and other measures complement and interpret that Convention, such as the International Management Code for the Safe Operation of Ships and for Pollution Prevention (ISM Code) adopted by the International Maritime Organization (IMO) through Assembly Resolution A.741(18) of 4 November 1993.[386] The main objective of the SOLAS Convention is to specify minimum standards for the construction, equipment and operation of ships, compatible with their safety. Flag States are responsible for ensuring that ships under their flag comply with its requirements.[387]

It is also worth mentioning here Regulation (EU) 2017/352 of the European Parliament and of the Council of 15 February 2017 establishing a framework for the provision of port services and common rules on the financial transparency of ports.[388] It applies to the provision of several categories of port services, either inside the port area or on the waterway access to the port.[389] The Regulation applies to all maritime ports of the trans-European transport network, as listed in Annex II to Regulation (EU) No 1315/2013 (Article 1).

In Poland, for example, there are no specific rules on ports regarding only cruises, but general rules on ports are applicable to cruise ships and refer to safety of navigation and environmental protection, maintenance of order, forms and registration of passenger traffic, supervision by its crew member of passengers embarking and disembarking, among others. These rules are issued by territorial authorities of maritime administration and vary from one port to the other.[390]

In Romania general rules on ports and on specific issues like the authorization of commercial operators for the activity of public transport of passengers and/or goods on inland waterways that apply to cruises.[391]

---

[383] http://www.imo.org/es/OurWork/Security/Instruments/Paginas/ISPSCode.aspx.

[384] Belgian Report, V.27.

[385] USA Report, III.

[386] Belgian Report, II.9.6.

[387] USA Report, III.

[388] https://eur-lex.europa.eu/legal-content/EN/TXT/?uri=CELEX:32017R0352.

[389] Those categories are: bunkering, cargo-handling, mooring, passenger services, collection of ship-generated waste and cargo residues, pilotage and towage.

[390] Polish Report, V.27.

[391] Romanian National Report, III.15 and V.27.

In Spain there are no specific rules on ports that are relevant concerning cruises, but there are references and sectorial regulation in different State and infra-State regulations. The Spanish Constitution provides for the distribution of competences concerning ports, granting the State the exclusive competence on ports of general interests and the Autonomous Communities that on safe havens, marines and those not carrying business activities. Main regulation regarding ports is in the Royal legislative Decree 2/2011, its annexes and some ministerial rank regulations.[392] There is a dual regime depending on the public or private character of services. Ports of general interest are under the State's competence and are managed by Port's Authorities. They are public entities subject to private law.[393]

7.1.2 In the Americas

Few jurisdictions have reported information on this topic. For example, Brazilian legal system contains specific rules on ports that are relevant regarding cruises. They cover several tourism issues, general principles on water transportation, customs services and taxes.[394]

In Argentina, in addition to the objectives of the International Code for the Protection of Vessels and Port Facilities (CPBIP OMI) and the SOLAS Convention of 1974, there are several rules on maritime and port security.[395]

7.1.3 In Asia

Also in this region, little information was reported. The Chinese national reporter informs that in China there are specific rules on construction and planning of cruise ports.[396]

7.2 *Costs, Taxes and Rates Charged by Ports to Cruises*

7.2.1 In Europe

In Europe Regulations CEE 4.055/86, 4.056/86, 4.057/86 and 4.058/86, 22/12/86 and Regulation CEE 3.572/92, 7/12/92 held the principle of freedom to provide maritime transport services between Member States and third countries, modified by

[392] See very detailed information in Spanish Report, V.27–30.
[393] Ariza Herrerías (2014), pp. 15 and 57.
[394] See for a detailed list, Brazilian Report, V.27.
[395] See further information on this topic in Barone (2008).
[396] Chinese Report, V.27.

the Council Regulation (EC) No 1/2003 of 16 December 2002 on the implementation of the rules on competition laid down in Articles 81 and 82 of the Treaty.[397]

There is some case-law of the European Court of Justice reported. For example, in the case C-435/00[398] the European Court of Justice held that "Article 1 of Council Regulation (EEC) No 4055/86 of 22 December 1986 applying the principle of freedom to provide services to maritime transport between Member States and between Member States and third countries precludes the application in a Member State of different harbour dues for domestic or intra-Community traffic and traffic between a Member State and a third country if that difference is not objectively justified".[399]

Regarding national jurisdictions reported, in Poland, as in most countries, port fees are charged to cruises, consisting of "1) tonnage fee charged for entrance and departure of the ship into and from the port, transit through the port area and reception of wastes from ships in order to dispose or retrieve them; not exceeding 1.10 euro per 1 GT; 2) demurrage fee collected for the use of quays or piers, not exceeding 0.17 euro per 1 GT; 3) passenger fee collected for passengers embarking and disembarking, that may not be higher than 1.74 euro per passenger.[400] Tonnage fee is collected by the port authority whereas demurrage and passenger fee is collected by the quay owner. The exact amount of fee is determined by its collector, within the limits prescribed above". There are other fees and also tax relieves.[401] In Romania, the system of taxes and rates that ports charge is available on line.[402]

In Spain applicable taxes to cruises are those regarding maritime signalling or navigation aid, ship tax, passenger tax, encompassed as deployment taxes, pilot service, mooring service and reception facilities for the waste generated by the ship. It is reported that cruises are subject to important allowances, considering the economic impact they have, not only in the port but also in the city where it is located.[403] Ports usually charge several taxes and rates for the use of their space and waters and for different services provided by ports.[404]

There are cruises with particular characteristics that pose some problems regarding tax exemptions and have given rise to case-law from the EU Court of Justice. These are very short cruises, sometimes lasting just a few hours, which aim only at

---

397 http://eur-lex.europa.eu/legal-content/en/ALL/?uri=CELEX:32003R0001 See on this topic Estepa Montero (2012), p. 138; and Ariza Herrerías (2014), p. 10.

398 https://eur-lex.europa.eu/legal-content/EN/ALL/?uri=ecli%3AECLI%3AEU%3AC%3A2002%3A661.

399 See further information in Belgian Report, V.29.

400 Ports and Maritime Piers Act of 20th December 1996 (consolidated text in Journal of Laws 2010 No 33, item 179).

401 See further information in Polish Report, V.29.

402 In www.portofconstantza.com, at the "Port tariffs" section in the main menu, the website of the Constanta Maritime Ports Administration National Company. See Romanian National Report, V.29.

403 See very detailed information in Spanish Report, V.29–30.

404 Ariza Herrerías (2014), p. 15.

allowing passengers to shop on board and profit from tax exemptions. This practice may distort competition with mainland traders.[405]

For the purpose of the fiscal exemption regime of sales on board of the cruise vessel, the EU Court of Justice ruled that "the transit stops (intended for excursion and sightseeing) as opposed to the turnaround stops (intended for the embarkation of new passengers or for final disembarkation) in the port of a third (non EU) country were also qualified as 'stops'".[406]

7.2.2 In the Americas

We will briefly analyse four American jurisdictions: Argentina, Brazil, Uruguay and the USA. In Argentina there are some general rules on ports that are applicable to cruises, like the Navigation Act N° 20.094, the Ports Act N° 20.093 and its Regulatory Decree 769/93, and also some specific rules like the Regulation on cruise ships entering the Buenos Aires Port, incorporated into Resolution 052/16 of the Ports General Administration. Each port issues its own Regulation.[407] As for taxes and rates, in Argentina each port has its own system, but on the whole, they are all very expensive, much more that regarding cargo vessels.[408]

In Brazil it is Ordinance N° 188/02 and Act N° 10.233/01 that regulate taxes and rates charged by ports. Taxes are annually adjusted by the Maritime Authority, following the provisions set forth by the Ministry of Treasury in the Ordinance N° 188/02. Rate of adjustment must be set forth in each concession agreement and adjustment of taxes must be based on the fluctuation of the Port's operational costs or a price index.[409] The tax rules are contained in the Normative Resolution N° 137/98 of the Federal Revenue (concerning the tax and customs regimes that apply to cruise vessels).

Uruguayan port authorities charge costs to each vessel that uses a port for docking, fresh water supply, electricity supply, among other services. The *Prefectura Nacional Naval* (Coast Guard) collects a rate for the use of the navigation aids on Uruguayan waters, called "rate for aid to maritime navigation", created under Article 216 of Act No. 13.637.[410]

In Uruguay, logistic regarding scales of cruises in Uruguay include maritime agents, who coordinate with different actors that intervene in cruises scales in

[405] Belgian Report, II.9.11 and case-law referred there, and V.27.

[406] Case C-58/04, see further information in Belgian Report, II.9.14. See also http://curia.europa.eu/juris/liste.jsf?language=en&num=C-58/04.

[407] Argentine Report, V.27.

[408] See more details in Argentine Report, V.29.

[409] Brazilian Report, III.29.

[410] Uruguayan Report, V.29.

Uruguay, public authorities;[411] terminals and port operators, airports and border points, pilots services, tugs and boats, customs brokers, maritime providers, cargo agents, touristic operators; Ministry of Tourism and Sports, Ministry of Transport and Public Works, and Ministry of Interior.[412]

It has been reported that U.S. lawmakers are concerned with the costs to the government for maintaining the ports used by cruises and to the Coast Guard, which is responsible for all prevention activities associated with the safe operation of vessels and facilities,[413] and thus for search and rescue operations. However, the cruise line industry pays very little in income taxes.[414]

7.2.3 In Asia

In Japan, the Yokohama Port, which is the main port for cruises, charges the port arrival fee for an amount of JPY2.70/GT per arrival in the case of a foreign vessel exceeding 700/GT. The wharfage is 10.05/GT per mooring of less than 12 hours. In case mooring exceeds 12 hours, cost is calculated at 6.7/GT for every extra 12-hours.[415]

7.3 Final Remarks

There are several legal instruments on port issues like customs, maritime and port security, a framework for the provision of port services and common rules on the financial transparency of ports and on costs, taxes and rates charged by ports to cruises. Some rules are of supranational character, others international and also some national rules. Therefore, some degree of harmonisation is achieved regarding certain topics, like safety standards, port services and financial transparency of ports.

---

[411] *Sanidad Marítima y Fluvial, Prefecturas, ANP, Hidrografía, Migración, Aduanas, Política turística.*

[412] González (2013).

[413] *See* United States Coast Guard, http://www.uscg.mil/.

[414] See USA Report, I, regarding measures proposed to recover those costs and the lobby of the cruise industry against them.

[415] Japanese Report, V.29.

8 Rules on Environmental Impact of Cruises

8.1 General Remarks

Nowadays environmental law is a specific and generally autonomous branch of law, with its own international and national sources of law. Therefore, it is not only impossible but also would exceed this general report to deal with this matter thoroughly here. This chapter will try to analyse the main Conventions in the area of maritime environmental protection and other relevant rules for cruises. Almost all of them are applicable to all kinds of ships, not only cruise ships, but are applicable to the latter.[416]

It is worth pointing out that the cruise industry is inextricably linked to the environment, since its aim is to bring people to interesting places in the world, by travelling via water. Cruise ships produce pollution from the day-to-day operations of the ship and its inhabitants and contribute a significant portion of pollution, especially in at-risk natural areas.[417] The CLIA document titled "Waste management best practices and procedures" describes waste management practices and procedures that CLIA Members agree shall be incorporated into their respective Safety Management Systems (SMS). The development of industry practices and procedures is based upon the fundamental principles outlined in CLIA's Waste Management policy. There are many other waste management practices and procedures not described in the referred document; therefore, CLIA Members have agreed to use best waste management practices and to comply with all local, state, national, and flag State operational waste management laws and requirements.[418]

The standards of MARPOL (the International Convention for the Prevention of Pollution from Ships) have in turn been adopted by most flag and port States and subsequently enacted into national legislation and regulation. Additional national and local legislation have been adopted by many port States. The cruise industry demonstrates its commitment to protecting the environment through the use of a broad spectrum of waste management technologies and procedures employed on its vessels.[419]

---

[416] See German Report, VI.32.

[417] USA Report, V.

[418] https://www.cruising.org/about-the-industry/regulatory/industry-policies/environmental-protection/waste-management.

[419] https://www.cruising.org/about-the-industry/regulatory/industry-policies/environmental-protection/waste-management.

8.2 *Regional and National Regulations*

8.2.1 International Conventions

There are some important international instruments on environmental matters, like the IMO International Convention for the Control and Management of Ships' Ballast Water and Sediments (BWM),[420] adopted 13 February 2004 and entered into force 8 September 2017, and the IMO International Convention for the Prevention of Pollution from Ships (MARPOL), adopted in 1973 (Convention), 1978 (1978 Protocol), 1997 (Protocol—Annex VI); it entered into force on October 2, 1983 (Annexes I and II).[421]

The International Convention for the Prevention of Pollution from Ships (MARPOL 73/78) was established in 1973 to prevent oil spillage from ships. It afterwards covered also pollution from noxious liquid substances in bulk, harmful substances carried by sea in packaged form, sewage, garbage, (1983–1988) and air pollution (in 2005). A section on limitation of greenhouse gas emissions was added in 2011.[422] MARPOL is also working on the problem of the marine industry's relying on heavy fuel oil and passing some regulation on the matter.[423]

The MARPOL's regulation of shipping in a number of areas, defined in its Annexes I, II, and V, that are in need of extra protection from environmental damage, is particularly relevant for cruises. They are designated as either "Special Areas" and given appropriate regulatory protection, or "Particularly Sensitive Sea Areas" (PSSAs).[424]

---

[420] http://www.imo.org/en/About/Conventions/ListOfConventions/Pages/International-Convention-for-the-Control-and-Management-of-Ships'-Ballast-Water-and-Sediments-(BWM).aspx.

[421] http://www.imo.org/en/about/conventions/listofconventions/pages/international-convention-for-the-prevention-of-pollution-from-ships-(marpol).aspx.

[422] As explained with detail in the USA Report, II: "MARPOL Convention, annexes I-VI. The relevant Annexes are:

Annex I Regulations for the Prevention of Pollution by Oil (entered into force 2 October 1983); Annex II Regulations for the Control of Pollution by Noxious Liquid Substances in Bulk (entered into force 2 October 1983): "In any case, no discharge of residues containing noxious substances is permitted within 12 miles of the nearest land"; Annex IV Prevention of Pollution by Sewage from Ships (entered into force 27 September 2003): "[S]ewage which is not comminuted or disinfected has to be discharged at a distance of more than 12 nautical miles from the nearest land"; Annex V Prevention of Pollution by Garbage from Ships (entered into force 31 December 1988): "the most important feature of the Annex is the complete ban imposed on the disposal into the sea of all forms of plastics"; Annex VI Prevention of Air Pollution from Ships (entered into force 19 May 2005): "Sets limits on sulphur oxide and nitrogen oxide emissions from ship exhausts and prohibits deliberate emissions of ozone depleting substances; designated emission control areas set more stringent standards for SOx, NOx and particulate matter. A chapter adopted in 2011 covers mandatory technical and operational energy efficiency measures aimed at reducing greenhouse gas emissions from ships"."

[423] See further information in the USA Report, III.

[424] See further information in the USA Report, III.

8.2.2 European Rules

In Europe, the Directive 2000/59/EC addressed Port Reception Facilities (PRF) for ship-generated waste. The main objective of the Directive is to eliminate uncontrolled dumping from vessels, whatever their activities. The dumping must be done in the facilities designed for that.[425] Its main precepts are the creation of an adequate port reception facility for garbage from ships that call at the port, the development of a waste removal plan, a timely declaration by the ship of the quantity of ship's garbage to be discharged, the contribution by the ship in the cost of reception, removal, processing, and exchange of information on discharge for the purpose of enforcement.[426]

Regulation (EU) No 1143/2014 of the European Parliament and of the Council of 23 October 2014 on the prevention and management of the introduction and spread of invasive alien species[427] recognises the BWM Convention as one of the possible management measures for invasive species of concern.[428]

In case C-537/11 the European Court of Justice ruled that a cruise ship falls within the scope of Article 4a(4) of Council Directive 1999/32/EC of 26 April 1999 relating to a reduction in the sulphur content of certain liquid fuels with regard to the criterion of 'regular services', as laid down in its art. 2(3g), if it operates cruises, with or without intermediate calls, finishing in the port of departure or another port, provided that those cruises are organised at a particular frequency, on specific dates and, in principle, at specified departure and arrival times, with interested persons being able to choose freely between the various cruises offered, which is a matter for the referring court to ascertain.[429]

In some countries, like Romania,[430] Poland,[431] and Germany[432] there are national and international rules on environmental protection that are applicable to cruises, though not specific on cruises. In Poland there is "the Prevention of Pollution from Ships Act of 1995[433] which implements into the Polish law the MARPOL Convention (with the London Protocol), the HELCOM Convention, the Dumping Convention 1972 (Convention on the Prevention of Marine Pollution by Dumping of Wastes and Other Matter) and the AFS Convention (International Convention on the Control of Harmful Anti-fouling Systems on Ship). It also meets the Vienna Convention on the protection of the Ozone Layer, to the extent applicable to ships (in respect to

[425] Ariza Herrerías (2014), p. 19 y ss.

[426] Belgian Report, VI.31.

[427] https://www.eea.europa.eu/policy-documents/ec-2014-regulation-eu-no.

[428] See further information in Belgian Report, VI.31.

[429] Belgian Report, II.9.10 and https://eur-lex.europa.eu/legal-content/EN/TXT/?uri=CELEX%3A62011CJ0537.

[430] Romanian National Report, VI.31.

[431] Polish Report, VI.31.

[432] German Report, VI.31–32.

[433] Consolidated text in Journal of Laws 2015 item 434.

ships implemented into the Polish law by Article 20 and 39 of the Act on Substances Depleting the Ozone Layer and on Certain Fluorinated Greenhouse Gases of 2015[434])".[435]

In Germany, "on the basis of § 15 of the Law relating to the Tasks of the Federal Government in the Area of Maritime Traffic (Seeaufgabengesetz, SeeAufG), the Federal Ministry for Transport and Digital Infrastructure had issued the Environmental Maritime Behaviour Regulation (Seeumweltverhaltensverordnung, SeeUmwVerhV) on the basis of which offences committed against the MARPOL Convention, against other international environmental agreements and other behavioural provisions for the protection of the environment in maritime traffic can be punished. The Federal Maritime and Hydrographic Agency (Bundesanstalt für Seeschifffahrt und Hydrographie, BSH) is the authority responsible for prosecuting the vast majority of offences committed pursuant to the SeeUmwVerhV".[436]

It must be noticed, as pointed out by the German reporter,[437] that "the SeeUmwVerhV is no implementation of the MARPOL Convention to German law, but gives power to the BSH to enforce the Convention. The Convention is applicable in Germany as such, as it was ratified by the German legislator in 1996 including all the six annexes.[438] The SeeUmwVerhV empowers the BSH also to enforce the Convention on the Control of Harmful Anti-Fouling Systems on ships (AFS Convention)[439] and the Convention on the Control and Treatment of Ballast Water".[440]

In Spain, Act 27/1992[441] refers to the right to a balanced, sustainable and healthy environment and to enjoy natural resources and the environment and landscape (Article 28).[442] Act 21/2007[443] provides that the respect to environmental values must be guaranteed, and forbids any kind of dumping or pollutant emission, whatever its origin, within the port's public domain. If it occurs, damages must be compensated under an objective liability regime.[444]

---

[434] Consolidated text in Journal of Laws 2015 item 881.

[435] Polish Report, VI.31.

[436] German Report, VI.31.

[437] German Report, VI.32.

[438] Bundesgesetzblatt (Federal Official Journal) 1996 II, p. 399.

[439] Bundesgesetzblatt 2008 II, p. 520.

[440] Bundesgesetzblatt 2013 II, p. 42.

[441] *Ley 27/1992, 24/11/92, de Puertos del Estado y de la Marina Mercante.*

[442] Ariza Herrerías (2014), pp. 20–21.

[443] Ley 21/2007, de 18 de diciembre, de Régimen Jurídico y Económico de los puertos de Andalucía, Título V, "Puertos y medio ambiente".

[444] Ariza Herrerías (2014), p. 22.

8.2.3 South American Rules

In some countries, like Argentina,[445] there are national rules on environmental impact of vessels, which are applicable to cruise ships. Similarly, though Brazil has no specific rules on environmental impact of cruises, there are several national rules and international conventions that are applicable to environmental damages caused by cruises. There are national rules on prevention, control and inspection, control and inspection of pollution caused by oil and its by-products and other noxious or dangerous substances in waters under Brazilian jurisdiction (Act N° 9.966/2000), on criminal and administrative penalties for environmental damage (Act N° 9.605/1998), administrative penalties for acts and activities harmful to the environment (Decree N° 6.514/2008), the procedure for notifying the ANP of oil pollution incidents (ANP Resolution N° 44/2009), among others.[446]

In the Uruguayan legal system there are some general rules that are applicable to the environmental impact of the operation of cruise ships, of national, bi-national and international origin. They refer mainly to the prevention and surveillance regime for possible contamination of the waters of national jurisdiction or other elements of that medium, the repressive and preventive regime of pollution, the prevention of polluting actions in the Río de la Plata, among others. Several international instruments are applicable in Uruguay regarding this topic, like the International Convention for the Prevention of Pollution from Ships (MARPOL 73/78), ratified by Act N°14.885; the International Convention on the Control of Harmful Anti-fouling Systems on Ships (AFS) 2001, ratified by Act N° 18.971; the International Convention on Civil Liability for Oil Pollution Damage (CLC) 1969, ratified by Act N° 16.820; the 1992 Protocol to the International Convention on the Establishment of an International Fund for Compensation for Oil Pollution Damage (FUND 1992), ratified by Act N° 16.820; and the United Nations Convention on the Law of the Sea (UNCLOS), ratified by Act N° 16.287.[447]

8.2.4 Antarctic Continent

Since the late fifties of the twentieth century tourists began visiting the Antarctic continent, mainly by ship but also by airplane flying over the region throwing correspondence and other supplies from the air. During the past 50 years the cruise tourism has increased significantly, with vessels that carry from 200 to 2500 passengers plus 1200 crew members, like the *Golden Princess*. This phenomenon obviously puts environmental security at risk. In the XXXth Advisory Meeting of the Antarctic Treaty a Resolution was approved recommending the parties to discourage or prohibit disembarkment of passengers from vessels carrying more

[445] See the list in Argentine Report, V.31.

[446] See more details in Brazilian Report, III.31.

[447] See more detailed information in the Uruguayan Report, VI.31–32.

than 500 passengers in the Area of the Antarctic Treaty. Moreover, there were some proposals to reduce or block touristic activities or others that may affect the environment.[448]

8.2.5 Federal and State Legislation in the USA

Both the U.S. Environmental Protection Agency and the U.S. Coast Guard can set regulations for cruise ship pollution under different legislative acts. However, national environmental protections alone would not be sufficient because of the limited jurisdictional reach of any national act. Therefore, Congress has incorporated international standards set by the International Maritime Organization into U.S. law. The most relevant instruments reported are the Marine Protection, Research, and Sanctuaries Act (MPRSA, also known as the Ocean Dumping Act),[449] the Clean Water Act (CWA) and the Clean Air Act (CAA).[450]

The Clean Water Act states, under the title "Restoration and maintenance of chemical, physical and biological integrity of the Nation's waters; national goals for achievement of objective", among other goals, that "it is the national goal that the discharge of pollutants into the navigable waters be eliminated by 1985".[451] It is "the primary Federal statute regulating the protection of the nation's water. The CWA aims to prevent, reduce, and eliminate pollution in the nation's water in order to "restore and maintain the chemical, physical, and biological integrity of the Nation's waters", as described in CWA section 101(a). A stated goal of the CWA is to eliminate discharge of pollutants into navigable waters, as that term is defined in CWA § 502(7) and corresponding case law".[452] As reported by the national experts, "discharges are only allowed under the National Pollution Discharge Elimination Program (NPDES), which creates a system for state and federal environmental agencies to issue discharge permits".[453] Moreover, under the CWA, "the administrator of the EPA "shall promulgate Federal standards of performance for marine sanitation devices (hereafter in this section referred to as "standards") which shall be designed to prevent the discharge of untreated or inadequately treated sewage into or upon the navigable waters from new vessels and existing vessels, except vessels not

[448] Aramburu (2008), p. 3.

[449] Marine Protection, Research, and Sanctuaries Act (16 U.S.C. § 1431 and 33 U.S.C. § 1401).

[450] See further information in the USA Report, V.

[451] Clean Water Act. §101, 33 U.S.C. § 1251 (a)(1). See further information at: https://www.law.cornell.edu/uscode/text/33/1251.

[452] See further information in https://www.epa.gov/enforcement/clean-water-act-cwa-and-federal-facilities and in the USA Report, V.

[453] See further information in the USA Report, V.

equipped with installed toilet facilities."[454] However, the Act only applies to "vessels owned and operated by the United States."[455]

Regarding U.S. national legislation, national reporters consider that it was "insufficient to control maritime pollution. The Act to Prevent Pollution from Ships[456] implements MARPOL and its annexes, and applies to all U.S. flagged ships and all ships in navigable waters of the United States or at port in the U.S. Recent efforts are underway in the cruising industry to meet the MARPOL targets of reducing sulfur in fuel from the current 3.5 percent to 0.5 percent by 2020,[457] other new IMO regulations are also responsible for developments in wastewater discharge levels of nitrogen and phosphorous,[458] and the industry is also cognizant of the Polar Code promulgated by the IMO, but not especially enthusiastic about its prospects for a good result.[459]"[460]

Federal Legislation

It has been reported that: "The U.S. Environmental Protection Agency estimates that a single 3,000-person cruise ship produces 150,000 gallons of sewage per week, and that the cruise ship industry can produce more than one billion gallons of sewage per year.[461] Untreated human waste can cause a host of environmental problems, such as nitrogen and phosphorus in sewage, causing algae blooms, which can deplete oxygen and suffocate sea-life; human waste transmits harmful bacteria and viruses, including Hepatitis A, Norovirus, and E. Coli,[462] and human pathogens emitted near coastlines can infect swimmers and bathers, or infect shellfish and later be consumed by humans".[463]

Water Pollution

There are some differences in the regulation of graywater, blackwater and ballast water.

---

[454] Environmental Protection Agency. *Clean Water Act*, CWA § 312 33 U.S.C. 1332 (b)(1), https://www3.epa.gov/npdes/pubs/cwatxt.txt.

[455] USA Report, V.

[456] 33 U.S.C. §§1905–1915.

[457] See Mia Bennett, Cruising's Environmental Impact: "The industry strives to go green and atone for past missteps," Jan.-Feb. 2017, https://maritime-executive.com/magazine/cruisings-environmental-impact#gs.eOzkd98 [hereinafter Mar-Ex].

[458] *Id.* See IMO Marine Environment Protection Committee (MEPC) Resolution 227(64).

[459] Mar-Ex, *supra* note 160.

[460] USA Report, V.

[461] Friends of the Earth, *2016 Cruise Ship Report Card*, https://1bps6437gg8c169i0y1drtgz-wpengine.netdna-ssl.com/wp-content/uploads/wpallimport/files/archive/Cruise_Report_2016.pdf.

[462] Centers for Disease Control and Prevention, National Center for Environmental Health Vessel Sanitation Program, *Health Practices on Cruise Ships: Training for Employees*, Transcript. https://www.cdc.gov/nceh/vsp/training/videos/transcripts/water.pdf.

[463] USA Report, V.

Graywater Regulation

For the purpose of the 2008 Vessel General Permit (VGP), "graywater" means "gallery, bath and shower waters, as well as wastewater from lavatory sinks, laundry, and water fountains".[464] Pursuant to the U.S. Environmental Protection Agency (EPA) Regulation, "ordinary graywater discharges currently are exempt from the CWA's NPDES[465] permit requirement. Environmental groups and other interested parties, however, are pushing EPA to eliminate or modify the exemption" (40 C.F.R. § 122.3(a). However, as reported by the EPA, "in December 2003, the long-standing exclusion of discharges incidental to the normal operation of vessels from the NPDES program became the subject of a lawsuit in the U.S. District Court for the Northern District of California. On March 30, 2005, the same court determined that the exclusion exceeded the Agency's authority under the CWA, and issued a court order vacating that exclusion. As a result, discharges incidental to the normal operation of a vessel, including graywater, became subject to CWA section 301's prohibition against discharging without a NPDES permit, unless covered under an NPDES permit".[466]

33 U.S.C. § 1362(6) defines the term "pollutant" very broadly, including "dredged spoil, solid waste, incinerator residue, sewage, garbage, sewage sludge, munitions, chemical wastes, biological materials, radioactive materials, heat, wrecked or discarded equipment, rock, sand, cellar dirt and industrial, municipal, and agricultural waste discharged into water". It adds: "This term does not mean (A) 'sewage from vessels or a discharge incidental to the normal operation of a vessel of the Armed Forces' within the meaning of section 1322 of this title; or (B) water, gas, or other material which is injected into a well to facilitate production of oil or gas, or water derived in association with oil or gas production and disposed of in a well, if the well used either to facilitate production or for disposal purposes is approved by authority of the State in which the well is located, and if such State determines that such injection or disposal will not result in the degradation of ground or surface water resources".[467]

Nevertheless, it has been stated that "because graywater is not sewage, it is probably a "pollutant" and vessels clearly are "point sources." Thus, graywater discharges into navigable waters (within the three-mile limit of the territorial seas) arguably fall within the scope of CWA § 301 (a) and thereby require an NPDES permit". "EPA, however, has excluded, by regulation, the wastewater stream ordinarily referred to as 'graywater' from the NPDES permitting requirements of the CWA".[468]

---

[464] https://www3.epa.gov/npdes/pubs/vgp_graywater.pdf, p. 4.

[465] CWA stands for Clean Water Act, and NPDES stands for National Pollutant Discharge Elimination System.

[466] https://www3.epa.gov/npdes/pubs/vgp_graywater.pdf, p. 5.

[467] https://www.law.cornell.edu/uscode/text/33/1362.

[468] Courtney et al. (2004), p. 51.

It is worth mentioning that the London Dumping Convention,[469] which regulates ocean dumping of "wastes or other matter", was implemented in the United States through the Ocean Dumping[470] Act, which generally applies to waters beyond the three-mile limit of the territorial seas and prohibits unpermitted disposal at sea.[471] However, "unlike the London Dumping Convention, the Ocean Dumping Act does not appear to exclude graywater". (...) "it remains unclear whether graywater discharges are exempted from the Ocean Dumping Act, and there is no case law or regulation addressing the applicability of the Ocean Dumping Act or the London Dumping Convention to graywater discharges". (...).[472]

Blackwater Regulation

Blackwater is "water that contains animal, human, or food waste".[473] It is "any waste from toilets or urinals. It is defined either as treated or untreated (raw), and contains disease-causing bacteria and viruses that can result in human illness from direct contact, or by consumption of affected fish and shellfish. It contributes to nutrient build-up in ecosystems that result in changes to habitat and the proliferation of nuisance pest species". The problem with blackwater (sewage) discharged from vessels is that it is more concentrated than domestic blackwater and therefore, though discharged in relatively small amounts, it is an important source of pollution that can and should be avoided.[474]

---

[469] See text of the Convention on the Prevention of Marine Pollution by Dumping of Wastes and Other Matter (1972) and further information in http://www.imo.org/en/OurWork/Environment/LCLP/Pages/default.aspx.

[470] "Dumping" is defined in 33 U.S.C. § 1402 (f) as "a disposition of material: Provided, That it does not mean a disposition of any effluent from any outfall structure to the extent that such disposition is regulated under the provisions of the Federal Water Pollution Control Act, as amended [33 U.S.C. 1251 et seq.], under the provisions of section 407 of this title, or under the provisions of the Atomic Energy Act of 1954, as amended [42 U.S.C. 2011 et seq.], nor does it mean a routine discharge of effluent incidental to the propulsion of, or operation of motor-driven equipment on, vessels: Provided, further, That it does not mean the construction of any fixed structure or artificial island nor the intentional placement of any device in ocean waters or on or in the submerged land beneath such waters, for a purpose other than disposal, when such construction or such placement is otherwise regulated by Federal or State law or occurs pursuant to an authorized Federal or State program: And provided further, That it does not include the deposit of oyster shells, or other materials when such deposit is made for the purpose of developing, maintaining, or harvesting fisheries resources and is otherwise regulated by Federal or State law or occurs pursuant to an authorized Federal or State program".

[471] 33 U.S.C. § 1402(b), https://www.law.cornell.edu/uscode/text/33/1402.

[472] Courtney et al. (2004), p. 52.

[473] https://ofmpub.epa.gov/sor_internet/registry/termreg/searchandretrieve/termsandacronyms/search.do?matchCriteria=Contains&checkedTerm=on&checkedAcronym=on&search=Search&term=blackwater.

[474] https://www.epa.sa.gov.au/environmental_info/water_quality/programs/grey_and_black_water_discharge/black_water.

Annex IV to MARPOL 73/78 exclusively addresses sewage.[475] It is generally considered that, "on the high seas, the oceans are capable of assimilating and dealing with raw sewage through natural bacterial action and, therefore, the regulations in Annex IV prohibit ships from discharging sewage within four miles of the nearest land, unless they have in operation an approved treatment plant". Nowadays, "...all cruise ships and large passenger ships already have sewage treatment plants on board".[476] This Annex IV has about 136 State Parties,[477] though the USA has not ratified it yet.

Ballast Water Regulation

Ballast water "is used to stabilise vessels and maintain their structural integrity. Typically ballast water is pumped in to special tanks while cargo is being unloaded, and discharged while cargo is being taken on board. Safety, weather conditions, the ship's load, and the route taken are the primary factors that determine how much ballast water is taken on board a vessel for a particular voyage. More ballast is necessary for ships to sit lower in the water during stormy weather to avoid bottom impact from waves. Ballast water is also adjusted so as to balance the ship as it consumes fuel during a long voyage".[478] It must be treated because "taken on in one ecological zone and released into another can introduce invasive and nuisance aquatic species that may have detrimental impacts on the biodiversity, economy or human health of the receiving community and may in time become a serious threat to the environment".[479] In September 8, 2017, the IMO Ballast Water Management Convention (BWMC) entered in full force for all participating nations (73 contracting States), though the USA has not ratified it.[480]

The situation in the USA has been described as follows: "The regulatory standards applicable to ballast water discharges primarily derive from Coast Guard programs under the Nonindigenous Aquatic Nuisance Prevention and Control Act (NANPCA) of 1990, 16 U.S.C. §§ 4701 et seq. and the National Invasive Species Act (NISA) of 1996, Pub. L. No. 104-332, 1120 Stat. 4073. Additionally, certain international guidelines exist. (Many states have also initiated regulatory programs that are not described in this article due to their wide variation.) These regulatory

[475] http://pmg-assets.s3-website-eu-west-1.amazonaws.com/140729annexiv.pdf.

[476] http://pmg-assets.s3-website-eu-west-1.amazonaws.com/140729annexiv.pdf, Regulation 8. Courtney et al. (2004), pp. 53–54.

[477] See complete list and dates in https://www.ecolex.org/details/international-convention-for-the-prevention-of-pollution-from-ships-annex-iv-sewage-tre-000988/participants.

[478] http://www.damengreen.com/en/bwt?gclid=CjwKCAjwpIjZBRBsEiwA0TN1r5NO2z91W8uz2ByeJUs6U4CgJZvlmCZy9_HhXprNEDkQ6N-q7vl0HBoC_8QAvD_BwE.

[479] http://www.damengreen.com/en/bwt?gclid=CjwKCAjwpIjZBRBsEiwA0TN1r5NO2z91W8uz2ByeJUs6U4CgJZvlmCZy9_HhXprNEDkQ6N-q7vl0HBoC_8QAvD_BwE.

[480] http://www.imo.org/en/About/Conventions/StatusOfConventions/Pages/Default.aspx.

programs are in a state of flux as old standards and guidelines are reviewed and new ones are proposed".[481]

Air Pollution

USA national reporters inform that "Cruise ship exhaust contains greenhouse gasses, sulfur oxides, nitrogen oxides, and particulate matter. According to a 2017 undercover study, a single cruise ship produces more ultra-fine particulate matter (PM) per day than one million cars.[482] Researchers recorded PM concentrations as high as 226,000 particles per cubic centimeter near the exhaust stacks on deck, and concentrations of 84,000 particles per square centimeter downwind from the exhaust.[483] Cruise vacationers are exposed to air quality worse than many major metropolitan areas; the research team recorded PM concentrations of 38,400 in central London's congested Piccadilly Circus[484]".[485]

State Legislation: Alaska

We will take the case of Alaska, as an example, since it exceeds the length of this report to analyse all the States of the Union, and because there is great concern in Alaska because of the fact that cruises are one of the largest threats to its environment. The State of Alaska takes great care to protect its uniquely fragile environment from the effects of its status as an immensely popular cruise destination, so its situation provides a good case in point. In 2017, the state expected more than one million visitors via visiting cruise ships.[486]

The government is caught between "protecting the environment or protecting the economy", since "many of the residents and business owners in Alaskan port cities depend on the money spent by cruise ship passengers". Marrin states that so far, "there has been a mixed response from both the judiciary and the legislature"[487]

It was stated that "In response to significant controversy concerning cruise ship discharges in southeast Alaska, Congress passed legislation in December 2000 that regulates the discharge of blackwater and graywater from cruise ships capable of carrying more than five hundred passengers operating in the waters of the Alexander Archipelago and "navigable waters" within the State of Alaska. Pub. L. No. 106-554, 114 Stat. 2763". The federal legislation arose out of a number concerns, including allegations that beyond three miles from shore, some cruise ships were discharging untreated blackwater and graywater into areas, known as "doughnut

[481] Courtney et al. (2004), p. 54.

[482] Chloe Farand, *Air quality on cruise ship deck 'worse than world's most polluted cities,' investigation finds*. Independent, July 3, 2017, http://www.independent.co.uk/news/world/pollution-cruise-ships-po-oceana-higher-piccadilly-circus-channel-4-dispatches-a7821911.html.

[483] Id.

[484] Id.

[485] See further information in the USA Report, V.

[486] See, e.g., AP News, Alaska pollution regulators gear up for cruise ship season, May 3, 2017, https://www.apnews.com/d26c8908b52b41b1bbd579bd28427f85/Alaska-pollution-regulators-gear-up-for-cruise-ship-season USA National Report.

[487] Marrin (2002), p. 325.

holes," surrounded by Alaskan waters. The legislation also authorized EPA and the Coast Guard to develop regulations. The Coast Guard promulgated regulations on July 26, 2001, largely recasting the requirements established in Pub. L. No. 106-554* 66 Fed. Reg. 38,926, 33 C.F.R. §§ 159.300-321.[488]

Alaska is served by EPA's Region 10 office.[489] The State of Alaska enacted its own statute and regulations that are similar to the requirements contained in the federal legislation and implementing regulations.[490] The joint federal/state regulatory program in Alaska is viewed as a success.[491] The Commercial Passenger Vessel Environmental Compliance (Cruise Ship) Program was established in July 2001.[492] The Alaska Department of Environmental Conservation (ADEC) worked with a facilitator and a Negotiated Regulations Committee to draft regulations to accompany this law. The regulations that were drafted by the Committee became effective November 15, 2002.[493]

On July 8, 2004 the state law AS 46.03.460–46.06.490 was changed based on Chapter 153, SLA 04 which was passed by the Alaska Legislature and became final and effective May 18, 2006. Changes were made in 2006 to state laws governing the operation and regulation of large cruise ships while those ships are in Alaska Marine waters. These changes passed with voter approval under Ballot Measure 2. In 2013 state law was changed regarding large cruise ship permitting and the small cruise ship BMPs. Regulation changes to match the statute changes were completed. The intent of HB 80 was to make small cruise ship Best Management Practices (BMP) permanent, however the BMP law expired at the end of 2015. SB 3 in 2017 reintroduced the BMP program.[494]

As explained by the USA national reporters, under the Commercial Passenger Vessel Environmental Compliance Program,[495] ships must be registered and agree to follow discharge regulations.[496] "The law 'bars discharge of treated sewage, greywater, or other waste water without a permit' and requires the shipper to comply with very strict standards maintained to prevent the vessel traffic from unduly harming the local sea".[497]

---

[488] Courtney et al. (2004), p. 54.

[489] See further information in https://www.epa.gov/aboutepa/epa-region-10-pacific-northwest.

[490] ALASKA STAT. § 46.03.460–490 (2001); Alaska Admin. Code tit. 18, ch. 69 (2002).

[491] Courtney et al. (2004), p. 54.

[492] by AS 46.03.460—AS 46.03.490.

[493] https://dec.alaska.gov/water/cruise_ships/Law_and_Regs/index.htm.

[494] https://dec.alaska.gov/water/cruise_ships/Law_and_Regs/index.htm.

[495] Alaska Commercial Passenger Vessel Environmental Compliance Program, http://www.legis.state.ak.us/basis/statutes.asp#46.03.462.

[496] *Id.* Para. 2.

[497] *See, e.g.,* Alaska Dept of Environmental Conservation [DEC], Division of Water, Frequently Asked Questions—Cruise Ship Wastewater Discharge Regulation and HB 80, Dec. 5, 2017, http://dec.alaska.gov/water/cruise_ships/faq.htm. See also Graywater Regulations 33-CFR Part 150, Marine Exchange of Alaska, pt. 159.3, et seq., sec. 1(a)(4), Pub. L. 106-554, 114 Stat. 2763;

It is well known that in addition to the problem of congestion and noise pollution affecting any place that is frequented by cruise ships, the problem of greywater is a main one. The Consolidated Appropriations Act of 2001,[498] is a federal legislation regulating chemicals and general waste water generated by cruise ships, which reflects "a compromise reached by diverse interests including certain Alaska economic interests, the Clinton Administration, the cruise ship industry and environmental groups". The legislation also requires inspections by the Coast Guard to ensure full compliance by cruise ships. Since 2001, "cruise ships that operate within the borders of Alaska must submit to Alaska's Department of Environmental Conservation solid waste plans".[499]

The problem is how to reach balanced solutions that contemplate the protection of the environment and the economy, since it has been reported that "the cruise ship economy is vital to Alaska's very economic existence". Nevertheless, "citizens have started resenting the large crowds and pollution –noise, air and water- that accompanies the presence of large cruise ships". Anyhow, "Alaska is still very economically dependent upon the money brought into the state by the passengers of the cruise ships, and do not seek to ban cruise ships, just merely regulate them, keeping the balance between their invaluable natural resources and the ability to profit from them".[500]

8.3 International Convention on Civil Liability for Oil Pollution Damage, Brussels, 1969

This Convention[501] states in Article I that State Parties "may take such measures on the high seas as may be necessary to prevent, mitigate or eliminate grave and imminent danger to their coastline or related interests from pollution or threat of pollution of the sea by oil, following upon a maritime casualty or acts related to such a casualty, which may reasonably be expected to result in major harmful consequences". It rules the measures to be taken by coastal States in accordance with Article I (Article III) and mandates that those measures shall be proportionate to the damage actual or threatened to it (Article V). It includes a compatibility clause stating that "Except as specifically provided, nothing in the present Convention shall prejudice any otherwise applicable right, duty, privilege or immunity or deprive any

https://www.gpo.gov/fdsys/pkg/CFR-2017-title33-vol2/xml/CFR-2017-title33-vol2-part159.xml. See further information in the USA national report.

[498] Pub. L. No. 106-554, 114 Stat. 2763 (2000) (enacted).

[499] Marrin (2002), pp. 329–330, where case law is mentioned.

[500] Marrin (2002), pp. 335–337.

[501] http://www.admiraltylawguide.com/conven/civilpol1969.html; https://treaties.un.org/doc/publication/unts/volume%20970/volume-970-i-14049-english.pdf.

of the Parties or any interested physical or corporate person of any remedy otherwise applicable" (Article VII).

There may be cases where the provisions in the Convention clash with the principle of full compensation of the damage (*Restitutio in Integrum*) incorporated in many national legal systems, like those of Brazil.[502] The solution to this conflict depends on the hierarchy of the different sources of law in each country. For example, in Brazil, the Convention has the status of a common or ordinary Law. Therefore, the Brazilian Constitution and subsequent Federal Laws on the same subject will prevail over the Convention in the event of a conflict. As a consequence, the convention has not been applied by Brazilian courts.[503]

8.4 International Convention for the Prevention of Pollution from Ships, as Modified by the Protocol of 1978 (MARPOL 73/78)

This is the main international Convention covering prevention of pollution of the marine environment by ships from operational or accidental causes. It was adopted on 2 November 1973 at the International Maritime Organization (IMO). As explained by the IMO, the Protocol of 1978 "was adopted in response to a spate of tanker accidents in 1976–1977. As the 1973 MARPOL Convention had not yet entered into force, the 1978 MARPOL Protocol absorbed the parent Convention. The combined instrument entered into force on 2 October 1983. In 1997, a Protocol was adopted to amend the Convention and a new Annex VI was added which entered into force on 19 May 2005. MARPOL has been updated by amendments through the years".[504]

The Convention includes regulations aimed at preventing and minimizing pollution from ships—both accidental pollution and that from routine operations—and currently includes six technical Annexes: Annex I Regulations for the Prevention of Pollution by Oil (entered into force 2 October 1983), Annex II Regulations for the Control of Pollution by Noxious Liquid Substances in Bulk (entered into force 2 October 1983), Annex III Prevention of Pollution by Harmful Substances Carried by Sea in Packaged Form (entered into force 1 July 1992), Annex IV Prevention of Pollution by Sewage from Ships (entered into force 27 September 2003), Annex V

[502] The Brazilian Constitution and Federal laws incorporate the principle of full compensation of the damage. In addition, the principle of full reparation of environmental damage is provided for, among others, by Law N° 6.938 regarding the Brazilian National Policy on the Environment, on article 4th, VII, and states that any party held liable for the incident must be held liable for the totality of damage incurred. See Brazilian National Report, VI.33.

[503] See Brazilian National Report, VI.33.

[504] http://www.imo.org/en/about/conventions/listofconventions/pages/international-convention-for-the-prevention-of-pollution-from-ships-(marpol).aspx.

Prevention of Pollution by Garbage from Ships (entered into force 31 December 1988), and Annex VI Prevention of Air Pollution from Ships (entered into force 19 May 2005). Special Areas with strict controls on operational discharges are included in most Annexes.[505]

8.5 *Problems Regarding the Implementation of the Environmental Protection Rules*

Cruises have great environmental impact, as explained before, since they release a significant amount of polluting gases, wastewater and other waste generated by the ship.[506]

Some problems are reported regarding the implementation of the environmental protection rules, like in Poland, the collision between the Prevention of Pollution from Ships Act and the Law on Environmental Protection. "Polish administrative courts have ruled that ships are obliged to pay for the emission permits as prescribed by the Law on Environmental Protection,[507] notwithstanding the fact that Article 36a p. 9 of the Prevention of Pollution from Ships Act puts a fine of up to 50,000 SDR for those who use the ship which introduces into the air substances depleting the ozone layer, NOx[508] in excess of the limits as well as fluorinated greenhouse gases". The national reporter adds that: "According to the judgment of the Administrative Supreme Court, the Law on Environmental Protection is dedicated to the whole Polish territory, including internal waters and the Polish territorial sea, as well as the airspace above them. That is the basic reason why, ships operators are obligated to cover the cost of the emission permits as a result of "using the environment" by the emission of gas and dust".[509]

8.6 *Final Remarks*

Cruise industry is particularly dangerous for the environment, since it contributes a significant portion of pollution, especially in at-risk natural areas. To eliminate or at least diminish such dangers, the cruise industry demonstrates—in general—its commitment to protecting the environment through the use of a broad spectrum of

[505] http://www.imo.org/en/about/conventions/listofconventions/pages/international-convention-for-the-prevention-of-pollution-from-ships-(marpol).aspx.

[506] See further information in Spanish Report, VI.33.

[507] See rulings of the Supreme Administrative Court of 25 January 2007 (II OSK 151/06), Woivodship, Administrative Court in Gdańsk of 21 June 2007 (II SA/Gd 257/07).

[508] "NOx" stands for nitrogen oxides.

[509] Polish Report, VI.33.

waste management technologies and procedures employed on its vessels. Notwithstanding, there is probably still room to improve rules, measures and consequently, results in the protection of the environment and technology will surely help to achieve that target.

9 Jurisdiction and Arbitration

9.1 Specific and General Provisions on Jurisdiction Applicable to Cruises

9.1.1 At the International Level: The Athens Convention Relating to the Carriage of Passengers and Their Luggage by Sea

Jurisdiction

Article 17 of the Athens Convention gives the claimant the possibility to choose among several reasonable and concurrent jurisdictions that enable access to justice for both parties. It states that: "1. An action arising under this Convention shall, at the option of the claimant, be brought before one of the courts listed below, provided that the court is located in a State Party to this Convention: (a) The court of the place of permanent residence or principal place of business of the defendant, or (b) The court of the place of departure or that of the destination according to the contract of carriage, or (c) A court of the State of the domicile or permanent residence of the claimant, if the defendant has a place of business and is subject to jurisdiction in that State, or (d) A court of the State where the contract of carriage was made, if the defendant has a place of business and is subject to jurisdiction in that State. 2. After the occurrence of the incident which has caused the damage, the parties may agree that the claim for damages shall be submitted to any jurisdiction or to arbitration".

Time-Bar for Actions

Article 16 of the Athens Convention refers to time-bar for actions for damages arising out of the death of or personal injury to a passenger or for the loss of or damage to his luggage. It states a period of 2 years and the way in which that period shall be calculated. Paragraph 3 is a conflict-of-laws rule that leaves to the law of the court seized of the case to govern the grounds of suspension and interruption of limitation periods. It adds a substantive rule that limits the competence of the court's law, since it states that "in no case shall an action under this Convention be brought after the expiration of a period of three years from the date of disembarkation of the passenger or from the date when disembarkation should have taken place, whichever is later. However, "the period of limitation may be extended by a declaration of the carrier or by agreement of the parties after the cause of action has arisen. The declaration or agreement shall be in writing".

9.1.2 In the Americas

In Argentina maritime issues are of federal competence.[510] Jurisdiction issues are ruled by the Navigation Act N° 24.094, by the 1940 Montevideo Treaty on International Commercial Navigation and by the 1974 Athens Convention Relating to the Carriage of Passengers and their Luggage by Sea, depending on which instrument is applicable in each particular case.

The Uruguayan legal system does not provide for specific provisions on jurisdiction on cruises, but some general provisions are applicable. That is the case of the Montevideo Treaties on International Civil Law of 1889[511] and 1940,[512] both regulating international jurisdiction. Their main and general bases of jurisdiction are that of the State whose law is applicable, and that of the defendant's domicile (Articles 56). The 1889 Montevideo Treaty on Commercial Law provides for several special rules of jurisdiction, among which it is worth mentioning that of the place where the company acts (Article 7) and that of the domicile of the branches or agencies.[513] On the other hand, the 1940 Montevideo Treaty on International Commercial Navigation Law expressly provides for the carriage of passengers, regulating it in the same articles that govern the transport of cargo (articles 25–27). The bases of jurisdiction are, at the plaintiff's option, the place of performance of the contract or the defendant's domicile.[514] In fact, though with a different drafting, they basically coincide in the chosen criteria.

When the aforementioned treaties are not applicable to the case, in Uruguay, under Article 7.2 of Act N° 19.246 of August 15, 2015 on Maritime Commercial Law,[515] the referred rules of the 1940 Montevideo Treaty on International Commercial Navigation Law are applicable. The applicable law to carriage of passengers is that of the place of performance, construed as that of the place of disembarking of the passenger. Any contractual clause providing for something different is void.[516] In Argentina, under Article 604 of the Navigation Act N° 20.094[517] the provisions in the Navigation Act are applicable to the carrier's liability in carriage of passengers and its luggage in any case where the contract was entered into in Argentina or where the place of performance starts or terminates at an Argentine port, whether the vessel is national or foreign, among other circumstances.

In Brazil, under the Civil Procedural Code the general rule on jurisdiction is that of the defendant's domicile. Brazilian courts have also jurisdiction when the contract

[510] Article 116 of the National Constitution. See Argentine Report, VII.35.

[511] Ratified by Uruguay, Argentina, Paraguay, Colombia, Bolivia and Peru.

[512] Ratified by Uruguay, Argentina and Paraguay.

[513] See further information in the Uruguayan Report, VII.35 and in Fresnedo de Aguirre (2009), pp. 168–181.

[514] Uruguayan Report, VII.35.

[515] https://legislativo.parlamento.gub.uy/temporales/leytemp2250106.

[516] Fresnedo de Aguirre (2015), pp. 127–168, p. 150.

[517] http://servicios.infoleg.gob.ar/infolegInternet/anexos/40000-44999/43550/texact.htm.

was entered into in Brazil and when the fact or event giving rise to the case occurred in Brazil. Regarding consumers, like cruises' passengers, under Article 101 of the Consumers Code the courts of the consumer's domicile have jurisdiction and this provision prevails over the general rules in the Civil Procedural Code. In labour cases, under Article 651 of the Labour Act or CLT (Decree N° 5.452/43) the courts of the place where the worker performs his duties have jurisdiction.[518]

In the USA the Constitution authorizes federal courts to adjudicate "all Cases of admiralty and maritime Jurisdiction."[519] Subsequently, Congress adopted the Judiciary Act of 1789[520] and authorized this grant of original jurisdiction. However, state courts have concurrent general maritime jurisdiction, as the Florida Supreme Court stated in the 2007 case of *Carnival Corp. v. Carlisle.*[521] The CVSSA applies extraterritorially in accordance with another U.S. law, 18 U.S.C. § 7, Special Maritime Jurisdiction of the United States Defined.[522] Under its provisions, the U.S. can exercise extraterritorial maritime jurisdiction when: the vessel is owned in whole or part by U.S. nationals, the offense was committed by or against a U.S. national on the high seas, the incident occurs in a territorial sea of the U.S., or the incident was by or against a U.S. person during a voyage to or from a U.S. port.[523]

In Canada, though jurisprudence generally respects and enforces choice of laws and choice of forum clauses in commercial contracts, when it comes to passenger contracts those clauses are frequently and sometimes successfully challenged.[524]

9.1.3 In the European Union

Supranational Sources on Jurisdiction

In the European Union, supranational sources are mainly the applicable rules, without prejudice of national private international law rules. European Union secondary legislation has direct effect in the Member States legal orders, therefore European Union unified law on jurisdiction applies,[525] and that is the Regulation (EU) No. 1215/2012 of the European Parliament and the Council of 12 December

[518] Brazilian National Report, VII.34, 36.

[519] U.S. Const., art. III, § 2, cl. 1.

[520] 28 U.S.C. § 3033(1).

[521] See further information in USA Report, II.

[522] Government Publishing Office. *18 U.S.C. § 7. Special maritime and territorial jurisdiction of the United States defined.*

[523] See USA Report, II. Government Publishing Office. *18 U.S.C. § 7. Special maritime and territorial jurisdiction of the United States defined;* https://www.gpo.gov/fdsys/pkg/USCODE-2010-title18/pdf/USCODE-2010-title18-partI-chap1-sec7.pdf.

[524] Chircop et al. (2016), p. 659.

[525] With the exemption of Denmark.

2012 on jurisdiction and the recognition and enforcement of judgments in civil and commercial matters (Brussels Ia Regulation, recast).[526]

The general rule on jurisdiction is that of the defendant's domicile (Article 4.1), a criterion applied worldwide,[527] though the recast includes several detailed and specific rules on the matter. Article 7 refers to special jurisdictions; those relevant to cruise issues are those on contracts, which provide that the courts of the place of performance of the obligation in question have jurisdiction and defines the connecting factor (Article 7 (1) (a)), and those on torts, which resource to the traditional connection of the place where the harmful event occurred or may occur (Article 7 (2)), also accepted worldwide. Rules on consumer protection included in the recast are dealt with later in Sect. 9.2

National Sources on Jurisdiction and Application of Supranational and International Sources in EU State Members

In Germany there are no specific rules on jurisdiction and arbitration regarding cruises, so general European Union rules on jurisdiction and consumer protection apply.

In Poland the Athens Convention relating to the carriage of passengers and their luggage by sea, 1974 and the Regulation (EU) No 1215/2012 of the European Parliament and of the Council of 12 December 2012 on jurisdiction and the recognition and enforcement of judgments in civil and commercial matters (recast) (Brussels I bis)[528] are applicable. Under Article 71 of the Brussels I bis Regulation, where there is a clash between the provisions of the Regulation and the international convention, the convention prevails.[529] The Athens Convention protects consumers by providing for limitations on party autonomy (Article 17).[530]

In Romania, private international law rules on jurisdiction included in the Civil Code are applicable to cases related to cruises, since there are no specific rules on the topic. However, general rules on consumer protection prevail in cases involving cruise passengers.[531]

In Spain, rules on jurisdiction regarding cruise matters are in the Spanish Law on Judiciary (*Ley Orgánica del Poder Judicial*) amended by Act 7/2015 of July 7, in the Spanish Law on Shipping (*Ley 14/2014, 24 de Julio, de Navegación maritima*) and in the Council Directive 93/13/EEC of 5 April 1993 on unfair terms in consumer contracts and its Annex containing an indicative and non-exhaustive list of terms which may be regarded as unfair. This Directive has been implemented in Spain by

[526] OJ No. L 351 of 20.12.2012, p. 1. This Regulation replaces the Brussels I-Regulation, Council Regulation (EC) 44/2001 of 22 December 2000 on jurisdiction and the recognition and enforcement of judgments in civil and commercial matters, OJ No. L 12 of 16.1.2001, p. 1.

[527] For example, in the Montevideo Treaties on International Civil Law of 1889 and of 1940, in both, Article 56.2; also in the Uruguayan Civil Code, Article 2401.

[528] OJ L 351, 20.12.2012, pp. 1–32.

[529] Polish National Report, VII.35.

[530] Polish National Report, VII.36.

[531] Romanian National Report, VII.34–36.

Act 7/1999 of 13 April on general contract terms and Articles 80 *et seq* of Royal Decree-Legislative 1/2007 of 16 November approving the Recast text of the General Law on Consumer Protection and other supplementary laws. Article 82 deals with terms not individually negotiated and Article 90(2) with forum selection clauses and are to be held as overriding mandatory provisions because they are meant to protect the general interests of consumers.[532]

In the *Costa Crociere SpA* case, decided by the Court of Appeals in Madrid, Section 28, judgment N° 165/2015 of 8 June 2015, "on an injunction action for the protection of consumers' interest brought by a consumer association before the Spanish jurisdiction against *Costa Crociere SpA*, an Italian company", the court stated that some of the challenged terms were unfair under Articles 80 *et seq* of the Royal Decree-Legislative 1/2007 and Spanish Act 7/1998, and granted the injunction.[533]

9.1.4 In Asia

In Japan, general rules on jurisdiction are applicable in cruise cases. The Code of Civil Procedure (Act No. 109 of 1996. hereinafter, CCP) only had rules on domestic jurisdiction until 2011,[534] when it incorporated rules on international jurisdiction. The amended CCP protects weaker parties, like consumers and employees. Japanese courts have jurisdiction when the defendant's principal office, the representative's domicile or the place of performance of the contract is in Japan, or when the cruise operator's office is in Japan and the passenger's claim is related to the activities carried out by the office, or when the cruise operator engages in business in Japan whether it has an office in Japan or not, and the passenger's claim is related to the business in Japan. If the passenger is a 'consumer' under Article 3–4 of the CCP ('consumer' is defined as a natural person except where he or she becomes a party to a contract in or for its business), when his or her domicile is located in Japan either at the time of bringing an action against the cruise operator or at the time of concluding the consumer cruise contract. There are other special rules on jurisdiction for torts actions and maritime claims, among others.[535]

Under the protective rules in the Japanese CCP, a consumer passenger living in Japan or who lived in Japan at the time of contracting will be usually able to bring an action against a cruise operator before a Japanese court. The cruise passenger will not be forced to appear before a foreign court by a cruise operator, and if the latter gets a rendered by a foreign court, it will not be recognized or enforced in Japan on the grounds of lack of jurisdiction of the foreign court under Japanese jurisdiction

[532] See more detailed information in Spanish National Report, VII.34–36.

[533] See more detailed information in Spanish National Report, III.19 and VII.36.

[534] The amendment came into force on April 1, 2012.

[535] See detailed information in Japanese Report, VII.35.

rules. Even a consumer having no domicile in Japan may in some cases, as long as the disputes have a sufficient connection with Japan.[536]

9.1.5 Final Remarks

In spite of the variety of sources of laws on jurisdiction in the jurisdictions considered in this report, general solutions are not so different. It is worth remarking that in all of them it is the option of the claimant to choose among several concurrent jurisdictions. Most, though not all of those concurrent jurisdictions are frequently repeated in the analysed texts. The jurisdictions most generally recognised are that of the place of domicile or of permanent residence or principal place of business of the defendant, that of the domicile of the branches or agencies acting in the contract or where the contract was entered into, the place of departure or of destination of the passenger, courts of the consumer's domicile, courts of the place where the worker performs his duties. There are other criteria used by some jurisdictions like for example those of the domicile or permanent residence of the claimant, if the defendant has a place of business and is subject to jurisdiction in that State, or the place where the contract of carriage was made, if the defendant has a place of business and is subject to jurisdiction in that State.

9.2 *Forum Selection Clauses Included in General Conditions of Cruise Contracts and Consumer Protection Rules*

9.2.1 In the Americas

In Brazil forum selection clauses included in general conditions of cruise contracts would not be recognized as valid unless the passenger—who is a consumer—voluntarily files his claim in the chosen jurisdiction.[537]

In principle choice of jurisdiction clauses are not recognised in Uruguay.[538] The Buenos Aires Protocol on international jurisdiction in contracts has a limited scope of application and would rarely apply to cruise contracts.[539] However, under Article 7.3 of Act N° 19.246, *post-litem* prorogation is admitted, *i.e.*, whatever the jurisdiction is under the applicable rules, after the litigious facts occurred the parties may agree to submit litigation to another state jurisdiction or to arbitration. In Argentina,

[536] See detailed information in Japanese Report, VII.36.

[537] Brazilian National Report, VII.37.

[538] Under Article 2403 of the Civil Code, party autonomy is not admitted unless the applicable law—*i.e.*, the law referred to by the applicable conflict of laws rule—admits it.

[539] For more detailed information see Uruguayan Report, VII.37 and Fresnedo de Aguirre (2009), pp. 168–176.

Article 621 of the Navigation Act N° 20.094 provides for a very similar solution, admitting the *post-litem* prorogation.[540]

In the USA the matter has been definitively ruled by the US Supreme Court's decision in *Carnival Cruise Lines v. Shute*, where the Court held that forum selection clauses in passenger contracts are enforceable if they are fair and reasonable.[541]

9.2.2 In the European Union

Regulation (EU) 1215/2012 of the European Union and of the Council of 12 December 2012 on Jurisdiction and the Recognition and Enforcement of Judgments in Civil and Commercial Matters (Brussels Ia Recast)

In the European Union the Brussels Ia Regulation provides for a high standard of consumer protection with regard to jurisdiction and jurisdiction clauses.[542] Under Article 18.1 a consumer has the choice to bring proceedings against the other party "either in the courts of the Member State in which that party is domiciled or, regardless of the domicile of the other party, in the courts of the place where the consumer is domiciled". The other party may bring proceedings only in the courts of the Member State in which the consumer is domiciled (Article 18.2). Rules on jurisdiction in Article 18 are mandatory[543] and may only be departed from by an agreement that meets the requirements in Article 19.

In the hypothesis ruled in Article 18(c), when the consumer has concluded a contract "with a person who pursues commercial or professional activities in the Member State of the consumer's domicile or, by any means, directs such activities to that Member State or to several States including that Member State, and the contract falls within the scope of such activities", the words "direct to that Member State" are of utmost importance, as pointed out by the German reporter, "because this includes internet bookings. It has to be decided, whether a web site is directed to the Member State of the consumer. The CJEU developed in a leading case (*Pammer*)[544] criteria under which circumstances a web site may be regarded as being directed to the Member State of the consumer' domicile. Subject of the *Pammer* case was a cruise on a cargo ship".[545]

Regarding forum selection clauses included in general conditions of carriage of passengers in cruises under Article 25.5 of the Recast "an agreement conferring

---

[540] Argentine Report, VII.35.

[541] See further information in USA Report, II, and its reference to *Artistic Stone Crafters, Inc. v. Safeco Ins. Company of America*, 2010 WL 317472 (S.D. Ga. 2010), *citing Carnival Cruise Lines, Inc. v. Shute*, 499 U.S. 585, 593–95 (1991), legislatively overruled on other grounds, by 46 U.S.C § 30509.

[542] German Report, VII.36.

[543] German Report, VII.36.

[544] CJEU 7.12.2010, combined cases C-585/98 and C-144/09—Pammer and Hotel Alpenhof.

[545] German Report, VII.36.

jurisdiction which forms part of a contract shall be treated as an agreement independent of the other terms of the contract. The validity of the agreement conferring jurisdiction cannot be contested solely on the ground that the contract is not valid". This provision is applicable to the agreement's existence, validity and effects whenever the claim is filed in the jurisdiction of a Member State of the European Union, regardless the parties' domicile. If the contract includes a choice-of-court clause that submits the carriage of passengers to a third country and not to a Member State of the European Union, then domestic rules of each Member State are applicable, and not the Brussels I Recast.[546]

Transport contracts are in principle excluded from the scope of Section 4 on jurisdiction over consumer contracts of the Recast. However, it applies to "a contract which, for an inclusive price, provides for a combination of travel and accommodation" (Article 7(3)). Therefore, and since cruises are regarded by the CJEU as packages in the sense of the Package Travel Directive, the consumer jurisdiction rules of the Recast apply, even if the consumer had booked the cruise without transportation to and from the port of embarkment and disembarkment.[547]

The Athens Convention Relating to the Carriage of Passengers and Their Luggage by Sea

Under Article 18 of the Athens Convention, "Any contractual provision concluded before the occurrence of the incident which has caused the death of or personal injury to a passenger or the loss of or damage to the passenger's luggage, purporting to relieve any person liable under this Convention of liability towards the passenger or to prescribe a lower limit of liability than that fixed in this Convention except as provided in Article 8, paragraph 4, and any such provision purporting to shift the burden of proof which rests on the carrier or performing carrier, or having the effect of restricting the options specified in Article 17, paragraphs 1 or 2, shall be null and void, but the nullity of that provision shall not render void the contract of carriage which shall remain subject to the provisions of this Convention".[548]

Under Article 17 of the Athens Convention the claimant may choose between four jurisdictions: "(a) the Court of the State of permanent residence or principal place of business of the defendant, or (b) the Court of the State of departure or that of the destination according to the contract of carriage, or (c) the Court of the State of the domicile or permanent residence of the claimant, if the defendant has a place of business and is subject to jurisdiction in that State, or (d) the Court of the State where the contract of carriage was made, if the defendant has a place of business and is subject to jurisdiction in that State", as far as the court is located in a State Party to the Convention and "and subject to the domestic law of each State Party governing proper venue within those States. . .".

[546] Spanish Report, VII.37.

[547] German Report, VII.36.

[548] See Polish Report, VII.37 and case law mentioned there, particularly from the Court of Justice of the European Union.

9.2.3 In Asia

In China forum selection clauses included in general conditions of cruise contracts seem to be recognized as valid.[549]

9.2.4 Final Remarks

It seems clear that in general, at least in the jurisdictions dealt with in this report, jurisdiction cannot be unilaterally imposed to the passenger/consumer by the carrier and that the carrier cannot restrict the passenger's options between concurrent jurisdictions granted by law. The only exception seems to be China.

9.3 Arbitration Clauses Included in General Conditions of Cruise Contracts

9.3.1 In the Americas

In Brazil arbitration clauses included in general conditions of cruise contracts are not valid under Article 51, VII of the Consumer Code unless the passenger chooses to submit his claim to an arbitration court.[550]

In Uruguay, arbitration clauses included in general conditions of international contracts that are not signed or otherwise consented by the adherent party to the contract are not admitted, since they do not comply with Article II of the 1958 New York Convention on the Recognition and Enforcement of Foreign Arbitral Awards, or Article 1 of the 1975 Inter-American Convention on International Commercial Arbitration. In those cases the clause is considered a unilateral provision not validly consented by the adherent party. There are several judgments confirming this approach.[551] However, if the clause complies with those requirements, it could be considered valid.

In the USA, arbitration clauses are usually included in the Seafarer's Employment Agreement, and the U.S. courts have traditionally upheld them.[552]

---

[549] Chinese Report, VII.37.

[550] See case-law in Brazilian National Report, VII.38.

[551] See: Fresnedo de Aguirre (2004), pp. 420–435; Fresnedo de Aguirre (2012), pp. 217–251.

[552] See *Bautista v. Star Cruises* and *Yuzwa v. M/V Oosterdam,* and further information, in the USA Report, II.

9.3.2 In the European Union

In the European Union there are some relevant instruments regarding our subject matter, particularly the Regulation (EU) N° 524/2013 of the European Parliament and of the Council of 21 May 2013 on online dispute resolution for consumer disputes and amending Regulation (EC) N° 2006/2004 and Directive 2009/22/EC (Regulation on consumer ODR) and the Directive 2013/11/EU of the European Parliament and of the Council of 21 May 2013 on alternative dispute resolution for consumer disputes and amending Regulation (EC) No 2006/2004 and Directive 2009/22/EC (Directive on consumer ADR).[553]

However, it has been reported that cruise lines do not have their own arbitration schemes yet, though with some exceptions. Therefore, "consumer disputes arising from this Regulation play only a minor role compared with disputes arising from the package travel rules, which use to go to court if they cannot be settled amicably".[554]

In Bulgaria general rules on arbitration are contained in the International Commercial Arbitration Act, which is based on the UNCITRAL Model Law. Arbitration clause must be valid. These clauses are generally included in general conditions of international contracts of carriage of passengers by sea, not only in cruise contracts.[555]

In Germany, arbitration did not play a significant role for the settlement of consumer disputes in the past due to accessibility and low costs of state courts, but things changed in the last years. The Directive 2013/11/EU on online dispute resolution for consumer disputes was implemented in German law by a Verbraucherstreitbeilegungsgesetz (VSBG, Consumer Dispute Settlement Act). Although under the referred Act arbitration must be offered to consumers, a consumer cannot be obliged to go to arbitration before filing a claim into court, because the right to go to court is regarded as a fundamental right, granted by the Grundgesetz (Basic Law, German Constitution) and the EU Charter of Fundamental Rights as well. Arbitration is only possible if the consumer agrees after the harmful event occurred.[556]

In Belgium, cruise lines may stipulate the travel contract conditions of the Belgian Travel Dispute Commission (*Commission de Litiges Voyages*). These conditions provide for alternative dispute resolution (ADR) via mediation or arbitration for package travel contract disputes. The referred Commission is not competent for bodily injury claims, extra-contractual disputes, non-inclusive travel or assistance insurance, etc.[557]

In Spain under Article 90(1) of the Royal Decree-Legislative 1/2007 "arbitration clauses are null and void if submission to arbitration is made to a system other than

[553] http://eur-lex.europa.eu/legal-content/EN/TXT/?uri=OJ:L:2013:165:TOC.

[554] German Report, VII.38.

[555] Bulgarian national Report, VII.

[556] German Report, VII.38.

[557] Belgian Report, VII.38.

consumer arbitration save the case of sector-specific arbitration established by law". In addition, the Royal Decree 231/2008 of 15 February deals with the Spanish Consumer Arbitration System, which is in accordance with the Directive 93/13/ECC of 5 April 1993 on unfair terms in consumer contracts, is applicable to cruise passengers.[558]

9.3.3 Final Remarks

It might be concluded that in general, and at least in the jurisdictions dealt with in this report, although arbitration may be offered to consumers, a consumer cannot be obliged to go to arbitration, because the right to go to court is regarded as a fundamental right. Arbitration is only possible if the consumer agrees after the harmful event occurred. If submission to arbitration is made to a consumer arbitration system, like the Spanish Consumer Arbitration System, it is considered valid in some jurisdictions.

10 Choice of Law

In most countries legal systems do not provide for specific provisions on choice of law regarding cruises.[559] Therefore, general rules on carriage of passengers by sea and on international contracts in general apply.

10.1 In the Americas

That is the case, for example, of Uruguay, where as it was explained *supra*, the general rule is that choice-of-law clauses are not valid unless the applicable law admits it. Under Article 2399 of the Civil Code, the law of the place of performance, construed as the place of disembarking of the passenger,[560] is applicable.[561] If it is a round trip ticket, the place of disembarking is that of the final destination, which coincides with the place of departure.[562] Regarding carriage of passengers by sea

[558] Spanish Report, VII.38.

[559] That is the case, for example, of Brazil, Bulgaria, China, Germany, Poland, Romania, Spain, and Uruguay.

[560] Article 34.b) of the 1889 Montevideo Treaty on International Civil Law, referred to by Article 2399 of the Civil Code.

[561] For further information see: Fresnedo de Aguirre (2009), pp. 160–167.

[562] Fresnedo de Aguirre (2015), pp. 127–168, p. 150. See Case N° 185 "*DFPO vs. Transporte Turismo Ltda.*", *RTYS* (Revista de Transporte y Seguros) N° 10.

contracts, Article 7 of Act N° 19.246 and its reference to the 1940 Montevideo Treaty on International Commercial Navigation are applicable.

In Brazil, under Article 9 of Decree N° 4.657/42, the law of the place where the obligation was entered into applies, unless the obligation must be complied with in Brazil, when the Brazilian law applies. However, it must be taken into account that Brazilian courts are very reluctant to applying foreign law and therefore, if a Brazilian court has jurisdiction, it is very likely that Brazilian legislation will be applied.[563] Choice of law clauses included in general conditions of carriage of passengers in cruises are not valid and effective in Brazil, as explained before regarding jurisdiction, and may be considered abusive for hampering the defence of the consumer.[564]

In Canada, a choice of law clause in a passenger ticket is sometimes challenged, though not always successfully, like in *Roy v. North American Leisure Group et al*, where the Ontario Court of Appeal "found the clause enforceable despite the expiry of a statutory limitation period under the stipulated law". The court stated that "the contract between the parties, reflected in the cruise brochure, specified England as the choice of law in any action arising out of the contract" and adds that "the mere fact that the plaintiffs failed to read the term was not determinative of the result".[565]

If there is no choice of law clause in the passenger contract, or if the clause is not binding, the identification of the applicable law "becomes less certain and more difficult" in Canada, where jurisprudence states that the law governing the contractual relationship is that of the place with which the contract "has its closest and more substantial connection, which regarding passenger contracts could be the place of registration and flag of the ship, the place where the owner or person in possession of the ship has its place of business, the place of residence of the passenger, where the contract was made or where it was to be performed, among others. Regarding tort claims, the *lex loci delicti* applies.[566]

10.2 In the European Union

10.2.1 Supranational Sources on Choice of Law and Applicable Law

The main source on the matter is the Regulation (EC) No 593/2008 of the European Parliament and of the Council of 17 June 2008 on the law applicable to contractual obligations (Rome I), which is applicable to all contractual obligations in civil and commercial matters. Freedom of choice of law is the general rule though with some

[563] Brazilian National Report, VIII.41–42.

[564] Brazilian National Report, VIII.43.

[565] http://ctdj.ca/en/jurisprudence/roy-al-v-north-american-leisure-group-inc-al/; Chircop et al. (2016), p. 659.

[566] Chircop et al. (2016), pp. 661–662.

limitations, like those in consumer contracts, insurance contracts, and employment contracts.

Article 5 §2, which is applicable to cruise passengers, provides that: "To the extent that the law applicable to a contract for the carriage of passengers has not been chosen by the parties in accordance with the second subparagraph, the law applicable shall be the law of the country where the passenger has his habitual residence, provided that either the place of departure or the place of destination is situated in that country. If these requirements are not met, the law of the country where the carrier has his habitual residence shall apply. The parties may choose as the law applicable to a contract for the carriage of passengers in accordance with Article 3 only the law of the country where: (a) the passenger has his habitual residence; or (b) the carrier has his habitual residence; or (c) the carrier has his place of central administration; or (d) the place of departure is situated; or (e) the place of destination is situated".

This limitation to party autonomy is based on the fact that the passenger is the weaker party in the contract of carriage.[567] Moreover, such constraints to party autonomy stem not only from the general limitations in the Regulation but mainly from the overriding mandatory provisions in Article 9: "1. Overriding mandatory provisions are provisions the respect for which is regarded as crucial by a country for safeguarding its public interests, such as its political, social or economic organisation, to such an extent that they are applicable to any situation falling within their scope, irrespective of the law otherwise applicable to the contract under this Regulation. 2. Nothing in this Regulation shall restrict the application of the overriding mandatory provisions of the law of the forum. 3. Effect may be given to the overriding mandatory provisions of the law of the country where the obligations arising out of the contract have to be or have been performed, in so far as those overriding mandatory provisions render the performance of the contract unlawful. In considering whether to give effect to those provisions, regard shall be had to their nature and purpose and to the consequences of their application or non-application."[568]

It must be noted that contracts of carriage of passengers "are not deemed consumer contracts for choice-of-law purposes save the case of 'a contract relating to package travel within the meaning of Council Directive 90/314/EEC of 13 June 1990 on package travel, package holiday and package tours' (Article 6(3)(b) Rome I). In such cases and 'provided that the professional: (a) pursues his commercial or professional activities in the country where the consumer has his habitual residence, or (b) by any means, directs such activities to that country or to several countries including that country, and the contract falls within the scope of such activities', the choice of law by the parties is feasible as long as it does not deprive the consumer of

[567] Bulgarian National Report, VIII.41.

[568] See Spanish Report, VII.43.

the protection afforded to him by provisions that cannot be derogated from by agreement by virtue of the law of his habitual residence".[569]

In other words, the provision in the Rome Ia Regulation that excludes carriage contracts from the consumer protection rule of its Article 6 does not affect neither package travel nor cruises, since the latter are regarded as package travel. Thus, Article 6 of the Rome Ia Regulation is applicable to cruises.[570]

However, for other kinds of carriage of passengers, like a ferry service, Article 5 is applicable and allows a choice of law between the law of the place where the passenger has his habitual residence, or the carrier has his habitual residence, or the place of departure or arrival.[571]

Therefore, under Article 6 of the Rome I-Regulation, a consumer contract shall be governed by the law of the country where the consumer has his habitual residence, provided that the professional directs his commercial or professional activities to that country. The expression "directs his commercial or professional activities" has the same meaning than in the Brussels Ia-Regulation.[572]

However, choice of law is not prohibit in consumer contracts, as far as it does not deprive the consumer from the mandatory rights he would have in the absence of such a choice of law clause, that are provided for by the law of the country of his habitual residence.[573]

10.2.2 National Sources on Choice of Law and Applicable Law

In Bulgaria, the Private International Law Code has been harmonized with the Regulation (EC) No 593/2008 of the European Parliament and of the Council of 17 June 2008 on the law applicable to contractual obligations (Rome I).

In Poland, the Polish Maritime Code (Article 181) implements the Athens Convention relating to the carriage of passengers and their luggage by sea, 1974. Besides, as a Member State of the EU, the Regulation (EC) No 392/2009 of the European Parliament and of the Council of 23 April 2009 on the liability of carriers of passengers by sea in the event of accidents and the Regulation (EC) No 593/2008 of the European Parliament and of the Council of 17 June 2008 on the law applicable

[569] See also Spanish Report, VIII.42.

[570] German Report, VIII.42.

[571] German Report, VIII.42.

[572] See previous references to this topic and to the leading case CJEU 7.12.2010, combined cases C-585/98 and C-144/09—*Pammer and Hotel Alpenhof* already mentioned. See German Report VII.36 and VIII.42.

[573] German Report VIII.42.

to contractual obligations (Rome I)[574] are applicable.[575] Some of those rules, like the Athens Convention, protect passengers, who are very frequently also consumers.[576]

10.3 In Asia

In China, choice of law clauses, even those included in general conditions of contracts of carriage of passengers in cruises are considered valid. As a consequence of that, in most cruise tickets the law of the cruise corporation is selected. For example, if the cruise corporation is Royal Caribbean, the choice of law clause included in the ticket selects the American Law.[577]

In Japan, consumer contracts like cruise contracts between passenger and cruise operators, are subject to special rules in Article 11 of the Act on General Rules for Application of Laws (Act No. 78 of 2006). "The parties to a consumer contract may choose a law applicable to a contract in accordance with Article 7, and they may change the chosen law pursuant to Article 9 as well. However, despite such choice, a consumer may invoke any specific provision(s) which would otherwise be mandatorily applicable to the consumer contract under the law of the place where the consumer has its habitual residence (Article 11 (1)), in addition to the chosen law". In the absence of choice of law, the law applicable to the consumer contract and its formalities is that of the place where the consumer has its habitual residence, though there are some special cases with different solutions.[578]

10.4 Final Remarks

It might be concluded that in general and at least in the jurisdictions dealt with in this report, the law applicable to cruise contracts is that of the place of performance, construed as the place of disembarking of the passenger, or the law of the place where the obligation was entered into applies, or the law of the country where the passenger has his habitual residence. As for the latter, some jurisdictions require that in addition, either the place of departure or the place of destination is situated in the country of the passenger's residence. The law of the place with which the contract has its closest and more substantial connection is also indicated as the applicable law by some conflict of laws rules.

574 OJ L 177, 4.7.2008, pp. 6–16.

575 See also Spanish Report, VIII.41.

576 See further information in Polish Report, VIII.42–43.

577 Chinese National Report, VIII.42.

578 See more detailed information in Japanese Report, X.41. See also X.44 for some specific problems regarding the implementation of the referred choice of law rules.

Choice of law clauses included in general conditions of carriage of passengers in cruises are not valid and effective in some jurisdictions. In others, freedom of choice of law is the general rule though with some limitations, based on the fact that the passenger is the weaker party in the contract of carriage.

However, in some countries like China, choice of law clauses, even those included in general conditions of contracts of carriage of passengers in cruises are considered valid. As a consequence of that, in most cruise tickets the law of the cruise corporation is selected.

11 General Conditions Used by Companies Offering Cruise Services

11.1 Preliminary Considerations

Only some clauses or sections included in some general conditions used by companies offering cruise services will be analysed hereinafter in this chapter. The chosen clauses are those considered particularly relevant for the legal regime of cruises. Besides, it would be beyond the scope of this report to deal with all of them.

General Conditions in cruise contracts used by several companies have been studied by the Confederation of Consumers and Users (CECU) and reach some interesting conclusions.[579] For example some of them make erroneous references to the law in force,[580] they determine incorrectly the different issues to pay to the agency in case of consumer withdrawal and its amounts and they do not properly distinguish between cruises and air and hotels contracts. In all the General Conditions analysed by the CECU there is an express resignation to submit any possible conflict to arbitration.[581]

Usually, general conditions impose the consumer a specific deadline to claim, when in some countries, like Spain, there is no legal deadline for the consumer to file an extra-judicial claim and that those deadlines imposed by the Agency do not prevent the consumer from asking for a mediation at the General Direction of Tourism of the corresponding Autonomous Community, or even to go to court to exercise actions derived from the rights recognised by the Legislative Real Decree 1/2007 within a time-bar of 2 years.[582]

There are other examples mentioned by the CECU, regarding the establishment of non-binding prices and itineraries for excursions, insurance subscriptions, incomplete information on implicit risks at destination, imprecise references to services included in the price, prohibition to check prices upwards in the 20 days before the

---

[579] http://cecu.es/campanas/cuadernos/CRUCEROS09.pdf.

[580] See below N° 4 in this same chapter.

[581] See below N° 2 in this same chapter, where some exceptions are mentioned.

[582] http://cecu.es/campanas/cuadernos/CRUCEROS09.pdf.

trip, setting of excessive advances, modification of essential elements in the contract and custody of values.[583]

11.2 Arbitration

Many companies offering cruise services do not include in their general conditions an arbitration clause.[584] However, some of them require the use of arbitration for certain disputes, like those used by *Celebrity Cruises*, which advises in its first page, under the title "Important Notice to Guests" and in capital black letters, that "This agreement requires the use of arbitration for certain disputes". Moreover, section 10 provides:

> Notice of claims and commencement of suit or arbitration; security: a. Time limits for personal injury/illness/death claims: no suit shall be maintainable against carrier, the vessel or the transport for personal injury, illness or death of any passenger unless written notice of the claim, with full particulars, shall be delivered to carrier at its principal office within six (6) months from the date of the injury, illness or death and suit is commenced (filed) within one (1) year from the date of such injury, illness or death and process served within 120 days after filing, notwithstanding any provision of law of any state or country to the contrary.
>
> b. **Arbitration of all other claims:** any and all other disputes, claims, or controversies whatsoever, except for personal injury, illness or death of a passenger, between passenger and carrier, vessel or transport, whether based on contract, tort, statutory, constitutional or other legal rights, including but not limited to alleged violation of civil rights, discrimination, consumer or privacy laws, or for any losses, damages or expenses, relating to or in any way arising out of or connected with this contract or passenger's cruise, no matter how described, pleaded or styled, shall be referred to and resolved exclusively by binding arbitration pursuant to the United Nations Convention on the recognition and enforcement of foreign arbitral awards (New York 1958), 21 U.S.T. 2517, 330 U.N.T.S. 3, 1970 U.S.T. LEXIS 115, 9 U.S.C. §§ 202–208 ("the Convention") and the Federal Arbitration Act, 9 U.S.C. §§ 1, et seq., ("FAA") solely in Miami, Florida, U.S.A. to the exclusion of any other forum. The arbitration shall be administered by the American Arbitration Association under its commercial dispute resolution rules and procedures, which are deemed to be incorporated herein by reference. Any question about the arbitration administrators mentioned above may be directed to them as follows: American Arbitration Association, Bank of America Tower, 100 Southeast 2nd street, ste. 2300, Miami, Fl 33131 (305) 358-7777. Neither party will have the right to a jury trial nor to engage in prearbitration discovery except as provided in the applicable arbitration rules and herein, or otherwise to litigate the claim in any court. The arbitrator's decision will be final and binding. Other rights that passenger or carrier would have in court also may not be available in arbitration. An award rendered by an arbitrator may be entered in any court having jurisdiction under the convention or FAA. Passenger and carrier further agree to permit the taking of a deposition under oath of the passenger asserting the claim, or for whose benefit the claim is asserted, in any such arbitration. In the event this provision is deemed unenforceable by an arbitrator or court of competent jurisdiction for any reason, then and only then the provisions of section 9 above governing venue and

[583] http://cecu.es/campanas/cuadernos/CRUCEROS09.pdf.

[584] Spanish Report, VII.39.

jurisdiction shall exclusively apply to any lawsuit involving claims described in this section 10(b). (. . .).[585]

11.3 Jurisdiction and Applicable Law

The standard passenger ticket terms and conditions of the major international cruise lines, generally published on the website of each cruise line, "contain a choice of law clause and also a mandatory choice of forum for the resolution of disputes between the passenger and the cruise line".[586] This is the case, for example, of the *Celebrity Cruises*, that in its Cruise/CruiseTour Ticket Contract includes section 9, providing:

9. **Forum selection clause** for all lawsuits; class action waiver:

a. Except as provided in section 10 (b) with regard to claims subject to binding arbitration, it is agreed by and between passenger and carrier that all disputes and matters whatsoever arising under, in connection with or incident to this agreement, passenger's cruise, cruisetour, RCT land tour or transport, shall be litigated, if at all, in and before the United States District Court for the Southern District of Florida located in Miami-Dade county, Florida, U.S.A., (or as to those lawsuits to which the federal courts of the United States lack subject matter jurisdiction, before a court located in Miami-Dade County, Florida, U.S.A.) to the exclusion of the courts of any other state, territory or country. Passenger hereby consents to jurisdiction and waives any venue or other objection that he may have to any such action or proceeding being brought in the applicable court located in Miami-Dade County, Florida.

b. Class action relief waiver. Passenger hereby agrees that except as provided in the last sentence of this paragraph, passenger may bring claims against carrier only in passenger's individual capacity. Even if the applicable law provides otherwise, passenger agrees that any arbitration or lawsuit against carrier, vessel or transport whatsoever shall be litigated by passenger individually and not as a member of any class or as part of a class or representative action, and passenger expressly agrees to waive any law entitling passenger to participate in a class action. If your claim is subject to arbitration as provided in section 10 below, the arbitrator shall have no authority to arbitrate claims on a class action basis. You agree that this section shall not be severable under any circumstances from the arbitration clause set forth in section 10.b below, and if for any reason this class action waiver is unenforceable as to any particular claim, then and only then such claim shall not be subject to arbitration.[587]

General Conditions used by *Goldium Cruceros* state that any dispute derived from the use of the offered services or from the contents of the web site of the parties, accepting this Conditions, must be filed to the courts of the place of performance of the contract. However, it states that the parties submit, at their option, for the

[585] Clause 10.c) refers to time limits for non-injury/illness or death claims and d) to the event of an in rem proceeding against the vessel. http://media.celebritycruises.com/celebrity/content/en_US/pdf/Celebrity_CTC_Eff_08_01_10.pdf.

[586] Chircop et al. (2016), p. 661. Spanish Report, VII.43.

[587] Clause 10.c) refers to time limits for non-injury/illness or death claims and d) to the event of an in rem proceeding against the vessel. http://media.celebritycruises.com/celebrity/content/en_US/pdf/Celebrity_CTC_Eff_08_01_10.pdf.

resolution of conflicts and waiving any other jurisdiction, to the courts and tribunals of the user's domicile (section 17).[588]

In the General Conditions used by *MSC Cruises S.A.*, a choice of law and jurisdiction clause is included *in fine*, providing that the present conditions and the contract are ruled by the Swiss laws and courts of Geneva, Switzerland, have exclusive jurisdiction to hear any dispute arising from them.[589]

11.4 Legal References in General Conditions

Some general conditions used by companies offering cruise services contain some legal references, like for example those of *Goldium Cruceros*, which state that the present General Conditions are subject to the provisions in the Real Legislative Decree 1/2007, of November 16, and amendments of Act 3/2014, of March 27, as well as those of *Viajes El Corte Inglés* and of *Pullmantur*. The Decree approves the refunded text of the General Act for Consumers and Users Defence and other complementary Acts (B.O.E. 30-11-2007), as well as, when applicable, to the provisions in the Athens Convention and amendments and other rules in international Conventions related to carriage of passengers.[590] General Conditions in the Cruise/CruiseTour Ticket Contract used by *Celebrity Cruises* make reference to the Athens Convention relating to the carriage of passengers and their luggage by sea of 1974, as well as the Protocol to the Athens Convention relating to the carriage of passengers and their luggage by sea of 1976 and to some specific rules in the laws of the United States (section 11). Section 10 refers to the United Nations Convention on the recognition and enforcement of foreign arbitral awards (New York 1958) and to the Federal Arbitration Act, 9 U.S.C. §§ 1, et seq.[591]

It was reported by Spanish national reporters that some general conditions used by companies offering cruise services contain erroneous legal references. They mention some examples.[592]

---

[588] http://www.goldiumcruceros.com/informacion-legal.php?id=3.

[589] See more details in http://www.msccruceros.com.ar/ar_es/Guia-Crucero/Condiciones-Generales.aspx.

[590] http://www.goldiumcruceros.com/informacion-legal.php?id=3; https://www.viajeselcorteingles.es/documento/condiciones/pdf_condiciones_cruceros.pdf; https://www.pullmantur.travel/general/condiciones-generales.html.

[591] http://media.celebritycruises.com/celebrity/content/en_US/pdf/Celebrity_CTC_Eff_08_01_10.pdf.

[592] See Spanish Report, VII.39.

11.5 Limitation of Liability

Most general conditions used by companies offering cruise services contain sections that intend to limit the carrier's liability. For example the Cruise/CruiseTour Ticket Contract used by *Celebrity Cruises* includes in its first page, in black capital letters and under the title "Important Notice to Guests", the following advice:

> Your cruise/cruisetour ticket contract contains important limitations on the rights of passengers. It is important that you carefully read all terms of this contract, paying particular attention to section 3 and sections 9 through 11, which limit our liability and your right to sue, and retain it for future reference.[593]

Section 3.b) provides:

> Liability for Loss of or Damage to Baggage. Unless negligent, Carrier is neither responsible nor liable for any loss of or damage to Passenger's property, whether contained in luggage or otherwise. Liability for loss of or damage to Passenger's property in connection with any air or ground transportation shall be the sole responsibility of the provider of the service and in accordance with applicable limitations.[594]

Section 3.c) provides:

> Limitation of Liability for Lost or Damaged Property. Notwithstanding any other provision of law or this Agreement, Carrier's liability for loss or damage to property during the RCT Land Tour portion of a CruiseTour is limited to $300.00 per Passenger. Notwithstanding any other provision of law or this Agreement, Carrier's liability for loss or damage to property for the cruise (or for the cruise only portion of a CruiseTour) is limited to $300.00 per Passenger, unless Passenger declares the true value of such property in writing and pays Carrier within 10 days of final payment for the cruise, a fee of five percent (5%) of the amount that such value exceeds $300.00. In such event, Carrier's liability shall be limited to its true declared value, but not exceeding $5,000.[595]

Section 11 provides:

> Limitations of liability: a. Carrier shall not be liable for injury, death, illness, damage, delay or other loss to person or property, or any other claim by any passenger caused by act of God, war, terrorism, civil commotion, labor trouble, government interference, perils of the sea, fire, thefts or any other cause beyond carrier's reasonable control, or any act not shown to be caused by carrier's negligence. b. Passenger agrees to solely assume the risk of injury, death, illness or other loss, and carrier is not responsible for passenger's use of any athletic or recreational equipment; or for the negligence or wrongdoing of any independent contractors, including but not limited to photographers, spa personnel or entertainers; or for events taking place off the carrier's vessels, launches or transports, or as part of any shore excursion, tour or activity. c. Carrier hereby disclaims all liability to the passenger for damages for emotional distress, mental suffering or psychological injury of any kind under any circumstances, when such damages were neither the result of a physical injury to the passenger, nor

---

[593] http://media.celebritycruises.com/celebrity/content/en_US/pdf/Celebrity_CTC_Eff_08_01_10.pdf.

[594] http://media.celebritycruises.com/celebrity/content/en_US/pdf/Celebrity_CTC_Eff_08_01_10.pdf.

[595] http://media.celebritycruises.com/celebrity/content/en_US/pdf/Celebrity_CTC_Eff_08_01_10.pdf.

the result of passenger having been at actual risk of physical injury, nor were intentionally inflicted by the carrier. Without limiting the preceding sentence, in no event will carrier be liable to passenger for any consequential, incidental, exemplary or punitive damages. d. On cruises which neither embark, disembark nor call at any port in the United States, carrier shall be entitled to any and all liability limitations, immunities and rights applicable to it under the "Athens Convention relating to the carriage of passengers and their luggage by sea" of 1974, as well as the "Protocol to the Athens Convention relating to the carriage of passengers and their luggage by sea" of 1976 ("Athens Convention"). The Athens Convention limits the carrier's liability for death or personal injury to a passenger to no more than 46,666 special drawing rights as defined therein (approximately U.S. $70,000, which amount fluctuates, depending on daily exchange rate as printed in the wall street journal). In addition, and on all other cruises, all the exemptions from and limitations of liability provided in or authorized by the laws of the United States (including title 46, United States Code Sections 30501 through 30509 and 30511) will apply.[596]

In the General Conditions used by *MSC Cruises S.A.*, clause 12.1 states that the Company accepts liability for death, damage or disease caused by its negligent acts or omissions or those of any of those who provide services that are part of the cruise. It adds that it limits its liability, when applicable, to the provisions of the Conventions mentioned in the same clause, numbers 4–8: the International Air Conventions, including the Warsaw Convention of 1929 amended by The Hague Protocol of 1955 or the Montreal Protocol of 1999, or the Montreal Convention of 1999; the Athens Convention of 1974, and the EU Regulation N° 392/2009. It declines liability in case of guilt of the passenger, *force majeur* and others.[597]

The General Conditions used by *Deluxe Travel S.A.S.* provide that since the company is an intermediary of tourist services, it does not assume liability for specific non compliance by the providers of touristic services and for events like accidents, strikes, assonate, political factors, earthquakes, climatic or natural phenomena, damage of the vessel, mechanical failure, fire, collision or labour conflicts that affect navigation, among others.[598]

The General Conditions used by *Viajes El Corte Inglés*, provide in clause 9.2 that limits of compensation for damages resulting from non performance or bad performance in the rendering of services are ruled by the Athens Convention of 1974 as amended by the London Protocol of 1976, when applicable, or by the Brussels Convention of 1970 and other legal rules in force.[599]

The General Conditions used by *Pullmantur* provide in clause 8 that the organising Travel Agency and the retailer are liable to the consumer in relation to each one's scope of travel management and that compensation for damages are ruled by national norms and international conventions ruling such services, particularly the Regulation (CE) N° 392/2009 which incorporates the Refunded Text of the

---

[596] http://media.celebritycruises.com/celebrity/content/en_US/pdf/Celebrity_CTC_Eff_08_01_10.pdf.

[597] See more details in http://www.msccruceros.com.ar/ar_es/Guia-Crucero/Condiciones-Generales.aspx.

[598] http://www.deluxetravel.com.co/agencia-de-cruceros-medellin-colombia/terminos-legales.

[599] https://www.viajeselcorteingles.es/documento/condiciones/pdf_condiciones_cruceros.pdf.

Athens Convention of 1974 and its 2002 Protocol, and the London Convention of 1976 amended by its Protocol of 1996 and further amendments in force on limitations of liability derived from maritime law claims.[600]

11.6 Final Remarks

General conditions used by companies offering cruise services are in general rather similar, at least regarding the topics they deal with. As for arbitration, many companies offering cruise services do not include in their general conditions an arbitration clause. However, some of them require the use of arbitration for certain disputes, like those used by *Celebrity Cruises*.

Regarding applicable law and jurisdiction, it can be stated that the standard passenger ticket terms and conditions of the major international cruise lines, generally published on the website of each cruise line, contain a choice of law clause and also a mandatory choice of forum for the resolution of disputes between the passenger and the cruise line. Regarding the core issue of liability, most general conditions contain clauses or sections dealing with this matter which clearly intend to limit the carrier's liability.

It can be concluded that in spite of what companies include in their unilateral general conditions, it will be the applicable law[601] that will determine whether those clauses are valid or not. In case they are considered abusive, or against a mandatory rule of the court's legal system, or a prevailing consumer rule, those clauses will be null and void and with no effect in that case. Anyhow, they continue to be included in most general conditions just in case they might be validated in some jurisdiction.

12 Sources of Law Applicable to Cruises

This chapter aims at providing a list of sources of law that are relevant to cruises, organised according to their origin and nature, though not exhaustive. Some of them are briefly analyzed while others are just mentioned since they are commented in the corresponding thematic chapter.

[600] https://www.pullmantur.travel/general/condiciones-generales.html.

[601] See Sect. 10 on this matter.

12.1 *European Union Supranational Sources of Law: Regulations*

European Union Regulations are binding legislative acts that must be applied in their entirety across the EU.[602] They are directly applicable in the Member States; therefore, it is supposed that all Regulations dealt with hereinafter are applicable in all the European Union's Member States.

- Regulation (EC) 593/2008 of the European Parliament and of the Council of 17 June 2008 on the law applicable to contractual obligations (Rome I)
- Regulation (EC) N° 392/2009 of the European Parliament and of the Council of 23 April 2009 on the liability of carriers of passengers by sea in the event of accidents
- Regulation (EU) No 1177/2010 of the European Parliament and of the Council of 24 November 2010 concerning the rights of passengers when travelling by sea and inland waterway and amending Regulation (EC) No 2006/2004 (EU Sea Passengers' Rights Regulation)
- Regulation (EU) 1215/2012 of the European Union and of the Council of 12 December 2012 on jurisdiction and the recognition and enforcement of judgments in civil and commercial matters (Brussels I Recast)

  It must be noted that The Hague Convention of 20 June 2005 on Choice of Court Agreements is not applicable to contracts of carriage of passengers, including cruise passengers, since consumer and labour contracts are excluded from its scope of application (Articles 2.1 and 2.f).[603]
- Regulations CEE 4.055/86, 4.056/86, 4.057/86 and 4.058/86, 22/12/86 and Regulation CEE 3.572/92, 7/12/92
- Regulation (EU) No 692/2011 of the European Parliament and of the Council of 6 July 2011 concerning European statistics on tourism and Commission Regulation (EU) No 1051/2011 implementing Regulation (EU) No 692/2011 concerning European statistics on tourism, as regards the structure of the quality reports and the transmission of the data
- Council Regulation (EEC) N° 2658/87 on the tariff and statistical nomenclature and on the Common Customs Tariff

  This Regulation identifies cruise ships as a particular type of goods. It established a nomenclature, known as 'Combined Nomenclature' or abbreviated to the 'CN', based on the International Convention on the Harmonised Commodity Description and Coding System (WCO) known as 'the Harmonised System' or abbreviated to the 'HS'.[604]
- Regulation (EC) N° 451/2008

[602] https://europa.eu/european-union/eu-law/legal-acts_en.

[603] Spanish Report, VII.35.

[604] Belgian Report, II.9.1.

It establishes a new statistical classification of products by activity (CPA), contains several cruise specific categories and identifies cruise ships as a particular type of goods. It is in accordance with the United Nations' Central Product Classification (CPC) and aligned with the Harmonised System (HS) (International Convention on the Harmonised Commodity Description and Coding System (WCO[605]) and the Combined Nomenclature (CN).[606]

- Commission Regulation (EU) 2017/2119 of 22 November 2017

  It establishes the 'Prodcom list' of industrial products provided for by Council Regulation (EEC) No 3924/91.[607]

- Regulation (EU) 2016/399 on a Union Code on the rules governing the movement of persons across borders (Schengen Borders Code)

  This Regulation provides for a special immigration regime for cruise passengers (exemption from entry/exit stamping of travel documents) (art. 11, 3 (d) and specific check procedures for cruise ships and depending on whether their itineraries comprise ports situated inside or outside the EU territory (Annex VI art. 3.2.).[608]

- Regulation N° 164/2010 on technical specifications for electronic ship reporting in inland navigation[609]
- Regulation EC/3577/92 on the freedom to provide maritime transport services within E.U. Member States (maritime cabotage)
- Regulation (EU) 2017/352 of the European Parliament and of the Council of 15 February 2017 establishing a framework for the provision of port services and common rules on the financial transparency of ports
- Regulation (EU) N° 524/2013 of the European Parliament and of the Council of 21 May 2013 on online dispute resolution for consumer disputes and amending Regulation (EC) N° 2006/2004 and Directive 2009/22/EC (Regulation on consumer ODR) and the Directive 2013/11/EU of the European Parliament and of the Council of 21 May 2013 on alternative dispute resolution for consumer disputes and amending Regulation (EC) No 2006/2004 and Directive 2009/22/EC (Directive on consumer ADR)

12.2 European Union Supranational Sources of Law: Directives

European Union Directives are legislative acts that set out a goal that all EU countries must achieve. However, "it is up to the individual countries to devise

[605] World Customs Organisation.

[606] Belgian Report, II.9.1.

[607] See further information in Belgian Report, II.9.1.

[608] Belgian Report, II.9.2.

[609] See Belgian Report, II.9.6.

their own laws on how to reach these goals. One example is the EU consumer rights directive, which strengthens rights for consumers across the EU, for example by eliminating hidden charges and costs on the internet, and extending the period under which consumers can withdraw from a sales contract".[610]

- Directive 90/314/EEC of 13 June 1990 on package travel, package holidays and package tours[611] (the Package Travel Directive of 1990) currently superseded by the Directive 2015/2302
- Directive (EU) 2015/2302 of the European Parliament and of the Council of 25 November 2015 on package travel and linked travel arrangements, amending Regulation (EC) No 2006/2004 and Directive 2011/83/EU of the European Parliament and of the Council and repealing Council Directive 90/314/EEC
- Directive 2009/45/EC of the European Parliament and of the Council of 6 May 2009 on safety rules and standards for passenger ships[612]

  This is the most extensive instrument on the matter at the EU level and regulates ships made of steel or equivalent material and high speed craft (HSC) engaged in domestic voyages. It does not contain specific rules on cruise vessels.[613]
- Directive 2009/13/EC of 16 February 2009

  This Directive incorporates the Maritime Labour Convention, 2006[614]
- Directive 2009/21/EC of the European Parliament and of the Council of 23 April 2009 on compliance with flag State requirements[615]
- Directive 2009/42/EC on statistical returns in respect of carriage of goods and passengers by sea
- Directive 2013/54/EU of the European Parliament and of the Council of 20 November 2013 concerning certain flag State responsibilities for compliance with and enforcement of the 2006 Maritime labour Convention.[616]
- Directive 2013/38/EU of the European Parliament and the Council of 12. August 2013, amending Directive 2009/16/EC on port State control, OJ no. L 218, p. 1 of 14.8.2013

  The purpose of these Directives is not only to enforce labour law, but also environmental law.[617]
- Directive 93/13/EEC of 5 April 1993 on unfair terms in consumer contracts
- Directive 2005/29/EC concerning unfair business-to-consumer commercial practices in the internal market ('Unfair Commercial Practices Directive')

---

[610] https://europa.eu/european-union/eu-law/legal-acts_en.

[611] OJ L 158, 23.6.1990, pp. 59–64.

[612] OJ L 163, 25.6.2009, pp. 1–140.

[613] Belgian Report, II.9.6.

[614] http://www.ilo.org/wcmsp5/groups/public/%2D%2D-ed_norm/%2D%2D-normes/documents/normativeinstrument/wcms_554767.pdf See Spanish Report, IV.22 and Belgian Report, IV.20.

[615] Spanish Report, IV.20, 22.

[616] Spanish Report, IV.22.

[617] German Report, IV.20.

- Directive 2011/83/EU of the European Parliament and of the Council of 25 October 2011 on consumer rights, amending Council Directive 93/13/EEC and Directive 1999/44/EC of the European Parliament and of the Council and repealing Council Directive 85/577/EEC and Directive 97/7/EC of the European Parliament and of the Council
- Directive 2000/59/CE
  Its main objective is to eliminate uncontrolled dumping from vessels, whatever their activities. The dumping must be done in the facilities designed for that.[618]
- Directive (EU) 2016/1629
  It lays down technical requirements for inland waterway vessels for passengers but does not include any specific rule on cruises.
- Council Directive 1999/32/EC of 26 April 1999 relating to a reduction in the sulphur content of certain liquid fuels and amending Directive 93/12/EEC[619]
- Directive 2006/123/EC of the European Parliament and of the Council of 12 December 2006 on services in the internal market[620]

12.3 *International Sources of Law*

It must be considered here that the International Maritime Organization (IMO), the United Nations specialized agency, with 173 state members[621] that accounts for 99 % of the world's shipping,[622] establishes standards for all kinds of shipping in order to promote the safe use of the seas and to protect the seas from the polluting effects of transport, and that the global shipping industry, including cruise ships, is subject to its international legal regulation. The IMO's International Convention for the Prevention of Pollution from Ships (MARPOL)[623] and the Convention for the Safety of Life at Sea (SOLAS)[624] are perhaps the most relevant instruments for the cruise industry.

---

[618] Ariza Herrerías (2014), p. 19 y ss.

[619] https://publications.europa.eu/en/publication-detail/-/publication/a093e44c-bf78-434b-92c7-d726dc5ad012/language-en.

[620] https://eur-lex.europa.eu/legal-content/EN/TXT/?uri=celex:32006L0123.

[621] As at Jan. 23, 2018. United Nations Treaty Collection, International Maritime Organization, https://treaties.un.org/Pages/ViewDetails.aspx?src=TREATY&mtdsg_no=XII-1&chapter=12&clang=_en.

[622] USA Report, II.

[623] International Maritime Organization. *International Convention for the Prevention of Pollution from Ships (MARPOL)*. Adoption: 1973 (Convention), 1978 (1978 Protocol), 1997 (Protocol—Annex VI); Entry into force: 2 October 1983 (Annexes I and II). http://www.imo.org/en/about/conventions/listofconventions/pages/international-convention-for-the-prevention-of-pollution-from-ships-(marpol).aspx [hereinafter MARPOL].

[624] IMO, International Convention for the Safety of Life at Sea (SOLAS), 1974, www.imo.org/en/About/Conventions/ListOfConventions/Pages/International-Convention-for-the-Safety-of-Life-at-

- The United Nations Convention on the Law of the Sea (Montego Bay, 1982)
- United Nations Convention on the Law of the Sea, Geneva, April 29, 1958
- Convention and Statute on the International Regime of Maritime Ports, Geneva, 9 December 1923
- The Athens Convention relating to the Carriage of Passengers and their Luggage by Sea[625]
- The 1990 Protocol to amend the Athens Convention relating to Carriage of Passengers and their Luggage by Sea[626]
- The 2002 Protocol or "Athens Convention relating to the Carriage of Passengers and their Luggage by Sea, 2002"[627]
- 2006 Maritime Labour Convention
- International Convention on Civil Liability for Oil Pollution Damage/1969
- International Convention for the Control and Management of Ships' Ballast Water and sediments (BWM)
- International Convention for the Prevention of Pollution from Ships (MARPOL 73/78)
- International Convention on the Control of Harmful Anti-fouling Systems on Ships (AFS) 2001
- International Convention for the Safety of Life at Sea (1974 SOLAS Convention)
- International Regulations for the Preventing of Collisions at Sea, 1972 (COLREGS)

12.4 National Sources of Law

In this epigraph, only some national rules relevant for cruises reported by some national jurisdictions are listed. Further information can be found in National Reports and supra, Sect. 3.3.

12.4.1 In Europe

In Bulgaria

- Act on Consumers' Protection

Sea-(SOLAS),-1974.aspx [hereinafter SOLAS]. "The Convention in force today is sometimes referred to as SOLAS, 1974, as amended," as new amendments enter into force under a "tacit acceptance procedure" contained in the 1974 version that requires express objections from an agreed number of States Parties to prevent it.

[625] See *supra*, Sects. 3.3.2 and 9.1.1.

[626] See *supra*, Sect. 3.3.2.

[627] See *supra*, Sect. 3.3.2.

In Germany

- s. 651a et seq. of the Civil Code (BGB)
- Handelsgesetzbuch (Commercial Code)
- Civil Code (Bürgerliches Gesetzbuch), special chapter about package travel.

In Poland

- Consumer Rights Act of 2014
- Polish Maritime Code of 2001
- Maritime Safety Act of 2011

In Spain

- Royal Decree-Legislative 1/2007 of 16 November approving the Recast text of the General Law on Consumer Protection and other supplementary laws (*Real Decreto Legislativo 1/2007, de 16 de noviembre, por el que se aprueba el texto Refundido de la Ley General para la Defensa de los Consumidores y Usuarios y otras leyes complementarias*, B.O.E. 30 November 2007)
- Royal Decree 357/2015, 8 May 2015 on compliance and enforcement of the 2006 Maritime Labour Convention
- Travel Packages Act (*Ley 21/1995, de 6 de Julio reguladora de los viajes combinados*)
- Spanish Law on Shipping (*Ley 14/2014 de 24 de julio, Ley de Navegación Maritima*)
- Real Legislative Decree 2/2011, 5 September and its annexes, and some ministerial rank regulations
- Spanish Law on Judiciary (*Ley Orgánica del Poder Judicial*) amended by Act 7/2015 of July 7, and in the Spanish Law on Shipping (*Ley 14/2014, 24 de Julio, de Navegación maritima*).

12.4.2 In the Americas

In Argentina

- Act N° 24.240 on Consumer Defence
- Navigation Act N° 20.094
- REGINAVE Decree N° 4.516/73
- Travel Agents' Act N° 18.829 and its Regulatory Decree 2182/72

In Brazil

- Federal Act N° 8.078/90 (Consumer Code)
- Presidential Decree N° 7.381/2010

In Uruguay

- Act 17.250 on consumer relations and consumer's defence
- Civil Code (Articles 2399, 2401, 2403)

- Commercial Code (Articles 1282–1289)
- Act N° 19.246 of August 15, 2015 on Maritime Commercial Law
- Penal Code (Article 366)

USA

- U.S. Const., art. III, § 2, cl. 1; 28 U.S.C. § 3033(1);
- Passenger Vessel Services Act, 46 U.S.C. § 55103(b);
- Merchant Marine Act, also known as the Jones Act, 1920, and further amendments: Jones Act, 46 U.S.C. §30104;
- Death on the High Seas Act 46 U.S.C. app. §§ 761–768 (1920) (DOHSA), codified at 46 U.S.C. 303, et seq.,
- United States Code. Chapter 303 Death on the High Seas;
- Cruise Vessel Security and Safety Act of 2010, Pub. L. 111-207, 124 Stat. 2243, et seq., Jul. 27, 2010, enacted at 46 U.S.C. §3507;
- Marine Protection, Research, and Sanctuaries Act (16 U.S.C. § 1431 and 33 U.S.C. § 1401).

12.4.3 In Asia

In Japan

- Commercial Code, Part III (Maritime Commerce)

In Turkey

- Turkish Commercial Code's Fifth Book Maritime Law, Fifth Chapter Contract of Carriage of Passengers by Sea, Articles 1247–1271.

13 Conclusions

This general report dealt mainly with the following issues: (1) the importance of cruise business, (2) general and specific rules applicable to cruises, (3) cruise passengers as consumers, (4) package travels, (5) labour rules on cruises' workers, (6) rules on ports that are relevant to cruises, including taxes, costs and rates charged to cruises in different ports, (7) rules on environmental impact of cruises, (8) jurisdiction, arbitration, and choice of law in cruise contracts, and (9) general conditions used by companies offering cruise services, aiming at discovering which the existing sources of law on these matters are and whether they are appropriate and sufficient or not.

1. It has been corroborated throughout this comparative study the growing importance of cruise business almost all over the world. There is no doubt about that, as statistics show, though its importance varies depending on the region and

country. Policies favouring this business also vary, from regions and countries where they are relevant and others where they do not exist at all. The impact that cruise business has for many countries, including labour markets, is denaturalised by the worldwide practice of using flags of convenience instead of the natural ones. The results of the efforts done by the international community to obtain the proper flagging of ships are not too encouraging.

2. The comparative study carried out all through this general report demonstrate that there is quite a great amount of general rules on different law matters that are applicable to cruises, and only very few specific rules aiming particularly at cruises. Most of those general rules are quite specific and adequate because they refer to carriage of passengers by sea.
3. The protection of tourists and particularly of cruise passengers is guaranteed by consumer protection rules, which are mandatory and prevail over other applicable rules, in most jurisdictions analysed during this general report. That is because tourists and cruise passengers are qualified as consumers under most consumer regulations.
4. Cruises are usually part of a package travel, but cruises have also been declared to be a package in itself. Several service providers, like travel agents and tour providers, intervene in this business and sometimes have their own regulation and their own liability.
5. In most jurisdictions considered in this general report there are rules on seafarers' employment contracts, though not specific on cruise workers. Among them there are international and national, substantive and conflict-of-laws rules, the latter usually indicating the law of the flag as applicable. It has been reported by some jurisdictions to be quite frequent that cruises' workers are not enough protected by the labour law.
6. It has been discovered throughout this comparative study that there is a wide variety of general rules on different issues on ports that are relevant to cruises, including taxes, costs and rates charged to cruises, customs procedures and formalities, port facilities and security, maritime security measures. Few jurisdictions reported much information on these topics.
7. Environmental impact of cruises has proved to be a major topic regarding this contemporary way of travelling. Though environmental law is a specific and generally autonomous branch of law, with its own international and national sources of law, and a thorough study of it would absolutely supersede this general report, its main rules that are relevant for cruises were analysed in this comparative study. It can be concluded that cruise industry is inextricably linked to the environment and that cruises are a main source of pollution of water, air and visited coast areas. There is a variety of rules and measures that aim at controlling and preventing pollution from cruises, most of them with a wider scope of application, including all kinds of ships. It is not realistic—not even desirable—to attempt to eliminate or diminish the cruise business, since it is a growing and powerful business that is relevant for the economy of many regions and countries. Moreover, it is vital for some of them. Therefore the crux is, in my opinion, to reach balanced solutions that contemplate the need to protect the

environment, the convenience of protecting the economy, and the right of cruisers to enjoy the environment responsibly.

8. Most rules on jurisdiction, arbitration, and choice of law applicable to cruise contracts have a wider scope of application, and include carriage of passengers and their luggage by sea. Others are even more general and rule contracts. This comparative study enables us to state that solutions are not so different, since most jurisdictions offer several concurrent jurisdictions, at the claimant's option, that guarantee access to justice to both parties. In principle, jurisdiction cannot be unilaterally imposed to the passenger/consumer by the carrier and the carrier cannot restrict the passenger's options between concurrent jurisdictions granted by law. Arbitration may be offered to consumers, but a consumer cannot be obliged to go to arbitration. In most jurisdictions the law applicable to cruise contracts is that of the place of performance, construed as the place of disembarking of the passenger, or the law of the place where the obligation was entered into applies, or the law of the country where the passenger has his habitual residence. Choice of law clauses included in general conditions of carriage of passengers in cruises are not valid and effective in some jurisdictions, in others, freedom of choice of law is the general rule though with some limitations, and in seldom they are valid.
9. A comparative study of general conditions used by some companies offering cruise services was carried out in this general report, and it led us to the conclusion that they are rather similar. Most of them do not include in their general conditions an arbitration clause; contain a choice of law clause and also a mandatory choice of forum clause and clauses that clearly intend to limit the carrier's liability. Of course the validity or not of those clauses will depend on the law applicable.

Finally, I would dare state that the existing sources of law surveyed in this general report might be considered rather adequate and sufficient to rule legal aspects of cruises. That is because they cover the main issues relevant to cruises, though with a wider scope of application since they generally apply to all kinds of ships, in a reasonably appropriate manner. That does not mean that the existing regulation cannot be improved. Therefore, efforts shall continue to improve and harmonise the existing rules on legal aspects of cruises, meeting the requirements that may crop up in this fragile and changing world we live in.

Web Pages Visited[628]

- https://curia.europa.eu/jcms/upload/docs/application/pdf/2014-03/cp140041en.pdf

[628] Listed in the order they appear in the text of the general report.

- http://www.businessinsider.com/what-are-condo-cruise-ships
- https://eur-lex.europa.eu/legal-content/EN/TXT/?uri=CELEX%3A32015L2302
- http://abremar.hospedagemtemporaria.com.br/dados-do-setor/
- http://www.abremar.com.br/down/Cruzeiros_2017_Portugues_WEB_FINAL.pdf
- http://www.abremar.com.br/down/Cruises_2017_English_WEB_v2.pdf
- http://mintur.gub.uy/index.php/turismo-de-cruceros
- http://www.turismo.gub.uy/blog/por-que-tantos-cruceros-visitan-uruguay.html?utm_source=programatica&utm_medium=nativa&utm_campaign=cruceros&utm_content=crucero-punta-del-este
- https://allthingscruise.com/cruise-research/cruise-departure-ports/
- http://www.f-cca.com/downloads/2017-Cruise-Industry-Overview-Cruise-Line-Statistics.pdf
- https://www.cruising.org/docs/default-source/research/2016_clia_sotci.pdf
- https://www.cruising.org/docs/default-source/research/clia-2017-state-of-the-industry.pdf?sfvrsn=0
- https://www.cliaeurope.eu
- https://ec.europa.eu/transport/themes/strategies/2018_maritime_transport_strategy_en
- http://eur-lex.europa.eu/legal-content/EN/ALL/?uri=CELEX:52009DC0008
- https://directories.lloydslist.com/services-browse/ss/3123/country/Belgium
- http://www.tsakosmonte.com.uy
- http://www.un.org/depts/los/convention_agreements/texts/unclos/unclos_e.pdf
- http://uscode.house.gov/view.xhtml?path=/prelim@title46/subtitle3/chapter303&edition=prelim
- http://laws-lois.justice.gc.ca/PDF/M-0.7.pdf
- https://treaties.un.org/doc/Publication/UNTS/Volume%201463/volume-1463-I-24817-English
- http://www.imo.org/en/About/Conventions/StatusOfConventions/Documents/Status%20-%202018
- https://eur-lex.europa.eu/legal-content/EN/TXT/?uri=celex%3A32012D0022
- http://www.imo.org/en/About/Conventions/ListOfConventions/Pages/Athens-Convention-relating-to-the-Carriage-of-Passengers-and-their-Luggage-by-Sea-(PAL)
- http://uscode.house.gov/view.xhtml?path=/prelim@title46/subtitle3/chapter303&edition=prelim
- http://laws-lois.justice.gc.ca/PDF/M-0.7.pdf
- http://www.goldiumcruceros.com/informacion-legal.php?id=3
- https://www.viajeselcorteingles.es/documento/condiciones/pdf_condiciones_cruceros.pdf
- https://www.pullmantur.travel/general/condiciones-generales.html
- http://www.impo.com.uy/bases/leyes/17250-2000
- http://eur-lex.europa.eu/legal-content/EN/TXT/?uri=celex:32011L0083
- http://www.cec-msssi.es/en/CEC/web/secciones/viajes_combinados.htm
- http://freecases.eu/Doc/CourtAct/3611261

- https://www.eui.eu/Projects/CentreForJudicialCooperation/Documents/2012-05-25-26/C-585OpinionAGTrstenjak.pdf
- http://www.dictionary.com/browse/travel-agent?s=t
- http://www.dictionary.com/browse/tour-operator?s=t
- http://www.ilo.org/global/standards/maritime-labour-convention/lang%2D%2Den/index.htm
- http://www.ilo.org/dyn/normlex/en/f?p=NORMLEXPUB:11300:0::NO::P11300_INSTRUMENT_ID:312331
- http://servicios.infoleg.gob.ar/infolegInternet/verNorma.do?id=43550
- https://www.mtss.gub.uy/web/mtss/9-transporte-maritimo
- http://www.audm.com.uy/pdf/leyes/tratado-de-derecho-de-navegacion-comercial-internacional-1940.pdf
- http://www.ilo.org/global/standards/maritime-labour-convention/lang%2D%2Den/index.htm
- https://eur-lex.europa.eu/legal-content/EN/TXT/?uri=CELEX:31987D0594
- https://eur-lex.europa.eu/legal-content/EN/TXT/?uri=LEGISSUM:l33205
- http://www.imo.org/en/OurWork/Security/Guide_to_Maritime_Security/Documents/ILOIMOCodeOfPracticeEnglish.pdf
- http://www.imo.org/en/About/Conventions/ListOfConventions/Pages/International-Convention-for-the-Safety-of-Life-at-Sea-(SOLAS),-1974.aspx
- http://www.imo.org/es/OurWork/Security/Instruments/Paginas/ISPSCode.aspx
- https://eur-lex.europa.eu/legal-content/EN/TXT/?uri=CELEX:32017R0352
- http://eur-lex.europa.eu/legal-content/en/ALL/?uri=CELEX:32003R0001
- https://eur-lex.europa.eu/legal-content/EN/ALL/?uri=ecli%3AECLI%3AEU%3AC%3A2002%3A661
- http://curia.europa.eu/juris/liste.jsf?language=en&num=C-58/04
- https://www.cruising.org/about-the-industry/regulatory/industry-policies/environmental-protection/waste-management
- http://www.imo.org/en/About/Conventions/ListOfConventions/Pages/International-Convention-for-the-Control-and-Management-of-Ships'-Ballast-Water-and-Sediments-(BWM).aspx
- http://www.imo.org/en/about/conventions/listofconventions/pages/international-convention-for-the-prevention-of-pollution-from-ships-(marpol).aspx
- https://www.eea.europa.eu/policy-documents/ec-2014-regulation-eu-no
- https://www3.epa.gov/npdes/pubs/cwatxt.txt
- https://www.law.cornell.edu/uscode/text/33/1251
- https://www.epa.gov/enforcement/clean-water-act-cwa-and-federal-facilities
- https://www3.epa.gov/npdes/pubs/vgp_graywater.pdf
- http://www.imo.org/en/OurWork/Environment/LCLP/Pages/default.aspx
- https://ofmpub.epa.gov/sor_internet/registry/termreg/searchandretrieve/termsandacronyms/search.do?matchCriteria=Contains&checkedTerm=on&checkedAcronym=on&search=Search&term=blackwater
- https://www.epa.sa.gov.au/environmental_info/water_quality/programs/grey_and_black_water_discharge/black_water
- http://pmg-assets.s3-website-eu-west-1.amazonaws.com/140729annexiv.pdf

- https://www.ecolex.org/details/international-convention-for-the-prevention-of-pollution-from-ships-annex-iv-sewage-tre-000988/participants
- http://www.damengreen.com/en/bwt?gclid=CjwKCAjwpIjZBRBsEiwA0TN1r5NO2z91W8uz2ByeJUs6U4CgJZvlmCZy9_HhXprNEDkQ6N-q7vl0HBoC__8QAvD_BwE
- http://www.imo.org/en/About/Conventions/StatusOfConventions/Pages/Default.aspx
- https://www.apnews.com/d26c8908b52b41b1bbd579bd28427f85/Alaska-pollution-regulators-gear-up-for-cruise-ship-season
- http://www.legis.state.ak.us/basis/statutes.asp#46.03.462
- https://www.epa.gov/aboutepa/epa-region-10-pacific-northwest
- https://dec.alaska.gov/water/cruise_ships/Law_and_Regs/index.htm
- http://www.admiraltylawguide.com/conven/civilpol1969.html
- https://treaties.un.org/doc/publication/unts/volume%20970/volume-970-i-14049-english.pdf
- http://www.imo.org/en/about/conventions/listofconventions/pages/international-convention-for-the-prevention-of-pollution-from-ships-(marpol).aspx
- https://legislativo.parlamento.gub.uy/temporales/leytemp2250106
- https://www.gpo.gov/fdsys/pkg/USCODE-2010-title18/pdf/USCODE-2010-title18-partI-chap1-sec7.pdf
- http://cecu.es/campanas/cuadernos/CRUCEROS09.pdf
- http://media.celebritycruises.com/celebrity/content/en_US/pdf/Celebrity_CTC_Eff_08_01_10.pdf
- http://www.goldiumcruceros.com/informacion-legal.php?id=3
- http://www.msccruceros.com.ar/ar_es/Guia-Crucero/Condiciones-Generales.aspx
- https://www.viajeselcorteingles.es/documento/condiciones/pdf_condiciones_cruceros.pdf
- https://www.pullmantur.travel/general/condiciones-generales.html
- http://www.deluxetravel.com.co/agencia-de-cruceros-medellin-colombia/terminos-legales
- https://www.cruising.org/about-the-industry/regulatory/industry-policies/health/medical-facilities
- https://www.cruising.org/about-the-industry/regulatory/industry-policies/environmental-protection/waste-management
- https://www.vallettawaterfront.com/DetailPage.aspx?id=156262
- https://www.cruising.org/about-the-industry/regulatory/industry-policies/other/pbor
- https://www.cruising.org/about-the-industry/regulatory/industry-policies/health/medical-facilities

References

Aguirre Ramírez F, Fresnedo De Aguirre C (2011) Curso de Derecho del Transporte. Transporte marítimo, vol III. Fundación de Cultura Universitaria, Montevideo

Aguirre Ramírez F, Fresnedo De Aguirre C (2016) Curso de Derecho del Transporte. Transporte Marítimo, Tomo I, 2nd ed. FCU, Montevideo

Aramburu S (2008) Principio de precaución, turismo y Antártida. Thomson Reuters, Sup. Act. 05/02/2008, 05/02/2008, Online AR/DOC/87/2008

Ariza Herrerías Á (2014) Análisis Jurídico-Económico del Transporte Marítimo en el Sector Turístico, Trabajo Fin de Máster. Universidad de Málaga, Facultad de Turismo. http://riuma.uma.es/xmlui/bitstream/handle/10630/8729/TRABAJO%20FIN%20DE%20M%C3%81STER%20-%20def.pdf?sequence=1

Barone M (2008) Seguridad Marítima y Portuaria: la implementación del nuevo Código Internacional para la Protección para Buques e Instalaciones Portuarias (CPBIP OMI) en la República Argentina. Thomson Reuters, UNLP 2008-38, 01/01/2008, 319, Online: AR/DOC/469/2008

Barreiro KM (2008) In: Barreiro KM (ed) Protección legal del turista en el derecho comparado. Ladevi Ediciones, Buenos Aires

Beltrán Montiel L (1981) Curso de Derecho de la Navegación. Ed. Astrea, Buenos Aires

Borda A (2003). El contrato celebrado con organizadores de viajes turísticos es un contrato de consumo. UY/DOC/454/2014, La Ley, T. 2003-B

Cappagli AC (2016). El derecho de la navegación en el nuevo Código. La Ley 04/02/2016, 04/02/2016, 1 – LA LEY2016-A, 949; Online: AR/DOC/4547/2015

Chami D (n.d.). Limitación de responsabilidad por créditos marítimos. Thomson Reuters, Online: 0021/000299

Chami D, Adragna E (2013). Cruceros de Turismo. VII Jornadas Rioplatenses de Derecho Marítimo 2013, published in CD

Chircop A, Moreira W, Kindred H, Gold E (eds) (2016) Essentials of Canadian law – Canadian maritime law, 2nd edn. Irwin Law Inc., Toronto, ISBN 978-1-55221-404-6

Correa JL (2005) Transporte internacional de personas. Thomson Reuters, LLGran Cuyo2005 (octubre), 1005, Online: AR/DOC/3158/2005

Courtney A, Fjelstad E, Wildman SA (2004) Multijurisdictional regulation of cruise ship discharges. Nat Resour Environ 19(1):50–56. American Bar Association. http://www.jstor.org/stable/40925141

Delebecque P (2001) Le Droit International des Transports Maritimes, 1999. Centre D'Étude et de Recherche de Droit International et de Relations Internationales, Académie de Droit International de La Haye, Kluwer Law International, The Netherlands

Estepa Montero M (2012) El régimen jurídico y el tráfico de los cruceros marítimos. Anuario Jurídico y Económico Escurialense XLV(2012):133–154. ISSN: 1133-3677

Estepa Montero M (2013) Los puertos del Estado y el tráfico de cruceros marítimos (State seaports and maritime traffic cruises). Anuario Jurídico y Económico Escurialense XLVI:325-344. ISSN: 1133-3677

Facal J, Pezzutti M (2008) El Uruguay y las Normas de Protección al Turista. La Necesidad de una Reforma de la Ley de Turismo. In: Barreiro KM (ed) Protección legal del turista en el derecho comparado. Ladevi Ediciones, Buenos Aires, pp 292–321

Felder BO (2006) Get on board: yes, maritime law is different. Bus Law Today 15(4):25–31. http://www.jstor.org/stable/23296380

Fresnedo de Aguirre C (2004) El estado de situación del arbitraje comercial internacional en la jurisprudencia uruguaya. DeCITA 02.2004, Derecho del Comercio Internacional. Temas y Actualidades, Directores: A. Dreyzin de Klor y D. Fernández Arroyo, Argentina, Zavalía, pp 420–435

Fresnedo de Aguirre C (2009) Curso de Derecho Internacional Privado, Tomo II, Parte Especial, vol 2. FCU, Montevideo, pp 160–167

Fresnedo de Aguirre C (2012) El arbitraje internacional: presencia y evolución en el ámbito jurídico uruguayo. In: Oyarzábal MJA (Coordinador) *Derecho procesal transnacional. Homenaje al Profesor Doctor Gualberto Lucas Sosa.* Ed. Ábaco, Buenos Aires, pp 217–251 and in *Revista de Derecho* N° 7, 2012, Konrad Adenauer Stiftung – Universidad Católica del Uruguay, pp 115–151

Fresnedo de Aguirre C (2015) Normas de Derecho Internacional Privado en las Leyes N° 18.803 y N° 19.246 de Derecho Marítimo. In: Reforma del Derecho Marítimo Uruguayo, Asociación Uruguaya de Derecho Marítimo. FCU, Montevideo, pp 127–168

González A (2013). Cruceros: Unidad de Negocios con Calidad en Servicios. VII Jornadas Rioplatenses de Derecho Marítimo 2013, published in CD

GP WILD (International), Business Research and Economic Advisors (BREA) (2015) The cruise industry – contribution of cruise tourism to the economies of Europe. 2015 Edition, p 3

Haiek B (2012) Los seguros en el transporte de pasajeros por agua. In: Parés GAO (ed) Derecho de los Seguros Marítimos y Portuarios. Libro Homenaje al Dr. Alberto Baumeister Toledo, 1st edn. Caracas and others, Legis, pp 201–213

Hocsman HS, Buccheri S (2008). Contrato de agencia comercial. El contrato de viaje. Responsabilidad de la agencia de viajes y de la empresa organizadora intermediaria. Thomson Reuters, Online: 0003/013752

Marrin SS (2002) Rough seas ahead for Alaska cruises – the judicial and legislative battle over Glacier Bay. Fordham Environ Law J 13:323. Content downloaded/printed from HeinOnline

Mozuni M, Jonas W (2016) Rise of alternative business models in the era of expensive megaships. In: Papathanassis A (ed) Cruise business development, safety, product design and human capital. Springer, Cham

Phlypo L, Gheysen S (2014) Strategisch beleidsplan voor toerisme en recreatie aan de Kust 2015–2020. Westtoer, Brugge, p 41

Radovich JM (2012) Es aplicable la normativa de Defensa del Consumidor en el Derecho Marítimo? Revista Megatrade, junio de 2012

Ray JD (2002). La responsabilidad en el derecho y, en especial, en el marítimo. Thomson Reuters, Online: 0003/008661

Romero Basaldúa L (1996) Derecho Marítimo, 2nd edn. Ed. Marcos Lerner, Córdoba

Schüter RG, Winter G (2000) La Agencia de Viajes y Turismo. Estructura y Operaciones. Ed. Docencia, Buenos Aires

Sconfienza Pérez R (2003) El contrato de 'agencia turística' en el derecho positivo uruguayo. Revista de la Facultad de Derecho 22:81–89. http://revista.fder.edu.uy/index.php/rfd/article/view/199

Vasallo I (2015) El negocio de los cruceros. www.elsiglodeuropa.es/siglo/historia/2015/1119/1119Vasallo.pdf

Vázquez Ferreyra R, Fiscella ME (1997) Contrato de Transporte. Ed. Juris, Rosario

Cecilia Fresnedo de Aguirre Professor of Private International Law. University of the Republic, Uruguay. Director of the Uruguayan Institute of Private International Law. Professor at The Hague Academy of International Law (2015).

Part II
National Reports: Europe

Legal Aspects of Cruises from a Belgian Perspective

Kristiaan Bernauw

Abstract The European Union promotes the cruise tourism, but with due regard for environmental protection.

The cruise activity is seldom governed by a specific legal regime in the fields of safety, security, health and taxation, but may or may not qualify as a type of several other broader categories in public, labour and private law: passenger transport contract, tourism service contract, package travel contract, consumer contract, cabotage, regular service, fiscal transit, immigration, etc.

Professional organisations in the cruise sector have elaborated some self-regulation.

According to the type of cruise, the conveyance, accommodation or entertainment component may prevail.

The nuanced criterion to distinguish a package travel contract from a transport contract is the substantial nature of the accommodation or entertainment components. The prevalence of the conveyance component shall qualify the operation as transport.

For the purpose of carrier liability, the E.U. package travel regime is aligned with the international maritime passenger carrier liability regime.

The compatibility of state aid to cruise terminals and cruise vessel building with E.U. competition law is an often raised issue.

For the sake of marine environment protection, the compliance of cruise operations with waste disposal precepts are particularly critical.

The characteristics of personnel employment in the cruise industry (seasonal, mobile, cross-border, irregular working time, etc.) are however not specific for that sector.

Conflicts of laws issues are addressed by the E.U. Regulations: Brussels Ibis on jurisdiction and Rome I on choice of law.

The text reflects the situation as of 19 April 2018.

K. Bernauw (✉)
Ghent University, Ghent, Belgium
e-mail: Kris.Bernauw@ugent.be

C. Fresnedo de Aguirre (ed.), *Legal Aspects of Cruises*, Ius Comparatum - Global Studies in Comparative Law 56, https://doi.org/10.1007/978-3-030-83090-8_2

1 Cruise Policies and Strategies

1.1 On the Regional E.U. Level

The E.U. Commission laid out its strategic goals for the European maritime policy in the 2009 Communication on Strategic Goals and Recommendations for the E.U. Maritime Transport Policy until 2018, identifying key areas, where action by the E.U. would strengthen the competitiveness of the sector, while enhancing its environmental performance. The European Parliament highlighted the importance of cruise tourism for the growth of the tourism sector in Europe; it therefore called on the Commission, together with the Member States, to assess the resources required and existing port and nautical infrastructure, and to standardise the sorting of waste and recycling, in order to create innovative planning actions for these areas by developing the concept of the smart port city.[1] The promotion of the cruise business is part of the broader E.U. policy and strategy of sustainable development of the so-called "blue economy", that includes cruise tourism.

The E.U. maritime tourism policy[2] focuses on the following items:

- Promotion of the "blue" economy: "blue" growth,[3] also in jobs[4]
- Taking into account the seasonality of the tourism sector
- By a favourable fiscal regime for the sector
- Reducing the red tape for the sector.

The protection of the environment (marine ecosystem) is pursued by a sustainable "green" approach, i.a.:

[1] P8_TA(2015)0391, New challenges and concepts for the promotion of tourism in Europe, European Parliament resolution of 29 October 2015 on new challenges and concepts for the promotion of tourism in Europe (2014/2241(INI)) (2017/C 355/10).

[2] DG Maritime Affairs & Fisheries. (2013). *Study in support of policy measures for maritime and coastal tourism at EU level;* Opinion of the Committee of the Regions — European strategy for coastal and maritime tourism, 2014/C 415/03 (paragraphs 43–45 on the cruise sector).

[3] Communication from the Commission to the European parliament, the Council, the European economic and social committee and the Committee of the regions Blue Growth opportunities for marine and maritime sustainable growth /* COM/2012/0494 final */ (paragraph 5.3. on Maritime, coastal and cruise tourism); Opinion of the Committee of the Regions on 'Blue growth: opportunities for marine and maritime sustainable growth' (2013/C 62/10) (paragraphs 20–25 on maritime, coastal and cruise tourism).

[4] Communication from the Commission to the European Parliament, the Council, the European Economic and Social Committee and the Committee of the Regions a European strategy for more growth and jobs in coastal and maritime tourism, com(2014) 86 final, Brussels, 20.2.2014; Opinion of the European Economic and Social Committee on the Communication from the Commission to the European Parliament, the Council, the European Economic and Social Committee and the Committee of the Regions on 'A European Strategy for more Growth and Jobs in Coastal and Maritime Tourism COM(2014) 86 final (2014/C 451/10).

- waste management avoiding marine pollution from littering
- the development and use by the cruise industry of more energy-efficient ships with lower (even zero) emission, in particular cruise liners, based on the use of renewable energies from wind, solar and wave power, and linked with fuel-cell technologies.

In the field of Human Resources, development of skills in tourism and attracting skilled personnel is pursued.

With respect to port infrastructure[5] and services: the construction of cruise terminals[6] and in conformity with Schengen immigration requirements (cfr. the security factor below) is promoted. Interconnections with other modes of transport is thereby to be ensured.

Another goal is age-friendly tourism and accessibility for passengers with reduced mobility (i.a. by adapting port terminals to their needs).

The development of the next generation of passenger cruise ships (as means of transport) is one of the specific objectives pursued by the E.U.[7] With respect to cruise ship building, a threefold goal is pursued in the development of innovative cruise vessels:

- improved quality with regard to passengers' rights, on the basis of operators' best practices
- safety
- environmental friendliness (see above).

Also the security concern is an element of the policy: cfr. the Transport White Paper, Annex I, 1.4.[8]

1.2 On the Belgian National Level

The cruise ports of Oostende and Zeebrugge co-operate in the "Belgian Coast Cruise Project" in order to promote cruise tourism in their ports and to reinforce the market position of their ports in the world cruise market.[9] "The strategic policy plan for coastal tourism and recreation (2015-2020)" adopted by the Flemish regional

[5] Directorate General for Maritime Affairs and Fisheries. (2009). *Tourist facilities in ports - Growth opportunities for the European maritime economy :economic and environmentally sustainable development of tourist facilities in ports.*

[6] Communication from the Commission to the European Parliament, the Council, the European Economic and Social Committee and the Committee of the Regions—Strategic goals and recommendations for the EU's maritime transport policy until 2018 (COM/2009/0008 final).

[7] (Council decision of 3 December 2013 establishing the specific programme implementing Horizon 2020—the Framework Programme for Research and Innovation (2014–2020) (2013/743/EU).

[8] COM(2001) 370 of 12 September 2001.

[9] Haven Zeebrugge. (2014). *Belgian Coast Cruise Project*. http://www.poz.be/nl/node/807.

government and the Province of West-Flanders includes the promotion of cruise operations (departure and destination) in Belgian seaports.[10] The building of the cruise terminal infrastructure in Zeebrugge is one of the achievements in this respect.[11] As mentioned above, Zeebrugge port has built a cruise terminal, Brussels Seaport is building a cruise terminal and Antwerp Port plans to build a cruise terminal. Towards the end of the last century there was a general flagging-out of the Belgian merchant fleet (to Luxembourg) inspired by the intent to improve its competition position on the international market. The operational cost had risen too high, due to onerous social and fiscal legislation and regulation under socialist governments. A reverse evolution could be witnessed as from the turn of the century.

2 The Legal Regime

2.1 *Public Regulation*

2.1.1 Supranational Legislation

As a cross-border activity almost by its very nature, cruise shipping is governed by a legal regime that consists of national (Belgian), regional (E.U. secondary legislation/regulation) and global (I.M.O. generated) components. The supranational legislation either has direct effect (e.g. E.U. Regulation) or must be implemented (e.g. E.U. Directive) in the Belgian legal order.

2.1.2 Specific Regulation

The maxim "*lex specialis generali derogat*" expresses the principle that in the interrelationship between the general and the specific rules of the body of law, the specific legal regime prevails over the general regime. This principle applies both in private law and in public law. Hence cruise activity is subject to the general regime to the extent that specific rules do not deviate from it.

Cruise activities may be part of broader legal categories (e.g. package travel, (maritime) passenger transport/carriage,[12] consumer contracts, etc.) that are addressed by specific legal regimes.

Consumer protection legislation generally applies horizontally cross-sector wise, save specific exceptions. This is relevant as the cruise passenger is normally

---

[10] Phlypo and Gheysen (2014), p. 41 (www.toerismevlaanderen.bewww.toerismevlaanderen.be).

[11] Phlypo and Gheysen (2014), p. 37 and 49 (www.toerismevlaanderen.bewww.toerismevlaanderen.be).

[12] E.g.: Directive 2009/45/EC on safety rules and standards for passenger ships; Regulation (EC) Nr. 725/2004 enhancing ship and port facility security.

qualified as a consumer. Horizontal cross cutting consumer protection provisions apply also on cruise contracts.

Transport services (carrier liability) however are sometimes excluded from the consumer protection legislation, because they are already specifically addressed by the international transport related treaties (carrier liability conventions). For this reason E.U. consumer protection legislation generally excludes transport services from its scope of application.

The cruise activity and the cruise vessel are one of the many types of respectively maritime operations and concomitant types of sea-going vessels (besides e.g. passenger liner, ferry, tanker, bulk-carrier, container, ro-ro, dredger, ice-breaker etc. operations/vessels).

A number of legal/regulatory precepts are common for all types of maritime operations and vessels. Some may be specific for certain types, like cruise, but there are very few legal rules or regulations specifically applicable to cruises. A cruise vessel/operation in the first place belongs to the broader category of maritime passenger vessel/transport operation. Cruise activities are within the scope of the international public law instruments, such as UNCLOS,[13] SOLAS,[14] COLREGs,[15] MARPOL[16] and overall those with regard to the liability of the ship owner and operator (e.g. the Collision Convention, Athens Convention on passenger transportation (PAL), Ship Arrest Convention, Salvage Convention, Convention on Limitation of Liability for Maritime Claims ("LLMC"), Bunker Oil Convention, Wreck Removal Convention).

The International Convention for the Safety of Life at Sea (SOLAS) contains specific rules for specific classes of vessels, such as passenger vessels, but not for cruise vessels. The International Association of Classification Societies (IACS) issued Common Structural Rules (CSR) but did not develop technical standards specifically for cruise vessels.

Legal regimes generally also apply to cruises in their capacity of maritime activities next to other maritime activities (e.g. transportation) or to cruises as part of broader categories of maritime activities (supply of services).

The question is rather whether cruises qualify as those other specifically regulated categories of activities or are on the contrary in some instances excluded from the application of a specific legal regime, both in the field of private and public law (cfr. infra: e.g. maritime passenger transport and package travel, cabotage, etc.).

For that purpose, the qualification and definition of "cruise" services is crucial (cfr. infra).

[13] United Nations Convention on the Law of the Sea.

[14] International Convention for the Safety of Life at Sea, 1974 (SOLAS).

[15] International Regulations for the Preventing of Collisions at Sea, 1972 (COLREGS).

[16] International Convention for the Prevention of Pollution from Ships (MARPOL).

2.2 Self-Regulation

Where there is no (mandatory) legislation/regulation, self-regulation may be relevant. In this respect the following sources of self-regulation can be mentioned.

Current safety levels in IWT (Inland Waterway Transport) are not only a product of legislation in force but also of practices developed over many years by the profession. Navigation on large convoys or on cruise ships is an example. Although according to the regulatory framework a skipper can navigate these vessels with the patent/boatmaster certificate, shipping companies have put in place a career management system that includes additional requirements in terms of experience and lifelong training.[17]

Cruise Lines International Association (CLIA) Europe was previously known as the European Cruise Council (ECC). The European Cruise Council (ECC) represents the leading cruise companies operating in Europe. It is the European wing of Cruise Lines International Association (CLIA), the world's largest cruise industry trade association with representation in North and South America, Europe, Asia and Australasia.

CLIA advances policies and in some cases calls for best practices in excess of existing legal requirements, intended to enhance operational safety, shipboard security, fire protection, environmental protection (waste management), health (ship medical facilities, public health (pre-boarding health screening in the context of communicable diseases), and other (passenger bill of rights).

CLIA thus issues various "Cruise Industry Policies", but stresses that by promoting these practices and policies, it does not undertake to develop or enforce industry standards.

CLIA developed the *Cruise Industry Passenger Bill of Rights,* codifying cruise industry practices and expressing the cruise line's commitment to the safety, comfort and care of guests in the event of a mechanical failure or shipboard emergency.

The ECC requires all its members to meet the ECC Standard On Blackwater[18] Discharges (April 2011).[19] Reference can also be made to the ECC Statement of Commitment on the Environment.

---

[17] Commission staff working document Impact Assessment, Accompanying the document Proposal for a Directive of the European Parliament and of the Council on the recognition of professional qualifications in inland navigation and repealing Council Directive 91/672/EEC and Council Directive 96/50/EC (COM(2016) 82 final) (SWD(2016) 36 final).

[18] Waste from toilets, urinals, medical sinks and other similar facilities is called "blackwater."

[19] All blackwater is to be processed through a Marine Sanitation Device (MSD), certified in accordance with national and/or international regulations, prior to discharge. For ships travelling regularly on itineraries beyond the territorial water of coastal states, discharge must take place only when the ship is more than 4 miles from shore and when the ship is travelling at a speed of not less than 6 knots.

3 The Cruise Concept: Qualification

Depending on the legal context, the concept of cruises was classified differently, sometimes in a contradictory manner, as is illustrated below. In this respect the consideration was relevant that the cruise industry is part of the luxury segment of the maritime sector, that the ships include a complete hotel infrastructure, provide leisure activities and often bring passengers back to the port of departure.[20]

A basic distinction may be made between river cruises and maritime (ocean) cruises.

The differential cruise business or semi-cruise models may cause qualification problems for the purpose of application of the legal regime in various respects. The main model of the major cruise lines focuses on providing "Onboard Hospitality and Entertainment" (OHE), where the transportation element is servile to entertainment. They may even limit themselves to onboard entertainment and activities rather than destination-based activities, abandoning the multiple-coast-check program and offering long term ocean-only cruises. Another niche is the "Condominium/Residential Model" (CRM) that offers floating residency. "Shore to Shore Floating Services" (SSFS) mobilizes conventionally land-based services (events, festivity, casino, etc.) on a floating infrastructure often consisting of immobile ships. Ferry-services focus mainly on transportation and mobility with no or "Limited Onboard Involvement" (LOI):[21] in some cases only tax free shops.

In this context the following cases were assessed.

The journey of a passenger on board of a cargo ship was qualified as a package travel contract for the purpose of application of the package travel contract law[22] (cfr. infra).

The distinctive criteria between a package travel contract and a maritime transport contract, (e.g. overnight boat trip or ferry service that includes accommodation in a cabin with bed and catering services: the excess of 24 hours and the overnight stay criteria (as opposed to the entertainment element) are problematic to distinguish cruise operations from transport operations.

Art. 3 of the Directive (EU) 2015/2302 and Art. 2 of the Belgian of Act of 21 November 2017 on the sale of package travel, linked travel arrangements and travel services distinguish accommodation that is not intrinsically part of passenger transportation.

Recital 17 of the Directive (EU) 2015/2302 explains that only the combination of different types of travel services, such as accommodation, carriage of passengers by bus, rail, water or air, as well as rental of motor vehicles or certain motorcycles,

---

[20] Report from the Commission to the European Parliament and the Council on the application of Regulation (EU) No 1177/2010 concerning the rights of passengers when travelling by sea and inland waterway and amending Regulation (EC) No 2006/2004 (COM/2016/0274 final).

[21] Mozuni and Jonas (2016), pp. 59–60.

[22] E.U. Court of Justice, 7 December 2000, cases nr. C-585/08 and C-144/09.

should be considered for the purposes of identifying a package or a linked travel arrangement.

This means that in cases where (unlike in the case of a cruise), overnight accommodation is provided as part of passenger transport by road, rail, water or air, accommodation should not be considered as a travel service in its own right if the main component is clearly transport.

4 Specific Rules on Cruises

Specific rules on cruises were issued in various fields.

4.1 Goods and Services Classification and Nomenclature

Cruise related products and services are acknowledged for the purpose of statistics, customs and trade agreements, public procurement,[23] etc.

The E.U. instruments on statistics contain definitions and provisions that are specific to cruise activity, viz.:

- Regulation (EU) No 692/2011 of the European Parliament and of the Council of 6 July 2011 concerning European statistics on tourism.
- Commission Regulation (EU) No 1051/2011 implementing Regulation (EU) No 692/2011 concerning European statistics on tourism, as regards the structure of the quality reports and the transmission of the data
- Directive 2009/42/EC on statistical returns in respect of carriage of goods and passengers by sea.
- Council Regulation (EEC) No 2658/87 on the tariff and statistical nomenclature and on the Common Customs Tariff identifies cruise ships as a particular type of goods. It established a nomenclature, known as 'Combined Nomenclature' (abbreviated 'CN'), based on the International Convention on the Harmonised Commodity Description and Coding System (WCO) known as 'the Harmonised System' (abbreviated 'HS').
- The Regulation (EC) nr. 451/2008 establishing a new statistical classification of products by activity (CPA) contains several cruise specific categories and identifies cruise ships as a particular type of goods. It is in accordance with the United Nations' Central Product Classification (CPC) and aligned with the Harmonised System (HS) (International Convention on the Harmonised Commodity Description and Coding System (WCO[24]) and the Combined Nomenclature (CN).

[23] Commission Regulation (EC) No 213/2008 on the Common Procurement Vocabulary (CPV).

[24] World Customs Organisation.

- Commission Regulation (EU) 2017/2119 of 22 November 2017 establishes the 'Prodcom list' of industrial products provided for by Council Regulation (EEC) No 3924/91.

Those instruments define e.g.:

- "Cruise passenger" as a sea passenger making a sea journey on a cruise ship. Passengers on day excursions are excluded. (Annex I, art. 2 (h) Directive 2009/42)
- "Cruise ship" (89.01) as a passenger ship intended to provide passengers with a full tourist experience. All passengers have cabins. Facilities for entertainment on board are included. Ships operating normal ferry services are excluded, even if some passengers treat the service as a cruise. In addition, cargo-carrying vessels able to carry a very limited number of passengers with their own cabins are excluded. Ships intended solely for day excursions are also excluded (Annex I, art. 2 (i) Directive 2009/42).
- "Cruise passenger excursion" as a short visit by a cruise passenger to a tourist attraction associated with a port while retaining a cabin on board (Annex I, art. 2 (j) Directive 2009/42).

For the purpose of vessel classification, ICST[25]-COM distinguishes "Passenger ships" (sea passengers other than cruise passengers) (Annex VI, 35 Directive 2009/42) and "cruise ships" (cruise passengers only) (Annex VI, 36 Directive 2009/42). The cruise ship building is designated with the CPA code 30.11.21.30. The sea and coastal passenger water transport services on cruise ships are designated with the CPA code 50.10.12. The exploitation of cruise vessels was defined as a specific category (nomenclature code (NACE[26]) 6110002) of waterborne passenger transportation (Belgian Royal Decree of 9 August 2002 listing the commercial activities). NACE-BEL 2008 in accordance with the EC Regulation 1893/2006 no longer specifies cruises as a distinct category of waterborne passenger transportation in code 50.1.

4.2 *Immigration*

In the field of immigration, a Belgian interdepartmental circular letter dated 10 December 1998 was issued on the effect of the Schengen Agreement on border control and police and judicial cooperation. It applies to maritime transport, but for cruise operations it refers to specific control measures (art. 6M2, Chapter VI).

[25] International Classification of Ships by Type (for statistical purposes).

[26] Nomenclature statistique des Activités économiques dans la Communauté Européenne: cfr. Council Regulation (EEC) No 3037/90 of 9 October 1990 on the statistical classification of economic activities in the European Community.

Regulation (EU) 2016/399 on a Union Code on the rules governing the movement of persons across borders (Schengen Borders Code) provides for a special immigration regime for cruise passengers (exemption from entry/exit stamping of travel documents) (art. 11, 3 (d) and specific check procedures for cruise ships and depending on whether their itineraries comprise ports situated inside or outside the EU territory (Annex VI art. 3.2.).

'Cruise ship' is defined by the Regulation as "a ship which follows a given itinerary in accordance with a predetermined programme, which includes a programme of tourist activities in the various ports, and which normally neither takes passengers on nor allows passengers to disembark during the voyage" (art. 2, 17).

Clandestine disembarkation of illegal immigrants from cruise ships was judged a limited risk, as the operators themselves exert tighter controls.[27]

4.3 Customs Clearance

Cruises (especially maritime) are often operated cross-border. Council Decision 87/594/EEC of 30 November 1987 accepted, on behalf of the European Community, Annex F.3 to the International Convention on the simplification and harmonization of customs procedures. With respect to the location of customs offices at which customs formalities relating to travellers may be accomplished, this procedures standard specifies that in some instances, such as cruise ships, it may be possible for travellers to accomplish all the necessary customs formalities on board.

4.4 Cruise Passenger Security

Whereas the I.M.O. work on maritime security does not contain specific measures applicable to cruise ships, the E.U. Commission has addressed the subject of cruise passenger security in Europe in the Transport White Paper (see Annex I, 1.4.),[28] where it was considered that cruise passengers deserve special attention. Given the nature of their journeys and their large number on board, cruise ships could be a target in the same way as other means of collective transport. Consequently, it was felt necessary that access to cruise ships should be the subject of tighter controls on people, their belongings and the ship's provisions. The issue is part of port security requiring legislation on checks on cruise ship passengers and, where appropriate,

[27] Feasibility study on the control of the European Union's maritime borders, 11490/1/03, REV 1, LIMITE, FRONT 102, COMIX 458.

[28] COM(2001) 370 of 12 September 2001.

crew members in the context of the relevant provisions such as the Common Manual for External Borders (cfr. infra).

4.5 Health and Sanitation on Board

Ships sail from country to country where different hygiene standards and rules for controlling diseases exist. Mechanisms for communicable disease control in ships were elaborated under E.U. Decision No 2119/98/EC of the Council and the Parliament. Epidemic outbreaks have been associated to cruise ships. In the European Union, a common policy for dealing with health threats related to ships was needed. To address these issues the European Commission funded from 2006 until 2011 two European health programme projects in the area of maritime transport: 'Assessing the usefulness of an EU ship sanitation programme and coordinated action for the control of communicable diseases in cruise ships and ferries' (SHIPSAN) and 'EU Ship Sanitation Training Network' (SHIPSAN TRAINET).[29]

The SHIPSAN ACT is a European Joint Action funded by the European Commission under the Health Programme (2008–2013), in which 33 partners from 24 European countries participate. EU SHIPSAN ACT produced a State of the Art report, with a literature review on infectious diseases, surveys on practices of E.U. authorities on chemical, biological, radiological and nuclear (CBRN) incidents in maritime transport, hygiene inspection on fishing and inland vessels, and training needs on core capacities at points of entry. This action produced a ship inspection plan including competencies, roles and responsibilities and a code of conduct. The production of guidelines was planned to allow consistent preparedness planning in the E.U. based on shared and common standards, facilitating International Health Regulation (WHO) implementation.

The European Manual for Hygiene Standards and Communicable Disease Surveillance on Passenger ships[30] incorporates hygiene standards based on E.U. legislation and brings together best practice guidelines for passenger ships sailing within European waters. This manual is intended for passenger shipping companies and public health inspectors in European ports, who are responsible for passenger ship inspections.

[29] http://trainet.shipsan.eu.

[30] European Manual for Hygiene Standards and Communicable Disease Surveillance on Passenger Ships, edition 2, April 2016.

4.6 Passenger Safety

The safety of passenger ships is regulated at three levels: (i) through international conventions to which E.U. Member States (and in rare cases the E.U. itself as a whole) are party, (ii) E.U. passenger ship safety legislation and (iii) national law.

The 1974 International Convention for the Safety of Life at Sea (the 1974 SOLAS Convention), as amended, contains internationally agreed safety standards for passenger ships engaged on international voyages. For ships engaged in international voyages, including between two E.U. Member States, SOLAS is the most safety-relevant applicable convention. It is administered by the International Maritime Organization (I.M.O.), a U.N. body, and has been ratified by all E.U. Member States. Resolutions adopted by the I.M.O. and other measures complement and interpret that Convention, such as the International Management Code for the Safe Operation of Ships and for Pollution Prevention (ISM Code) adopted by the International Maritime Organization (I.M.O.) through Assembly Resolution A.741 (18) of 4 November 1993.

At E.U. level, the most extensive legislative instrument is Directive 2009/45/EC regulating ships made of steel (or equivalent material) and high speed craft (HSC) engaged in domestic voyages. Directive 2009/45/EC on safety rules and standards for passenger ships does not contain specific precepts for cruise vessels. Also it applies to ships operated in domestic services. For international service reference is made to I.M.O.

Similarly Directive (EU) 2016/1629 laying down technical requirements for inland waterway vessels, contains specific precepts for passenger vessels, but not exclusively for cruise ships.

4.7 Vessel Technical Specifications and Standards

Commission regulation (EU) No 164/2010 of 25 January 2010 on the technical specifications for electronic ship reporting in inland navigation referred to in Article 5 of Directive 2005/44/EC of the European Parliament and of the Council on harmonised river information services (RIS) on inland waterways in the Community and the Commission regulation (EC) No 415/2007 of 13 March 2007 concerning the technical specifications for vessel tracking and tracing systems referred to in article 5 of Directive 2005/44/EC of the European Parliament and of the Council on harmonised river information services (RIS) on inland waterways in the Community, recognise cruise ships and cruise activities as distinct categories.

Cruise ship tenders[31] are mainly made from materials other than steel or equivalent to minimise the weight to be carried on board the cruise ship. However, it is a moot point whether such vessels can be considered as passenger ships in their own

[31] Devices used to ferry passengers from cruise ships to shore and back.

right or simply equipment on board a cruise ship. Tender operation is regulated nationally, unless the tenders are deemed to operate outside the port area and are made of steel (a rare occurrence) in which case the Directive 2009/45/EC (cfr. supra) applies. The I.M.O. has developed and adopted non-mandatory guidelines for the construction, outfitting and use of tenders to provide a common standard for their use (MSC.1/Circ.1417 on Guidelines for passenger ship tenders).[32]

5 Cruises Meeting Characteristics of Other Legal Categories

The question arose whether cruises meet the characteristics to qualify as other legal categories in several respects.

5.1 Cabotage

Together with other types of maritime transport services, during (E.U. economic integration) transition periods, the category of cruise services in the Mediterranean has been exempted from the application of the Regulation EC/3577/92 on the freedom to provide maritime transport services within E.U. Member States (maritime cabotage), first in general for the E.U. founding member states and later on also upon the accession of Croatia to the European Union: exemptions were granted allowing Croatia till 31 December 2014 to reserve cruise services between Croatian ports by ships smaller than 650 gt, to Croatian ships.[33]

The Regulation (EEC) No 3577/92 of 7 December 1992 applying the principle of freedom to provide to maritime transport services within Member States (maritime cabotage), was declared applicable to cruise services.

In the case C-17/13 before the E.U. Court of Justice the question arose from the perspective whether a cruise which starts and ends, with the same passengers, in the same port of the Member State in which it takes place, is covered by the term 'maritime cabotage' within the meaning of Regulation No 3577/92. The Court held that a cruise which starts and ends, with the same passengers, in the same port of the Member State in which it takes place, is covered by the term 'maritime cabotage' within the meaning of Regulation (EEC) No 3577/92 of 7 December 1992 applying the principle of freedom to provide services to maritime transport within Member States (maritime cabotage). Consequently such a service falls under the European

[32] Commission staff working document accompanying the document Report from the Commission to the European Parliament and Council REFIT Adjusting course: EU Passenger Ship Safety Legislation Fitness Check, SWD/2015/0197 final.

[33] Act of 9 December 2011, amending Regulation n° EC/3577/92.

Union's transport policy. The Court considered that it is true that the transport services listed in Article 2(1)(a) to (c) of Regulation No 3577/92 are described as having different departure and arrival ports. However, according to the Court that list, which is introduced by the term 'in particular', is not exhaustive and cannot have the effect of excluding from the scope of that regulation transport services presenting all the essential characteristics of maritime cabotage contained in the above-mentioned phrase 'maritime transport services within a Member State' (referring to Case C-251/04 Commission v Greece, paragraphs 28 and 32). The question arose whether Greece could apply national manning rules to Community cruise liners exceeding 650 gt, which carry out island cabotage (See Case C-288/02 Commission v Greece, paragraph 29). The Court considered that all cruise services normally provided for remuneration in the maritime waters of a Member State fall within the ambit of the concept of 'maritime transport services within a Member State' defined in art. 1(1) and art. 2(1) of Regulation No 3577/92. The fact that its departure and arrival ports are one and the same and that its passengers are the same throughout the itinerary, cannot, according to the Court, render Regulation No 3577/92 inapplicable to such a cruise.

The Communication from the Commission on the interpretation of Council Regulation (EEC) No 3577/92 applying the principle of freedom to provide services to maritime transport within Member States (maritime cabotage) (COM/2014/0232 final) discusses (in 3.3.) the question whether the cabotage leg of an international cruise service falls within the scope of the Regulation. The Commission is of the opinion that the Regulation only applies when passengers are embarked and disembarked in the Member State where the cabotage leg takes place.

When reference is made to cabotage, the operations by E.U. carriers are meant. Greece has liberalised its cabotage market even more widely than required by the Regulation by opening the maritime cabotage to cruise ships registered in a third country (Law 3872/2010).

The qualification of E.U. carrier may be subject to substantive ownership (at least 50 percent national equity) and effective control requirements (management by nationals). The operation may require the manning by a majority of E.U. national crew.

5.2 *Passenger Transport*

Regulation (E.U.) No 1177/2010 concerning the rights of passengers when travelling by sea and inland waterway aims to ensure the basic protection of passengers who travel by sea and inland waterway using passenger services or cruises in the event of transport disruption (delayed or cancelled departures), by imposing duties on the service provider viz.: information, care/assistance (supply of food and beverage, accommodation, communication, transport), rerouting, compensation and reimbursement. It also imposes special duties on the operator vis-à-vis disabled passengers/customers or passengers with reduced mobility.

With certain exceptions, the Regulation applies to maritime and inland waterway passenger services operated from or to ports in the E.U. and to cruise services with a port of embarkation in the E.U. The interrelationship between the Regulation (EU) No 1177/2010 and the Package travel Directive 90/314/EEC is addressed by the Regulation: the former does not apply in cases where a package tour is cancelled for reasons other than cancellation of the passenger service or the cruise (recital 20 of Regulation 1177/2010).

The Regulation N° 1177/2010 distinguishes between "commercial passenger services" on the one hand and "cruise services" on the other hand and reflects their different characteristics in the different scope of the rights that it grants to passengers. Commercial passenger services are passenger transport services operated between ports according to a published schedule. Cruises are defined as waterborne (by sea or inland waterway) services operated exclusively for the purpose of pleasure or recreation, supplemented by accommodation and other facilities, exceeding two overnight stays on board (art. 3 (t) Regulation No 1177/2010).

The Regulation 1177/2010 applies in respect of passengers travelling on a cruise where the port of embarkation is situated in the territory of a Member State. However articles 16(2), 18, 19 and 20(1) and (4) of the Regulation do not apply to those passengers (art. 2 (c) Regulation 1177/2010).

Contrary to commercial passenger services, cruises do not have a binding published schedule, therefore cruise passengers have no right under the Regulation to choose between rerouting and reimbursement in the event of cancelled or delayed departure (this issue is referred to the contract that the passenger concludes for the cruise services), neither a right to compensation in the event of delayed arrival.

5.3 River Operation

In the case C-17/13 before the E.U. Court of Justice the issue of distinguishing maritime from river cruises arose. The non-E.U. (Swiss) river cruise operator claimed that the concept of 'maritime cabotage' applies only to services that involve true sea transport and that the river cruise at issue does not involve such transport because, with the exception of the short passage through territorial sea, it takes place in internal (non-maritime) waters. The Swiss operator had applied for an authorisation to cross a stretch of Italian territorial sea because the size of the cruise vessel did not permit it to navigate an inland canal connecting two points of its itinerary. Italy had rejected the application on the ground that maritime cabotage was reserved for ships flying the flag of a Member State of the European Union.

The European Court of Justice observed that river cruise services fall within the scope of Council Regulation (EEC) No 3921/91 of 16 December 1991 laying down the conditions under which non-resident E.U. carriers may transport goods or passengers by inland waterway within a Member State. The Court ruled that the term 'sea' referred to by Regulation No 3577/92 is not limited to territorial sea within the meaning of the United Nations Convention on the Law of the Sea, signed in

Montego Bay (Jamaica) on 10 December 1982, entered into force on 16 November 1994 and approved on behalf of the European Community by Council Decision 98/392/EC of 23 March 1998, but also covers internal maritime waters which are on the landward side of the baseline of the territorial sea (referring to Case C-323/03, paragraphs 25 to 27). It considered that even if the Swiss operator's claim that the sole crossing of a stretch of sea in itself is too short to confer a maritime nature on the cruise, were well founded, (although according to the Advocate General even where only a limited part of a cruise takes place at sea, that suffices for the transport service to be classified as 'maritime cabotage') also other sections of the river cruise itinerary were situated in areas of navigation that form part of the internal maritime waters of the Italian Republic.

5.4 Multimodal Operation

As opposed to cargo transportation, there is no enacted legislation on multimodal passenger transportation. For the application of the package travel contract regime the transport mode or combination of transport modes is irrelevant.

5.5 Regular Service

In the case C-537/11 the European Court of Justice ruled that a cruise ship falls within the scope of Article 4a(4) of Council Directive 1999/32/EC of 26 April 1999 relating to a reduction in the sulphur content of certain liquid fuels with regard to the criterion of 'regular services', as laid down in its art. 2(3g), if it operates cruises, with or without intermediate calls, finishing in the port of departure or another port, provided that those cruises are organised at a particular frequency, on specific dates and, in principle, at specified departure and arrival times, with interested persons being able to choose freely between the various cruises offered, which is a matter for the referring court to ascertain.

5.6 Tax Exempted Travel

Very short (lasting only a few hours) cruises, exiting the national customs territory either or not by leaving the territorial waters and proceeding to the high seas without making a call abroad or at best making only a token (symbolic) port call, are sometimes organised with the sole goal of allowing travellers to purchase goods on board, that are exempted from indirect taxes and charges, such as VAT, customs and excise duties on products (spirits, tobacco, coffee, tea, perfumes, ICT devices, etc.). After the boat trip, the goods bought on board benefit from the duty-free exemption allowance for personal use or consumption when entered into the national territory. In this way the practice may distort competition with mainland traders.

In the case C-158/80 the EU Court of Justice ruled that a person who, during a cruise departing from a port of a Member State, does not call at a non-member country or who makes only a token call there and does not remain there for an appreciable period, that is to say, a period during which he has in fact an opportunity of making purchases, cannot be considered as a traveller coming from a non-member country, within the meaning of the regulation. Consequently the exemptions of customs duties, excise and turnover taxes on import provided for by Regulation 1544/69 and Directive 69/169 for goods contained in the personal luggage of travellers coming from a non-member country, cannot apply. The argument of simulation or abuse of right/fraud was not advanced.

In the case C-74/91 The European Court of Justice rejected the position that on the basis of art. 27(5) of the Sixth Directive (VAT), which allows the Member States to maintain, under certain conditions, special derogating measures intended to simplify the collection of the tax, cruises must be exempted, for the sake of simplification, even where they take place between two ports in Member States, on the alleged ground that sea transport operations are as a general rule carried out almost exclusively on the high seas, that is to say outside Community waters. The Court considered such exemption to be contrary to art. 26 of the Sixth Directive, that limits the derogation to transactions performed outside the Community.

The proposal[34] for a differential monetary exemption value between on the one hand "sea ferry or cruise passengers" and on the other hand "air travellers" was not retained by the Council Directive 2007/74/EC of 20 December 2007 on the exemption from value added tax and excise duty of goods imported by persons travelling from third countries.

5.7 Tourism

Services in the field of transport, falling within the scope of Title VI of Part Three of the TFEU (Treaty on the Functioning of the European Union), are excluded from the field of application of the EU Services Directive n° 2006/123 (art. 2,2 (d)).

On the other hand, services in the field of tourism are covered by this Directive (Recital 33).

The question arises under which category (either "transport" or "tourism") cruise operations are to be classified in this respect.

In the case C-340/14, the European Court of Justice examined whether the transportation of passengers by open sloop on internal waterways with the main

[34] European Parliament legislative resolution on the proposal for a Council directive on the exemption from valued added tax and excise duty of goods imported by persons travelling from third countries (COM(2006)0076 - C6-0078/2006 - 2006/0021(CNS)).

purpose of providing, for payment, tours and rentals for festive occasions, is a service to which the provisions of Directive 2006/123 apply, having regard to the exception set out in art. 2(2)(d) of that directive in respect of services in the field of transport.

The Court considered that *prima facie* transport means: conveying people or goods from point A to point B, so that when the starting and end point of a boat trip are the same, it does not constitute a service in the field of transport.

The Court held that the main purpose of the activity forms the criterion to define cruise services either as transport (conveyance) or as tourism (event related purposes: entertainment/recreation).

5.8 Competitive Activity

The Commission of the European Union ruled on the compatibility of state aid for the building of cruise vessels with competition law precepts, thereby assessing the cruise market.[35] In concentration cases the Commission assessed the relevant market of cruise operators,[36] cruise terminal operators[37] and cruise shipbuilding.[38]

Also the competition distortion issue came up in the context of the public procurement on the basis of a tender for scheduled maritime passenger transport in order to fulfil a public service obligation. Besides the maritime public transport service obligation, the same operator also offered commercial cruise services outside of the public procurement tender. The duty to keep separate accounts of the public service obligation operations and the commercial cruise operations for the purpose of transparency in order to disclose state aid was at stake.[39]

---

[35] Commission decision of 20 May 2008 on State aid implemented by France for building the cruise vessel Le Levant (C 74/99 (ex-NN 65/99), notified under document number C(2007) 5419 (2008/746/EC); Commission decision of 20 July 2005 on the State aid implemented by France for two cruise ships with a view to the development of French Polynesia (notified under document number C(2005) 2731) (2006/219/EC).

[36] Commission decision of 24 July 2002 declaring a concentration to be compatible with the common market and the functioning of the EEA Agreement. (Case No COMP/M.2706—Carnival Corporation/P& O Princess) (notified under document number C(2002) 2851) (2003/667/EC).

[37] Commission Decision of 17/06/2010 declaring a concentration to be compatible with the common market (Case No COMP/M.5756 - DFDS / NORFOLK) according to Council Regulation (EC) No 139/2004.

[38] Commission Decision of 27/03/2006 declaring a concentration to be compatible with the common market (Case No IV/M.4104 - AKER YARDS/CHANTIERS DE L'ATLANTIQUE) according to Council Regulation (EEC) No 4064/89. Summary of commission decision of 5 May 2008 declaring a concentration compatible with the common market and the functioning of the EEA Agreement (Case COMP/M.4956—STX/Aker Yards).

[39] EFTA surveillance authority decision No 205/11/COL of 29 June 2011 on the Supplementary Agreement on the Hurtigruten service (Norway).

5.9 *Fiscal Transit*

The transit stops (intended for excursion and sightseeing) as opposed to the turn-around stops (intended for the embarkation of new passengers or for final disembarkation) in the port of a third (non E.U.) country were also qualified as "stops" for the purpose of the fiscal exemption regime of sales on board of the cruise vessel (case C-58/04).

The report from the Commission to the Council on the place of taxation of the supply of goods and the supply of services, including restaurant services, for passengers on board ships, aircraft, trains or buses drawn up in accordance with Article 37(3) of Council Directive 2006/112/EC of 28 November 2006 on the common system of value added tax (COM/2012/0605 final) addresses the specific situation of supplies offered on board cruises (3.5). In this context a mere stopover for the purpose of visit/sightseeing/excursion was distinguished from the first point of embarkation or the last point of disembarkation.

5.10 *Package Travel*

Package travel implies a combination of at least 2 out of 3 constituent components, that are prearranged and sold at an inclusive price, viz. (i) transport (travel), (ii) accommodation (lodging and catering) and (iii) other tourist services (entertainment, practice of sport, excursions, attendance of cultural or sport events, etc.).

In the case C-585/08 before the E.U. Court of Justice, the question arose whether the services offered in case of a voyage by a freighter (cargo carriage vessel) are comparable to a cruise. The European Court of Justice held that a contract concerning a voyage by freighter, is a contract of transport which, for an inclusive price, provides for a combination of travel and accommodation that corresponds to the concept of 'package' within the meaning of Article 15(3) of Council Regulation (EC) No 44/2001 of 22 December 2000 on jurisdiction and the recognition and enforcement of judgments in civil and commercial matters, in the sense of art. 2(1) of Directive 90/314.

The further qualification criteria require that the other tourist service is significant (substantial) and not ancillary (art. 3,1 (b) and that the travel exceeds 24 hours or includes an overnight stay (art. 2,2) (Directive 2015/2302).

Services, which are intrinsically part of another travel service, are not considered as travel services in their own right. This includes, for instance, transport of luggage provided as part of carriage of passengers, minor transport services such as carriage of passengers as part of a guided tour or transfers between a hotel and an airport or a railway station, meals, drinks and cleaning provided as part of accommodation, or access to on-site facilities such as a swimming pool, sauna, spa or gym included for hotel guests. This also means that in cases where, unlike in the case of a cruise, overnight accommodation is provided as part of passenger transport by road, rail, water or air, accommodation is not considered as a travel service in its own right if the main component is clearly transport (Recital 17 and art. 3,1 (b) EU Directive 2015/2302).

However Rome I (art. 6,4 (b) and Brussels Ibis (art. 17,3) Regulations qualify in an implied manner a package travel contract in the sense of Directive 90/314/EEC as a contract of carriage (cfr. infra).

The Directive (EU) 2015/2302 on package travel and linked travel arrangements replacing the Directive 90/314/EEC is to be transposed by the EU Member countries by 1 January 2018 and to become effective by 1 July 2018 (art. 28).

The new directive updates current E.U. rules on package holidays by aiming to adapt to travel market developments in order to meet the needs of consumers and businesses in the digital era.

The Belgian act of 21 November 2017 on the sale of package travel, linked travel arrangements and travel services has transposed the Directive (EU) 2015/2302 into Belgian law. Hence its origin is supranational. As mentioned below the International Convention on Travel Contracts (CCV), Brussels, April 23, 1970 was denounced by Belgium.

6 Cruises and Passenger Carrier Liability

As mentioned before, a cruise qualifies as a package travel. As a package travel, a cruise includes a component part that consists of passenger transportation. As passenger carrier liability is often governed by a supranational or an international instrument, the question of the interrelationship between the package travel contract liability regime and the passenger carriage liability regime arises.

Art. 5,2 EEC Directive 90/314[40] allows the Member States to limit the compensation for malperformance in accordance with the international conventions governing services included in the package and art. 19 § 3 (old) Belgian Act of 16 February 1994 allows the package travel organiser to invoke the exonerations and limitations in international conventions governing services included in the package. For maritime cruises this means the maritime passenger carrier liability conventions, viz. the Athens 1974 (PAL) as amended (PALProt).

The EU Directive 2015/2302 (Recital 35 and art. 14, 4 and 5) and the (new) implementing/transposing Belgian Act of 21 November 2017 (art. 51 and 52) are aligned with the provisions of international conventions on maritime carrier liability and address the interrelationship between the package travel contract liability regime and the supra- and international treaties governing the passenger carrier liability

[40]EU Council Directive 90/314/EEC of 13 June 1990 on package travel, package holidays and package tours.

regimes (EU Regulation 392/2009[41] adopting the PALProt on maritime passenger carrier liability and EU Regulation 1177/2010 on maritime and inland navigation passenger rights).

The International Convention on Travel Contracts (CCV), Brussels, April 23, 1970 was denounced by Belgium. This convention distinguishes the package travel organizer liability for damage due to malperformance in the organization on the one hand and liability from any component part service provided by the package travel organizer himself on the other hand. In the former case the CCV provides the limitation regime itself (art. 13) and in the latter case it refers to the rules governing such services (art. 14): for the passenger carriage services, in the case of cruises this means the maritime carrier liability convention(s).

7 Cruises and Consumer Protection

E.U. Consumer protection contract law is transposed and implemented in Book VI of the Belgian Code of Economic Law. It also applies on cruise contracts. A special regime is e.g. elaborated with respect to the withdrawal period in case of distance sale (art. VI. 47 Belgian Code of Economic Law), save for catering and leisure services on a certain date or in a certain period (art. VI.53,12° Code of Economic Law). The provider is however under a duty to inform the consumer that no withdrawal right will apply (art. VI.45,11° Code of Economic Law).

7.1 Package Travel

The EU Directive 2015/2302 on package travel and linked travel arrangements addresses its interrelationship with consumer protection legislation.

The information requirements laid down in this directive are without prejudice to the information requirements laid down in other applicable European Union legislation, such as Directive 2000/31/EC on certain legal aspects of information society services, in particular electronic commerce, in the Internal Market (Directive on electronic commerce), Directive 2006/123/EC on services in the internal market, and EU Regulation 1177/2010 concerning the rights of passengers when travelling by sea and inland waterway.

Also the general consumer protection legislation does not exclude package travel from its field of application. The Directive 2006/123/EC of the European parliament and of the council of 12 December 2006 on services in the internal market does not exclude from its scope the package travel contracts as tourism services. The council

[41]EU Regulation 392/2009 dated 23 April 2009, implementing the Athens Convention of 13 December 1974 (PAL) as amended by the 2002 Protocol (PALProt).

Directive 93/13/EEC of 5 April 1993 on unfair terms in consumer contracts does not exclude package travel contracts from its scope of application. The Directive 2005/29/EC concerning unfair business-to-consumer commercial practices in the internal market ('Unfair Commercial Practices Directive') does not exclude package travel contracts from its scope of application. The same goes for the Directive 98/6/EC on consumer protection in the indication of the prices of products offered to consumers and the Directive 2006/114/EG concerning misleading and comparative advertising.

EU Directive 2015/2302 adapted certain EU consumer protection legislative acts. In particular, EU Regulation 2006/2004 on cooperation between national authorities responsible for the enforcement of consumer protection laws (the Regulation on consumer protection cooperation) applies to infringements of this Directive.

Also EU Directive 2015/2302 amended Directive 2011/83/EU on consumer rights (i.a. distance and off-premises sale) to ensure that certain consumer rights laid down in that directive also apply to package travel. This Directive 2011/83/EU on consumer rights did not apply to contracts which fell within the scope of the former Council Directive 90/314/EEC on package travel, package holidays and package tours (art. 3, 3 (g)).

The Directive 2015/2302 is without prejudice to rules on the protection of personal data laid down in Directive 95/46/EC on the protection of individuals with regard to the processing of personal data and on the free movement of such data, to be replaced by the General Data Protection Regulation (GDPR) 2016/679,[42] and to the Union rules on private international law, including Regulation (EC) No 593/2008[43] and Regulation (EU) No 1215/2012.[44]

7.2 *Protected Consumer ?*

Another problem arises with respect to the protection (e.g. compensation for malperformance) of the traveller when the cruise contract was concluded and paid (cruise purchased) by another person for account or in favour of a beneficiary: e.g. by an employer for his employees (as rewards or in the context of team building activities, etc.) or by a merchant for his customers (as a gift). To whom does the protective legislation apply: the beneficiary natural person, who attended the cruise or the contracting legal person who ordered and paid for the cruise?

The issue was addressed and solved by art. 1,5 of the Belgian Package Travel Act of 16 February 1994, that defined the protected traveller as the person who enjoys the

[42]Regulation (EU) 2016/679 on the protection of natural persons with regard to the processing of personal data and on the free movement of such data, and repealing Directive 95/46/EC (General Data Protection Regulation).

[43]Regulation (EC) No 593/2008 on the law applicable to contractual obligations (Rome I).

[44]Regulation (EU) No 1215/2012 on jurisdiction and the recognition and enforcement of judgments in civil and commercial matters.

benefit of the contract, irrespective of who concluded the contract or paid the price for it. The repealed Directive 90/314/EEC also defined the consumer (protected by its regime) as "the person who takes or agrees to take the package ('the principal contractor'), or any person on whose behalf the principal contractor agrees to purchase the package ('the other beneficiaries') or any person to whom the principal contractor or any of the other beneficiaries transfers the package ('the transferee') (art. 2,4). This Directive 90/314/EEC explained in its preamble that "... the consumer should have the benefit of the protection introduced by this Directive irrespective of whether he is a direct contracting party, a transferee or a member of a group on whose behalf another person has concluded a contract in respect of a package".

The Belgian Supreme Court[45] ruled (against the EU Directive 90/314/EEC) on the other hand that according to the Belgian Package Travel Contract Act of 16 February 1994 the buyer of a package travel, non-traveller (i.e. who is not the physical person travelling), does not qualify as the protected traveller, so that in the relationship between this non-travelling buyer and the travel organiser the regime of the Package Travel Contract Act of 16 February 1994 does not apply.

The new EU Directive 2015/2302 defines in its art. 3 (6) the "traveller" (as protected by its regime) also as the person who is entitled to travel on the basis of a contract concluded within the scope of the Directive. The new EU Directive 2015/2302 excludes from its field of application the package travel that is bought by a general agreement for the arrangement of business travel between a travel organiser and another professional (art. 2,2,c). Consequently a framework contract between an employer of travellers and a cruise company is outside the scope of the EU Directive. Travellers who did not contract the cruise themselves, but travel outside the context of a framework contract, remain protected by the regime of the new directive.

7.3 *Transport*

E.g. the Directive 2011/83/EU on consumer rights did not apply to contracts for passenger transport services, with the exception of article 8(2) (information requirements for distance contracts) and articles 19 (cost of the payment transaction) and 22 (express consumer consent with extra payment) (art. 3,3 (k)).

The Directive 2006/123/EC of the European parliament and of the council of 12 December 2006 on services in the internal market excludes from its scope: services in the field of transport, including port services, falling within the scope of Title V of the Treaty; (art. 2, 2 (d)).

[45] Cass., 15 May 2014.

8 Cruises and Labour Law

The precepts of maritime labour law are very relevant for cruise operations, as they relate to passenger vessel operations, but they are not specific for cruise operations.

A few examples of relevant but not cruise specific rules and precepts follow.

In the "French sailors" Case 167/73 the European Court of Justice ruled that a French law requiring a certain proportion of a French-flagged ship's crew to be of French nationality could not be enforced and had to be repealed because it was contrary to the EU precept of the free movement of persons for E.U. nationals.

Council Regulation (EEC) No 3577/92 of 7 December 1992 applying the principle of freedom to provide services to maritime transport within Member States (maritime cabotage) divides the responsibilities of all matters relating to manning of cruise liners carrying out mainland and island maritime cabotage between the flag state and the host state (art. 3).

8.1 *Binding Sectoral Collective Agreements*

In Belgium Joint Committees (employer-employee occupational consultation committees) are endowed with legislative/regulatory initiative and powers in specific economic sectors. In the present subject matter this is the case for the relevant sectors of inland navigation (nr. 139), transport (nr. 226), port activities (nr. 301), hotel business (nr. 302), entertainment business (nr. 304), merchant navy (nr. 316). The Joint Committee nr. 316 for the Merchant Navy concludes the (binding) collective agreements between the employer and employee representative organisations.

There are no such bodies specifically for the cruise business.

8.2 *International Law Implemented by Belgium*

The Act of 3 June 2007 on the seafarers' employment contract has conformed the Belgian law to the international conventions.

8.2.1 Maritime Labour Convention (MLC)

The Maritime Labour Convention (MLC) 2006 of the International Labour Organisation (ILO) protects the sailors by setting minimum safety, wellbeing and labour conditions.

Its degree of specificity is limited to the distinction between passenger ship and other than passenger ships. It does not acknowledge cruise operations as a specific category.

Belgium has ratified the MLC on 20 August 2013.

Signatory countries are entitled to inspect and apply the MLC on vessels flying the flag of non-signatory countries, when they berth in a port of a signatory country (flag and port state control issue).

The ILO Maritime Labour Convention (MLC) was incorporated into EU law by means of Council Directive 2009/13/EC of 16 February 2009 implementing the Social Partners' Agreement.

The ILO's international standards for this sector establish the minimum conditions for "decent work" and address almost all aspects of work including minimum requirements for work on a ship (such as minimum age, medical fitness and training) provisions on the conditions of employment such as work and rest time periods, wages, leave, repatriation, accommodation, recreational facilities, food and catering, occupational safety and health protection, medical care, welfare and social security protection. In addition, they address issues such as pensions and an internationally recognized document for seafarers (a seafarers' identity document) to assist in border control matters.

8.2.2 Standards of Training, Certification and Watchkeeping for Seafarers (STCW)

The IMO Maritime Safety Committee, at its ninety-first session, first considered proposals to amend the existing requirements of the STCW Convention[46] and the Code relating to passenger ships to address new challenges posed by the increased size of modern passenger ships and the large number of passengers on board, in particular concerning cruise ships.

The amendments to the STCW Convention and Code relating to passenger-ship specific training and to Parts A and B of the STCW Code comprise 4 distinct levels of training and familiarization: (i) passenger ship emergency familiarization, (ii) passenger ship crowd management training, (iii) passenger ship crisis management and (iv) human behaviour training, and ro-ro passenger ship training.

E.U. Directive 2008/106/EC, in particular Regulation V/2 of Chapter V of Annex I, includes mandatory minimum requirements for the training and qualifications of masters, officers, ratings and other personnel on passenger ships.

Amendments to regulations I/14 and V/2 of the STCW Convention and section A-V/2 of the STCW Code to improve the safety of (ro-ro and non-ro-ro) passenger ship safety have been actively promoted by the E.U., in particular after the Costa Concordia accident in January 2012.

These amendments are set out in the Annex of MSC 96/25/add.1. Paragraph 12.6 of the MSC 96 report (MSC 96/25) indicates that the amendments were foreseen to be adopted at MSC 97th session.

[46]International Convention on Standards of Training, Certification and Watchkeeping for Seafarers (STCW Convention).

8.3 Conflicts of Labour and Social Security Laws

The cruise sector activities often raise issues of conflicts of labour and social security law in case of employment of migrant workers or when the operator is established abroad, but operates in an E.U. member state, employing personnel that lives locally.

In accordance with Article 13(2)(a) of EU Regulation Nr. 1408/71 on the application of social security schemes to employed persons and their families moving within the European Community, a person is in principle subject to the social security legislation of the State in whose territory he/she is employed and is to contribute to that State's social security scheme.

In the case C-620/15 before the European Court of Justice employees worked on board of cruise ships on French rivers and were for the full duration of their contracts posted to ships sailing exclusively in France. The German employer however claimed that Swiss social security legislation applies to the employees concerned, relying on E 101 certificates stating that they are affiliated to the Swiss social security scheme. Art. 14(2)(a)(i) of the EU Regulation Nr. 1408/71 provides that a person employed by a branch and who is a member of the travelling or flying personnel of an undertaking operating international passenger transport services is to be subject to the legislation of the State in whose territory such branch is situated. The European Court of Justice held that without prejudice to abuse of right or fraud on the part of the worker or his employer however that the E 101 certificate issued in accordance with Article 12a(1a) of Regulation (EEC) No 574/72 is binding.

In the case C-292/14 Greek seamen, living in Greece were employed by a non-E. U. Member State (Malta[47]) established cruise vessel operator, whose vessel flew the Maltese flag, but whose actual head office was established in Greece. The operator became insolvent and the sailors' salaries remained unpaid. The question arose whether the sailors could claim from the Greek state on the basis of the employee protection guarantee[48] in case of employer insolvency. The European Court of Justice ruled affirmatively.

The various transport sectors, including inland waterways are within the scope of the E.U. Working Time Directive 2003/88/EC. However, it was not possible to reach agreement to apply the Directive's general rules on minimum daily and weekly rest periods or on limits to night work to mobile workers in Inland Water Transport (IWT) and other transport sectors. This was due to the distinctive working conditions and particular features of their activities (e.g. working and living at the workplace for certain periods, mainly cross-border activities). It was therefore provided that Member States must take the necessary measures to ensure that such workers are entitled to "adequate rest", without expressing this principle in specific units of time.

The absence of EU rules on numerical limits on daily and weekly working time, and night work of (IWT) mobile workers opened the way to a diversity of national

---

[47] Before 2004.

[48] Cfr. Directive 80/987/EEC relating to the protection of employees in the event of the insolvency of their employer.

rules, which created difficulties for transport companies and did not in all cases ensure sufficient protection for workers. This is particularly true for hotel personnel working in the river cruise industry. As the passenger navigation season lasts around eight months, hotel staff is away from home for a very long time. They often have to put up with very long working days and being accommodated for protracted periods in very small cabins.

Article 14 of the Working Time Directive provides for other instruments at E.U. level containing more specific working time requirements for certain occupations or occupational activities. Such specific requirements have been laid down by specific Directives for seafarers and for mobile transport workers in civil aviation and in cross-border rail services, based on European agreements concluded by the social partners for the sectors concerned.

Directive 1999/63/EC on working time for seafarers[49] does not contain any specific provisions for cruise workers.

Council Directive 2014/112/EU of 19 December 2014 implementing the European Agreement concerning certain aspects of the organisation of working time in inland waterway transport, concluded by the European Barge Union (EBU), the European Skippers Organisation (ESO) and the European Transport Workers' Federation (ETF), provides for a working time regime for seasonal work of mobile workers in inland waterway transport on passenger vessels. It defines:

– 'mobile worker' : as a worker employed as a member of travelling personnel by an undertaking which operates transport services for passengers or goods by inland waterway.
– 'season' : as a period of no more than 9 consecutive months out of 12 months in which activities are tied to certain times of the year as a result of external circumstances, e.g. weather conditions or tourist demand.

9 Cruises and Port Law

9.1 Waste Disposal

The Directive 2000/59/EC addressed Port Reception Facilities (PRF) for ship-generated waste (cfr. infra).

[49] *OJ L* 167, 2 July 1999, p. 33.

9.2 Competition Distortion by State Aid

State aid (within the meaning of Article 107 of the Treaty on the Functioning of the European Union (TFEU) issues were raised with respect to the public funding for the building of cruise terminals. Council Regulation (EC) No 659/1999 laying down detailed rules for the application of article 93 of the EC Treaty applies.

The E.U. Commission considered that:[50]

- For a measure to be qualified as State aid within the meaning of Article 107 (1) TFEU, the following cumulative criteria must be met: (i) use of state resources (public funds) (ii) selective advantage to the beneficiary undertaking and (iii) (potential) distorting effects on competition and trade between Member States.
- According to the European Court of Justice jurisprudence, whenever an entity is engaged in an economic activity, regardless of its legal status and the way in which it is financed, it can be considered as an undertaking for the purpose of the E.U. competition law. The Commission established in a series of decisions that the exploitation of some types of ports infrastructure, including cruise terminals,[51] can be considered as being of an economic nature.

  The use of the infrastructure, i.e. whether the infrastructure shall be commercially exploited or not, determines whether its construction constitutes an economic activity and falls within the scope of the E.U. state aid rules. It is irrelevant for the classification of a certain activity as economic whether a private investor would carry it out or not.[52]
- The public grant selectively advantages the beneficiary terminal operator as it strengthens its position vis-à-vis other competing port operators. The grant does not distort competition between the users (cruise shipping companies) if they are all eligible for equal and non-discriminatory access to the Terminal for use at market rates.
- The lifting of the restriction in the use of the cruise terminal from only as a "port of call" to a "turnaround port", was not found relevant in this respect. Ports of call handle only transit vessels, in contrast to "turnaround ports" where cruise journeys start and end. The latter are considered more attractive as they generate more income for cruise terminal operators.

[50]Commission Decision of 11 March 2014 in State aid case SA.35720 (2014/NN) — United Kingdom — Liverpool City Council Cruise Liner Terminal.

[51]For cruise terminals see Commission Decision of 19.06.2013 in State Aid case no. SA.35738 (2012/N) - *Aid for the upgrading of Katakolo port*, OJ C 204 of 18.07.2013;Commission Decision of 02.07.2013 in State Aid case no. SA.35418 (2012/N) – *Extension of Piraeus port*, OJ C 256 of 05.09.2013.

[52]Joined cases T-455/08 *Flughhafen Leipzig-Halle GmbH and Mitteldeutsche Flughafen AG v. Commission* and T—443/08 *Feistaat Sachsen and Land Sachsen Anhalt v. Commission* [2011] ECR II-0000. See also Case T-128/89 *Aéroports de Paris v. Commission* [2000] ECR II-3929, confirmed by the ECJ in Case C-82/01P [2002] ECR I-9297 and Case T-196/04 *Ryanair v. Commission* [2008] ECR II-3643, paragraph 88.

- The investment contributes to an objective of common interest, in particular the E.U. maritime transport policy.
- The public funding was necessary because for lack of it, neither the beneficiary nor any market investor would have undertaken the investment.
- With respect to proportionality, the cruise industry is subject to high seasonal variations, since transport of passengers by cruise ships is significantly reduced during winter time, which means that port revenues from cruise passengers are more volatile (i.e. subject to higher risk) and lower than the revenues from other types of ports that operate throughout the whole year. In view of this, a relatively higher aid intensity for cruise terminals than for other types of port infrastructure (e.g. freight ports) should not be regarded as unusual.

Consequently the aid was found necessary and proportional to address a well-defined objective of common interest and does not affect competition and trade between Member States to the extent that would be contrary to the common interest. On these grounds, the Commission concluded that the aid is compatible with the internal market pursuant to Article 107(3)(c) TFEU.

The General Block Exemption Regulation nr. 651/2014 (GBER) was amended in 2017 by extending it to ports and airports as regards aid for infrastructure building.

9.3 Port Services

Regulation (EU) 2017/352 of the European Parliament and of the Council of 15 February 2017 establishing a framework for the provision of port services and common rules on the financial transparency of ports pursues accessibility of ports and facilitation via simplification, but exempts passenger services from its application (art. 10), because the market access for providers of cargo-handling and passenger services is granted by means of public contracts (recital 38).

9.4 Port Fees and Charges

In the case C-435/00 the European Court of Justice held that art. 1 of Council Regulation (EEC) No 4055/86 of 22 December 1986 applying the principle of freedom to provide services to maritime transport between Member States and between Member States and third countries does not allow the application in a Member State of different harbour dues for domestic or intra-Community traffic on the one hand and traffic between a Member State and a third country on the other hand, if that difference is not objectively justified by the cost of the harbour services provided.

The Council[53] authorised a reduced rate of electricity tax for electric power directly provided to vessels at berth in a port ('shore-side electricity') pursuant to Article 19(1) of Directive 2003/96/EC and in line with Commission recommendation 2006/339/EC on the promotion of shore-side electricity for use by ships at berth in Union ports.

It is an environmentally less harmful way to satisfy the electricity needs of vessels lying at berth in ports, compared with the burning of bunker fuels by those vessels for on- board generation of electricity.

The measure pursues the reduction of ship CO2 emissions at berth in ports, thus improving overall air quality.

The measure is however not specific for cruise ship, as it also applies to other passenger and cargo vessels.

9.5 Port Security

The matter of port security (the question of checks on cruise ship passengers and, where appropriate, crew members) is addressed in the Common Manual for External Borders.

The EU Schengen Catalogue, EU Council, External Border Control, Removal and Readmission, Recommendations and Best Practices, February 2002, contains Recommendation 9.1.3. on cruise ships.

The Code of Practice on Security in Ports (Geneva 2003), is the product of the cooperation between the International Labour Organization (I.L.O.) and the International Maritime Organization (I.M.O.).

The amendment of the International Convention for the Safety of Life at Sea, 1974 (SOLAS) created a new Chapter XI-2 on special measures to enhance maritime security. This Chapter XI-2 of SOLAS is supplemented by the International Ship and Port Facility Security (ISPS) Code, which contains, inter alia, requirements that relate to the security of the ship and to the immediate ship/port interface. The overall security of port areas was left to further joint work between ILO and IMO.

The E.U. security policy is less developed in other transport domains than aviation. The overall objective of the EU's maritime transport security policy is to protect citizens and economies from the consequences of unlawful intentional acts against shipping and port operations. The basis of the E.U. legislation was the International Ship and Port Security (ISPS) Code on security in ports and on ships laid down by the International Maritime Organization (I.M.O.). The ISPS Code was introduced in the EU legislation in 2004 with the Maritime Security Regulation

[53] Council Implementing Decision (EU) 2015/993 of 19 June 2015 authorising Denmark to apply a reduced rate of taxation on electricity directly provided to vessels at berth in a port, in accordance with Article 19 of Directive 2003/96/EC; Council Implementing Decision 2014/722/EU of 14 October 2014 authorising Germany to apply a reduced rate of taxation on electricity directly provided to vessels at berth in a port in accordance with Article 19 of Directive 2003/96/EC.

725/2004. It was complemented by Directive 2005/65/EC that addressed elements of port security not covered by the Regulation. The EU maritime security legislation transposing and enhancing the ISPS Code, provides a harmonised interpretation, implementation and monitoring of the international rules. It is applicable to ships engaged in international and domestic voyages and the ports and port facilities serving them. The Member States ensure that security assessments are periodically reviewed, taking into account changing threats. The E.U. Commission undertakes inspections to monitor the application of this legislation. An alleged option would be to consider some security issues for ferries and cruise ships based on a dialogue with the Member States and the stakeholders.

10 Cruises and Environment Protection

The Commission decision (EU) 2016/611 of 15 April 2016 on the reference document on best environmental management practice, sector environmental performance indicators and benchmarks of excellence for the tourism sector under Regulation (EC) No 1221/2009 on the voluntary participation by organisations in a Community eco-management and audit scheme (EMAS) (notified under document C(2016) 2137) must be mentioned.

This sectoral reference document (SRD) primarily covers Best Environmental Management Practices (BEMPs) within organisations that provide accommodation, food and beverage services, or that manage tourism destinations or offer and reserve travel, accommodation or activities for tourism (travel agents and tour operators). This document does not directly target the cruise sector. However, a number of the BEMPs described may, to a certain extent, also be applicable to cruises.

10.1 Ballast Water

The I.M.O. International Convention for the Control and Management of Ships' Ballast Water and Sediments (Ballast Water Management or BWM Convention), London 3 February 2004, entered into force on 8 September 2017 and applies indiscriminately to all types of vessels (art. 1,12). At present there is no direct E.U. law on ballast water, although Regulation (EU) No 1143/2014 of the European Parliament and of the Council of 23 October 2014 on the prevention and management of the introduction and spread of invasive alien species recognises the BWM Convention as one of the possible management measures for invasive species of concern. See also the European Environment Agency.

10.2 Air Pollution

The International Convention for the Prevention of Pollution from Ships (MARPOL 73/78) (e.g. also Annex VI Regulations for the Prevention of Air Pollution from Ships) apply indiscriminately to all types of vessels.

The Energy Efficiency Design Index (EEDI) sets technical standards for improving the energy efficiency of certain categories of ships which will, in turn, lead to less CO2 emissions. The EEDI applies only to the new ships and there are no specific measures in place for existing ships. The 63rd Marine Environment Protection Committee of the I.M.O. in 2012 stressed that the EEDI cannot be used for existing ships and the use of Energy Efficiency Operational Index (EEOI) is currently not mandatory. Furthermore, vessel types with high relevance in Europe such as cruise ships and ferries are not yet covered by the EEDI. Therefore, developing such a measure in a European context would require the E.U. to replace or supplement existing efficiency standards adopted at the global level. In this respect special attention was paid by the E.U.[54] to environmental standards for Arctic cruise ship tourism (cfr. I.M.O. Polar Code).

Directive 2014/94/EU on the deployment of alternative fuels infrastructure provides for the shore-side electricity supply during mooring time for inland waterway vessels and seagoing ships in maritime and inland ports in conformity with the technical specifications set out in point 1.7 of Annex II.

10.3 Waste (Garbage from Ships (Marine Litter)

The International Convention for the Prevention of Pollution from Ships (1973) and its Protocol (1978) (MARPOL73/78), address in particular sewage (Annex IV) and garbage (Annex V).

The EU Directive 2000/59 on port reception facilities for ship-generated waste and cargo residues (PRF Directive) has the same aim as MARPOL, viz. the protection of the marine environment. Its main precepts are:

- Creation of an adequate port reception facility for garbage from ships, that call at the port
- Development of a waste removal plan
- Timely declaration by the ship of the quantity of the ship's garbage to be discharged
- Contribution by the ship in the cost of reception, removal and processing
- Exchange of information on discharge for the purpose of enforcement.

[54] Joint staff working document: The inventory of activities in the framework of developing a European Union Arctic Policy Accompanying the document Joint communication to the European Parliament and the Council Developing a European Union Policy towards the Arctic Region: progress since 2008 and next steps (SWD/2012/0182 final) nr. 2.3.

On the Belgian national (federal) level, the EU directive 2000/59 was transposed via the Royal Decree on the ships inspection with respect to discharge of ship garbage and cargo residue, amending the Royal Decree of 20 July 1973 containing the Maritime Inspection Regulation.

On the Belgian Flemish (regional) level it was transposed by the Decree of the Flemish Government containing the Flemish Regulation on the sustainable management of recyclable and waste material (VLAREMA) (see section 5.2.10).

Directive 2000/59/EC on port reception facilities for ship-generated waste and cargo residues (PRF Directive) applies to recreational craft, including cruise ships, but it does not contain any specific provisions on cruise activities.

However in this context the cruise operations show a few special features. Given the increasing size and the number of passengers transported by its vessels, the cruise sector was said to produce significant amounts of waste to be delivered in accordance with the Directive. The on-board treatment of sewage is significant: for cruise ships it is assumed to be up to 80% and can be up to 100% for the larger sized modern cruise ships. In the shipping sector, cruise vessels in particular have incinerators on board. Regarding the information obligation burden imposed by the PRF Directive, it was indicated that it generally takes between 30 and 60 min to complete and submit the advance waste notification, but an average sized cruise ship spends roughly 8 man-hours to retrieve and/or estimate the necessary information on the amounts of waste to discharge.[55]

A proposal was launched for a Directive of the European Parliament and of the Council on port reception facilities for the delivery of waste from ships, repealing Directive 2000/59/EC and amending Directive 2009/16/EC and Directive 2010/65/EU.[56] The Commission staff working document, accompanying the document Communication from the Commission "A European Strategy for Plastics in a Circular Economy" (COM(2018) 28 final) addresses the issue of plastic waste from sea-based sources such as shipping, including cruise ships. The Packaging and Packaging Waste Directive (PPWD) n° 94/62/EC applies on top of these legal requirements: in most Member States, packaging is governed by Extended Producers Responsibility (EPR) schemes, defining the fees to be paid by producers. Those rules on sewage deliveries intending to avoid illegal discharges and thus to protect the marine environment, apply indiscriminately to cruise activities.

[55] Commission staff working document, impact assessment, Accompanying the document Proposal for a Directive of the European Parliament and of the Council on port reception facilities for the delivery of waste from ships, repealing Directive 2000/59/EC and amending Directive 2009/16/EC and Directive 2010/65/EU (COM(2018) 33 final, SWD(2018) 22 final).

[56] Cfr. the The Commission staff working document containing an impact assessment, accompanying the document.

11 Jurisdiction and Arbitration

11.1 Jurisdiction

EU Regulation n° 1215/2012 dated 12 December 2012 on jurisdiction and the recognition and enforcement of judgments in civil and commercial matters (Brussels 1bis) contains the jurisdiction regime. Consumer contracts providing for an inclusive price a combination of travel and accommodation, are governed by the special jurisdiction regime of the Regulation (art. 17,3 Regulation). The consumer is protected by mandatory (save limited party autonomy as per art. 19) rules to the effect of guaranteeing the consumer the opportunity to institute proceedings in the court of the country of his/her domicile (art. 17) and by the restriction to bring actions against the consumer only in the court of the country of his/her domicile (art. 18).

The contractual forum selection clause is valid and effective, subject to:

- the restrictions as per art. 19 Regulation Brussels Ibis Regulation, referred to above
- substantive validity under the national law of the designated court
- evidence in writing or equivalent (electronic) format (art. 25 Brussels Ibis Regulation).

11.2 Arbitration

U.K. established cruise lines may apply the ABTA[57] code of conduct that provides for an arbitration scheme to resolve disputes. In Belgium cruise lines may stipulate the travel contract conditions of the Belgian Travel Dispute Commission (Commission de Litiges Voyages). These conditions provide for Alternative Dispute Resolution (ADR) via mediation or arbitration for package travel contract disputes. This Commission is not competent for bodily injury claims, extra-contractual disputes, non-inclusive travel or assistance insurance, etc. The same issue as the one discussed below with respect to the choice of law arises, viz. the distinction between the legal status of the consumer contract partner and the consumer third party beneficiary of a contract concluded by a professional.

[57] Previously: Association of British Travel Agents.

12 Choice of Law

The E.U. Regulation 593/2008 (Rome I) contains a conflicts of laws regime, with universal application: it means that it applies regardless whether the applicable law is or is not the law of a Member State (art. 2). The normal regime is party autonomy in the choice of law (art. 3 Rome I Regulation). For lack of an express choice of law, the law of the service provider's country of residence applies (art. 4,1(b) Rome I Regulation). The Rome I Regulation contains however specific conflicts of laws rules for (i) passenger transportation (art. 5,2) and (ii) for consumer contracts and in particular for package travel contracts (art. 6).

In case of a passenger transportation contract, for lack of an express choice, the law of the passenger's country of residence applies if the place of departure or destination are situated there (art. 5,2 first subparagraph). The choice of law for a contract of passenger transportation is further restricted to a limited number of options (art. 5,2 second subparagraph).

In case of consumer contracts the law of the consumer's country of residence mandatorily applies (art. 6,1). A limited party autonomy in the choice of law is offered, provided that the mandatory protections guaranteed by the law of the consumer's country of residence are respected (art. 6,2).

In case a passenger transport contract qualifies as a consumer contract, it is however excluded from the consumer contract regime, except when it amounts to a package travel in the sense of Directive 90/314/EEC (art. 6,4 (b)).

As a consumer, the passenger is protected by the mandatory application of the protective legal provisions of his/her country of residence (art. 6 Rome I Regulation).

The contractual choice of law is valid and effective, subject to:

- the restrictions referred to above
- the consent and material validity according to the designated national law (art. 10 Rome I Regulation)
- the formal validity according to the law of the consumer's country of residence (art. 11 Rome I Regulation).

The criterion for the application of the conflicts of laws regime protecting the consumer, is the capacity of the customer concluding the contract (art. 6 Rome I Regulation). However the customer concluding the contract may be a person acting in a professional capacity (e.g. the employer or the merchant) whereas the beneficiary may be a natural person acting in a private capacity outside any trade or profession. The Regulation does not expressly acknowledge the case where the contract is concluded by a customer acting in a professional capacity (e.g. employer or merchant) in favour of a third natural person acting in a private capacity. With respect to the case of passenger transportation the problem is solved, because the Rome I Regulation directly imposes the application of the law of the passenger's country of residence, irrespective of the contracting customer's country of residence (art. 5,2 Regulation). The same solution however cannot be found in case the beneficiary is a consumer.

Art. 8 of the Rome I Regulation determines the national law applicable to the employment contract.

13 Conclusion

Cruise operations are to a large extent governed by the legal regime of maritime passenger activities. In that capacity the applicability of the consumer protection, package travel and carrier liability regimes are relevant issues. A few interesting qualification issues have arisen, such as: cabotage, maritime or river operation, transit.

References

Mozuni M, Jonas W (2016) Rise of alternative business models in the era of expensive megaships. In: Papathanassis A (ed) Cruise business development, safety, product design and human capital. Springer, Cham, pp 59–60

Phlypo L, Gheysen S (2014) Strategisch beleidsplan voor toerisme en recreatie aan de Kust 2015–2020. Brugge, Westtoer, p 41. www.toerismevlaanderen.bewww.toerismevlaanderen.be

Des aspects légaux des croisières en Bulgarie

Diana Marinova

Résumé Le rapport presenté est consacré surtout aux questions suivantes – l'importance de croisières, les rulles générales et spécifiques applicables aux croisières, les passagers croisières, le choix applicable aux croisières, la jurisdiction et l'arbitrage. Dans le droit bulgare il n'existe assez de règles concernant les problèmes particulières de croisières.

Le but général de ce papier est de présenter la réglementation bulgare dans cette domaine. Le contenu consiste en analyse sur l'importance des croisières, les règles générales et spécifiques applicables aux croisières, les passagers aux croisières comme consommateurs, les voyages combinés, les tours en paquet, les excursions organisées, les règles de travail relatives aux travailleurs de croisières, les règles sur les ports concernant les croisieres, la jurisprudence et l'arbitrage, le choix de la loi applicable et les sources juridiques dans le domaine de cette recherche.

Une attention spéciale est donné aux questions relative au droit international privé et surtout à l'autonomie de la volonté.

Dans la conclusion on mentionne les poins dans lesquels doit etre concentré la strategie nationale et la possibilité à créer sur cette base une réglementation juridique spéciale concernante les croisières.

1 Introduction

Pendant les dernières années on développe les voyages par des charges de courses, ainsi des croisières thématiques. Cependant, il faut souligner que dans ces cas les passagers et les charges de courses sont bulgares, mais les navires ne départent de ports bulgares et ils ne débarquent dans ces ports non plus. Le plus souvent il s'agit de croisières à la Mer Noire et la Mer Méditerranée.

La popularisation de villes maritime bulgares d'une façon convenable au niveau global pourrait attirer l'attention de compagnies croisières. Ce sont des villes avec une histoire très ancienne et très riche, ou on pourrait connaitre la culture unique de

D. Marinova (✉)
Universite d'Economie Nationale et Mondiale (UENM), Sofia, Bulgaria

C. Fresnedo de Aguirre (ed.), *Legal Aspects of Cruises*, Ius Comparatum - Global Studies in Comparative Law 56, https://doi.org/10.1007/978-3-030-83090-8_3

notre pays. De telle façon ce type de tourisme pourrait se développer en tourisme culturel.

Ce rapport est consacré surtout aux questions suivantes - l'importance de croisières, les rulles générales et spécifiques applicables aux croisières, les passagers croisières, le choix applicable aux croisières, la jurisdiction et l'arbitrage, etc... En ce qui concerne les autres problèmes de croisières dans le droit bulgare n'existe assez de règles convenantes.

Le but général de ce papier est de présenter la réglementation bulgare dans cette domaine. Cependant, il est très important à souligner que ce rapport est le premier et l'unique à ce moment essai en Bulgarie à faire un papier concernant les problèmes légaux de croisières. Pour cette raison il est possible parfois à trouver dans ce recherche des imperfections.

2 L'importance des croisières

C'est un problème de notre politique nationale en général concernant le droit maritime en principe.

L'intérêt vers les croisières de la part de bulgares est constant, mais malheureusement les grands navires qui servent les meilleures destinations débarquent rarement de Bulgarie à cause de deux raisons générales:

Premièrement, la Bulgarie n'est pas assez intéressante destination croisière, non seulement parce que la cote bulgare de la Mer Noire n'a pas de ports convenables, mais aussi à cause du fais que les villes maritimes bulgares ne sont pas populaires au niveau global. De plus, notre pays se trouve en direct voisinage avec la République Turque et la République Grèce, avec ses dizaines îles. Le tourisme dans ces pays est parfaitement organisé et développé. Pour cette raison nous ne sommes pas en condition à proposer un produit touristique ayant la possibilité de se porter concurrent.

Deuxièmement, l'autre cause, ce sont les passagers, qui départent de Bulgarie et qui débarquent en Bulgarie. Ces passagers sont d'un nombre assez limité. Par comparaison d'autres nationalités, qui préfèrent ce type de tourisme, les bulgares sont très peux. Pourtant, il y a quelques compagnies qui proposent des voyages incluant des visites de villes bulgares. On pourrait mentionner Azamara Club Cruises incluant l'ancienne ville maritime Nessebar (monument, protégé par l'UNESCO) dans son programme croisière à Mer Noire. Ainsi, Holland American Line inclue les grandes villes maritimes bulgares Varna et Bourgas dans ses grands voyages méditerranéens, durant plus d'un mois. On pourrait mentionner aussi les compagnies MSC, Costa Cruises, Norwegian Cruise Line et Celestrial Cruises.

3 Des règles générales et spécifiques applicables aux cruisières

Notre système juridique contient une régulation générale applicable aussi aux croisières. Au niveau international c'est la Convention d'Athènes de 1974 relative au transport de passagers et leur bagage par mer et le Protocole de 2002 dont la République de Bulgarie fait partie. La convention contient des termes juridiques – transporteur, transporteur de fait, contrat de transport, navire, passager, bagage, transport international, etc. . .Le champ d'application de la Convention est établi dans l'article 2. Elle est applicable au chaque transport international si les conditions les suivantes ont été accomplies:

- Le navire navigue sous le pavillon d'un pays-membre de la Convention ou
- Il a été enregistré dans un pays-membre de la Convention ou
- La place de départ ou d'arrivée selon le contrat de transport se trouve dans un pays-membre de la Convention.

La responsabilité des parties du contrat de transport est aussi un objet de règles juridiques détaillées dans la Convention, ainsi que la prescription. On applique des règles conventionnelles directes, mais aussi des règles de collision qui renvoient vers la législation nationale.

En ce qui concerne la forme de preuve du contrat, on applique la loi de la place de formation du contrat (lex loci contractus), même si le passager est monté au bord du navire dans un autre pays. En ce qui concerne le contenu du contrat des formules d'attachement (connecting formulae – engl.) différentes sont possibles et notamment les suivantes:

- La loi du pays de transporteur (lex patriae) – la commodité de cette loi s'exprime dans le fait que les passagers d'une nationalité différente montent et débarquent aux ports différents. L'application d'autres formules (comme des lois applicables) est soit impossible, soit non convenable.
- La loi de pavillon (lex banderae) qui peut être la loi du pays du transporteur, mais il est possible aussi le navire d'être loué par un transporteur d'une autre nationalité, différente de celle du navire.
- La loi du pays d'exécution d'action (lex loci actus) – aux actions, effectuées avant le moment auquel le passager monte au bord du navire et après le moment auquel le passager débarque du navire.

En ce qui concerne les règles spécifiques sur les croisières, il faut constater que malheureusement en Bulgarie il n'y a pas de règles pareilles.

4 Passagers aux cruisières comme consommateurs

Les passagers débarquent dans notre pays rarement. Il n'existe pas de statistiques concernant ces passagers. En Bulgarie l'offre de voyages croisières n'est pas assez grande. Chez nous est encore visible la conviction que les croisières sont très chères pour les bulgares, car non seulement qu'ils doivent acheter le paquet croisière, mais aussi les billets d'avion vers le point de départ. Cependant, les grandes compagnies touristiques proposent des paquets au prix convenable pendant des périodes de promotion.

Ici il est convenable à mentionner des règles relatives aux consommateurs qui s'agissent aussi aux passagers croisières.

Au niveau national c'est la Loi de protection de consommateurs. Cette loi est applicable aussi aux passagers en croisières, car ils sont des consommateurs du produit touristique croisière. Ce produit est un service selon la loi si mentionnée. De plus, la République de Bulgarie est un membre à part entière de l'Union Européenne et les actes de l'Union relatifs à la protection de consommateurs font partie de la législation interne bulgare. Ces actes ont une priorité si les règles nationales sur les matières identiques sont contradictoires aux actes européens. Plus spécialement, il s'agit de Régulation "Rome I" (Régulation № № 593/2008 du Parlement Européen et du Conseil de 17.06.2008). Pourtant, il faut souligner que notre loi nationale est complétement harmonisée avec les actes de l'Union Européenne.

5 Voyages combinés, tours en paquet ou excursions organisées

Une partie de compagnies touristiques s'efforcent á développer des produits effectifs et se portant concurrent, dans le but d'innover ses offres. Le développement de l'industrie touristique et l'augmentation de nécessités de consommateurs incite la nécessité de création de méthodes alternatives de divertissements et recréation.

L'un des éléments de base dans le processus de développement d'une politique de marketing, c'est l'analyse des parts fortes et faibles du produit proposé.

Dans le but d'examiner les possibilités de développement du produit croisière au niveau national, il est admissible à présenter une analyse, surnommé "SWOT". Selon cet analyse les parts fortes sont comme suit: l'attraction du produit; l'accessibilité; presque tous les groupes de passagers sont couvertes;les prix pourraient être en concurrence;une haute qualité de produits proposés;un haut niveau de service;des traditions crées dans les compagnies différentes;des prix et des tarifs en promotion;le prix inclue tous les services nécessaires (all inclusive);facile à planifier;repos et excursion ensemble;une riche gamme de produits et services; innovations;des conditions souples d'annulation. D'autre part, il faut pas oublier les parts faibles et notamment - itinéraires saisonniers;publicité insuffisante au marché bulgare;manque d'itinéraires départant de Bulgarie;des hauts prix des billets d'avion vers les points de départ.

6 Règles de travail relatives aux travailleurs de croisières

Le Code du travail contient une réglementation générale, car il est applicable à toutes les relations juridiques concernant les contrats du travail individuels. Le Code du travail est harmonisé avec toutes les règles européennes. Ces règles juridiques sont nationales et elles sont particulièrement appliquées aux cases de travailleurs de croisières, qui sont des citoyens bulgares. Dans le droit bulgare il n'y a pas de règles de travail spécifiques relatives aux travailleurs de croisières.

7 Règles sur les ports qui sont importants en ce qui concerne les croisières

Les croisières débarquent rarement aux ports nationaux bulgares et ils ne sont jamais un point de départ. Pour cette raison en Bulgarie il n'y pas de règles sur les ports concernant les croisières.

8 Jurisprudence et arbitrage

La loi de l'arbitrage international commercial contient les règles générales en Bulgarie. Cette loi est applicable à la réglementation de litiges concernant les contrats internationaux et leur résolution par l'arbitrage. Ce sont les cas, auqels dans les contrats il y a une clause arbitrale. Cette clause doit être valide. La loi nationale est applicable, indépendamment de son nom, a tous les litiges résolus par l'arbitrage. Le nom de la loi est conforme et corresponde à la Loi-type de l'UNCITRAL sur la base de laquelle cette loi a été adoptée. En effet, la loi est applicable à l'arbitrage aux contrats nationaux et internationaux. Le Code de Procédure Civile contient la résolution de litiges par la cour.

On pourais ici mentionner les clauses d'arbitrage, généralement inclus dans les conditions générales de contrat de transport de passagers par mer, c'est-à-dire, non seulement en croisières.

Il n'y a pas de règles spécifiques relatives aux croisières. Pour cette raison on ne peut pas indiquer une jurisprudence nationale.

9 Choix de la loi

Le système juridique bulgare possède des règles juridiques générales sur le choix de la loi relatives aux contrats internationaux qui soient applicables aux croisières. Le Code de droit international privé contient la réglementation générale. Ainsi, la Régulation Européenne Rome I (la Régulation № 593/2008 du Parlement Européen et du Conseil de 17.06.2008) possède des règles générales. Selon l'article 93, §1 du Code de droit international privé les contrats sont réglementés par la loi choisie. Le choix doit être express ou doit poursuite d'une façon claire de clauses du contrat ou de circonstances de la relation contractuelle. Selon le §2 du même article on suppose, que les parties ont accepté comme applicable la coutume, qu'elles connaissent ou qu'il est bien connu dans le commerce international et constamment observe par les parties de contrats de même type dans ce domaine de commerce. Les parties peuvent choisir la loi applicable au contrat ou à une partie du contrat. Elles ont la possibilité toujours à changer la loi applicable choisie. Il est nécessaire à observer des règles impératives du pays, dont le droit est lié avec tous les éléments du contrat. La Convention de Rome de 1980 relative à la loi applicable aux contrats s'applique et le Code de droit international privé est harmoniseé avec cette convention. Selon ces sources juridiques générales du droit international privé est admissible l'autonomie de la volonté aux contrats avec un élément international (art. 93, §1 du Code de droit international privé et art. 3, §1, préposition première de la Convention de Rome). Cette admissibilité poursuit seulement de lex fori. La liberté du choix de la loi est réglementée maintenant selon la Régulation Européenne Rome I (la Régulation № 593/2008 du Parlement Européen et du Conseil de 17.06.2008). Selon l'art. 3 de cette Régulation le contrat est réglementé par la loi choisie par les parties du contrat. La réglementation est identique avec la réglementation si mentionnée du Code de droit international privé et de la Convention de Rome, c'est-à-dire la Régulation rétablie les règles de la Convention de Rome concernant les questions de l'admissibilité du choix non-express de la loi applicable, ainsi que les questions d'admissibilité de "dépeçage" du contrat et de la possibilité de choix de la loi applicable suivie après le première choix. Le §4 de l'art.3 de la Régulation Rome I est un nouveau moment par comparaison à la Convention de Rome et au Code de droit international privé. Si au moment du choix de la loi tous les éléments du contrat se trouvent dans une ou plusieurs pays-membres, le choix de la loi, différente du droit d'un pays-membre, n'est pas au préjudice de l'application du droit communautaire. Si c'est admissible, ce choix n'est pas au préjudice du droit national du pays-membre (le pays de la cour), dans lequel sont introduites les règles du droit communautaire. Le choix de la loi applicable ne doit pas être contradictoire aux normes impératives de la loi et aux beaux mœurs (l'art.93, §1 et art.3 du Code du droit international privé; art. 9 de la Loi des obligations et des contrats). La jurisprudence arbitraire de la cour d'arbitrage auprès de Chambre du commerce et de l'industrie bulgare (BCCI – angl.) est la même. Cette cour est la plus grande et la plus vieille cour d'arbitrage en Bulgarie et elle fonctionne auprès de la plus grande organisation d'employeurs en Bulgarie.

Les raisons d'appliquer une loi étrangère selon la législation bulgare sont les suivantes:

- Choix d'une loi applicable par les parties du contrat;
- Exigence du droit international privé bulgare;
- Exigence du droit international privé d'un autre pays d'en face;
- Exigence d'un traité international, dont la Bulgarie fait partie.

L'application du droit étranger est indépendante de la présence ou non de la réciprocité. Pour les cas, dans lesquels la réciprocité est demandée, la loi a établi une présomption réfutable – la réciprocité est présumée jusqu'on prouve le contraire (l'art. 47, §2 du Code de droit international privé). En manque de choix de la loi on applique la loi, qui est la plus proche au contrat (lex proxima). On présume que c'est la loi du pays ou la partie avec la prestation caractéristique a son séjour habituel ou son siège central au moment de la formation du contrat. Si le contrat est d'une liaison plus proche avec un autre pays, on applique le droit de ce pays. C'est la surnommée "clause de dérogation". La réglementation de la Convention de Rome (l'art.4) et du Régulation Rome I (l'art.4, §4) est identique. Le Code bulgare a été harmonise avec la Régulation Européenne. Cette réglementation ne s'applique aux transports de marchandises, mais les transports de passagers, et plus spécialement, les croisières, ne sont pas exclues d'une façon expresse. A la différence de la Convention de Rome, ou il n'y a pas de règles relatives à la loi applicable aux contras de transport de passagers, §2 de l'art.5 de la Régulation Rome I prévoit une réglementation spéciale, selon laquelle les parties ne peuvent choisir comme applicable que la loi du pays où se trouve:

- le séjour habituel du passager, ou
- le séjour habituel du transporteur, ou
- la place du siège central du transporteur, ou
- la place de départ, ou
- la destination.

Cette limitation prenne en considération le fait que le passager est plus faible partie de la relation juridique et l'autonomie de volonté sans limites pourrait courir des risques. En manque de choix de la loi du pays, où se trouve le séjour habituel du passager, la loi applicable est la loi du pays où se trouve le séjour habituel du transporteur ou la place du siège central du transporteur, à condition que la place de départ ou la destination se trouve dans le même pays. Si c'est n'est pas le cas, on applique la loi du partie avec la prestation caractéristique du contrat – le pays du séjour habituel du transporteur. La surnommée „clause de dérogation" (au sens mentionnée) ici aussi est en vigueur.

Pour les croisières on applique la réglementation générale du Code du droit international privé et de la Régulation Rome I, consacrée aux contrats de consommateurs, car les passagers sont des consommateurs. Pour cette raison on applique ainsi la loi nationale spéciale – la Loi de protection de consommateurs. Pour ces contrats l'autonomie de la volonté est ainsi admissible. Des limitations de choix de cette liberté sont imposées par les règles impératives du pays, où se trouve le séjour habituel du consommateur. En manque de choix de la loi on applique la loi du pays où se trouve le séjour habituel du consommateur.

10 Sources juridiques applicables aux croisières

Comme il a été mentionné au paragraphes précédants, dans le domaine analysé la réglamentation juridique est nationale et internationale. Ainsi, il faut souligner qu'une partie considérable de cette réglamentation est inclue dans les acts européens et surtout, dans le régulations europeenes. Ces acts font partie de règles nationales de pays membres de l'UE et elles sont obligatoires pour ces pays, pour la Bulgarie y compis. D'autre part, la réglamentation jurisique de croisières en Bulgarie n'est que générale. Il n'y a aucune loi ou n'importe quel act normatif relatif spéciallement aux croisières.

Au niveau international les sources les plus importantes contennant des règles générales sont la Convention d'Athènes de 1974 relative au transport de passagers et leur bagage par mer et le Protocole de 2002 dont la République de Bulgarie fait partie.

Au niveau national la première place possèdent les acts européens impératifs et plus spécialement la Régulation "Rome I" (Régulation № 593/2008 du Parlement Européen et du Conseil de 17.06.2008). Ces règles juridiques sont nationales et elles sont particulièrement appliquées aux cases de choix de la loi concernant les croisières.

Finalement, parmi les sources juridiques nationales on pourrait mentionner encore une foi la Loi de protection de consommateurs, le Code du travail, la Loi de l'arbitrage international commercial et le Code de droit international privé qui contienne la réglementation générale en Bulgarie relative à la choix de la loi applicable, harmonisée avec la Régulation Rome I.

11 Conclusion

Les croisières présentent une niche non-développée au niveau national du tourisme. De plus cette constatation est relative pour les aspects juridiques aux croisières.

Les aspects de base, dans lesquels doit être concentrée la stratégie bulgare de marketing, sont liés aux points suivants:

- Développement d'une stratégie active de publicité dans le but de populariser des produits croisières au niveau national;
- Etablissement de relations durables avec les compagnies croisières, dans le but d'engager les ports maritimes et fluviaux bulgares dans les itinéraires croisières;
- Renouvellement de contrats avec les compagnies croisières et établissement d'itinéraires ayant comme un point de départ des ports bulgares.

En ce que concerne plus spéciallement les aspects juridiques il est nessesaire à souligner qu'il manque une réglementation spéciale et se probleme pourrait etre résolu après la réalisation des aspects de base ici mentionnés.

Ce recherche est le début d'une analyse plus approfondie de cette matière assez intéressante.

Bibliographie

Басмаджиева, С. Д., Позициониране на круизния продукт на туроператорите като възможност за повишаване на конкурентоспособността на българския туризъм, в: Сборник от Научно-приложна конференция на Нов Български Университет (НБУ), Департамент „Администрация и управление" на тема: Стратегически визии:ефективно управление за икономически, организационни и социални трансформации (иновации-институции-бизнес), София, 2013, с.422-428 (Basmadjieva, S. D., Positionnement du produit croisière d'agences touristiques comme une possibilité d'augmenter le capacité de concurrence du tourisme bulgare, dans : Recueil d'une Conférence scientifique et pratique "Des visions stratégiques: management effective dans le bit de transformations économiques, organisationnelles et sociales" (innovations-institutions-business), Sofia, 2013, pp 422–428)

Градева, В. К., Тенденции в развитието на круизния туризъм през 2015 г., в: Сборник от Пета научна студентска конференция, София, УНСС, с.33-39 (Gradeva, V. K., Des tendencies dans le développement du tourisme croisière en 2015, dans: Recueil de la Cinquième Conférence scientifique d'étudiants, Sofia, Université d'économie nationale et mondiale, pp. 33–39)

Грозева, М., Тенденции на развитие на българския туризъм на модерния пазар, Географски институт на БАН, София, 2006 (Groseva, M., Des tendencies de développement du tourisme bulgare dans le marché modern, Institut de géographie auprès de l'Académie Bulgare des sciences, Sofia, 2006)

Димитрова, Д., Туристическа агенция "Александър Тур", Малка история на круизните пътувания, 2010 (Dimitrova, D., Agence touristique Alexander tour, Une petite histoire de voyages en croisières), http://www.kruizi-blog.alexandertour

Министерство на икономиката и енергетиката, Стратегия за устойчиво развитие на туризма в България 2014-2030 (Ministère de l'économie et de l'énergétique, Stratégie de développement du tourisme en Bulgarie 2014-2010), http://www.tourism.government.bg/bg/kategorii/strategicheski-documenti/nacionalna-strategiya-za-ustoychivo-razvitie-na-tourizma-v-Bulgaria

Цонев, Н., Маркетинг в туризма, София, Издателски комплекс – УНСС, 2013 (Tzonev, N., Marketing en tourisme, Sofia, Maison d'édition – Université d'économie nationale et mondiale, 2013)

Christopher Holloway, J., Marketing for Tourism, 2004

Middleton VTC, Clarke JR, Marketing in Travel and Tourism

Seaton AV, Bennett MM (2006) The marketing of tourism products: concepts, issues and cases. Ed. Thomson, UK

Legal Aspects of Cruises from a German Perspective

Klaus Tonner

Abstract There is no specific cruise law in Germany separated from other laws. The general rules of consumer law and maritime law apply to cruises. As far as the relation to the passenger is concerned a cruise is regarded as a package travel. This is to say that the German implementation of the Package Travel Directive of the European Union is applicable. This transposition is part of the Civil Code (Bürgerliches Gesetzbuch, BGB). With regard to labour law and environmental law the German legislator implemented international Conventions by national acts. The most important are the Seearbeitsgesetz (Maritime Labour Act), which implemented the Maritime Labour Convention, and the Seeumweltverhaltensordnung (Maritime Environmental Regulation), which is relevant for the enforcement of the MARPOL Convention.

In the field of jurisdiction and choice of law Regulations of the European Union directly apply without being transposed to German law. These Regulations include consumer protection rules, which are applicable to cruises.

1 Introduction

Cruise law is no separate, well structured body of law. It is composed by elements of other fields of law. In relation to passengers, this is consumer protection law, in relation to seamen employment law. Consumer law and employment law are contract law, this is to say that the principle of freedom of contract is applicable, but as both—consumers and employees as well—are regarded as the weaker party to the contract, many rules were adopted by the states, which protect the weaker party by mandatory provisions in contract law. This is the case not only with regard to national, but also to supranational rules. In particular consumer protection law in Germany is today dominated by European law, which leaves only little autonomy to the national legislator. But also international law applies, with regard to cruises

K. Tonner (✉)
University of Rostock, Rostock, Germany
e-mail: klaus.tonner@uni-rostock.de

C. Fresnedo de Aguirre (ed.), *Legal Aspects of Cruises*, Ius Comparatum - Global Studies in Comparative Law 56, https://doi.org/10.1007/978-3-030-83090-8_4

especially the Athens Convention.[1] Also in labour law the sailor as the weaker party shall be protected. Here an international Convention, the Maritime Labour Convention (MLC) dominates the applicable law.[2]

But not only contract law is relevant for cruises. The protection of the environment is today an issue of utmost relevance. Again, it is an International Convention, drafted by the International Maritime Organisation, which is the core of International Maritime Environmental Law. This Convention enables authorities of the states to act against polluters. This kind of law is, in terms of German law, public law (öffentliches Recht).[3]

After discussing in short the economic background of the German cruise industry (Sect. 2), we will summarize the national, supranational and international provisions which apply to the cruise industry and their customer and employees (Sect. 3). Then we will deal more deeply with the sectors of consumer law (Sect. 4), in particular package travel law (Sect. 5), labour law (Sect. 6), environmental law (Sect. 7), jurisdiction and arbitration (Sect. 8), and choice of law (Sect. 9).

2 The Importance of Cruises

2.1 Germany as Destiny and as Source Market

Germany is more a source market than a destiny for cruises, at least sea cruises. In 2016, there was a passenger revenue of 2.018 billions compared to 1.812 in 2015 and 1.219 in 2010.[4] This number includes cruises, which were sold in Germany including those cruises, which began outside of Germany.

The number of passengers, who booked a cruise to North and West Europe including the British Islands and the Baltic Sea is 36.0% of the above mentioned number of 2.018 billions. These passengers usually embark for their cruise in a German port. The biggest German ports, where cruises use to begin, are Hamburg, Rostock-Warnemünde and Kiel. These ports are relevant mainly for embarkation and disembarkation, not for port visits. The second biggest area is the Mediterranean Sea. It has a market share of 33.5% of the above mentioned 2.018 billions of passengers. Passengers, who book a cruise in the Mediterranean Sea, usually travel by air to the port of embarkation. They either book a package consisting of the cruise and the flight, or they book cruise and flight separately. This distinction causes legal problems, with which we will deal later.

[1] As introduction to consumer protection in cruise law cf. Tonner (2013).

[2] As introduction to the German maritime labour law cf. Maul-Sartori (2013).

[3] As introduction to international maritime law cf. Heintschel von Heinegg, in: Ipsen (2014), p. 817 et seq.

[4] Source: Cruise Lines International Association Germany and Deutscher ReiseVerband (2016).

Passengers, who book a cruise beginning in a German port, use to travel to this port by their own car or by railway. They may stay one or two days at the port of embarkation before the cruise begins.

It is difficult to sort out the number of non German passengers, who embark in one of the German ports. The Baltic Sea is a famous area for cruises during the summer with cities as Riga, Stockholm or St. Petersburg, which attracts not only Germans, and Kiel and Warnemünde are conveniently located at the southern part of the Baltic Sea to start a cruise. In particular Warnemünde developed as an embarkation and disembarkation port for Baltic Sea cruises not only for Germans. There is a near-by small airport, which serves for charter flights for cruise passengers from Italy and Spain. In 2016, 71,000 passengers reached their cruise ship in this way.

Warnemünde is the only port which plays a relevant role for port-of call visits. Even Berlin is offered as a destination for day excursions by bus or rail. Contrary, Kiel and Hamburg are ports nearly only for embarkation and disembarkation.

The statistics about Germany do not allow a distinction between German passengers and passengers of other nationalities. Only the total number of passengers who book a cruise is available. The same is true for the money they spend on land. Only Rostock Port published a study of the University of Rostock, according to which in 2015 passengers and crew members spent more than 15 millions EUR in local and regional retail sale, accommodation, and transport.[5]

Contrary to that European statistics are more instructive. According to a study of CLIA Europe,[6] the global source markets of Europe consisted in 2015 of 23.19 million passengers. 12.13 millions of them came from North America, 3.21 from Asia/Pacific, and only 28.4% of the total from countries of Europe.

We estimate that figures for Germany will show a higher percentage of passengers from European countries, as tourists from North America will probably show a greater interest in the Mediterranean Sea and in Western Europe than in the Baltic Sea and to Northern Europe, which is the main region for cruises departing from Germany.

It may be of interest to have a look to figures for embarkation, disembarkation and port visits of the three leading German ports to show the relation of port visits to embarkation/disembarkation. Hamburg had in 2015 232,000 embarking and 232,000 disembarking passengers and 55,000 port call visits, Warnemünde 132,000 embarking and 131,000 disembarking passengers and 222,000 port call visits, whereas Kiel had 209,000 embarking and 214,000 disembarking passengers and 35,000 port call visits.

---

[5] Source: www.rostock.port.de/Kreuzschifffahrt.html.

[6] CLIA Europe (2015).

2.2 *Importance of the Cruise Business for the German Economy*

CLIA Europe published figures about the total economic impacts of the cruise industry to the European economy.[7] The study distinguishes mining and construction, manufacturing, wholesale and retail trade, transportation and utilities, hospitality, financial and business, and personal service. The total amount for Europe is 40,946 million EUR for expenditures, and 360,571 jobs. Unfortunately the study includes only aggregated figures for Europe as a whole, but no detailed data for countries. Nevertheless, the study mentions that the direct expenditures for Germany were 2946 millions EUR in 2015, and 45,673 jobs.

German shipyards play a major role with regard to cruise ships. The Meyer Werft in Papenburg in Lower Saxonia (Niedersachsen) is one of the leading cruise shipyards in the world. The shipyards in Wismar, Warnemünde and Stralsund, located all at the Baltic Sea, are now overtaken by the Genting group of Malaysia and Hongkong and will also be active in building cruise ships.

Many cruises in Germany are offered by German based cruise lines. The biggest three are AIDA Cruises in Rostock, a branch of Costa Crociere in Genoa (Italy), part of the Carnival Group, TUI Cruises in Hamburg, a joint venture of TUI (Hanover) and Royal Carribean Cruises, and Hapag Lloyd in Hamburg, part of the TUI group.

2.3 *Relevance for the Labour Market*

Germany accounted for 12.7% of the total European employment impacts with an estimated 45,673 jobs. Manufacturing, with 12,241 impacted jobs, accounted for 27% of the total employment impact. As Europe's largest cruise passenger source market, Germany's transportation (excluding cruise line employees), trade, and hospitality industries accounted for a combined 19.5% of the total employment impacts. The cruise lines directly employed an estimated 4538 German residents as crew and administrative staff, which accounted for 10% of the total employment impacts.[8]

[7] CLIA Europe (2015).

[8] CLIA Europe (2015), p. 22.

3 General and Specific Rules Applicable to Cruises: International, European and National Law

Cruise law as applicable in Germany is a mixture of international, European and national rules. It is characterized by many international Conventions, which are ratified in Germany and directly applicable. Among them are the Athens Convention which grants for compensation to passengers in case of damages,[9] and the MARPOL Convention, which is the core legal instrument for environmental protection.[10] Both Conventions are drafted by The International Maritime Organisation (IMO). Contrary to that, the Maritime Labour Convention,[11] drafted by the International Labour Organisation (ILO), which is of utmost relevance for the protection of seamen, is not directly applicable, but transposed by a national act, the Seearbeitsgesetz (Sea Labour Act).[12] In case of a dispute the provisions of the Seearbeitsgesetz have to be applied, whereas in case of damages a passenger may base his claim directly on a provision of the Athens Convention. It is not unusual, that international Conventions are either directly enforceable or only addressed to the states which have to implement them by national legislation, but nevertheless it is somehow puzzling that in the same field—cruise law—both types of Conventions are applicable.

The matter is even more complicated. The MARPOL Convention is directly applicable, but needs national enforcement rules. The German legislator therefore adopted the Seeumweltverhaltensordnung.[13] Contrary to that, the Athens Convention needs no national amendment for enforcement, but a parallel Regulation at the level of the European Union exists.[14] In general, there is in most cases an interplay

---

[9] Athens Convention relating to the Carriage of Passengers and their Luggage by Sea, Adoption: 13. December 1974; entry into force: 28. April 1987; Protocol 2002, Adoption: 1. November 2002; Entry into force: 23. April 2014, www.imo.org/en/about/conventions/pages/Athens-convention-relating-to-the-carriage-of–passengers-and-_their-luggage-by-sea-(pal).aspx (last access 17.11.2017).

[10] International Convention for the Prevention of Pollution from Ships (MARPOL), Adoption: Convention 1973, Bundesgesetzblatt (BGBl.) 1982 II, p. 2; Protocol 1978 (1987), BGBl.. 1996 II, p. 399; 1997 (Protocol 1997); Entry into force: 2. October 1987 (Annexes I and II), 19. May 2005 (Annex VI), www.imo.org/en/about/conventions/pages/international-convention-for-the-preven tion-of-pulltion-from-ships-(MARPOL).aspx. (last access 17.11.2017).

[11] Maritime Labour Convention (MLC, 2006); adoption: 23.6.2006, entry into force: 20.8.2013; www.ilo/org/dyn/normlex/en/f?p=NORMLEXPUB:12100::NO21100:P:12100:ILO_CODE: C186; Amendments (2014) to the Maritime Labour Convention, adoption: 11.6.2014; entry into force: 18.1.2017, www.ilo.org/ilc/ILCSessions/103/reports/WCMS_248905lang—en/index/htm (last access 17.11.2017).

[12] Seearbeitsgesetz (SeeArbG) of 20.4.2013, Bundesgesetzblatt (BGBl.) I, p. 868.

[13] Seeumweltverhaltensordnung (SeeUmwVerhV) of 13.8.2014, Bundesgesetzblatt (BGBl.) I, p. 1371.

[14] Regulation(EU) No. 392/2009 of the European Parliament and of the Council of 23 April 2009 on the liability of carriers of passengers by sea in the event of accidents, OJ No. L 131 of 28.5.2009, p. 24.

between Conventions and amending national rules, but this interplay is different from sector to sector.

A similar interplay exists with regard to the relation between European and national law. There are regulations, which are directly applicable. The most important of them are the regulations dealing with the law of jurisdiction (Brussels Ia Regulation)[15] and of applicable law (Rome I Regulation).[16] These laws are completely European law; no amending national law applies. But the Athens Convention includes a provision dealing with jurisdiction. This rule precedes the European provisions. A further European regulation, which needs no national implementation, is the Sea Passengers' Rights Regulation, so that a claim of a passenger may be based on a provision of this Regulation.[17]

But European law also provides for Directives, which must be transposed by member states to their national law. The most important of them is the Package Travel Directive, which is applicable to cruises.[18] This Directive is implemented by §§ 651a et seq. of the BGB (Civil Code), so that a claim must be based on a provision of the BGB. The new Package Travel Directive of 2015, which replaces the Directive of 1990, is only recently implemented in Germany by an amendment of §§ 651a et seq. BGB.[19]

Nearly nothing is left to an autonomous law making process of the national legislator. Cruise law in Germany exists either in directly applicable international Conventions (Athens Convention, MARPOL Convention) and European Regulations (Sea Passengers' Rights Regulation), or in international Conventions (Maritime Labour Convention) and European Directives (Package Travel Directive) which need transposition to national law.

Cruise law is no separate body of law within or beside maritime law. The rules we have to deal with in this contribution are applicable to all sorts of ships, be it passenger ships or cargo ships. This is in particular true for environmental law and

---

[15] Regulation (EU) No. 1215/2012 of the European Parliament and of the Council of 12 December 2012 on jurisdiction and the recognition and enforcement of judgments in civil and commercial matter, OJ No. L 351 of 20.12.2012, p. 1. This Regulation replaces the Brussels I-Regulation, Council Regulation (EC) No. 44/2001 of 22 December 2000 on jurisdiction and the recognition and enforcement of judgments in civil and commercial matters, OJ No. L 12 of 16.1.2001, p. 1.

[16] Regulation (EC) No. 593/2008 of the European Parliament and of the Council of 17 June 2008 on the law applicable to contractual obligations (Rome I), OJ No. L 177 of 4.7.2008, p. 6.

[17] Regulation (EU) No. 392/2009 of the European Parliament and of the Council of 23 April 2009 on the liability of carriers of passengers by sea in the event of accidents, OJ No. L 131 of 28.5.2009, p. 24.

[18] Directive 2015/2302/EU of the European Parliament and of the Council of 25 November 2015 on package travel, linked travel arrangements, amending Regulation (EC) 2006/2004 and Directive 2011/83/EU of the European Parliament and of the Council and repealing Council Directive 90/314/EEC, OJ No. L 326 of 11.12.2015, p. 1.

[19] Drittes Gesetz zur Änderung reiserechtlicher Vorschriften v. 17.7.2017, Bundesgesetzblatt (BGBl.) I, p. 2394. Cf. overview by Führich (2017).

labour law. The passenger is protected as a consumer regardless whether he is on a cruise ship or a cargo ship, as the Pammer case of the CJEU clearly shows.[20]

4 Cruise Passengers as Consumers

4.1 General Remarks

As already mentioned, the Package Travel Directive and its transposition to the BGB is the core for consumer protection for cruises (below Sect. 4). Also other general consumer protection legal instruments apply to cruises, in particular those requiring the indication of a total price (below Sect. 5).

A further legal instrument of consumer protection is the Sea Passengers' Rights Regulation, which is an instrument of European law and—as a regulation—directly applicable in the member states and so in Germany (for details cf. below Sect. 4.3). As an international legal instrument the Athens Convention applies (cf. below Sect. 4.2).

The Conventions and Regulations discussed below are a mixture of international, supranational and national origin. The Athens Convention, which applies to international carriage, is of international origin, EU Regulations 392/2009[21] and 1077/2010, which apply to every carriage, which departs from an EU port, are of supranational origin. The Athens Convention and European law leave only little room for national law.

4.2 Athens Convention

There are three pieces of legislation which apply to carriage of passengers on sea in general including cruises. The first is the Athens Convention 2002, which deals with compensation for death and injury and for loss and damages of luggage. This Convention is applicable to international carriage. It was ratified by the EU member states and by the European Union as well and came into force in the EU on 23 April 2014.[22] Before that date the EU adopted Regulation (EU) 392/2009, which is identical with the Athens Convention 2002, but amended its scope to all carriages

[20] CJEU 7.12.2010, combined cases C-585/98 and C-144/09 – Pammer and Hotel Alpenhof.

[21] Regulation (EU) No. 392/2009 of the European Parliament and of the Council of 23 April 2009 on the liability of carriers of passengers by sea in the event of accidents, OJ No. L 131 of 28.5.2009, p. 24.

[22] Council Decision of 12 December 2011 concerning the accession of the European Union to the Protocol 2002 to the Athens Convention relating to the carriage of passengers by sea and their luggage, 1974, with the exception of Articles 10 and 11 thereof (2012/22/EU), OJ No. L 8 of 12.1.2012, p. 1.

by sea within the EU. So, a cruise, which calls only on ports of one member state, is not under the scope of the Athens Conventions, but the same liability rules apply according to the regulation mentioned.[23]

The German Commercial Code (Handelsgesetzbuch, HGB) also includes provisions about the liability of sea carriers (including cruises) to passengers (§§ 556 to 552). These rules were adapted to the Athens Convention and its Protocol 2002, so that is does not make a difference, whether the Athens Convention, Regulation (EU) No. 392/2009 of the provisions of the HGB are applicable. Also the Internal Waterways Act (Binnenschifffahrtsgesetz, BinSchG)[24] was adapted to the Athens Convention. This Act is of practical relevance, as it is applicable to national river cruises which are covered neither by the Athens Convention nor by Regulation (EU) No. 392/2009. With regard to liability § 77 BinSchG refers to the HGB. This link is the only practical relevance of the HGB provisions today. The HGB rules as such are not applicable to national river cruises, and national sea cruises are covered by Regulation (EU) No. 392/2009, which prevails over national law such as the HGB.

4.3 *Sea Passengers' Rights Regulation*

Within the frame of its "passengers' rights" policy the European legislator adopted the Sea Passengers' Rights Regulation in 2010. This Regulation is applicable to cruises, but in its main focus are carriages from A to B, this is to say in particular ferry services. It provides for compensation in cases of cancellation and delay in terms of a price reduction.

But it also includes provisions for passengers with reduced mobility, which are of relevance for cruises. Carriers and port authorities shall have in place non discriminatory access conditions for disabled passengers. Such passengers have a right to assistance in ports and on board ships free of charge.

[23]Cf. for the relation of the Athens Convention and the Sea Passengers' Rights Regulation Lagoni (2007). The Regulation was at that time a proposal of the Commission (COM [2005] 592).

[24]Gesetz betreffend die privatrechtlichen Verhältnisse der Binnenschifffahrt (Binnenschifffahrtsgesetz, BinSchG), Bundesgesetzblatt (BGBl. III No. 4103-1, as amended by BGBl. 2016, I, p. 1578.

5 Package Travels

The EU Package Travel Directive is the most important legislative instrument for complaints of cruise passengers against the cruise line. The Package Travel Directive came into force originally in 1990[25] and was implemented by Germany in 1995. The German legislator amended the contract law sections of the Civil Code (Bürgerliches Gesetzbuch) by a special chapter about package travel (originally §§ 651a to 651k BGB). As the original Package Travel Directive was a minimum standard Directive, the German legislator could maintain some rules which are more in favour for the consumer than the Directive, in particular rules about a strict liability for lacks of conformity which gives the consumer a right for a price reduction in many cases.

With regard to the wording of the Directive—and the German transposition provision (§ 651a BGB)—it is everything than clear whether a cruise is a package, as a package consists of at least two travel services, usually carriage and accommodation. But in a case of 2010[26] the CJEU declared that a cruise—in this case a voyage by freighter—is a package, because transport and accommodation are involved. The German Supreme Court (Bundesgerichtshof, BGH) declared in 2012, that a cruise is a package.[27] According to these decisions a cruise is a package notwithstanding whether it is combined with carriage to and from the embarkation respectively disembarkation port, or with other services as land excursions or special entertainment aboard.

If the cruise line sells the cruise and the carriage to and from the port, it is a package which includes the carriage. In the case the carriage is late and the passenger misses the ship, it is the responsibility of the cruise line either to bring him to the next port or to compensate him. But if the traveller books the carriage to the port separately, it is his own risk that the carriage is in time.

Another question is whether the retailer (travel agent) through whom the consumer books the cruise and—separately, but at the same occasion—the carriage to and from the embarkation port, may become liable. The Bundesgerichtshof originally decided that the travel agent is not liable, this is to say that he does not become a tour operator, who sells a package and is liable according to the package travel law, if he sells the cruise and the carriage to and from the port of embarkment and disembarkment.[28] But in another case, where the flight to the port of embarkment had to be cancelled due to volcano ash and the consumer could not reach the ship, the

[25] Council Directive of 13 June 1990 on package travel, package holidays and package tours, (90/314/EEC), OJ No. L 158 of 23.6.1990, p. 59.

[26] Court of Justice of the European Union (CJEU) 7.12.2010, combined cases C-585/98 and C-144/09 – Pammer and Hotel Alpenhof.

[27] Bundesgerichtshof (BGH) 18.12.2012, X ZR 2/12, NJW 2013, 1674 with note Tonner (2013), p. 1675.

[28] Bundesgerichtshof (BGH) 30.9.2010, Xa ZR 130/08, Neue Juristische Wochenschrift (NJW) 2011, p. 599.

Bundesgerichtshof decided, that this was a case of force majeure, so that the consumer could ask for repayment of the money paid for the cruise.[29]

But the new Package Travel Directive, which was adopted in November 2015 (Directive [EU] 2302/2015) and now transposed to German law,[30] provides for an intricate distinction between a tour operator and an intermediary. According to the new Directive a travel agent, who sells the cruise and the carriage, may become liable as if being a tour operator for carriage and cruise, if he does not book cruise and carriage separately. These new rules have to be applied as from 1. July 2018.[31]

Price reductions for lack of conformity play a big role in German travel law, also with regard to cruises. There are many lower court decisions, as the thresholds to go to court in Germany are lower than in many other states, and conciliation is not in the forehand. Here are some examples of lower court decisions, just to illustrate, about what German cruise passengers complain: The Amtsgericht München had to decide whether it is a lack of conformity if there is no water in the swimming pool, even if the sea is calm.[32] If the temperature in the cabin is sometimes too cold and sometimes to hot, this is a lack of conformity according to the Oberlandesgericht Koblenz.[33] There has to be information about a non smoking policy before departure.[34] A sofa, which is not long enough to sleep on it, also constitutes a lack of conformity.[35] These are only examples, the list of which could be easily amended.[36]

Typical lacks of conformity with regard to cruises are replacements of ships and shortfall of land excursions. The replacement of a ship gives the consumer the right to cancel the trip before departure.[37] Shortfall of land excursions are often the result of political unrests.[38] The cruise line and the passenger may cancel the whole cruise for that reason before departure, but after departure it is the risk of the cruise line whether they are able to call at the ports which are promised. It depends on the relevance of a port for the whole trip, whether the cruise line has to compensate the consumer if a port is missed, even if the reasons are political unrest or bad weather conditions.[39]

[29] Bundesgerichtshof (BGH) 18.12.2012, X ZR 2/12, NJW 2013, p. 1674.

[30] Supra n. 19.

[31] Cf. for the new rules Führich (2017).

[32] Amtsgericht (AG) München 27.4.2001, 274 C 23427/00, Reiserecht aktuell (RRa) 2002, 25.

[33] Oberlandesgericht (OLG) Koblenz, 13.6.2012, 5 U 1501/11, Neue Juritsiche Wochenschrift – Rechtsprechungsreport (NJW-RR) 2012, p. 1082.

[34] Oberlandesgericht (OLG) Rostock 27.10. 2008, 1 U 183/08, NJW 2009, p. 302.

[35] Amtsgericht (AG) Offenbach 31.1.2001, 31 C 6017/00, RRa 2001, p. 97.

[36] The so called Würzburger Tabelle (Würzburg list) includes a comprehensive list of court decisions, http://würzburger-tabelle.de.

[37] Bundesgerichtshof (BGH) 18.12.2012, X ZR 2/12, NJW 2013, p. 1674.

[38] Landgericht (LG) Leipzig 27.4.2005, 1 S 4/05, NJW-RR 2005, p. 995 (two Egyptian ports).

[39] Bundesgerichtshof (BGH) 14.5.2013, X ZR 15/11, NJW 2013, p. 3170 – Greenland; Amtsgericht (AG) Rostock 3.8.2016, 47 C 103/16, RRa 2017, p. 122.

5.1 *Price Indication*

In Germany, it was disputed whether the cruise line could charge aboard a service fee (tip, in German: Trinkgeld) in addition to the price for the cruise, because this might not be in line with the principle of indicating the total price, which is part of German and European law. In a recent judgment, the Bundesgerichtshof decided, that a compulsory service fee has to be included into the total price.[40] The clause about the service fee is regarded as void even in the case that the consumer may require the repayment of the fee or a part of it aboard if he is not satisfied with the services.

In principle, European consumer law requires the indication of the total price. This follows from the Unfair Commercial Practices Directive (UCPD) and the Consumer Rights Directive (CRD) as well. According to Art 7 (4) of the UCPD it is an unfair omission of an essential information, if the trader does not inform about "the price including taxes." This information must be given in the case of an invitation to purchase, this is to say in a brochure or on a website which enables the consumer to book the trip without seeking for further details. The UCPD is transposed to German law by the UWG (Gesetz gegen den unlauteren Wettbewerb, Act against unfair competition).

The CRD provides for pre-contractual information duties, among them the "total price including taxes", Art 5 (1) (c) for other than distance and off-premises contracts and Art 6 (1) (e) for distance and off-premises contracts. These provisions are implemented in German law by Art 246 and 246a EGBGB (Einführungsgesetz zum BGB, Introduction Act to the Civil Code).

6 Labour Rules on Cruises' Workers

The German legislator adopted in 2013 the Seearbeitsgesetz (SeeArbG, Sea Labour Act),[41] which supersedes general labour law. There is no general codification of general labour law in Germany, but it consists of a mixture of case law and specific statutes. The Seearbeitsgesetz is one of these many specific pieces of legislation.

The Seearbeitsgesetz is applicable for German ships, this is to say for ships under German flag. It is enforced by the Berufsgenossenschaft Verkehrswirtschaft (Employers' Liability Insurance Association for Transport). This authority is responsible with regard to sea transport not only for insurance but also for sea labour law, and in particular for the so called flag state control and for port state control of ships with a non German flag.

The port state control has its legal basis not only in the Maritime Labour Convention (MLC), but also in European law. In 2009, a Directive on port state

[40] Bundesgerichtshof (BGH) 7.5.2015, I ZR 158/14, Monatsschrift für Deutsches Recht (MDR) 2015, p. 1433 – Der Zauber des Nordens.

[41] For details of the SeeArbG cf. Bubenzer (2014) and Zimmer (2015).

control was adopted,[42] amended in 2013.[43] The purpose of these Directives is not only to enforce labour law, but also environmental law.

The Seearbeitsgesetz is a transposition of the MLC. The MLC came into force on 20. August 2013, and for Germany on 14. August 2014. There are no specific rules for workers on cruise ships. The Seearbeitsgesetz is applicable for cargo ships and all kind of passenger ships as well. Also the European legislator adopted a transposition of the MLC.[44]

The MLC—and so the Seearbeitsgesetz—provide for minimum rules for seamen (minimum age, medical fitness, training, recruitment), employment conditions (rest hours, leave, repatriation etc.), accommodation and health protection.

7 Rules on Environment

Emissions of cruise ships, in particular sulphur and CO_2, caused a political debate in Germany, which was not restricted to legal aspects.[45] In particular people living next to the ports complained. Local politicians have to balance the economic advantages of having the cruise ships within their ports, and the disadvantages caused by the significant emissions for the people living there. The term "Dreckschleuder" (colloquial for notorious polluter) was used very often in the public debates for cruise ships.

It was not the public debate, but international law, which determined the cruise industry to look for improvements. The MARPOL Convention, drafted by the International Maritime Organisation (IMO), came into force originally already in 1973. The Convention as such is only a framework; important are the annexes, which need separate ratification. The most important of them is annex VI, which came into force originally at 19.5.2005, revised at 1.7.2010. Its annex VI contains limit values for sulphur-, nitrogen oxide and Particulate Matter for Emission Control Areas (ECA) and higher limits for the worldwide maritime traffic.[46] The maximum sulphur oxide content in fuel in ECAs was since 2010 1.0% und reduced to 0.5% since 1.1.2015. For the worldwide maritime traffic it is for the moment 3.5% and will be reduced to 0.5% as from 2020. Similar standards apply for nitrogen oxide. Part of

---

[42] Directive 2009/16/EC of the European Parliament and of the Council of 23 April 2009 on port State control, OJ no. L 131, p. 57 of 28.5.2009.

[43] Directive 2013/38/EU of the European Parliament and the Council of 12 August 2013, amending Directive 2009/16/EC on port State control, OJ no. L 218, p. 1 of 14.8.2013.

[44] Council Directive 2009/13/EC of 16 February 2009 implementing the Agreement concluded by the European Community Shipowners Associations (ECSA), an the European Transport Workers' Federation (ETF) on the Maritime Labour Convention, 2006, and amending Directive 1999/63/EC, OJ No. L 124 of 20.5.2009, p. 30.

[45] Cf. Wiesenthal (2017).

[46] Koch (2015).

SECA (Sulphur Emission Control Area) are the Baltic Sea and the North Sea, this is to say all the German ports are concerned.

The European Union was active in this field, too. In 1999 the European legislator adopted a Sulphur Directive,[47] which was adapted to Annex VI of the MARPOL Convention in 2012[48] and amended again in 2016.[49] This Directive now provides for more or less the same standards than annex VI of the MARPOL Convention, so that its practical importance is reduced to the effect, that the MARPOL standards apply in all member states, regardless whether they had ratified Annex VI of the MARPOL Convention or not.

Cruise ships must conform to the new requirements. There is a debate which technology could be used.[50] Scrubber technology or LNG is discussed. Scrubber technology means that the cheap heavy oil can be used also in the future, but the fume must be cleaned. The cleaning causes the problem of wastewater. The problem of LNG is, that it is not available in all ports. A further alternative is hybrid power. For all the technics, conversions of the existing ships are necessary. Ships without such conversions, which operate in a SECA, must use—at least partly—expensive marine diesel.

German law does not provide for specific rules on environmental impacts of cruises, but the general shipping law applies. On the basis of § 15 of the Law relating to the Tasks of the Federal Government in the Area of Maritime Traffic (Seeaufgabengesetz, SeeAufG), the Federal Ministry for Transport and Digital Infrastructure had issued the Environmental Maritime Behaviour Regulation (Seeumweltverhaltensverordnung, SeeUmwVerhV) on the basis of which offences committed against the MARPOL Convention, against other international environmental agreements and other behavioural provisions for the protection of the environment in maritime traffic can be punished. The Federal Maritime and Hydrographic Agency (Bundesanstalt für Seeschifffahrt und Hydrographie, BSH) is the authority responsible for prosecuting the vast majority of offences committed pursuant to the SeeUmwVerhV.

The SeeUmwVerhV is no implementation of the MARPOL Convention and its annexes to German law, but gives power to the BSH to enforce the Convention. The Convention is applicable in Germany as such, as it was ratified by the German legislator in 1996 including all the six annexes.[51] The SeeUmwVerhV empowers the BSH also to enforce the Convention on the Control of Harmful Anti-Fouling

---

[47] Council Directive 1999/32/EEC of 26 April 1999 relating to a reduction in the sulphur content of certain liquid fuels, amending Directive 93/12/EEC, OJ No. L 121 of 11.5.1999, p. 13.

[48] Directive 2012/33/EU of the European Parliament and the Council of 21 November 2012 amending Council Directive 1999/32/EC as regards the sulphur contents of marine fuels, OJ No. L 327 of 27.11.2012, p. 1.

[49] Directive 2016/802/EU of the European Parliament and the Council of 11 May 2016 relating to a reduction in the sulphur content of certain liquid fuels, OJ No. L 132 of 21.5.2016, p. 58.

[50] Cf. Wiesenthal (2017).

[51] Bundesgesetzblatt (BGBl.) 1996 II, p. 399.

Systems on ships (AFS Convention)[52] and the Convention on the Control and Treatment of Ballast Water.[53] There are many more Conventions in the area of maritime environmental protection, which cannot be enumerated here. But none of them is applicable to cruise ships only. Maritime Environmental Law is a legal subject on its own, where much research is done.[54]

8 Jurisdiction and Arbitration

8.1 Jurisdiction

There are no specific provisions applicable to cruises, but the general rules on jurisdiction apply. They are of European origin and include specific consumer protection provisions.

Jurisdiction is regulated by the Brussels Ia Regulation (Regulation [EU] No. 1215/2012). This is to say that the law is unified within the European Union (with the exemption of Denmark). The basic principle is that persons domiciled in a member state shall be sued in that member state (Art 4). According to the list of special jurisdiction (Art 7) a person may be sued in a matter relating to a contract in the courts for the place of performance of the obligation in question, and in matters relating to tort, delict or quasi delict in the courts for the place where the harmful event occurred or may occur. These are principles which more or less apply worldwide. But the Regulation includes a chapter for consumer protection which is of utmost importance for cruises.

a. Consumer Law

The Brussels Ia Regulation provides for a high standard of consumer protection with regard to jurisdiction and jurisdiction clauses. According to its Art 18 the consumer has the choice to bring proceedings against the other party either to the courts of the member state where the other party is domiciled or to the courts where he/she him/herself is domiciled. The other party may bring proceedings only to the courts of the member state, where the consumer is domiciled. The jurisdiction according to Art 18 is mandatory.

Art. 18 is applicable only, if the consumer has concluded a contract with a person, who pursues commercial or professional activities in the member state of the consumer's domicile or direct such activities to that Member State. The words "direct to that Member State" are of utmost importance, because this includes internet bookings. It has to be decided, whether a web site is directed to the member

[52]BGBl. 2008 II, p. 520.
[53]BGBl. 2013 II, p. 42.
[54]Supra, n. 3.

state of the consumer. The CJEU developed in a leading case (Pammer)[55] criteria under which circumstances a web site may be regarded as being directed to the member state of the consumer' domicile. Subject of the Pammer case was a cruise on a cargo ship.

According to Art 17 (3) transport contracts are not covered by the consumer protection section of the Brussels Ia-Regulation. This is to say that a Swedish consumer who books a ferry service from Stockholm to Helsinki with a Finnish company, may not sue the company at home. But there is an exemption in Art 17 (3) for contracts with a combination of travel and accommodation. Such packages are covered by the consumer protection section of the Brussels Ia-Regulation. As explained earlier (supra IV 4), cruises are regarded by the CJEU as packages in the sense of the Package Travel Directive, and so the consumer jurisdiction rules apply, even if the consumer had booked the cruise without transportation to and from the port of embarkation and disembarkation.

The Athens Convention (death and injury, loss of luggage) includes a special provision for jurisdiction. According to its Art 17 the claimant has a choice between the courts of the state of the defendant, the state of departure or destination, and—in case the defendant has a place of business in that state, the state of the claimant or the state, where the contract is made. A deviating jurisdiction clause can be agreed only after the occurrence of the incident. This provision prevails over the Brussels Ia-Regulation.

A forum clause which deviates from the consumer protection rules of the Brussels Ia-Regulation to the detriment of the consumer is not valid. A choice of forum clause is valid only after a dispute has arisen (Art 19). It does not matter whether such a clause is part of the general terms or individually agreed.

b. Labour Law

A parallel section of the Brussels Ia Regulation protects the worker as the weaker party. Art 20 to 23 deal with jurisdiction over individual contracts of employment. An employee may be sued in the member state of his domicile, or in another member state, but only in the courts for the place where the employee habitually carries out his work (Art 21 [1] [a]) or if the employee does not habitually carry out his work in any one country, in the courts for the place where the business which engaged the employee, is situated (Art 21 [1] [b]). The employer may be sued even in another member state according to Art 21 (1) (b), if the employer is not domiciled in a member state (Art 21 [2]).

Art 22 deals with claims of the employer. An employer may bring proceedings against the employee only in the courts of the member states, in which the employee is domiciled (Art 22 [1]). This provision is mandatory (Art 23). This is to say that the employee is protected against jurisdiction clauses in his contract, which deprive him from the jurisdiction of his domicile.

[55] Court of Justice of the European Union (CJEU) 7.12.2010, combined cases C-585/98 and C-144/09 – Pammer and Hotel Alpenhof.

8.2 Arbitration

Arbitration did not play a significant role for the settlement of consumer disputes in the past. The reason is, that thresholds to go to court are relatively low in Germany compared with other countries. Procedures do not take very long, and costs are affordable. But things changed in the last years. The European legislator adopted an Alternative Dispute Resolution Directive,[56] which was recently implemented in German law by a Verbraucherstreitbeilegungsgesetz (VSBG, Consumer Dispute Settlement Act).[57] This law obliges business to offer arbitration to consumers. But a consumer cannot be forced to go to arbitration before filing a claim into court, because the right to go to court is regarded as a fundamental right, granted by the Grundgesetz (Basic Law, German constitution) and the EU Charter of Fundamental Rights as well. As a result, any arbitration clause, which shall deprive the other party to the contract of his right to go to court without a preceding arbitration procedure, is void. Arbitration is only possible if the consumer agrees after the harmful event occurred.

Nevertheless the new Directive and the VSBG obliges business to explain their arbitration policy in the contract. Until now, cruise lines do not have their own arbitration schemes. This is the ground why there are so many lower court decisions. There is one exemption: With regard to the Sea Passengers' Rights Regulation (supra IV 3), the Schlichtungsstelle für den öffentlichen Personenverkehr (Conciliation Centre for Public Passenger Transport) is in charge, which is operated by air, rail and sea carriers.[58] But consumer disputes arising from this Regulation play only a minor role compared with disputes arising from the package travel rules, which use to go to court if they cannot be settled amicably.

9 Choice of Law

9.1 Consumer Law

In Germany, the EU Rome I-Regulation applies.[59] There are no additional national rules insofar. The Rome I-Regulation is applicable to all contractual obligations. Its basic principle is the freedom of choice of law, but this freedom is limited in

[56] Directive 2013/11/EU of the European Parliament and of the Council of 21 May 2013 on alternative dispute resolution for consumer disputes and amending Regulation (EC) No 2006/2004 and Directive 2009/22/EC, OJ No. L 165 of 18.6.2013, p. 63.

[57] Gesetz über die alternative Streitbeilegung in Verbrauchersachen (Verbraucherstreitbeilegungsgesetz – VSBG) of 19. Februar 2016, BGBl. I, p. 254.

[58] www.soep-online.de. For the functioning of SÖP cf. Isermann (2016).

[59] Regulation (EC) No. 593/2008 of the European Parliament and the Council of 17 June 2008 on the law applicable to contractual obligations (Rome I), OJ No. L 177 of 4.7.2008, p. 6.

consumer contracts, insurance contracts, and employment contracts. There is also a specific provision for carriage contracts.

According to Art 6 of the Rome I-Regulation, a consumer contract shall be governed by the law of the country where the consumer has his habitual residence, provided that the professional directs his commercial or professional activities to that country. "Directing his activity" means the same as in the Brussels Ia-Regulation (supra 1.a.).

This rule does not totally exclude a choice of law clause. But such a choice may not deprive the consumer from mandatory rights he would have without such a choice of law clause, in other words, from the rights according to the law of the country of his habitual residence. So, a choice of law clause has only a limited effect in favour of business.

There is an exemption for carriage contracts corresponding to the same exemption in the Brussels Ia-Regulation, which are not covered by the consumer protection rule of Art 6 of the Rome I-Regulation. But this exemption does not affect package travel. As cruises are regarded as package travel, this means, that Art 6 is applicable to cruises.

For a mere carriage, e.g. for a ferry service, Art 5 is applicable, which allows a choice of law between the law of the place, where the passenger has his habitual residence, or the carrier has his habitual residence, or the place of departure or arrival. This means that a passenger, who books a flight to the place of embarkation separate from the cruise, is for his flight under the regime of a wide range of possible choices of law (Art 5), but for the cruise he more or less enjoys the law of the country of his domicile. But if the cruise line arranges the flight to and from the embarkation port, it is a "package", which includes the flight, and for the whole package Art 6 is applicable.

A choice of law clause within the limitations laid down by Art 5 or 6 of the Rome I-Regulation is valid. There is no additional control by the law of unfair contract terms; a choice of law clause, which meets the requirements of the Rome I-Regulation, cannot be unfair. But such a clause must also meet the requirement of transparency; this is to say it must not be "hidden" somewhere in the small print of the contract.

9.2 Labour Law

There are corresponding provisions for the employee as the weaker party to the contract, which also apply to maritime labour law.[60] According to Art 8 a choice of law clause may not deprive the employee of the protection afforded to him by provisions that cannot be derogated from under the law that in absence of the choice, would have been applicable. If there is no choice of law clause, the law of the

[60] Martiny (2018) Art. 8 Rom I-VO no. 83 with further references.

country, in which the employee carries out habitually his work, is applicable (Art 8 [2]).

For seamen Art 8 (3) may be of relevance. According to this provision, the place of the business, which engaged the employee, is the relevant place for the applicable law, if the law applicable cannot be determined according to Art 8 (2). Some legal writers are of the opinion that the applicable law must be determined according to this provision, but others are of the opinion, that the flag determines the law applicable, as the ship is the habitual working place, so that the law applicable can be determined according to Art 8 (2).[61]

German law provides for an international shipping register (GIS).[62] This allows to employ seamen form other states than Germany (and EU member states) to the conditions of their home country. It is discussed, whether the GIS is in line with the principle of non discrimination of the German constitution and with EU law such as Art 8 of the Rome I-Regulation, but the majority of legal writers is of the opinion that there are no contradictions of the GIS Act and law of upper levels (Constitution or supranational law).[63]

10 Conclusion

There is no systematic approach to cruise law in German law. German cruise law is characterized by international Conventions and EU law, which have to be applied either directly or by national transposition acts. The multiplicity of this international and supranational law does not leave much discretion to the national legislator. Even the national provisions for national carriage were adapted to international and supranational law.

This is not surprising as cruises are international. But is has to be taken into account that every international law, which is transplanted to the body of the national law, starts after the implementation a life of its own within the surrounding national law.

References

Bubenzer C (2014) Das deutsche Seearbeitsgesetz, Transportrecht (TranspR), p 393

Cruise Lines International Association (CLIA) Germany and Deutscher ReiseVerband (DRV) 2016: Der Hochsee-Kreuzfahrtmarkt Deutschland 2016

[61] Martiny (2018) Art. 8 Rom I-VO no. 90 with further references.

[62] Gesetz zur Einführung eines zusätzlichen Registers für Seeschiffe unter der Bundesflagge im internationalen Verkehr (Internationales Seeschifffahrtsregister – ISR), BGBl. 1989 I, p. 550.

[63] Cf. for references to this debate Martiny (2018), Art. 8 Rom I-VO, nos. 95 et seq.

Cruise Lines International Association (CLIA) Europe (2015): Contribution of Cruise Tourism to the Economies of Europe

Führich E (2017) Das neue Pauschalreiserecht, Neue Juristische Wochenschrift (NJW), p 2945

Ipsen J (2014) Völkerrecht, 8th edn

Isermann E (2016) soep-Schlichtung: Wie funktioniert das?, Reiserechr aktuell (RRa), p 104

Koch S (2015) (Cruise) ship emissions and international maritime law, IFTTA Law Review (supplement to Reiserecht aktuell no. 4), p 10

Lagoni R (2007) Die Haftung des Beförderers von Reisenden und das Gemeinschaftsrecht, Zeitschrift für Europäisches Privatrecht (ZEuP), p 1079

Martiny D (2018) Rom I-Verordnung in Münchener Kommentar zum BGB, 7th edn, vol 12

Maul-Sartori M (2013) Das neue Seearbeitsrecht, Neue Zeitschrift für Arbeitsrecht (NZA), p 821

Tonner K (2013) Reiserecht maritim, Reiserecht aktuell (RRa), p 206

Wiesenthal (2017) Schluss mit schmutzig!, fvw (Magazin für Touristik & Business Travel) no. 23, p 18

Zimmer R (2015) Umsetzung des Seearbeitsübereinkommens der Internationalen Arbeitsorganisation, Zeitschrift für Europäisches Arbeitsrecht (EuZA), p 297

Legal Aspects of Cruises in Poland

Maria Dragun-Gertner and Zuzanna Pepłowska-Dąbrowska

Abstract Poland is not a main cruise destination. Majority of passengers are carried on ferries rather than participating in a cruise. However, number of cruise ships entering Polish ports steadily increases (at least prior to 2020). In fact, there are favourable conditions for development of cruising in Poland, including good quality port services, ship management sector or shiprepair yards. In general there are no particular provisions on cruises, in respect of liability, labour or environmental issues, nor jurisdiction or arbitration. Instead more general rules are applicable to cruises. Those rules are of international, supranational and national origin. They are discussed extensively in below chapter, which is divided into parts referring to rules on: liability, consumer protection, package travelling, labour, port, environmental protection, as well as jurisdiction and choice of law rules. Moreover, the chapter presents current case law concerning cruise related issues (This chapter is an extended and amended version of a paper published in a collection of Polish reports for the XXth International Congress of Comparative Law: Dragun-Gertner and Pepłowska-Dąbrowska (Rapports Polonais XXe Congrès International de Droit Comparé Fukuoka 22–28 VII 2018, Wydawnictwo Uniwersytetu Łódzkiego, Łódź, pp. 173–181).

Research conducted by Zuzanna Pepłowska-Dąbrowska was funded by National Science Centre, Poland, under the contract UMO – 2016/22/E/HS5/00050. Problems of contemporary maritime codes.

M. Dragun-Gertner
WSB University in Torun, Torun, Poland
e-mail: mgertner@uni.torun.pl

Z. Pepłowska-Dąbrowska (✉)
Nicolaus Copernicus University in Toruń, Toruń, Poland
e-mail: zpeplow@umk.pl

C. Fresnedo de Aguirre (ed.), *Legal Aspects of Cruises*, Ius Comparatum - Global Studies in Comparative Law 56, https://doi.org/10.1007/978-3-030-83090-8_5

1 Introduction

Poland is not a major cruise destiny state. However, the statistics show that the number of cruise passengers and cruise ships has been growing in recent years. Favourable environment for increase of those numbers exist. It includes, *inter alia*, good quality of port services and shiprepair yards. There are no specific rules relating to cruises in Poland. In terms of liability issues general rules concerning carriage of passengers by sea or rules on package travel. Similarly, labor rules, rules on environmental impact or ports are not designed solely for cruises but are of more general applicability. Finally, there are no specific jurisdiction and collision rules on cruises. Applicability of multiple norms of more general character flowing from separate legal acts creates complexity of the legal regime relating to cruises (Dragun-Gertner and Pepłowska-Dąbrowska (2018)).

2 Importance of Cruises

In general, the Baltic Sea basin is not a main cruise destination. Among the users of maritime transport means within the Baltic, the cruise passengers constituted small, nevertheless growing percentage of 0.1% in 2010, 1.2% in 2016 and 1.7% in 2017.[1] Passengers visiting Polish ports are mainly those using passenger ships and passenger-cargo ferries. Polish ports are behind other main Baltic Sea ports in respect of the number of entering cruise ships. Number of passengers (those carried on different types on ships, mainly ferries) in Polish ports has been steadily growing though: from 2.2 mil in 2013 to 2.72 mil in 2018 and 2.78 mil in 2019.[2] Until 2017 major cruise ships operators as Carnival or Norwegian Cruise Line has not been present in the Polish ports. However, in 2017 the Port of Gdynia welcomed the largest cruise ship in the history of Polish ports with 145 thousands of GT (Norwegian Getaway of Norwegian Cruise Line). There are other indicators showing the growth of Poland's attractiveness as a cruise destiny. Until recently only cruise ships on voyages through the Baltic Sea called at the Polish ports. In 2017 Viking Cruises has added the Port of Gdańsk into the schedule of its 50-day voyage including *inter alia* ports of Greece, Italy, Spain, Great Britain and Russia.

[1] Data found in Statistical Yearbooks of Maritime Economy provided by Statistics Poland at http://stat.gov.pl/en/; specifically: The maritime economy in Poland in years 2017 and 2018, p. 140 [partly in English], last access on 10.03.2020.

[2] *Ibid*, Gospodarka morska w Polsce w 2013 r., p 1 [in Polish]; The maritime economy in Poland in years 2017 and 2018, p. 21 [partly in English]; 2020 Statistical Yearbook of Maritime Economy, p. 312 [partly in English].

2.1 *Statistics on the Evolution of the Number of Cruises and Cruise Passengers*

Essentially statistics prior to year 2020[3] show the growth of attractiveness of the Baltic Sea for cruise ships. The number of cruise passengers onboard ships calling at Polish seaports after a relative breakdown has been growing steadily, counting 97 thousands in 2013, 100.5 thousands in 2016, almost 127 thousands in 2017, more than 142 thousands in 2018 and 145.5 thousands in 2019.[4]

The cruise ships passengers visited mainly Gdynia, less frequently Gdańsk and Szczecin (f.ex. in 2018 almost 72% visited Gdynia, 19.5% visited Gdańsk and Szczecin 6.5%; in 2016 in 81% of them visited Gdynia, 10.5% Gdańsk and 5.9% Szczecin).[5] There is no data available on money spent on land by cruise ships passengers. However, there are general statistics indicating how much money has been spent by foreigners entering Polish sea ports. The record shows that numbers are rather low and constant. For example, in 2016 expenses of foreigners carried by sea equalled 1% of the total expenses of foreign visitors in Poland (travelling by all means of transport) with the amount of 408.4 mil PLN (almost 91 mil EUR[6]) and 1.1% in 2017 with amount of 447.6 mil PLN (99.5 mil EUR). Most recent data show similar number of 477.6 mil PLN (approximately 106 mil EUR) what constitutes 1.1% of the total expenses of foreign visitors in Poland.[7] In respect of the cruise passengers solely it is known that they usually spend between 6 and 8 hours on land, participating in various organized trips.

2.2 *Policies and Other Factors Aimed at Development of Cruise Industry*

Cruise industry is gradually developing in Poland despite the fact that there is no specific policy run on a national scale that favours the cruise business and attracts cruises to Polish ports. On the other hand, there are some initiatives undertaken by local authorities and ports. An example may be given of the Port of Gdańsk which

[3] At the time of final submission of this paper official statics on 2020 were not yet available.

[4] 2017 Statistical Yearbook of Maritime Economy, p. 386; 2020 Statistical Yearbook of Maritime Economy, p. 172, available at http://stat.gov.pl/en/, last access on 10.03.2020.

[5] The maritime economy in Poland in years 2017 and 2018, p. 140; The maritime economy in Poland in years 2015 and 2016, p. 110, available at http://stat.gov.pl/en/, last access on 10.03.2020.

[6] Exchange rate of EUR 1=4.5 PLN.

[7] Central Statistical Office, Border traffic and expenses made by foreigners in Poland and Poles abroad in 2016, p. 49; Statistical analyses: Border traffic and expenses made by foreigners in Poland and Poles abroad in 2017, p. 33; Statistical analyses: Border traffic and expenses made by foreigners in Poland and Poles abroad in 2019, p. 31, available at http://stat.gov.pl/en/, last access on 10.03.2020.

has introduced discounts on port fees for cruising companies that visit the port multiple times in a year. Moreover, a more coordinated cooperation of tourist service providers has been arranged making Gdańsk a more attractive spot from a cruise passengers' perspective. Those initiatives include providing mobile tourist information points next to gangways or dedicated taxis allocated near a cruise ship with tariffs to the main city attractions. Other facilitations are provided as special safety zones for cruise ships passengers in the port.

In general, there are good conditions for development of cruise industry in Poland. Ship management industry has been developing effectively to become important and strong element of the Polish maritime economy. Furthermore, services offered to cruises in Polish ports are of good quality, comparable to those available in other European ports. Multiple port services are available as pilotage, towage, mooring, supply of fresh water and bunker oil, as well as port reception facilities for collection of slops and wastes or safe ferry quays. Passenger terminals in ports of Świnoujście and Gdynia provide boarding bridges for maintenance of pedestrian traffic of passengers. Companies delivering food, supplying technical support and specialized services are common in all Polish ports. Moreover, shipyards in Poland are considered of good quality, including services rendered to cruises. In particular Gdańsk has become a renowned center with shipyard's specializing in passenger ships and ferries. However there are some limitations due to restrictions on size of ships entering and depth of the docks. In general shiprepair yards sustained large crisis period and they continue to offer shipping industry with wide range of service, from minor to class repairs and ships' conversions.[8]

3 General and Specific Rules on Cruises

Polish legal system does not contain any specific regulation aimed at cruises solely. Instead, general provisions on carriage of passengers by sea are applicable. The laws in question are: the Athens convention relating to the carriage of passengers and their luggage by sea, 1974; the Polish Maritime Code of 2001;[9] the Regulation (EC) No 392/2009 of the European Parliament and of the Council of 23 April 2009 on the liability of carriers of passengers by sea in the event of accidents,[10] the Regulation (EU) No 1177/2010 of the European Parliament and of the Council of 24 November 2010 concerning the rights of passengers when travelling by sea and inland waterway and amending Regulation (EC) No 2006/2004.[11] Also, rules of public law character are applicable, including the Directive 2009/45/EC of the European

[8] Section 2.2. was prepared on basis of information provided by Dariusz Szymankiewicz, Maritime Academy in Szczecin.

[9] Consolidated text in Journal of Laws 2018 item 2175.

[10] OJ L 131, 28.5.2009, pp. 24–46.

[11] OJ L 334, 17.12.2010, pp. 1–16.

Parliament and of the Council of 6 May 2009 on safety rules and standards for passenger ships[12] which has been implemented in Poland by the Maritime Safety Act of 2011.[13]

3.1 General Provisions on Carriage of Passengers by Sea

Poland ratified the 1974 Athens Convention in 1986. The provisions of the Polish Maritime Code incorporate the 1974 Athens Convention, making it the law applicable to all carriages governed by the Code, including solely national sea carriage, carriage performed free of charge with the agreement of the carrier, as well as carriage exercised on basis of other contract than passenger carriage contract (Article 181). The Polish Maritime Code supplements the 1974 Athens Convention provisions with the obligation of the carrier to insure its liability up to the limits of liability stated in Articles 7 and 8 of the Convention. Due to the Regulation (EC) No 392/2009 the regime of the Protocol of 2002 to the Athens Convention (PAL 2002) is applicable to any international carriage within the meaning of point 9 of Article 1 of the Athens Convention and to carriage by sea within a single Member State on board ships of Classes A and B under Article 4 of Directive 98/18/EC, where:

(a) the ship is flying the flag of or is registered in a Member State;
(b) the contract of carriage has been made in a Member State; or
(c) the place of departure or destination, according to the contract of carriage, is in a Member State.

Poland has used the opportunity provided in the Regulation to suspend until the end of 2018 the application of the Regulation to national carriages on passenger ships of B class by relieving the carriers of those ships from an obligation to obtain financial security as provided in Article 4bis of the PAL 2002. Moreover, Poland has not decided to broaden the application of the Regulation to national carriages on ships of C and D class. Accordingly, dichotomy exists in respect of liability regimes depending on type of a sea carriage. In cases of carriages governed by the Regulation (EC) No 392/2009 the more favorable to passengers PAL 2002 applies, while other carriages, specifically national carriages on passenger ships of C and D class are governed by the 1974 Athens convention. The Polish Codification Commission for Maritime Law has advised ratification of the PAL 2002. It opted for incorporation of the PAL 2002 into the Polish Maritime Code and its application to all national carriages, including those on ships of C and D class to eliminate dichotomy in liability regime. However, simultaneously it advised relieving the carriers of ships of C and D class from the obligation to obtain financial security of 250 thousand SDR per passenger on each distinct occasion. The reason for such proposal was the fact

[12] OJ L 163, 25.6.2009, pp. 1–140.

[13] Consolidated text in Journal of Laws 2020 item 680.

that for the smaller carriers obtaining affordable insurance coverage at the level required by the PAL 2002 might be impossible.

The Regulation (EU) No 1177/2010 of the European Parliament and of the Council of 24 November 2010 concerning the rights of passengers when travelling by sea and inland waterway and amending Regulation (EC) No 2006/2004 concentrates on securing rights of passengers—weaker parties to a transport contract—in instances of cancellation or delay of any passenger service or cruise. Among others, it also determines availability and special requirements of carriage of disabled persons and persons with reduced mobility. It is applicable, though not wholly, to passengers travelling on cruises where the port of embarkation is situated in the territory of an EU Member State. Accordingly, cruise passengers may benefit from information and assistance duty of a cruise carrier in cases of delay or cancellation of a cruise.

3.2 *Case Law on Carriage of Passengers by Sea*

In the Polish case law concerning the passenger carriage there has been a question raised whether a passenger claiming compensation for personal injury under the 1974 Athens Convention has a direct action against the carrier's insurer. As mentioned above the Polish Maritime Code supplements provisions of the 1974 Athens Convention by obliging the carrier to insure its liability up to the limitation limits provided in the Convention. A woman who suffered personal injury on board of a ship sued directly the carrier's insurer. The Appellate Court in Gdańsk dismissed the claim finding no basis for direct action under the provisions of the Polish Maritime Code.[14]

Moreover, the case law on passenger carriage indicates that the aggrieved parties sought to avoid the application of the 1974 Athens Convention as it requires in some instances of personal injury proof of a fault of the carrier. Since that requirement might be very difficult for claimants, they based their claims on more general provision of the Polish Civil Code[15] providing for strict liability of a person who runs on his own account an enterprise or a business set in motion by natural forces (Article 435 of the Polish Civil Code). The Polish courts have repeatedly stated that the carrier's liability for personal injury is governed by the specific provisions of the 1974 Athens Convention.[16]

[14] Judgment of the Appellate Court in Gdańsk from 3.11.2015, V ACa 240/15.

[15] Consolidated text in Journal of Laws 2020 item 1740.

[16] Judgment of the Supreme Court from 3.10.2012, II CSK 25/12.

4 Cruise Passengers as Consumers

Consumer protection law in Poland flows mainly from the European Union law. Some of the protective rules concerning consumers in general are applicable to cruises, while others are explicitly excluded.

Among the rules applicable to the cruises are those on unfair contract terms which are defined in the Polish Civil Code (Articles 385^1–385^4) implementing the Council Directive 93/13/EEC on unfair terms in consumer contracts.[17] Moreover, the control of unfair contract terms is regulated by the recently amended Act on the Protection of Competition and Consumers.[18]

On the other hand, provisions on the protection of consumers in respect of contracts negotiated away from business premises and distance contracts which flow from European directives and are implemented into the Polish law in the Consumer Rights Act of 2014[19] are not applicable to the contracts on package as defined in the Act on Package Travel and Linked Travel Arrangements of 2017,[20] implementing Directive (EU) 2015/2302 of the European Parliament and of the Council of 25 November 2015 on package travel and linked travel arrangements, amending Regulation (EC) No 2006/2004 and Directive 2011/83/EU of the European Parliament and of the Council and repealing Council Directive 90/314/EEC.[21] As a cruise tour often fulfills the prerequisites of a package, a consumer in such contracts may not benefit from the protection afforded in the Consumer Rights Act, with the exclusion of several provisions protecting consumers.[22] Instead, rights of a traveller are protected by the Act on Package Travel and Linked Travel Arrangements itself, which—to some extent—provides for similar solutions as the Consumer Rights Act. For instance, Polish legislator used an opportunity given by the 2015/2302 directive to safeguard a right of withdrawal from a contract concluded off-premises without giving any reason within a period of 14 days (Article 47.7 of the Act on Package Travel and Linked Travel Arrangements).

---

[17] OJ L 95, 21.4.1993, pp. 29–34.

[18] Consolidated text in Journal of Laws 2021 item 275.

[19] Consolidated text in Journal of Laws 2020 item 287.

[20] Consolidated text in Journal of Laws 2020 item 2139.

[21] OJ L 326, 11.12.2015, pp. 1–33.

[22] Including those on consumer's agreement in relation to any additional payments, fees for telephone communication with entrepreneur, specific information required from entrepreneur at the moment of contracting and confirmation of oral agreement.

5 Combined Trips, Package Travels, Package Tours or Package Holidays

Polish legal system includes specific rules on package (travel) which will very often be applicable to cruises. Definition of a package travel is included in 2017 Act on Package Travel and Linked Travel Arrangements which implements directive 2015/2302 on package travel and linked travel arrangements from 2015. The definition is elaborated and quite complicated due to the fact that it is aimed at covering not only traditional contracts between a single trader and traveler, but also—to some extent—packages created via process of so-called *dynamic packaging*, i.e. when traveler puts together his own holiday's components from different organizers, usually via internet. A package is defined as a combination of not less than two different touristic services for the purpose of the same trip or holiday, if (1) touristic services were combined by one tourist trader, including at the request of or in accordance with the selection of the traveler, before a contract containing all those services was concluded; or (2) irrespective of whether separate contracts are concluded with individual travel service providers, those services are: (a) purchased from a single point of sale and have been selected before the traveller agreed to pay, or (b) offered, sold or charged at an inclusive or total price, or (c) advertised or sold under the term 'package' or under a similar term, or (d) combined after the conclusion of a contract by which a trader entitles the traveller to choose among a selection of different types of travel services, or (e) purchased from separate traders through linked online booking processes where the traveller's name, payment details and e-mail address are transmitted from the trader with whom the first contract is concluded to another trader or traders and a contract with the latter trader or traders is concluded at the latest 24 h after the confirmation of the booking of the first travel service.

It is worth however to realize that the directive 2015/2302 is not limited to protection of consumers. Excluded from its scope are only those packages and linked travel arrangements which are purchased on the basis of a general agreement for the arrangement of business travel between a trader and another natural or legal person who is acting for purposes relating to his trade, business, craft or profession. Thus, the directive is applicable to representatives of small businesses or professionals who book trips related to their business or profession. A rational behind such solution is that those entities often require a similar level of protection as consumers. Accordingly, the 2017 Polish act on package travel and linked travel arrangements employs a notion of a traveler not limited to consumer, including any person who is seeking to conclude a contract, or is entitled to travel on the basis of a contract concluded within the scope of the act. Excluded are only those contracts between tourist trader and entrepreneur that are based on a general agreement relating to organization of a business travel. In this way Polish act correctly implements the directive. That was not the case under former package travel directive of 1990,[23]

[23] Council Directive 90/314/EEC of 13 June 1990 on package travel, package holidays and package tours (OJ L 158, 23.6.1990, p. 59), superseded by the directive 2015/2302.

which was implemented by the 1997 act on touristic services.[24] Under the former regime Polish act incorrectly limited protective scope of the 1990 package travel directive by applying it only to persons contracting or intending to contract for tourist services not in connection with the subject matter of their economic activity.

6 Labour Rules on Cruises' Workers

Polish legal system does not contain specific labour rules on cruises' workers. In absence of these, general rules applicable to all maritime workers apply. Also, to some extent, rules governing all workers are binding. The rules in question are of international, supranational as well as national origin. They include Maritime Labour Convention 2006 and European directives, as well as national acts: Maritime Labour Act of 2015[25] and Labour Code from 1974.[26]

7 Rules on Ports That Are Relevant Regarding Cruises

In Poland there are no specific rules on ports regarding cruises solely. Relevant to cruises are general port regulations issued by territorial authorities of maritime administration. They determine safety of navigation and environmental protection, as well as maintenance of order in a specific port. For example, according to port regulations issued by the Director of the Maritime Office in Szczecin passenger ships entering port are obliged to deliver FAL forms and register passenger traffic with the use of PHICS system. It is required that embarking and disembarking of passengers from or at the ship is supervised by its crew member. Quays and piers ought to be equipped with information signs including passenger ships' and ferries' itinerary, as well as conditions of the carriage. Passages on a ferry and passenger piers should be construed in such a way as to provide safe passage, maintenance of the order and control over the number of passengers carried. They should exclude the possibility of the emergence of a crowd among passengers. Ships are under the obligation to use the pilotage services in ports with difficult navigation conditions as in Szczecin.

Moreover, ro-ro passenger ships and high speed passenger crafts are under special surveillance executed in ports. If such a ship does not fulfill any safety standard the inspecting authority prohibits the use of the ship.

Additionally, according to the Maritime Code shipmaster has a right to detain in isolation a person infringing safety of the ship, persons or property and leave such a person in the port.

---

[24] Consolidated text in Journal of Laws 2016 item 187.

[25] Consolidated text in Journal of Laws 2020 item 1353.

[26] Consolidated text in Journal of Laws 2020 item 1320.

With regard to system of port fees applicable to cruises, until 2019 in Polish ports different port fees were charged: tonnage dues, wharfage (quay) and passenger dues. Tonnage dues were charged for entrance and departure of the ship into and from the port, transit through the port area and reception of wastes from ships in order to dispose or retrieve them. They might not exceed 1.10 euro per 1 GT. Wharfage was collected for the use of quays or piers and may not exceed 0.17 euro per 1 GT. Passenger dues were collected for passengers embarking on and disembarking from a ship, they might not be higher than 1.74 euro per passenger. Exact amount of port fees depended on its type, kind and size of a ship and period for which the infrastructure was used.[27]

However, revision of the Act on Ports and Maritime Piers from 2019 repealed above closed catalogue of fees together with their statutory. Currently, decision on type of port fee and its rate is left at the discretion of ports' governing bodies on the condition that they are non-discriminatory and according to port's needs in respect of modernization and development of port infrastructure.[28]

Some ports promote passenger ships entering frequently. For instance, port in Gdańsk offers discounts on tonnage dues depending on number of calls in a calendar year. Fees amount ought to be made publicly accessible.

We do not experience in Poland any particular complications regarding implementation of the rules on port fees. The only problem is of practical nature and relates to lack of payment of the dues.[29]

8 Rules on Environmental Impact of Cruises

There are no specific rules on cruises' environmental impact. Instead, general rules applicable to ships are relevant. Those rules include 1995 Act on Prevention of Pollution from Ships,[30] which implements into the Polish law multiple international acts: the MARPOL convention,[31] the HELCOM convention,[32] the Dumping convention,[33] the AFS convention.[34] Moreover, the 1995 Act meets the requirements of the Vienna Convention on the protection of the Ozone Layer, to the extent applicable

[27] Act on Ports and Maritime Piers of 20th December 1996 (consolidated text in Journal of Laws 2017 item 1933), art. 8.

[28] Act on Ports and Maritime Piers of 20th December 1996 (consolidated text in Journal of Laws 2020 item 998), art. 8.

[29] Sections 7.1 and 7.2. were prepared partly on basis of information provided by Ewa Krzysztoporska, Maritime Office in Szczecin.

[30] Consolidated text in Journal of Laws 2020 item 1955.

[31] 1973 International Convention for the Prevention of Pollution from Ships, with 1978 and 1997 London Protocols.

[32] 1992 Convention on the Protection of the Marine Environment of the Baltic Sea Area.

[33] 1972 Convention on the Prevention of Marine Pollution by Dumping of Wastes and Other Matter.

[34] 2001 International Convention on the Control of Harmful Anti-fouling Systems on Ships.

to ship. As it flows from above, those general rules applicable also to cruises are of international, supranational, as well as national origin.

8.1 Case Law Concerning Rules on Environmental Impact

The problem arising on grounds of the aforementioned rules concerns collision of the Act on Prevention of Pollution from Ships and—more general act—the 2001 Law on Environmental Protection.[35] Polish administrative courts have ruled that ships are obliged to pay for the emission permits as prescribed by the Law on Environmental Protection,[36] notwithstanding the fact that Article 36a p. 9 of the Prevention of Pollution from Ships Act puts a fine of up to 50,000 SDR for those who use the ship which introduces into the air substances depleting the ozone layer, NOx, as well as fluorinated greenhouse gases. According to the judgment of the Administrative Supreme Court, the Law on Environmental Protection is dedicated to the whole Polish territory, including internal waters and the Polish territorial sea, as well as the airspace above them. That is the basic reason why, ships operators are obligated to cover the cost of the emission permits as a result of "using the environment" by the emission of gas and dust.[37]

9 Jurisdiction and Arbitration

In Poland there are no specific provisions on jurisdiction applicable to cruises. General provisions on jurisdiction that are relevant to cruises are incorporated in the Athens Convention relating to the carriage of passengers and their luggage by sea, 1974; the Regulation (EU) No 1215/2012 of the European Parliament and of the Council of 12 December 2012 on jurisdiction and the recognition and enforcement of judgments in civil and commercial matters (recast)(Brussel I bis).[38]

The Brussel I bis Regulation provides in Article 71 that where there is a clash between the provisions of the Regulation and the international convention the convention prevails.

According to the Athens Convention 1974 the right of choice of forum of the parties to a contract for carriage of passengers by sea mentioned in Article 2 of the Convention is limited. The purpose of this article is the protection of passengers.

[35] Consolidated text in Journal of Laws 2020 item 1219.

[36] See rulings of the Supreme Administrative Court of 25 January 2007 (II OSK 151/06), Woivodship, Administrative Court in Gdańsk of 21 June 2007 (II SA/Gd 257/07).

[37] Sections 8 and 8.1. were prepared on basis of information provided by Justyna Nawrot and Maciej Nyka, Law and Administration Faculty, University of Gdańsk.

[38] OJ L 351, 20.12.2012, pp. 1–32.

Specifically, the Athens Convention states that the court before which the proceedings are being conducted must be the court of the State Party to the Convention. Moreover, it does not allow for the anticipated exclusion of the plaintiff's right to choose the most convenient place for the dispute to proceed from the jurisdictions specified by the Convention. The above restriction of option concerns only contractual provisions concluded before the occurrence of the incident.

Arbitration clauses are not usually included in general conditions of carriage of passengers in cruises celebrated in Poland.

9.1 Forum Selection Clauses

The effectiveness of jurisdiction clauses in contracts of carriage of passengers by sea may be affected by the overriding nature of the provisions of the Convention, as well as the internal or European law based on it. According to Article 18 of the Convention any contractual provision purporting to relieve the carrier of his liability towards the passenger or to prescribe a lower limit of liability than that fixed in this Convention except as provided in paragraph 4 of Article 8, and any such provision purporting to shift the burden of proof which rests on the carrier, shall be null and void.

It has been emphasized however in decisions of the Court of Justice of the European Union (previously The European Court of Justice) concerning Brussels I and Brussels I bis Regulations that the possibility of violating of the mandatory liability provisions does not render a jurisdiction agreement invalid. The aim of legal certainty which lies right in the middle of this Regulation regime would be violated by a public policy regulation of jurisdiction agreements. Courts assessing jurisdictions cannot analyze substantive aspects of the dispute, what automatically excludes the possibility of examining the substantive consequences of jurisdictional agreements. The regime of the Regulation incorporates substantial safeguards and no additional review of the legitimacy of the agreement is necessary. Questions concerned with public policy are transferred to the stage of recognition and enforcement of court decisions.

According to Article 25 of the Brussels I bis Regulation courts are obliged to verify the effectiveness of the jurisdiction agreement because of its form whenever a court of the Member State is chosen to have jurisdiction to settle the dispute.

The agreement conferring jurisdiction shall be either:

(a) in writing or evidenced in writing,
(b) in a form which accords with practices which the parties have established between themselves or,
(c) in international trade or commerce, in a form which accords with the usage of which the parties should have been aware and which in such trade or commerce is widely familiar and frequently experienced by parties to contracts of the type involved in a specific branch concerned.

Any communication by electronic means which provides a durable record of the agreement shall be equivalent to writing.

10 Choice of Law

Similarly to jurisdiction, there are no specific Polish provisions concerning choice of law in relation to cruises. As stated above, Poland is a party to the Athens Convention 1974 and its provisions are also implemented in the Polish Maritime Code (Article 181). Moreover, in Poland as the Member State of the EU, rules of the following Regulations are applied:

(a) the Regulation (EC) No 392/2009 of the European Parliament and of the Council of 23 April 2009 on the liability of carriers of passengers by sea in the event of accidents, and
(b) the Regulation (EC) No 593/2008 of the European Parliament and of the Council of 17 June 2008 on the law applicable to contractual obligations (Rome I).[39]

Importantly, the Athens Convention is an instrument of protection granted to a passenger who very frequently is also a consumer. However, it does not limit its regulation to the business-consumer relationship. It implements a broader idea of the protection of this contracting party, which is weak or even deprived of its negotiating position. Its purpose is also to increase maritime safety. This makes the Convention a legitimate regulation of public order law. Its provisions require application in any situation falling within their scope since they are crucial for the safeguarding a State Party public interests.

Such nature of the provisions of the Convention is expressed by its Article 2 which specifies that the Convention shall apply to any international carriage mentioned in this article. In respect of such carriage this provision mandates the obligatory application of the Convention.

Because of their nature, provisions of the Athens Convention (as well as the EU and internal Polish regulation based on the 1974 Convention or PAL 2002) may be applied by the Polish courts as overriding mandatory provisions, and as such they entertain protection in conflict rules. As is provided in Article 9(2) of the Regulation Rome I nothing shall restrict the application of such provisions of the law of the forum.

Contract of carriage of passengers has not been considered in the EU system of conflict rules as consumer contract. It is excluded from the scope of Article 6 of the Rome I Regulation providing the proper law for consumer contracts (Article 6 (4) "b") with the exception of the contract relating to package travel within the meaning of Council Directive 90/314/EEC of 13 June 1990 on package travel, package holidays and package tours. However it was decided that owing to the

[39] OJ L 177, 4.7.2008, pp. 6–16.

particular nature of contracts of carriage specific provisions should ensure an adequate level of protection of passengers (Recital 32). On the one hand such contracts are regarded as contracts concluded with parties being weaker which should be protected by conflict-of-law rules that are more favourable to their interests than the general rules but on the other hand the special nature of transport contracts requires a compromise between the interests of passengers and carriers. It cannot be expected from the carriers that they adapt to different legal systems of all countries whose laws could govern the consumer contracts.

10.1 Choice of Law Clauses

Under the Rome I Regulation the proper law of a contract of carriage of passengers may be chosen by the parties to the contract, but in accordance with the second subparagraph of Article 5 the parties' freedom to choose the applicable law is limited to the law of the country where:

(a) the passenger has his habitual residence; or
(b) the carrier has his habitual residence; or
(c) the carrier has his place of central administration; or
(d) the place of departure is situated; or
(e) the place of destination is situated.

To the extent that the law applicable to a contract for the carriage of passengers has not been chosen by the parties the applicable law shall be the law mentioned in the first subparagraph of Article 5 of the Rome I Regulation. It is the law of the country where the passenger has his habitual residence, provided that either the place of departure or the place of destination is situated in that country. If these requirements are not met, the law of the country where the carrier has his habitual residence shall apply. When it is justified there is also possibility of the application of the law manifestly more closely connected (Article 5(3)).

It is important to mention the restriction on the effect of an express choice imposed by Article 3(4) of the Rome I Regulation which specifies that where all other elements relevant to the situation at the time of the choice of law are located in one or more Member States, the parties' choice of applicable law other than that of a Member State shall not prejudice the application of provisions of Community law, where appropriate as implemented in the Member State of the forum, which cannot be derogated from by agreement. The Regulation (EC) No 392/2009 is the legal instrument containing such mandatory provisions of Community law and parties' choice of law other than the law of a Member State for a contract of carriage of passengers covered by this Regulation shall not prejudice the application of its provisions.

In cases where the agreement is entirely domestic in content and its all other elements relevant to the situation at the time of the choice are located in Poland mandatory provisions of the Polish law should be applied and choice of law should not be effective (Article 3(3) of the Rome I Regulation).

Reference

Dragun-Gertner M, Pepłowska-Dąbrowska Z (2018) Legal aspects of Cruises (Poland). In: Lewaszkiwiecz-Petrykowska B (ed) Rapports Polonais XXe Congrès International de Droit Comparé Fukuoka 22-28 VII 2018. Wydawnictwo Uniwersytetu Łódzkiego, Łódź, pp 173–181

Legal Aspects of Cruises from a Romanian Perspective

Gabriel Mihai

Abstract The Harbour of Constanta, Romania is a relatively new destination for the cruise industry, on maritime routes in the Mediterranean Sea and the Black Sea.

In Romania, there is no self-sustaining policy in favor of cruise shipping, but this type of business is a mean of promoting tourism activity on the Romanian Black Sea coast, both in the tourist resorts and in the city of Constanta.

The Romanian legal system doesn't contain special regulations for passenger transport. The general navigation rules and port regulations apply to cruises.

The consumer protection legislation, the law of international commercial contracts and the provisions of private international law are also applicable.

Concerning specific education programs devoted to legal aspects of cruises, it is worth mentioning that "Ovidius" University in Constanta holds a master's degree course *Maritime Law* (2 years), the only program of this kind in Romania, where curricula focuses on internal and international legislation and jurisprudence in the field of maritime transportation and legal institutions regarding the cruise transport regime are studied.

1 Introduction

This is a brief description of some legal aspects of cruises in Romania. There is not much available information on the topic, but we think it is worth sharing this perspective on the country's reality nowadays.

G. Mihai (✉)
"Ovidius" University of Constanța, Faculty of Law and Administrative Sciences, Constanța, Romania

C. Fresnedo de Aguirre (ed.), *Legal Aspects of Cruises*, Ius Comparatum - Global Studies in Comparative Law 56, https://doi.org/10.1007/978-3-030-83090-8_6

2 The Importance of Cruises

Romania is not a main cruise destiny for maritime passenger ships. The port of Constantza is home port for river passenger vessels and mainly for cargo ships and oil tanker ships.

The Harbour of Constantza, in Romania, is a second-choice destination for cruise routes in the Mediterranean Sea and the Black Sea. The Black Sea is a relatively new destination for the cruise industry. This is due to the current geopolitical situation: the Crimean and Ukrainian ports have been removed from the cruise map, and the Black Sea Cruise ships' routes are avoiding this conflict area, moving their focus to Constantza.

At the same time, there is no important interest in the legislative or marketing field of this segment.

There are some statistics in Romania on the evolution of the number of cruises and cruise passengers arriving in your country, of passengers disembarking and of their nationalities, and of the money they spend on land, but at the port level only. These refers to the number of passengers, how many embarked and disembarked in Constantza and how many vessels (maritime and river) are docking in the port of Constantza.

The new passengers' terminal is located in the northern part of the Harbour of Constantza, being located on the North Dive, at the passenger dock. Being a destination of many Danube and maritime cruise routes, Constantza now offers the proper conditions of boarding both river cruise ships which make a layover here, and maritime passenger ships. The depths of the new terminal facilitate this opportunity.

Located very close to the historical city of Constantza and Tomis Tourists Harbour, the new Passenger Terminal has an operating capacity of 100,000 passengers per year, being the latest investment meant to increase tourism activity on the Romanian seaside. The terminal is managed by CN Maritime Port Administration SA Constantza. The figures are the following:

2013: 69 ships boarded, having 54,616 tourists
2014: 92 layovers took place, with ships having 70,000 tourists aboard
2015: 35 layovers took place, with ships having 35,000 tourists aboard
2016: 14 ship visited with 8632 tourists aboard
2017: 21 sea and river ships are scheduled to board at the Constantza Port

Therefore, it could be said that cruise business is important in Romania because it facilitates the development of the Romanian tourism on the Black Sea Seaside and the city of Constantza (the ancient Tomis), Danube Delta and Bucharest, the capital of Romania.

In spite of the fact that this type of business is a mean of promoting tourism activity on the Romanian Black Sea coast, both in the tourist resorts and in the city of Constantza, at present there is no self-sustaining policy in favour of cruise industry.

The services offered to cruises in Romanian ports are of medium to good quality. There were no complaints from tourists on this matter. In the port of Constantza all services are available for all vessels. Some of them as waste removal, power and water supply are performed by port administration, in time to other services as ship chandlering, bunker supply is performed by private authorized companies.

Regarding labour market in Romania, it can be said that though it is not a significant industry yet, the activity of maritime navigation, cargo transport at sea and port activity are relevant for Constantza and Romania.

As for the ship management industry important, it is relevant to Romania and the port of Constantza.

There are several construction and repair yards for sea and river vessels. Some of them have a good reputation and their activity is appreciated by external clients. The most important shipyards in Romania are "Constanta Naval Shipyard", "Daewoo Mangalia Heavy Industries Shipyard", and "Damen Shipyard Galatzi".

3 General and Specific Rules Applicable to Cruises

The Romanian legal system contains some general legal rules that are applicable to general navigation and ports, and to carriage of passengers by sea, though not specifically on cruises. An example of these general rules is the Order of the Ministry of Transport no. 37/2014 regarding the authorization of commercial operators for the activity of public transport of passengers and/or goods on inland waterways. The general provisions on international commercial contracts also apply to cruises. Some of these rules are of international origin and others of national origin.

However, there are not special regulations for cruises or passengers maritime transport in the Romanian judicial system, except the port regulations which allow the captain to decide the number of tugs to use on the manoeuvre without imposing a minimum number and power of these tugs. These rules are both of international or supranational origin, and of national origin. The scope of application of those rules is the development of cruise transport and tourism in the near area.

4 Cruise Passengers as Consumers

There is no available information or developments in Romania regarding cruise passengers as consumers. As for its regulation, there are general rules on consumer protection that are applicable to passengers in cruises.

5 Combined Trips, Package Travels, Package Tours or Package Holidays

De lege lata, there are no specific regulations on combined trips in Romania. However, there are certain regulations on delegation and the allowance paid for the delegation of an employee, but applying them in this case would be debatable only if the first trip can be taken into consideration as the permanent work station, according to the individual labour agreement. National Law no. 53/2003 (Labour Code) provides such regulations on these topics.

6 Labour Rules on Cruises' Workers

The Romanian legal system does not provide specific labour regulations applicable to cruises' workers. Therefore, general international and national labour rules apply.

Even if its origin is contractual, the mobility clause is regulated in the Romanian legal system and states that the execution of the work obligations is not achieved in a stable place of work, and so the employee is entitled to benefits, in money or in nature.

Moreover, the Romanian legal system contains regulations regarding the working hours and the rest time, which are applicable to all categories of workers, therefore to cruises' workers as well. According to these regulations, in Romania one can work for 12 full hours, but with a subsequent 24-hour rest period.

Those rules are both of international or supranational origin, and of national origin. Law no. 53/2003 (Labour Code) provides the referred regulations on working hours and alike; and Directive 2003/88/CE also regulates aspects regarding the working hours in the European Union.

It is well-known that cruises' workers are not that well protected by the labour law once the ship leaves the port, because there are cases when they work more than 12 hours a day. Under the Romanian law, an employee who works more than 12 hours a day is entitled to supplementary rest time or to additional pay for the overtime work.

The provisions applicable for cruises' workers can be the CJUE cause nr. C-266/14 in response to a preliminary question regarding art. 2 of Directive 2003/88/CE. The court stated that the "work time" notion for workers who do not have a fixed or regular workplace should be interpreted in the sense that these "daily journeys from home to places where the first and last customer is working time".

7 Rules on Ports That Are Relevant Regarding Cruises

There are no special rules for the cruise industry in Romania. The general rules are established in the Commercial Code- Maritime Commerce and Navigation Chapter and also the general port rules and conditions apply to cruises as well. The rules on the matter are both of international or supranational origin, and of national origin.

The port charges system is available on www.portofconstantza.com at the "Port tariffs" section in the main menu, the website of the Constanta Maritime Ports administration National Company.

8 Rules on Environmental Impact of Cruises

The Romanian legal system does not contain specific rules on environmental impact of cruises. Therefore, national and international environmental protection laws are applicable.

9 Jurisdiction and Arbitration

The Romanian legal system does not contain specific regulations on jurisdiction or arbitration applicable to cruises. Therefore, international provision on jurisdiction of private international law contained in the Civil Code apply.

Only General Provisions on Consumer Protection (Consumer Code) regarding jurisdiction protect the passenger as a consumer.

Regarding forum selection clauses included in general conditions of carriage of passengers in cruises, there are contractual provisions based on the provisions of private international law that apply.

The inclusion of arbitration clauses in general conditions of carriage of passengers in cruises depends on the will of the contracting parties. In some contracts there is an arbitration clause.

10 Choice of Law

The Romanian legal system does not contain specific provisions on choice of law regarding cruises. Therefore, the Civil Code in the part relating to the private international law relations applies.

These general provisions on choice of law protect the passenger as a consumer, since they have an important contribution in terms of insurance, quality of passenger transportation, comfort and safety of passengers. There are no special provisions for the choice of applicable law in the case of passengers' carriage.

11 General Conditions Used by Companies Offering Cruse Services

The Romanian legal system does not contain specific or general provisions on liability or any other aspect of general conditions regarding cruises.

12 Sources of Law Applicable to Cruises

The following are some general sources of law that are applicable to cruises:

Order of the Ministry of Transport no. 37/2014
National Law no. 53/2003 (Labour Code)
Directive 2003/88/CE
Commercial Code- Maritime Commerce and Navigation Chapter
Consumer Code
Civil Code

13 Conclusions

Though Romania is not a main cruise destiny for maritime passenger ships, there are some indicators that show that cruises activities are growing, particularly regarding the port of Constantza. There are not specific rules on cruises in the Romanian legal system, but general international and general rules on maritime law, private international law, contracts, and consumer protection law, among other issues, apply.

Spanish Report on Cruises

Rosario Espinosa Calabuig, José Roberto Pérez Salom, and Laura Carballo Piñeiro

Abstract The cruise industry has experienced a significant boost all over the world in last years. Until the Covid-19 outbreak, Spain was taking a leading position within the European market as both departure and destination country. As a member of the International Maritime Organisation (IMO), the International Labour Organisation (ILO) and the European Union (EU), Spain has implemented a number of international and EU instruments that apply to the cruise industry. Hence, the approach is not industry-driven, but dependent on the matters at stake, being (general) provisions dealing with consumer, worker and environmental protection of particular significance in this sector. Specific measures can only be found at a port authority level and mainly seek to promote the industry. This chapter provides a general overview on the situation of the cruise industry in Spain with an emphasis on the regulatory framework that has been developed to rule the sector.

1 Introduction

Spanish ports have become in recent years a European landmark in cruise traffic. Spain is the second European country in number of cruise passengers, just behind Italy as indicated by the *Cruise Lines International Association (CLIA)*. The Spanish port system, of State ownership, comprises 46 ports of general interest. They are managed by 28 Port Authorities whose coordination and efficiency control is allocated to the public body *Puertos del Estado* (State Ports). This public body is attached to the *Ministerio de Fomento* (Ministry of Public Works and Transport),

R. E. Calabuig (✉) · J. R. P. Salom
University of Valencia, Valencia, Spain
e-mail: Rosario.Espinosa@uv.es; Jose.R.Perez@uv.es

L. C. Piñeiro
Nippon Foundation Chair Maritime Labour Law and Policy, World Maritime University, Malmö, Sweden
e-mail: laura.carballo@usc.es; lc@wmu.se

C. Fresnedo de Aguirre (ed.), *Legal Aspects of Cruises*, Ius Comparatum - Global Studies in Comparative Law 56, https://doi.org/10.1007/978-3-030-83090-8_7

which has been appointed by law for the implementation of government policy on ports.

The cruise industry makes an important economic impact in the cities that host Spanish ports and their surroundings with regard to both, direct expenditure and employment. Barcelona, Balearic Islands, Malaga and Valencia in the Mediterranean Sea; Bay of Cádiz, Vigo and A Coruña in the Atlantic region of the Iberian Peninsula; and the Canary Islands are the main attraction region of this kind of tourism, concentrating 96% of the domestic cruise traffic. Barcelona is the first European port and the fourth in the world with 3 million of cruise passengers in 2018 and a growth of 12.4%.[1]

Spain does not have a tailor-made legislation on the cruise sector, but it does have a significant number of laws and regulations that apply to the sector. Most of them have been drafted by way of implementation of international instruments issued by the International Maritime Organization (IMO), the International Labour Organization (ILO) and the European Union (EU). Accordingly, the cruise sector is actually heavily regulated in Spain, although the piecemeal approach implies a number of shortcomings. The absence of specific regulation on cruises in Spain requires to break down the different activities and areas linked to the cruise industry in order to determine the legal framework within which the sector is operating.

This report follows this pattern by acknowledging the role in cruise activities of provisions dealing with travel package contracts, the international contract of carriage of passengers, and in general consumer protection rules. In this regard, Spanish law—in line with EU law and the Court of Justice's case law (*Pammer/Alpenhof*)—considers cruise-related contracts as travel package contracts (*viaje combinado*). At the same time, EU law on package travel overlaps to a certain extent with EU and international substantive regulation regarding transport of passengers what will be analysed in section six. Section seven will address employment and labour law in the sector, mainly driven by the Maritime Labour Convention, 2006 (MLC, 2006) while the next sections will be devoted to rules on port where most sector-specific rules can be found, and finally environment protection rules. Finally, the international nature of the cruise sector makes it necessary to refer to the Spanish system of private international law, in order to resolve questions on jurisdiction and applicable law. The chapter closes with an overview of Spanish case law and some conclusions.

---

[1] See *Puertos del Estado*. Press release http://www.puertos.es/en-us/Pages/Noticias/Fitur2019_ENG.aspx (13.02.2019). This upward trend broke at the end of 2016. Spain came to a close in 2016 with 8.5 million cruise passengers, which shows a decrease of 1.15% (99,810 less passengers) compared to the previous year.

2 The Significance of the Cruise Industry in Spain

The last report published by the abovementioned CLIA shows that the cruise sector would have got 32 millions of passengers in 2020,[2] This report also highlights the significance of the sector for the Spanish economy, As confirmed by statistics to be found in the report *Contribution of the Cruise Tourism to the Economies of Europe 2018* published in November 2019,[3] as well as in the report *Statistics & Markets. Europe 2017* is a report also published by CLIA, although focused on its European section.[4] More detailed information can be found in the country report provided by CLIA Spain.[5] *Puertos del Estado* also publishes statistics concerning the activity of Spanish ports which include data regarding cruises and cruisers.[6] More specific information is available in the relevant port authority database.

According to *Puertos del Estado*, the cruise industry had in 2018 a direct economic impact in Spain of €1255 million. There were 26,400 jobs related to the industry in Spain, which represent the 10% of the national industry of tourism. As a result, Spain became the fourth country more benefited in the European market of cruises because of its accelerated increase of 6.5% in 2017 after the 4% in 2016. From 2008 onwards, the economic contribution of that sector increases about 22.5% in Europe, an 8% of which is represented by the Spanish cruise industry.[7] Regrettably, the Covid-19 crisis has put all these data in brackets and placed the sector in a very serious risk of insolvency. For the time being, it is too early but the bankruptcy of *Pullmantur Cruceros*, a major Spanish company, seems to confirm the gloomiest predictions.

While ports start slowly to reopen, the European Maritime Safety Agency (EMSA) along with the European Centre for Disease Control and Prevention (ECDC) have produced an EU Guidance for Safe Cruise Ship Operations with a view to helping the sector to provide a safe experience to travellers. Cruise ship operators have welcomed the harmonization of approaches as to how to tackle this serious health crisis on board, but the uncertainty remains as countries take quick measures such as travel restrictions to diminish the spread of the Covid-19 disease. Other factors that do not help the cruise business are lack of air connectivity and a port-to-port legal approach as to how to handle operations. In the current situation,

[2] https://portaldeturismo.pe/noticia/clia-2020.

[3] The report is available at CLIA website in https://cruising.org/-/media/research-updates/research/global-cruise-impact-analysis%2D%2D-2019%2D%2Dfinal.pdf.

[4] The report is available at CLIA website: <https://www.cliaeurope.eu/images/News/Europe_2017_CCFinal.pdf>.

[5] The report is available at CLIA Spain website: <https://es.cruiseexperts.org/media/3006/informe-de-contribuci%C3%B3n-econ%C3%B3mica-de-la-industria-de-cruceros-en-europa-2017_espa%C3%B1a.pdf>.

[6] Statistics can be found at the Puertos del Estado website: <http://www.puertos.es>.

[7] See http://www.cliaspain.com/la-contribución-economica-de-la-industria-de-cruceros-alcanza-su-maximo-historico-en-europa/noticias (02.05.2017).

all last year's predictions are outdated while new ones are far from being straightforward.

Notwithstanding the abovementioned data showing how relevant the cruise industry has been, and still is, in Spain, there are no specific legislative or regulatory policies and measures, at a national or a regional level, for its promotion. The Spanish government has adopted several specific policies for the promotion of the cruise industry, but only at a port authority level. *Puertos del Estado* launched the campaign "*Blue Carpet: Adéntrate en España sobre una alfombra azul*" (Blue carpet: step into Spain on a blue carpet) in 2013, whose aim was to promote Spain worldwide as a cruise destination country and strengthen the cruise sector in our country from the perspective of the improvement of port facilities and the cultural and touristic offer.[8]

Promotion measures are usually coordinated with local authorities and, sometimes, regional ones. In the case of Valencia city, the established inter-institutional work group comprises representatives of the Valencian Port Authority, Valencia City Council (*Ayuntamiento de Valencia*) and Valencia Tourism (*Turisme València*); Valencian Shipping Association (*Asociación Naviera Valenciana*), Valencian Tourism Agency (*Agencia Valenciana de Turismo*), Valencian Chamber of Commerce (*Cámara de Comercio de Valencia*), Valencian Business Confederation (*Confederación Empresarial Valenciana*) and Council of Valencia (*Diputación de Valencia*) (Esteve Pérez and García Sánchez 2015).

According to *Puertos del Estado* data, services provided at Spanish port facilities are satisfactory and this fact contributes to improve their quality and prestige in the cruise business. In particular, the reference instrument on the quality of the services provided to cruises is the benchmark of quality service for cruise traffic adopted by *Puertos del Estado*. The Service General Benchmark (*Referencial Genérico de Servicio*) contains applicable quality service characteristics to the providers of passenger services in Spanish ports of general interest, and the concession holders or authorization of maritime stations, for cruise passenger ships who willingly wish

[8] In Spain, promotion measures for the cruise sector are usually adopted by port authorities, as they enjoy independence to apply incentives of different nature in pursuit of the acquisition and retention of cruise companies. For instance, the Valencian Port Authority approved on July 2016 the application of a 40% allowance, on the ship and the passenger tax, to the mooring of cruises. Under this measure, shipping companies can save around 600,000 euros per year, according to the forecasts of this Authority. See http://valenciaplaza.com/el-puerto-de-valencia-bonificara-al-maximo-las-tasas-portuarias-para-frenar-la-caida-de-cruceristas (02.05.2017). Other promotion measures include the improvement of the facilities in order to encourage the mooring of cruises. The Valencian Port Authority invested around 8 million euros in the construction of a cruise terminal for ships with a large passenger capacity, between 3000 and 4000. This investment fell within its promotion strategy of cruise tourism, with the aim to reach 600,000 cruisers in 2020, and to facilitate Valencia as base port for cruises, and not only stopovers. *See Las Provincias* website http://www.lasprovincias.es/economia/201604/15/puerto-valencia-construira-terminal-20160415161651.html (02.05.2017).

to undergo a third party certification required to obtain the quality service allowance. Indicators include waste management and the quality of the services provided.[9]

3 The Spanish Legal Framework for the Cruise Industry

The cruise industry does not benefit from tailor-made instruments at the international, national or regional level. As a matter of fact, they are not necessary to the extent that the legal framework already provides rules dealing with the different activities linked to the cruise industry. These provisions are related to issues such as ship pollution, death of passengers or crew members, commission of crimes on board, employment of seafarers, jurisdiction or arbitral clauses included in the general terms of cruise contracts, among many others. By the same token, the IMO and the ILO instruments are applicable to the industry. And the same applies to many other rules, in particular those issued by the EU.

As requested by the International Academy of Comparative Law, this report basically deals with private law rules relevant to the industry and, within this field, the focus is placed upon travellers/passengers and workers. To this end, particular attention will be paid to their protection from a contractual perspective. In this vein, travel package contracts, contracts of carriage of passengers, and other provisions concerning consumer matters, as well as employment contracts will be examined from a purely domestic and private international law perspectives. Environmental matters are also of relevance and some references will be made. The applicable rules to all these issues in Spain will be specifically mentioned in the following sections.

4 Travel Package Contracts in the Cruise Sector: The Traveller as a Consumer

In practice, the EU law on package travel coexists with EU and international regulation regarding transport of passengers. On the one hand, transport of passengers is usually a component of a package travel (often by air) and this can have consequences over passenger damages' claims. On the other hand, the transport of passengers is regulated by international uniform law as well as EU law—there are EU Regulations in air, sea and rail transport. Therefore, the legal operator faces to a complex legal framework in which the respective areas of application of the existing legislations in this field have to be identified (López de Gonzalo 2016).

[9] *Referencial de calidad de servicio para el trafico de cruceros* - ref-gen-cruceros version 1 1709.2012.

According to EU law as interpreted by the Court of Justice,[10] travel packages are classified as consumer matters. In particular, travellers as consumers are covered in Spain by Royal Decree-Legislative 1/2007 of 16 November approving the Recast Text of the General Law on Consumer Protection and Other Supplementary Laws [*Real Decreto Legislativo 1/2007, de 16 de noviembre, por el que se aprueba el Texto Refundido de la Ley General para la Defensa de los Consumidores y Usuarios y otras leyes complementarias* (LGDCU).[11] This instrument transposes into Spanish law, Directive 2011/83/UE of the European Parliament and of the Council of 25 October 2011 on consumer rights, amending Council Directive 93/13/EEC and Directive 1999/44/EC of the European Parliament and of the Council and repealing Council Directive 85/577/EEC and Directive 97/7/EC of the European Parliament and of the Council.[12]

LGDCU has already been amended by Law 3/2014 of 27 of March,[13] and by the Royal Decree-Law 23/2018 of 21 of December,[14] that has transposed several directives into Spanish law, including Directive (EU) 2015/2302 of the European Parliament and of the Council of 25 November 2015 on package travel and linked travel arrangements. The LGDCU—in the last version given by the Royal Decree-Law 23/2018—regulates travel package,[15] making it clear that this type of contract is considered a consumer contract (Tur Faúndez 2003).

The new provisions in the LGDCU have replaced the former Spanish law 21/1995 of 6 July on travel packages, by which Council Directive 90/314/EEC of 13 June 1990 on package travel, package holidays and package tours, was transposed in Spain (Benavides Velasco 2012). At the same time this directive has been replaced by the abovementioned Directive (EU) 2015/2302, whose provisions have been transposed into Articles 150 and 151 of the LGDCU.

As highlighted by Directive 2015/2302, "Tourism plays an important role in the economy of the Union, and package travel, package holidays and package tours ('packages') represent a significant proportion of the travel market. That market has undergone considerable changes since the adoption of the first Directive 90/314/EEC. In addition to traditional distribution chains, the internet has become an increasingly important medium through which travel services are offered or sold. Travel services are not only combined in the form of traditional pre-arranged packages, but are often combined in a customised way. Many of those combinations of travel services were either in a legal 'grey zone' or were clearly not covered by Directive 90/314/EEC. The new Directive 2015/2302 was elaborated to adapt the

[10] A concept of travel package was given by the ECJ in the judgment of 7 December of 2010 in the accumulated cases *Peter Pammer/Reederei Karl Schlüter GmbH & Co. KG* (C-585/08) and *Hotel Alpenhof GesmbH/Oliver Heller* (C-144/09).

[11] BOE 30.11.2007.

[12] OJ L 304, 22.11.2011.

[13] BOE n. 76, 28.3.2014.

[14] BOE n. 314, 27.12.2018.

[15] Article 150 and 151 LGDCU after RDL 23/2018.

scope of protection taking account of those developments, to enhance transparency, and to increase legal certainty for travellers and traders".[16] Notwithstanding these arguments, some literature has already emphasized the "lights and shadows" of the new legal regime (Berenguer Albaladejo 2016).

The former Directive 90/314 referred to "package travel, package holidays and package tours" and now Directive 2015/2302 refers to "package travel and linked travel arrangements". In the old one, the definition of 'package' meant "the pre-arranged combination of not fewer than two of the following when sold or offered for sale at an inclusive price and when the service covers a period of more than twenty-four hours or includes overnight accommodation: (a) transport; (b) accommodation; (c) other tourist services not ancillary to transport or accommodation and accounting for a significant proportion of the package".[17] Directive 2015/2302 is more specific as the result of the abovementioned changes occurred in the tourism market. In particular, "package means a combination of at least two different types of travel services for the purpose of the same trip or holiday, if:

(a) those services are combined by one trader, including at the request of or in accordance with the selection of the traveller, before a single contract on all services is concluded; or
(b) irrespective of whether separate contracts are concluded with individual travel service providers, those services are:
    (i) purchased from a single point of sale and those services have been selected before the traveller agrees to pay,
    (ii) offered, sold or charged at an inclusive or total price,
    (iii) advertised or sold under the term 'package' or under a similar term,
    (iv) combined after the conclusion of a contract by which a trader entitles the traveller to choose among a selection of different types of travel services, or
    (v) purchased from separate traders through linked online booking processes where the traveller's name, payment details and e-mail address are transmitted from the trader with whom the first contract is concluded to another trader or traders and a contract with the latter trader or traders is concluded at the latest 24 hours after the confirmation of the booking of the first travel service".[18]

Together with this definition, Article 3.2 of Directive 2015/2302 in its last paragraph, contains some cases that cannot be considered as "packages", including, "a combination of travel services where not more than one type of travel service as referred to in point (a), (b) or (c) of point 1 is combined with one or more tourist services as referred to in point (d) of point 1 is not a package if the latter services:

[16] Recital 2 Directive 2015/2302.

[17] *Article 2.1* Directive 90/314.

[18] Article 3.2. Directive 2015/2302.

(a) do not account for a significant proportion of the value of the combination and are not advertised as and do not otherwise represent an essential feature of the combination; or
(b) are selected and purchased only after the performance of a travel service as referred to in point (a), (b) or (c) of point 1 has started".

As already said, Directive 2015/2302, as before Directive 90/314/CEE, overlaps to a certain extent with EU and international regulations regarding transport of passengers. This forces the legal operator to identify the respective areas of application and to interpret the legislation in cruises are qualified as transport and not as package travel. For example, according to Article 14.3 of Directive 2015/2302, the organizer of the travel package could be free from his/her liability if (s)he proves that "the lack of conformity is: a) attributable to the traveller; b) attributable to a third party unconnected with the provision of the travel services included in the package travel contract and is unforeseeable or unavoidable; or c) due to unavoidable and extraordinary circumstances". In Directive 2015/2302 as well as in Directive 90/314, the organiser is responsible for the correct execution of all services included in the travel package, regardless of the fact services had been provided by the same organiser or by a third one, and therefore, in particular, of the transport services provided by a third carrier. In this respect, compensable damage would include non-patrimonial damages.[19] A comparative study of both directives shows that the content of the damages caused by the travel package organizer is more rigorous than that of those regulated for the carrier (at least in relation to maritime and air carriers) (López de Gonzalo 2016).

In practice, the coordination between the compensation of the traveller by the organizer according to Directive 2015/2302 and that by the carrier according to international conventions or EU regulations in transport matters is regulated by Article 14.5 of Directive 2015/2302. More specifically, claiming the first one "shall not affect the rights of travellers under Regulation (EC) No 261/2004, Regulation (EC) No 1371/2007, Regulation (EC) No 392/2009 of the European Parliament and of the Council, Regulation (EU) No 1177/2010 and Regulation (EU) No 181/2011, and under international conventions. Travellers shall be entitled to present claims under this Directive and under those Regulations and international conventions. Compensation or price reduction granted under this Directive and the compensation or price reduction granted under those Regulations and international conventions shall be deducted from each other in order to avoid overcompensation" (López de Gonzalo 2016).

The consideration of travel packages as consumer contracts has also an impact on the Spanish PIL system and the application, among others, of Regulation (EU) 1215/2012 of 12th December, on international jurisdiction, recognition and enforcement of judgments in civil and commercial matters (Brussels Ia),[20] and *Regulation*

[19]In this sense the judgment of the ECJ of 12 March 2002, Case C-168/00, *Leitner c. Tui Deutschland*.

[20]OJ L 351, 20.12.2012.

(EC) 593/2008 of the European Parliament and of the Council of 17th June on the law applicable to contractual obligations (*Rome* I) ,[21] as can be seen in section X. In both regulations, travel packages are considered an "exception of an exception", meaning that they are an exception to passenger transport contracts and considered as consumer contracts in EU PIL. In other words, travel packages are considered as consumer contracts and therefore the most favourable rules existing in this field are also applied (Feliu Álvarez de Sotomayor 2012).

5 Carriage of Passengers' Contract: The Traveller as a Passenger

The relevant Spanish rules on carriage of passengers by sea are also of international origin. More specifically, the EU has acquired by the Treaty of Amsterdam competence to ratify international conventions dealing with the carriage of passengers. Accordingly, Spanish provisions in these matters follow EU rules.

In this capacity, the EU has issued Regulation (EC) No 392/2009 of the European Parliament and of the Council of 23 April 2009 on the liability of carriers of passengers by sea in the event of accidents (in force since 31 December 2012).[22] This is the relevant instrument in Spain when it comes to the regime dealing with liability and insurance for the carriage of passengers by sea as set out in the relevant provisions of the Athens Convention relating to the Carriage of Passengers and their Luggage by Sea (PAL) of 13 December 1974 (Rosaeg 2010), and its London Protocol of 1 November 2002. That regulation is also the applicable one when it comes to provisions on liability of the carrier and liability limitation (Piras 2012). Regulation 392/2009 has also incorporated IMO Reservation and Guidelines for the Implementation of the Athens Convention as adopted by the IMO Legal Committee on 19 October 2006.

Spain ratified the Athens Convention on 22 September 1981,[23] as well as the London Protocol on 22 September 1981,[24] that entered into force on 11 September 2015 for Spain in accordance with Article 20, paragraph 2. Spain has also ratified the 1990 Protocol to amend the Athens Convention which, however, has not entered into force due to lack of ratifications, only four so far, being Spain one of them (Zuburi de Salinas 2017).

It is also worth noting Regulation (EU) No 1177/2010 of the European Parliament and of the Council of 24 November 2010 concerning the rights of passengers when travelling by sea and inland waterway and amending Regulation (EC) No 2006/2004, in force from 18 December 2012. Finally, the Spanish Law on Shipping (*Ley*

---

[21] *OJ L 177, 04.7.2008.*

[22] OJ L 131, 28.5.2009.

[23] BOE n. 108, 6.5.1987.

[24] BOE n. 242, 9.10.1990.

14/2014 de 24 de julio, de navegación marítima) regulates the passage contract in Articles 287 to 300, being applicable to cruise ships. Article 298 thereof deals with the liability of the carrier while Article 299 establishes its limitation. Both provisions follow the lines of the Athens Convention and its London Protocol.

In relation to air carriage contracts that are usually a component of the travel package, the relevant instrument is the Varsaw Convention on 12 October 1929, later modified by the Montreal Convention on 28 May 1999.[25] From a EU perspective, the relevant instrument is Regulation (EC) No 889/2002 of the European Parliament and of the Council of 13 May 2002 amending Council Regulation (EC) No 2027/97 on air carrier liability in the event of accidents.[26]

Finally, and regarding the rail carriage contracts, the Berne Convention on 9 May 1980 as amended by the Vilnius Protocol on 3 June 1999 (COTIF-CIV)[27] is applied and in the EU the Regulation 1371/2007 of the European Parliament and of the Council of 23 October 2007 on rail passengers' rights and obligations was enacted.[28]

6 Cruises and Labour Contracts

The Spanish legal system has already implemented the Maritime Labour Convention, 2006 (MLC, 2006) which covers cruises' workers. On account of the many different types of workers on board cruise ships, other general rules and collective bargaining agreements (CBAs) are applicable. In addition to this, there are specific CBAs concluded with companies managing, or related to, cruises such as those in charge of assistance services for passengers embarking and disembarking cruises.

The MLC, 2006 has been further implemented in the EU by Council Directive 2009/13/EC of 16 February 2009 implementing the Agreement concluded by the European Community Shippowners' Associations (ECSA) and the European Transport Workers' Federation (ETF) on the MLC, 2006, and amending Directive 1999/63/EC; Directive 2009/21/ EC of the European Parliament and of the Council of 23 April 2009 on compliance with flag State requirements; Directive 2013/54/EU of the European Parliament and of the Council of 20 November 2013 concerning certain flag State responsibilities for compliance with and enforcement of the MLC, 2006. Domestically, all these provisions have been implemented by Royal Decree 357/2015, of 8 May 2015, on compliance with, and enforcement of, the MLC, 2006. Chapter III of Title III of the abovementioned Spanish Law on Shipping deals with able seafarers on board Spanish ships. However, Articles 156 et seq have to be understood in line with the MLC, 2006 and other international conventions

[25] BOE n. 122, 20.4.2004.

[26] *OJ L 140, 30.5.2002.*

[27] *BOE n. 149, 23.6.2006.*

[28] OJ L 315, 3.12.2007.

such as the Standards on Training, Certification and Watchkeeping (STCW) Convention.

According to the MLC, 2006, seafarer is "any person who is employed or engaged or works in any capacity on board a ship", including cruise ships. This means that not only able seafarers, i.e. those that operate the ship or with an STCW-certificate, but all type of workers including entertainers, sport instructors, catering or cabin staff are deemed seafarers and thus covered by the MLC, 2006 and all rules implementing the latter. Nevertheless, there are still differences between able seafarers and other workers that are even taken into consideration in the MLC, 2006.[29] Anyway, other types of workers than able seafarers have their own specific regulations and CBAs that may be applicable here in addition to the MLC, 2006 and implementing legislation.

The broad definition of "seafarer" laid down in the MLC, 2006, requires national determination as to who is not deemed a seafarer, and Resolution of 18 April 2013 of the Directorate-General for Merchant Shipping provides for that list of workers not considered seafarers. On a positive stance, the same resolution specifies that seafarers are all workers, including room stewards and cleaning personnel, barmen/women, waiters, entertainers, singers, kitchen personnel, etcetera, who regularly work on board a ship and who do not habitually provide their services onshore.

Remarkably, the abovementioned resolution excludes from the MLC, 2006's definition catering staff with short-term contracts. This exclusion is controversial as it may result in abuses of this type contracts, but in particular it obeys to a restrictive interpretation of the MLC, 2006 contrary to the international obligations assumed by Spain with its ratification. In particular, it does not comply with Resolution VII adopted by the International Labour Conference at its 94th Maritime Session, of 9 February 2006. While indicating that workers not specifically complying maritime tasks and only on a short period on board may not be seafarers, the said resolution also indicates that, first, the intention of the MLC, 2006 is to be applicable to all workers on board, and second, the suggested criteria should not exclude general categories of workers, but be applied in the light of the MLC, 2006 principles.

One further problem arises from the concept of shipowner who is, according to Article II(1)(j) of the MLC, 2006, "the owner of the ship or another organization or person, such as the manager, agent or bareboat charterer, who has assumed the responsibility for the operation of the ship from the owner and who, on assuming such responsibility, has agreed to take over the duties and responsibilities imposed on shipowners in accordance with this Convention, regardless of whether any other organization or persons fulfil certain of the duties or responsibilities on behalf of the shipowner". On board cruise ships many different types of workers provide services, but all of them benefit from the MLC, 2006 and in particular, from the fact that the shipowner is the one responsible for all seafarers' rights, including the right to wages laid down in that convention. The point is very important because the shipowner will

[29] Guideline A2 of the MLC, 2006.

usually subcontract some services on board such as entertainment, sports or retail shops. Despite being artists, sport instructors or shop attendants hired by another employer, the ultimate responsible for their rights, including the right to repatriation, once they are classified as seafarers is the shipowner. This poses one issue not addressed by the Spanish jurisdiction and it is the employment relationship between shipowner and seafarer, i.e. despite having an employment contract signed with the company actually hiring them, seafarers such as catering or cabin staff will need to sign a seafarer's employment agreement (SEA) as requested by the MLC, 2006.[30]

7 Rules on Ports Relevant to Cruises

Although there are no specific rules on ports that are relevant concerning cruises in the Spanish legal system, there are sectorial regulations in this regard. However, no international or supranational rules on cruises have been found. In Spain, the distribution of competences concerning ports has its origins in the 1978 Constitution, which confers to the State the exclusive competence on ports of general interest (Article 149.1.20) and stipulates that the Autonomous Communities (*Comunidades Autónomas*) shall assume, among others, competences on safe havens, marinas and, on the whole, those not carrying business activities (Article 148.1.6). Actually, twelve *Comunidades Autónomas* have assumed competences on ports in their respective Statute of Autonomy (*Estatuto de Autonomía*): Andalucía, Asturias, Canarias, Cantabria, Cataluña, Ceuta, Comunidad Valenciana, Galicia, Islas Baleares, Melilla, Murcia and País Vasco.[31]

In both, regional laws and regulations, almost no specific mention to cruise ships is done. There are nevertheless references to passenger traffic with regard to the provision of port services such as the embarkation/disembarkation of passengers, vehicles and luggage. Only the Andalucian regulation provides expressly for the case of cruises in art. 2.4, stating that "a passenger ship is conducting a tourist cruise when it meets the following requirements:

[30] Regulation 2.1 and Standard A2.1 of the MLC, 2006, both of mandatory application.

[31] From the earlier, six have carried out a legislative development of such competences: Andalucía (*Ley 21/2007, de 18 de diciembre de régimen jurídico y económico de los puertos de Andalucía; Decreto 368/2011, de 20 de diciembre, sobre servicios públicos portuarios, actividades en puertos y tasas portuarias*); Canarias (*Ley 14/2003, de 8 de abril, de puertos de Canarias; Decreto 52/2005, de 12 de abril, que aprueba el reglamento de puertos de Canarias*); Cantabria (*Ley 5/2004, de 16 de noviembre, de puertos de Cantabria*); Cataluña (*Ley 5/1998, de 17 de abril, de puertos de Cataluña; Decreto 258/2003, de 21 de octubre, que aprueba el reglamento de puertos de Cataluña*); Islas Baleares (*Ley 10/2005, de 21 de junio, de puertos de las Islas Baleares; Decreto 11/2011, de 18 de febrero, que aprueba el desarrollo y ejecución de determinados aspectos de la Ley de puertos de las Islas Baleares*); and Murcia (*Ley 3/1996, de 16 de mayo, de puertos de la Región de Murcia*).

(a) That it enters a port or is dispatched with such nature by the competent authorities.
(b) That the number of passengers on cruise regime exceeds 75 per cent of the overall amount of passengers.

It shall be understood that a passenger is travelling on cruise regime when the stopover in a port is part of a closed trip that, by itself, has a touristic or recreational aim, not a transportation one.

The declaration filled by the passive subject will state, apart from the characteristics of the ship and the intended duration of the stay in port, the itinerary of the cruise, the number and the conditions of the passengers on board."

Nowadays, the main regulation in connection with ports, which also expressly regulates cruise ships, can be found in the *Real Decreto Legislativo 2/2011, de 5 del septiembre, por el que se aprueba el Texto Refundido de la Ley de Puertos del Estado y de la Marina Mercante* which essentially recasts the *Ley 27/1992, de 24 de noviembre, de Puertos del Estado y de la Marina Mercante*, and *Ley 48/2003, de 26 de noviembre, de régimen económico y de prestación de servicios en los puertos de interés general*. In its annex II, dedicated to provide definitions, the recast text states, for instance:

9.ª Tourist cruise passenger in embarkment or disembarkment: are those of the ship qualified and authorized to operate as tourist cruise which begin or end their trip in that port.

10.ª Tourist cruise passenger in a transit port: are those passengers of a ship qualified and authorized to operate as tourist cruise which begin or end their trip in another port.

12.ª Base port for cruises: port in which, for a certain stopover, any of the following requirements is met:

a) That at least 50 per cent of the overall number of passenger begin or end their cruise in that stopover.
b) That the overall number of passenger beginning or ending their trip in that stopover is not less than 250.

It is understood that the passenger beginning or ending their cruise are those who have not been declared tourist cruise passengers in transit.

13.ª Cruise company: shipping company or group of shipping companies, of the same company group, devoted to the operation of passenger ships, tourist cruise type.

20.ª Shipping service: the one provided to a certain type of traffic in a port, when the ship or group of ships belonging to the same shipping or cruise company join that port with others, transporting the same kind and nature of goods or a certain type of passenger, article of transport or loading unit.

21.ª Regular shipping service: The one provided to a certain type of traffic in a port, when a ship or group of ships belonging to the same shipping or cruise company (or a group of ships belonging to different shipping companies under a joint exploitation agreement) join that port with others, transporting the same kind and nature of goods or a certain type of passenger, article of transport or loading unit and, in addition, it is publicly offered and advertised to potential users, given under conditions of regularity, with predetermined origins, destinations and dates and a frequency of at least 24 stopovers per year in the corresponding port.

Similarly, certain ministerial rank regulation makes reference to cruises, such as the *Orden FOM/1392/2004, de 13 de mayo, relativa a la notificación y entrega de desechos generados por los buques*. The purpose of this order is the regulation of the conditions required for the grant, by the Maritime Authority, of the certifications for the partial or total exemption of the obligations contained in article 6 and in paragraph 1 of article 7 of *Real Decreto 1381/2002, de 20 de diciembre, sobre instalaciones portuarias de recepción de desechos generados por los buques y residuos de carga*. Besides, the *Orden FOM/1194/2011, de 29 de abril, por la que se regula el procedimiento integrado de escala de buques en los puertos de interés general*. The purpose of this order is to harmonise the procedure of request for stopover, berth assignment and dispatch of vessels in Spanish ports of general interest, as well as to regulate the management of the uniform stopover document (*Documento Único de Escala DUE*) and the information contained in it.

Port taxes are regulated in chapter II, articles 161 ff. of *RDL 2/2011* and consist of four types: occupation, activity, deployment and aid to navigation (art. 161). The bill itself raises certain exemptions to them in articles 169 to 171, but from a careful reading results that they do not apply in the case of cruises.[32]

In order to take into account, the cost structure of each Port Authority and guarantee the principle of economic and financial independence, in a framework of fair competition among ports, each Port Authority is allowed to promote, within the framework of an annual Business Plan, three reduction coefficients which will be applied, respectively, to the basic amount of the taxes of the ship (T-1), passengers (T-2) and goods (T-3), with the several limits (see Article 166).

Each Port Authority will make, where appropriate, the proposal of correction coefficients taking into account the forecast of traffic evolution, the level of debt, their needs of investment and their management objectives, as well as the annual performance target and the reasonable return on the net non-current asset for the corresponding years. In the event that none is proposed, it will be understood that the ones from the previous year remain, provided that they comply with the previous limits or the value is equal to a unit, in case they have not been approved before. The definitive correction coefficients for each Port Authority will be established on

[32]Port taxes are governed by the aforementioned *RDL 2/2011* and, in anything not foreseen, a regulatory reference to *Ley 8/1989, de 13 de abril, de Tasas y Precios Públicos, la Ley 58/2003, de 17 de diciembre, General Tributaria* and regulatory provisions to implement them is done (art. 162). Article 165 admits the possibility of allowances on port taxes subject to the terms and restriction established by law, with the aim to promote competitiveness and economic and environmental sustainability of port activity and the transport system, the application to a tax of more than one of the allowances foreseen in the law will be carried out in a successive and multiplicative way. To these effects, the total tax quota will be multiplied, successively, by the corresponding reduction coefficient, understanding by such the unit minus the allowance value for one unit.

annual basis in the State Budget Law (*Ley de Presupuestos Generales del Estado*) or the one which, where appropriate, is approved in this respect (Article 166.3). Every year, this law updates the applicable allowances at the ports of general interest to the taxes of occupation, passengers and goods; the correction coefficients applied to the taxes of ships, passengers and goods in ports of general interest; as well as conducts a review of the applicable taxes to the system of ports of general interest.

Concerning cruise ships, the applicable taxes are those regarding to: maritime signalling or navigation aid (T-0), art. 164 d) of *RDL 2/2011*; ship tax (T-1); passenger tax (T-2), encompassed as deployment taxes in art. 193 ff. of the same law; pilot service, art. 126; mooring service, art. 128; and reception facilities for the waste generated by the ship, art. 132. To those taxes or service cost, different coefficients and allowances might be applied.[33]

Even though the previous regulation on ports gave rise to a certain number of lawsuits concerning the legal nature of the port taxes, such problems do not seem to exist with the present regulation. The only problems that might arise are those regarding competency issues among port authorities of different regions. This is because the Port Authorities are who determine their reduction coefficients, the so called CAP (*Coeficientes de la Autoridad Portuaria*), which have a direct influence in the cost of each cruise stopover and ranges up to a 30% among the main Spanish ports. On the other hand, nearby ports of the same autonomous community tend to have similar prices. As a whole, cruises are subjected to important allowances, considering the economic impact they have; not only in the port, but also in the city where it is located.

8 Environmental Protection Rules and Cruise Ships

One of the biggest problems associated to cruise ships' traffic regards pollution and other harmful effects on the environment. In 2019, the shipping companies have increased in a 44% the stoppage of ships to adapt them to the climate change (in particular, container companies are reducing their cargo capacity to modify engines and install filters of smoke) and this initiative would be desirable also in the cruise sector.[34]

According to the last Report on the State of the Cruise Industry for 2018 issued by CLIA, cruise ships are also expected to be more and more compromised with environmental questions in a way that less contaminant ships would be leading the sector of maritime transport with a compromise assumed to reduce pollution in a 40% for 2030.

However, the real situation is different and notwithstanding the efforts done in this field, cruise ships go on being very pollutant. Some cities are reacting at an

---

[33] See http://www.tasasportuarias.es/tasas.php?op=0.

[34] See www.levante-emv.com, 2.8.2019.

individual level forbidding, for example, these ships to stop in certain zones of their ports because of the pollution effects. It has been the case of Venetia in Italy or Palma de Mallorca in Spain.[35]

In this regard, the Spanish legal system does not contain specific rules on the environmental impact of cruise ships. Nevertheless, cruises are also subject to provisions on environmental conservation which are relevant to them as ships, as well as to the corresponding environmental regulation. The rules governing the activities of ships are of international, EU, national and regional nature and, where appropriate, of each Port Authority. For instance, among the international rules, a mention may be made, regarding waste discharges, to the 1973 International Convention for the Prevention of Pollution from Ships, as modified by the Protocol of 1978, known as MARPOL 73/78 (Labrot 2015).

It is also worth mentioning the International Convention for the Control and Management of Ships' Ballast Water and Sediments (BWM), which entered into force on 8 September 2017 and requires all ships to apply ballast water and sediment management plans.[36] Moreover, all ships have to apply ballast water management procedures in accordance with a certain rule. It is required that the existing ships make the same after a period of gradual introduction (Golasch and David 2018).

Accordingly, the same different rules that govern the environmental impact of ships apply in the case of cruises. However, it is interesting to highlight the main environmental concerns stemming from cruises. In the first place, a cruise ship releases as many polluting gases as five million cars for the same distance and the type of fuel used is highly pollutant, according to the report on environmental impact of cruises of the German NGO NABU.[37] In the second place, the treatment of the waste generated by the ship, including wastewater, should be mentioned. Discharges from cruise ships can contain toxic substances, hydrocarbons, organic waste and pathogens, which can cause a potentially big harm in sensitive areas.

Another problem is the one posed by the big amount of ballast water used in these ships. It has been estimated that an average cruise can pour up to 70,000 ballast water per day, with the subsequent risk of introducing invasive species in the ecosystems, dinoflagellates which cause red tides and pathogens, according to the report issued by the NGO Oceana.[38]

---

[35] See www.elmundo.es, 12.8.2019.

[36] See www.imo.org/es.

[37] Report done by the German organization NABU (*Nature And Biodiversity Conservation Union*) in https://en.nabu.de/issues/traffic/cruiseships.html (02/05/2017).

[38] http://oceana.org/sites/default/files/reports/cruise_ships_pollution_Jun2004_SPA.pf (02/05/2017).

9 Rules on Jurisdiction and Arbitration Applicable to Cruise-Related Contracts

As already indicated, the Spanish legal system contains provisions on jurisdiction which have international, EU and national origin, depending on the nature of the claim (consumer protection, contract of carriage, employment contract . . .). In this vein, Brussels Ia Regulation provides for the international heads of jurisdiction in Spain as an EU member State. This instrument lives with the Hague Convention of 20 June 2005 on Choice of Court Agreements from which consumer and labour contracts, as well as the carriage of passengers and goods are excluded.[39] They are not excluded, though, from the Convention on jurisdiction and the recognition and enforcement of judgments in civil and commercial matters, made in Lugano on 30 October of 2007,[40] which applies to members of the European Free Trade Association (EFTA). In absence of EU or international law, Spanish law could be applied, in particular the Spanish Law on Judiciary (*Ley Orgánica del Poder Judicial*) amended by Law 7/2015 of 7 July, as well as the Spanish Law on International Judicial Cooperation (*Ley 29/2015, de 30 de julio, de cooperación jurídica en material civil)*, which also contains some provisions regarding jurisdiction (Belintxon Martín and Forner I Delaygua 2015).

9.1 Rules on Jurisdiction Applicable to the Traveller as a Consumer

As already mentioned, the consideration of travel packages as consumer contracts has important consequences on the Spanish PIL system and the application, among others, of Brussels Ia regulation[41] or *Rome* I regulation.[42] In both regulations, travel packages are assimilated to consumer contracts. Consumers are protected by the EU in two ways when it comes to access to justice:

In the first place, forum selection clauses not individually negotiated included in consumer contracts such as contracts for the carriage of passengers may be held null and void. Article 3 of Council Directive 93/13/EEC of 5 April 1993 on unfair terms in consumer contracts lays down that:

> 1. A contractual term which has not been individually negotiated shall be regarded as unfair if, contrary to the requirement of good faith, it causes a significant imbalance in the parties' rights and obligations arising under the contract, to the detriment of the consumer.

---

[39] Article 2(1) and (2)(f) of the 2005 Hague Convention.

[40] OJ L 339, 21.12.2007.

[41] OJ L 351, 20.12.2012.

[42] *OJ L 177, 04.7.2008.*

2. A term shall always be regarded as not individually negotiated where it has been drafted in advance and the consumer has therefore not been able to influence the substance of the term, particularly in the context of a pre-formulated standard contract.

   The fact that certain aspects of a term or one specific term have been individually negotiated shall not exclude the application of this Article to the rest of a contract if an overall assessment of the contract indicates that it is nevertheless a pre-formulated standard contract.

   Where any seller or supplier claims that a standard term has been individually negotiated, the burden of proof in this respect shall be incumbent on him.
3. The Annex shall contain an indicative and non-exhaustive list of the terms which may be regarded as unfair.

In accordance to letter (q) of the abovementioned Annex, a term may be regarded as unfair when "excluding or hindering the consumer's right to take legal action or exercise any other legal remedy, particularly by requiring the consumer to take disputes exclusively to arbitration not covered by legal provisions, unduly restricting the evidence available to him or imposing on him a burden of proof which, according to the applicable law, should lie with another party to the contract".

A forum selection clause may hinder the consumer's right to take legal action for which reason it could be held null and void as it has been ruled out in the *Costa Cruceros* case that will be later analysed.

Directive 93/13/EC has been implemented in Spain by Law 7/1999 of 13 of April on general contract terms (*Ley 7/1998, de 13 de abril, sobre Condiciones Generales de la Contratación*) and Articles 80 et seq of Royal Decree-Legislative 1/2007 of 16 November approving the Recast text of the General Law on Consumer Protection and other supplementary laws. More specifically, Article 82 of Royal Decree-legislative 1/2007 translates into the Spanish legal system the abovementioned Article 3 of Directive 93/13/CE. Article 90(2) thereof specially deals with forum selection clauses considering them unfair if they submit matters related to consumer contracts to courts other than those of the consumer's domicile, those of the place where the obligation has to be carried out or those of the place where the asset is located if this is an immovable. It is important to note that the abovementioned provisions, Articles 82 and 90 of Royal Decree-Legislative 1/2007, are to be held overriding mandatory provisions because they are meant to protect the general interests of consumers.

In the second place, there is another layer of consumer protection laid down in both, Section 4, Chapter II, of Brussels I Recast and Article 22 bis of the Spanish Law on Judiciary. A forum selection clause may be held existent and valid according to the abovementioned provisions, but still not be effective if it is included in a consumer contract as indicated by Article 17 of Brussels Ia Regulation and Article 22 quinquies (d). (Feliu Álvarez de Sotomayor 2015).

Article 17(3) of Brussels Ia Regulation excludes from Section 4, Chapter II, transport contracts save the case of travel packages. The latter are included in this section when the package including travel and accommodation for an inclusive price "has been concluded with a person who pursues commercial or professional activities in the Member State of the consumer's domicile or, by any means, directs such activities to that Member State or to several States including that Member State, and the contract falls within the scope of such activities".[43] For the consumer protection sake, Article 19 lays down that only a choice-of-court agreement

(1) which is entered into after the dispute has arisen;
(2) which allows the consumer to bring proceedings in courts other than those indicated in this Section; or
(3) which is entered into by the consumer and the other party to the contract, both of whom are at the time of conclusion of the contract domiciled or habitually resident in the same Member State, and which confers jurisdiction on the courts of that Member State, provided that such an agreement is not contrary to the law of that Member State.

serves to ascertain jurisdiction; otherwise, such forum selection clauses are to be disregarded as ineffective.

Article 22 bis(1) of the Spanish Law on Judiciary provides for a similar protection in its second paragraph: the express choice of the Spanish jurisdiction will only be effective if the agreement is concluded after the dispute is born, or both parties to the agreement already have their domicile or habitual residence in Spain at the time of the conclusion of the contract, or the plaintiff is the consumer.

9.2 *Rules on Jurisdiction Applicable to the Traveller as a Passenger*

Forum selection clauses included in general conditions of carriage of passengers in cruise ships are dealt with by Article 25 of Brussels Ia Regulation. This provision is applicable regardless of the country where both parties to the agreement are domiciled as long as the claim is submitted to the jurisdiction of an EU member State such as Spain. In principle, a choice of forum has to be made in writing, including the resorting to electronic means, save the case of pre-existent parties' practices and usages in the relevant area of international trade or commerce. As to its substantive validity, the applicable law is that of the chosen jurisdiction, including its conflict rules.[44] The status and legal capacity of the parties to the agreement are not covered by Brussels Ia Regulation, and paragraphs 1 and 11 of Article 9 of the Spanish Civil Code submit these issues to the national law of both, natural and legal, persons, respectively.

If the choice-of-court agreement submits the carriage of passengers in cruises to a third country, i.e. not an EU member State, Article 25 of Brussels I Recast seems not to be applicable because it only refers to the abovementioned case, that of being designated a member State's jurisdiction. In view of this gap and for the sake of the party autonomy principle, the most plausible interpretation is that this case is not

[43] Article 17(1)(c) of Brussels I Recast.

[44] Recital 20 of Brussels I Recast.

addressed by the uniform rules on international jurisdiction of Brussels Ia Regulation, Chapter II, but by the relevant domestic rules of each member State.

In this vein, Articles 22 bis and 22 ter of the Spanish Law on Judiciary are applicable to the choice of third country courts. As to the formal validity, Article 22 bis closely follows Article 25 of Brussels I Recast, but not when it comes to the law applicable to the substantive validity of these agreements. As a matter of fact, this provision is silent on this issue and the gap should be filled up in line with Article 25 of Brussels Ia Regulation. Article 22 ter lays down the derogatory effect of choice-of-court agreements meaning that Spanish courts have to decline their jurisdiction if the agreement to a third country's jurisdiction is held valid.

The gap in Article 25 of Brussels I Recast could, however, be filled up in accordance with two other interpretations. As to the second interpretation, Article 25 could be applied by analogy and taking into account the party autonomy principle. Nevertheless, the fact that the EU was already aware of this gap at the time of reviewing its predecessor, Brussels I Regulation, is a powerful argument against this interpretation. As to the third one, it relies on the normal operation of Brussels Ia Regulation, namely, if Article 25 is not applicable because the agreement points to a non-member State jurisdiction, other heads of jurisdiction laid down in Chapter II of Brussels Ia Regulation could be applicable such as the defendant's domicile. In other words, only if Chapter II is not applicable because the defendant's domicile is also in a non-member State, national heads of jurisdiction are applicable in accordance with Article 6 of Brussels Ia Regulation. Obviously, the weak point of this interpretation is the disregarding of the party autonomy principle which is a settled principle in the EU and international jurisdiction framework. Accordingly, and as said before, the abovementioned interpretation submitting the existence, validity and effects of third countries' forum selection clauses to domestic legislation is the most adequate in view of the underlying conflicts of interests.

In short, should a member State jurisdiction have been chosen, it is up to Article 25 of Brussels Ia Regulation to establish the agreement's existence, validity and effects; otherwise, domestic rules such as Articles 22 bis and 22 ter of the Spanish Law on Judiciary have the last word as regards to the selection of a non-member State jurisdiction.

When the transport contract, that is not a travel package, does not contain any forum selection clause or when it has to be considered null and void because of its abusive nature, the passenger can choose between the general forum of the defendant's domicile[45] and the special forum of the place where the services were, or should have been, provided,[46] as access to the protective heads of jurisdiction in Article 17 of Brussels Ia Regulation is excluded.[47] Article 7 of Brussels Ia Regulation points out to the place of performance of the obligation in question. However, if

[45] Article 4(1) of Brussels I Recast.

[46] Article 7(1)(b) of Brussels I Recast.

[47] Article 17(3) of Brussels I Recast.

the defendant shipping company is domiciled in a EU member State, that place would be, unless otherwise agreed, "the place in a Member State where, under the contract, the services were provided or should have been provided". If the defendant domicile is located outside of the EU the rest of jurisdiction rules of the Spanish PIL system will be applied.

9.3 Rules on Arbitration Applicable to Cruise-Related Matters

An analysis of the general terms used by several companies offering cruise services, in both paper form and paperless available on the internet, reveals that there is a refusal to solve disputes through transport arbitration. The said general terms include the express relinquishment to submit any possible dispute to an arbitration proceeding. In so doing, this path becomes limited beforehand for those cases when the costumer wants to file a claim against the travel agency and/or the organizer.[48] In some cases, exclusively the regulation on travel packages of Royal Decree Legislative 1/2007 is mentioned. In other cases, already repealed laws such as the former and already outdated Spanish law on travel packages or the LGDCU are mentioned.

According to Article 90(1) of Royal Decree-Legislative 1/2007 dealing with the protection of passengers as consumers, arbitration clauses are null and void if submission to arbitration is made to a system other than consumer arbitration save the case of sector-specific arbitration established by law. In other words, if passengers are consumers, arbitration is restricted to those cases in which the system has been legally set up (Carballo Piñeiro 2016).

In Spain, Royal Decree 231/2008 of 15 February deals with the Spanish Consumer Arbitration System (hereafter CAS). The consumer arbitration administrative system was set up on the basis of the 1984 Law on Consumer Protection, although it was not legally established until 1993. In 2008, CAS was rearranged as a consequence of Law 60/2003, which abrogated the 1988 Law on Arbitration, with a view to filling in the gaps and shortfalls in the former system, such as the lack of collective arbitral proceedings. CAS only applies to disputes over consumer matters between consumers and professionals or businesses and does not cover cases involving poisoning, injury and death, or that show reasonable signs of a criminal offence. Such a system is pervaded by the principle of consumer protection, and that is why only consumers are entitled to claim their legal and contractual rights before an arbitral tribunal, i.e. professionals and businesses cannot initiate this type of arbitration. CAS is in line with Directive 93/13/ECC of 5 April 1993 on unfair terms in consumer contracts, according to which consumer arbitration is only feasible and any arbitral awards are only enforceable in Spain when the arbitration agreement

[48] Available at: http://cecu.es/campanas/cuadernos/CRUCEROS09.pdf.

either submits the dispute to a system established by law or was concluded after the dispute arose.

Arbitration agreements can either be incorporated into contracts or separate contracts can be drawn up, but they always record the parties' willingness to submit their differences to CAS. In line with Article II of the New York Convention on the recognition and enforcement of foreign arbitral awards, arbitration agreements must be written, signed by the parties or contained in an exchange of letters, telegrams, telexes, faxes and any other means of electronic communication allowing written documentation of the agreement, even when it is only electronically or optically available. So far, nothing here stands out as being particularly innovative.

However, there is one feature that makes the system unusual, and it is that companies and professionals can join CAS on an *ex ante* basis, meaning that they publicly declare themselves to be engaged in CAS, thereby accepting any arbitration requested by any consumers trading with them. The benefit in doing so lies in the fact that all those agreeing publically to join the system can sell this as an extra-service to consumers, who receive a clear signal that they can claim against the respective professional or business by resorting to CAS should conflict arise.

Professionals and businesses who are interested in sending this signal have to offer publically to submit to CAS, and then registered. Should a dispute arise later on, consumers simply have to request arbitration before the competent arbitration board. Hence, the arbitration agreement may consist of an *ex ante* public offer to submit to CAS plus the consumer's request for arbitration. In cases where there had not been a public offer to submit to CAS, or this one had not been accepted, consumer's request is equally admitted, but the respondent must expressly accept arbitration. In short, CAS admits both pre- and post-dispute submission agreements (Carballo Piñeiro 2016).

It is also important to note that the EU has established an Online Dispute Resolution System that is applicable to passengers as consumers. To this end, Directive 2013/11/EU of the European Parliament and of the Council of 21 May 2013 on alternative dispute resolution for consumer disputes and amending Regulation (EC) 2006/2004 and Directive 2009/22/EC; and Regulation (EU) 524/2013 of the European Parliament and of the Council of 21 May 2013 on online dispute resolution for consumer disputes and amending Regulation (EC) No 2006/2004 and Directive 2009/22/EC (Regulation on consumer ODR), have been issued. In order to put the system in motion, it is also to highlight the Commission implementing Regulation (EU) 2015/1051 of 1 July 2015 on the modalities for the exercise of the functions of the online dispute resolution platform, on the modalities of the electronic complaint form and on the modalities of the cooperation between contact points provided for in Regulation (EU) 524/2013 of the European Parliament and of the Council on online dispute resolution for consumer disputes. The Online Dispute Resolution System is already in place in all countries of the EU, including Spain.[49]

[49] See details in Centro Europeo del Consumidor website: <https://cec.consumo.gob.es/CEC/web/noticias/litigios_linea.htm> (06.08.2020).

10 Conflict Rules Applicable to Cruise-Related Contracts

The relevant instruments containing conflict rules applicable to the matters herein discussed are the abovementioned Rome I Regulation on the law applicable to contractual matters, and Regulation (CE) 864/2007 of the European Parliament and of the Council of 11 July 2007 on the Law applicable to non-contractual obligations (Rome II).[50]

10.1 Conflict Rules Applicable to Travellers as Consumers in Their Contractual Relationships

As package travellers are considered as consumers, Article 6 of Rome I Regulation is applicable. According to this provision and without prejudice to Articles 5 and 7 of Rome I Regulation, "a contract concluded by a natural person for a purpose which can be regarded as being outside his trade or profession (the consumer) with another person acting in the exercise of his trade or profession (the professional) shall be governed by the law of the country where the consumer has his habitual residence", provided that the professional:

(a) pursues his commercial or professional activities in the country where the consumer has his habitual residence, or
(b) by any means, directs such activities to that country or to several countries including that country,

and the contract falls within the scope of such activities".

Notwithstanding paragraph 1, "the parties may choose the law applicable to a contract which fulfils the requirements of paragraph 1, in accordance with Article 3. Such a choice may not, however, have the result of depriving the consumer of the protection afforded to him by provisions that cannot be derogated from by agreement by virtue of the law which, in the absence of choice, would have been applicable on the basis of paragraph 1".[51]

If the requirements in points (a) or (b) of paragraph 1 are not fulfilled, the law applicable to a contract between a consumer and a professional shall be determined pursuant to Articles 3 and 4.[52]

Accordingly, travel packages are included in Article 6 of Rome I Regulation. By the same token, contracts for the carriage of passengers are not deemed consumer contracts for choice-of-law purposes save the case of a "contract relating to package travel within the meaning of Council Directive 90/314/EEC of 13 June 1990 on

---

[50] OJ L 199, 31.7.2007.

[51] Article 6(2) Rome I Regulation.

[52] Article 6(3) Rome I Regulation.

package travel, package holidays and package tours" (article 6.4. b) replaced by the actual Directive 2015/2002 (Feliu Álvarez de Sotomayor 2015). This meaning is no longer similar as the one given by the Brussels Ia Regulation referred just to "a contract which, for an inclusive price, provides for a combination of travel and accommodation".[53]

10.2 *Conflict Rules Applicable to Travellers as Passengers in Their Contractual Relationships*

Rome I Regulation has included a new rule—in respect to the 1980 Rome Convention—regarding the contracts for the carriage of passengers. In general, the examination of this type of contracts shows that choice-of-law clauses are usually included among the general terms. However, they might not be valid in accordance with Article 5(2) of Rome I Regulation:

> To the extent that the law applicable to a contract for the carriage of passengers has not been chosen by the parties in accordance with the second subparagraph, the law applicable shall be the law of the country where the passenger has his habitual residence, provided that either the place of departure or the place of destination is situated in that country. . . .

Therefore, the parties may choose as the law applicable to a contract for the carriage of passengers in accordance with Article 3 only the law of the country where:

(a) the passenger has his habitual residence; or
(b) the carrier has his habitual residence; or
(c) the carrier has his place of central administration; or
(d) the place of departure is situated; or
(e) the place of destination is situated.

Hence, the principle of freedom of choice is clearly limited, much further than the limitations established in the Article 3 of the Rome I Regulation to that principle for other contractual obligations (for example, in Article 4 thereof). The limitation of the freedom of choice in the field of carriage of passengers lives with that deriving from overriding mandatory provisions as defined by Article 9 of Rome I Regulation.

In the absence of a choice of law, according to the requirements of Article 5 (2) "the law of the country where the carrier has his habitual residence shall apply". This is a concept that has traditionally involved many problems of characterization in maritime disputes (Espinosa Calabuig 1999).

This can lead to its non-application and instead of it, to the application of Article 5.3 of Rome I Regulation. According to this rule, where it is clear from all the circumstances of the case that the contract is "manifestly more closely connected" with a country other than that indicated in paragraphs 1 or 2, the law of that other

[53] Article 17(3) Brussels I Recast.

country shall apply. In this case, other connecting factors will be taken into consideration to show that there is in fact other law manifestly more closely connected with a concrete country. In any case, these conflict rules will be probably not applied in practice (Espinosa Calabuig 2011).

10.3 Conflict Rules Applicable to Seafarers' Employment Contracts

All personnel working on board a cruise ship in any capacity is considered in principle a seafarer according to the MLC, 2006 save the abovementioned cases in which they are not consider seafarers in accordance with the Spanish legislation implementing the said convention. This characterization problem does not affect, nevertheless, the applicable conflict rule to employment matters to the extent that seafarers as any other worker are submitted to the conflict rule laid down in Article 8 of Rome I Regulation. The latter is thus applicable to determine the law applicable to a seafarer's employment agreement (SEA).

This conflict rule allows the choice of law by the parties to the contract. However, as workers are at a disadvantage during the contracting process, one correction is introduced by only allowing an unrestricted choice of law provided that the choice does not deprive the employee of the protection afforded by the mandatory provisions of the law that would govern the contract in the absence of choice of law. Worker protection is thus achieved by applying the most favourable law to the worker.

In absence of choice of law, result-oriented considerations are, however, absent in the conflict rule, i.e. the applicable law is determined according to the principle of proximity and predictability for both parties to the contract and not taking into consideration the weaker party. The connecting factors are the habitual place of work, and failing that, the place of the engaging business at the time of hiring the employee. Both are rigid factors, although flexibility is achieved through the inclusion of an escape clause in the conflict rule. This is especially interesting in the maritime sector, given that the flag State may lack sufficient contacts with the employment relationship.

The peculiarities of the conflict rule when it comes to maritime employment appear in its application to the extent that habitual place of work is a connecting point that requires interpretation as it refers to the jurisdiction of a State. The latter is, however, lacking when a worker provides services on board a ship that is sailing on the high seas or through different jurisdictions and non-sovereignty areas. In these cases, public international law comes to the aid of private international law by locating the habitual workplace of seafarer in the flag State (Carballo Piñeiro 2014, 2016). However, in view of the impact of flags and crews of convenience on the maritime labor market, there has been a move away from the codification of this rule. In contrast, it has been understood that a vessel's flag should be weighed against other factors to determine a jurisdiction sufficiently close to the employment relationship (Carballo Piñeiro 2015a).

Nevertheless, the fact remains that public international law and the jurisdiction of the flag State continue to have a role in determining seafarers' habitual workplace (Carballo Piñeiro 2015a, 2017). This has been made clear by the Court of Justice in its *Weber v Ogden* judgment of 27 February 2002.[54] In this case, the Court resorted to the Geneva Convention on the Continental Shelf of 29 April 1958 to resolve a case in which it was necessary to establish the habitual workplace of a cook who had mainly worked on different platforms and vessels adjacent to the Dutch continental shelf. Moreover, the MLC, 2006 mainly addresses flag States, *ergo* confirming the role that the flag State jurisdiction still plays today in specifying the habitual workplace of workers who perform their duties aboard a ship sailing on the high seas or through different jurisdictions, including those on board cruise ships. Both parties to the contract expect the application of the law of the place where the work has to be carried out, making it also possible for the same law to govern the employment relationships of all seafarers working in the same workplace, thereby ensuring equality of opportunities, and thus avoiding distortion of competition and social dumping.

In cases in which the employee provides services in different countries, for example while not attached to one specific cruise or carrying out both sea and land-based activities, the law of the business which engaged the employee could come into play. Another solution, enshrined first in Court of Justice's case-law and later on in Articles 21(1)(a)(i) of Brussels Ia Regulation and 8 of Rome I Regulation, is based on locating, wherever possible, the place from which the employee habitually carries out his or her duties. This logic is also to be found in the Court of Justice's *Voogsgeerd v Navimer* judgment of 15 December 2011[55] dealing with the case of a machine engineer serving in two vessels for a Luxembourg-based company. The worker sued in Antwerp (Belgium), since the office where he signed his employment contract, received his instructions and to which he was meant to return once his transport tasks had finished, was located. The judgement, which accepted the employee's approach, reveals a controversial category of workers, that is, mobile workers serving in more than one country for whom the relevant elements should be assessed for the purposes of determining the place where they discharge their basic duties.

Surprisingly, the Court of Justice does not even mention in *Voogsgeerd v Navimer* the flag of the vessels in question, which could indicate that the approach to identifying the habitual workplace in this case law may be generalized to all cases involving seafarers. However, applying this factual approach to cases in which an employee performs services on one and the same vessel not only sacrifices legal certainty, but also it does not lead to jurisdictions which are more closely linked than the flag State, namely, the said approach may give consideration to the base port or

[54] Case C 37/00, *Herbert Weber v Universal Ogden Services Ltd.*

[55] Case C-384/10, *Jan Voogsgeerd v Navimer SA.*

the business through which seafarers receive their instructions, however both contacts are also susceptible to manipulation by the employer (Carballo Piñeiro 2016).

Furthermore, the question of establishing the effective centre of working activities, which is the vessel, would not really be addressed, and the already weakened principle of equal treatment of workers on board a cruise ship, a further goal underlying this connecting factor, would be broken. Hence, the factual approach advocated by the Court of Justice's case-law ought to be applied only in the case of mobile workers (Carballo Piñeiro 2015a, 2017). It must be noted that their case is different from that of temporarily posted workers who do not change their habitual workplace during the posting, as indicated by Recital 36 Rome I Regulation following the proposal of the European Group of Private International Law (GEDIP).

The interpretation of the Court of Justice in *Voogsgeer v Navimer* further reduces the role of the law of the country where the business which engaged the employee is located, which is only operative in the absence of a habitual workplace or a place from which services are habitually provided. In fact, this connecting factor is in itself controversial as it leaves location in the hands of employers and is hence open to manipulation, thereby this case law is to be welcome as it advances worker protection (Carballo Piñeiro 2015a).

Nevertheless, even in cases in which the employee only works on board a vessel, the flag State jurisdiction may not be indeed the closest law to SEA. In this vein, the escape clause responds better to the legislative objective of applying the closest law (Carballo Piñeiro 2015a). While in principle this is presumed to be the law of the habitual place of work, there might be a closer law than the flag State jurisdiction if all circumstances of the case are taken into account. Against this background, there has also been a debate as to the exact application terms of the escape clause. In this vein, a strict interpretation has been proposed, according to which the escape clause would only operate when two prerequisites concur, namely, the law designated by the conflict rule lacks sufficient contacts with the claim, and there is a closer law than the latter.

However, in its judgment of 12 September 2013, *Schlecker v Boedeker*,[56] the Court of Justice follows those advocating a broader interpretation. The latter does not require the designated law by the conflict rule to have a weak link to the claim, thereby the "significant contacts" factor is considered another connecting factor within the conflict rule laid down in Article 8 and thus on equal terms as the habitual workplace and the engaging business.

A final remark is nevertheless necessary. The closest link test is based on proximity and not on finding the law which will best protect the worker. In order to apply the escape clause, the seized jurisdiction has to take into account only the circumstances surrounding the employment relationship, but not those concerning the location of the place where the employee discharges their duties towards the employer because they are already taken into account when specifying the habitual workplace. Accordingly, the escape clause requires to weight the place of wage

[56]Case C-64/12, *Anton Schlecker v Melitta Josefa Boedeker*.

payment and other labour conditions, the parties' nationality or residence, and the place of payment of social security contributions and taxes (Carballo Piñeiro 2015a). As said, and in general, this assessment may be in contradiction with the worker protection principle.

11 Spanish Case Law on Cruise Matters

Spanish case law in cruise matters is very rare and there have not been identified specific problems regarding the implementation of the abovementioned rules. Nevertheless, the sinking of cruises has given risen to litigation in Spain and several cases are worth mentioning.

After the sinking of the *Sea Diamond* cruise ship in front of the Greek coast, passengers with residence in Spain have claimed for damages before the Spanish jurisdiction. The Court of Appeals, Section 20, in Madrid granted them damages for material and non-material losses by judgment of 21 June 2012. Noteworthy is that the Spanish courts apply the Supreme Court doctrine on non-material damage, i.e. in accordance with judgment 906/2011 of 20 November 2011, the Spanish Supreme Court understands that damages for non-material loss are included in compensation as legally granted by law. This judgement refers to road accidents whose compensation package is determined by a legal scale. The Madrid Court of Appeals understands in the *Sea Diamond* case that the same case-law is applicable to liability for the carriage of passengers by sea. In other words, this legal scale of compensation has been used by analogy in order to establish due damages to each passenger.

Later on, the sinking of the *Costa Concordia* cruise ship in front of the Italian coast on 13 January 2012 triggered a string of litigation (Dickerson 2014). One aspect of the litigation focused on the claim for damages, including material and non-material loss. Remarkably, damages granted in this case were higher than those in the *Sea Diamond* case, not only because of the greater stress suffered by the passengers in this sinking as the death toll shows, but also because Regulation (EC) 392/2009 was applicable to this claim and it establishes a higher compensation than the abovementioned applicable rules previous to its entering into force. Moreover, judgment 147/2014 of 29 April 2014 rendered by the Madrid Court of Appeals, Section 14, in this case granted compensation for non-material loss in addition to compensation for other damages.

The latter judgment was challenged before the Supreme Court which, by judgment 232/2016 of 8 April 2016, concluded, on the one hand, that passengers have to be compensated for any damage, either material or non-material; while on the other, the amount of compensation could be determined taking into account the scale of compensation legally laid down for liability arising out of road accidents. However, this is only indicative and it does not have to include non-material loss which can be compensated in addition to other damage.

The other aspect of the litigation in the *Costa Concordia* case depended on the characterization of passengers as consumers. In particular, it has to be mentioned the claim decided by the Court of Appeals of Madrid, Section 28, judgment 165/2015 of 8 June of 2015. The case involved an injunction action for the protection of consumers' interest brought by a consumer association before the Spanish jurisdiction against *Costa Crociere SpA*, the Italian company. This collective action is laid down in the already indicated *Ley 7/1998, de 13 de abril, sobre Condiciones Generales de la Contratación* and Articles 80 et seq of Royal Decree-Legislative 1/2007 dealing with unfair terms.

According to the plaintiff, *Costa Crociere SpA* was including unfair terms in consumer contracts, including contracts electronically concluded. The Spanish court finally stated that some of the challenged terms were unfair and granted the injunction. Among those terms considered null and void, there were a choice-of-forum and a choice-of-law clauses submitting all contractual matters to the Italian jurisdiction and legislation. Other clauses considered unfair limited the company's liability as regards to trips' or excursions' cancellations and prize variation, contract modifications such as on the type of ships, travel routes, hotels or flights as well as regards to damage caused to passengers or their belongings.

It is also important to note that this injunction action was not brought by passengers, but by a consumer association, and it did not involve questioning travel packages or contracts for the carriage of passengers already concluded; the injunction sought to prevent *Costa Crociere SpA* from employing unfair terms in its trade in Spain. Accordingly, the case was not about declaring terms already included in existing contracts unfair, but about ensuring that this type of terms is out of the Spanish legal system as a whole. In general, the point is significant because it excludes this type of injunction action from a contractual characterization and obliges to characterize it as a non-contractual matter (Carballo Piñeiro 2015b).

Against this backdrop and although the Spanish courts dealing with the *Costa Crociere SpA* case did not address this issue, their international jurisdiction was to be asserted on grounds of paragraph 2 of Article 7 of Brussels Ia Regulation on jurisdiction in non-contractual matters (Carballo Piñeiro 2015b). This provision covers injunction actions for the protection of consumers' interests that are characterized as a non-contractual matter, thereby they can be brought before the courts of the place where the harmful event may occur. Where that place might be, has been interpreted by the Court of Justice in its judgment of 1 October 2002, *Verein für Konsumenteninformation v Karl Heinz Henkel*, Case C-167/00.

As to the applicable law and according to the abovementioned characterization, Article 6(1) of the mentioned Rome II Regulation regarding non-contractual obligations indicates that "the law applicable to a non-contractual obligation arising out of an act of unfair competition shall be the law of the country where competitive relations or the collective interests of consumers are, or are likely to be, affected". Accordingly, and applying to the *Costa Crociere* case both provisions, Spanish jurisdiction and legislation were applicable as a matter of fact (Carballo Piñeiro 2015b).

Lastly, it is worth also mentioning a case relating to employment matters resolved by the High Court of Andalucía (*Tribunal Superior de Justicia*), Labour Section, in its judgment 2098/2016 of 18 July 2016. The Spanish court had to decide the following case: *Croisimer Belle de L Adriatique* hired on a temporary basis a Spanish captain in 2007 to operate a cruise ship flying the Belgian flag. Further contracts followed until he was fired in 2013. All contracts were apparently submitted to the Belgian law. Nevertheless, the judgment does not deal with the law applicable, but with the assertion of Spanish jurisdiction put into question by the employer and the judge of instance. The High Court rightly applied Brussels I Regulation, in force at that time, and resorted to the habitual workplace head of jurisdiction in absence of a forum selection clause. The interesting point made in this decision is that the cruise ship on board which the captain was sailing was basically navigating the Spanish rivers *Guadiana* and *Guadalquivir* with rare berthing at Portuguese ports. Accordingly, the Spanish court settled the case asserting jurisdiction as the habitual workplace of the captain was in Spain.

12 Conclusions

This report on cruises provides an overview of the Spanish legal framework applicable to the complex human activities related to cruise ships. Despite the lack of specific legislation, the fact that the industry is included within the shipping sector leaves no room for gaps as the IMO and ILO framework for the sector fully applies. Spain is a party to that framework and also to that of the EU, which has also issued a significant number of instruments implementing and supplementing the international legal framework in shipping. In fact, and as a consequence of the international nature of cruise ship operations, most Spanish rules applicable to the sector have an international or EU origin.

Noteworthy for this report are those provisions that are not included within the IMO and ILO framework because they deal with consumer protection. The latter overlap with the IMO and EU regulatory framework for the contract of carriage of passengers adding an extra level of protection in the event of travel packages, package tours and packages holidays. This distinction between one type of contract and packages has also a reflection on the applicable PIL rules that, in the case of Spain, are also mainly to be found at EU level. In any case, Spanish law according to EU law and the ECJ case law (*Pammer/Alpenhof*) considers cruise ships contracts as contracts of travel packages (*viaje combinado*), so the rules existing in this context are particularly relevant.

As to employment contracts on board cruise ships, while the MLC, 2006 covers all employment and labour relationships on board, PIL aspects are to be mainly dealt with the international jurisdiction and conflict rules laid down in Brussels I Regulations, and Rome I and Rome II Regulations. In other words, Spanish PIL provisions laid down in the Law on Judiciary only residually apply.

The increase of the cruise phenomenon in Spain and the relevance of ports such as Barcelona, Valencia or Cadiz might imply an increase of disputes arising out of this industry. For the time being, the Spanish judiciary has only been involved in some cases. However, some of them have been remarkable as a result of the number of passengers involved in the case. At least, one of them has provided an opportunity to test the Spanish system of collective actions and the outcome from the Judiciary perspective has been positive. In light of the figures in terms of passengers and employees behind the industry, this is an interesting development that might help to deal with the many (potential) issues arising from a sector that is constantly increasing.

References

Belintxon Martín U, Forner I Delaygua J (2015) La nueva Ley 14/2014 de navegación marítima desde la óptica del Derecho Internacional Privado. Revista Española de Derecho Internacional 67(1):340–344

Benavides Velasco P (2012) La directiva de viajes combinados: perspectivas de futuro. In: Aguado V, Casanovas O (Coord.) El impacto del derecho de la Unión Europea en el turismo. Atelier, pp 135–152

Berenguer Albaladejo C (2016) Luces y sombras de la nueva Directiva (UE) 2015/2302 del parlamento europeo y del consejo, de 25 de noviembre de 2015, relativa a los viajes combinados y a los servicios de viaje vinculados. Int J Sci Manag Tour 2(2):33–49

Carballo Piñeiro L (2014) La convención sobre el derecho del mar y la ley aplicable a la relación laboral marítima. In: Sobrino Heredia JM (dir.) La contribución de la convención de las Naciones Unidas sobre el derecho del mar a la buena gobernanza de los mares y océanos 1, pp 33–53

Carballo Piñeiro L (2015a) International maritime labour law. Springer, Heidelberg

Carballo Piñeiro L (2015b) La construcción del mercado interior y el recurso colectivo de consumidores. In: Esteban de la Rosa F (ed) La protección del consumidor en dos espacios de integración: Europa y América. Una perspectiva de Derecho internacional, europeo y comparado. Valencia: Tirant lo Blanch, pp 1055–1088

Carballo Piñeiro L (2016) Port state jurisdiction over labour conditions: a private international law perspective on extra-territoriality. Int J Mar Coast Law 31(3):531–551

Carballo Piñeiro L (2017) Employment, maritime. In: Basedow J et al (eds) European encyclopedia of private international law. Edward Elgar Publishing House, Cheltenham

Dickerson TA (2014) The cruise passenger's rights and remedies 2014: the Costa Concordia disaster: one year later, many more incidents both on board megaships and during shore excursions. Tulane Marit Law Rev 38:515–581

Espinosa Calabuig R (1999) El Contrato Internacional de Transporte Marítimo de Mercancías: Cuestiones de Ley Aplicable. Granada, Comares

Espinosa Calabuig R (2011) Cuestiones de jurisdicción y ley aplicable tras las Reglas de Rotterdam y el Reglamento Roma I. Il Diritto marittimo 1/2011, pp 18–36

Esteve Pérez J, García Sánchez A (2015) La industria de cruceros: características, agentes y sus funciones. Valencia, Fundación ValenciaPort, pp 36–44

Feliu Álvarez de Sotomayor S (2012) El tratamiento legal del contrato de viaje combinado en el derecho internacional privado. CDT 4(2):123–139

Feliu Álvarez de Sotomayor S (2015) Nulidad de las cláusulas de jurisdicción y ley aplicable a la luz de la ley 3/2014 por la que se modifica el texto refundido de la ley general para la defensa de consumidores y usuarios. Revista electrónica de estudios internacionales (REEI), n. 29, pp 5–36

Golasch S, David M (2018) Ballast Water Management Convention implementation challenges. Ocean Yearbook 32:456–476

Labrot V (2015) Marine pollution: introduction to international law on pollution caused by ships. In: Monaco A, Prouzet P (eds) Governance of seas and oceans, pp 77–106

López de Gonzalo M (2016) La nuova direttiva sui pacchetti turistici e la normativa internazionale e comunitaria in tema de trasporto di persone. Il Diritto marittimo, pp 405–418

Piras M (2012) International recent developments: European Union-Maritime passengers transport. Tulane Law Rev 36:627–639

Rosaeg E (2010) The Athens Convention on passengers liability and the EU. In: Basedow et al (eds) The Hamburg lectures on maritime affairs 2007&2008, Hamburg studies on maritime affairs, vol 16. Springer, Heidelberg, pp 55–75

Tur Faúndez MN (2003) La protección del turista en el contrato de viaje combinado. In: Torres Lana JA, Tur Faúndez MN, Janer Torrens JD (eds) La protección del turista como consumidor, Valencia, Tirant lo Blanch

Zuburi de Salinas M (Dir.) (2017) El contrato de transporte de viajeros. Nuevas perspectivas. Pamplona, Aranzadi/Thomson Reuters

Case Law Concerning Cruises (Listed by Dates in Chronological Order)

C-37/00. Judgment of the ECJ (Sixth Chamber) of 27 February 2002. *Herbert Weber v Universal Ogden Services Ltd*

C-384/10. Judgment of the ECJ (Fourth Chamber) of 15 December 2011. *Jan Voogsgeerd v Navimer SA*

C-64/12. Judgment of the ECJ (Third Chamber), 12 September 2013. *Anton Schlecker v Melitta Josefa Boedeker*

Judgment *Audiencia Provincial de Madrid*, Sec. 20, of 21 June 2012, n° 355/2012, rec 549/2011 *(Cruise Sea Diamond)*

Judgment Audiencia Provincial de Madrid, sec. 14ª, of 29 April 2014, n° 147/2014, rec. 725/2013 (Costa Concordia)

Judgment Audiencia Provincial de Madrid, sec. 28ª, of 8 June 2015, n° 165/2015, rec. 359/2013 (Costa Crociere)

Judgment of Tribunal Superior de Justicia de Andalucía, sec.1ª, of 18 July 2016, n° 2098/2016, rec. 2176/2015 (Croisimer Belle de l'Adriatique)

Judgment Tribunal Supremo, Sala Primera, of 8 April 2016, n° 232/2016, rec. 1741/2014 (Costa Concordia)

Part III
National Reports: North and South America

Legal Aspects of Cruises in Argentina

Giselle Javurek and Martín Lautaro Vega Correa

Abstract The emerging cruise market in Argentina is, although still without a proper legal and material infrastructure, and despite the lack of detailed official statistics on the field, a promisingly growing one. Recent satellite photos and CONICET studies have revealed that Argentina Atlantic litoral is 2000 km longer than thought, i.e. over 6800 km long. Along this territory an amazing variety of landscapes, fauna, views, etc. have become an international attraction. Argentina is therefore now part of Southamerican itineraries and offers its own national maritime roads as well. In addition, a river waterway project is being worked on. The country has already taken and implemented various measures to encourage the arrival of cruisers to the national ports. These include, among others, modifications to reduce fees and taxes, to improve costal facilities and to ease legal procedures for the commercial development of this branch. In this way Argentina expects to foster the national as well as the international cruise business in the coming years.

1 Introduction

For several years now, cruises have ceased to be a tourist activity only reserved for a few. The number of people who choose to take their vacations on board a ship is increasing year by year, making the cruise ship itself the main destination for their rest.

By offering the cruise service, the shipping company is obliged, not only to transport the passenger, but also to provide his/her accommodation, food,

This chapter has been written in collaboration with: Julio Córdoba, Attorney, National Board of Tourism, (Former Ministry of Tourism, Minister Gustavo Santos).

G. Javurek (✉)
National University of Cordoba, Cordoba, Argentina

University of Chilecito, Chilecito, Argentina

M. L. V. Correa
National University of Chilecito, UNdeC, Chilecito, Argentina

C. Fresnedo de Aguirre (ed.), *Legal Aspects of Cruises*, Ius Comparatum - Global Studies in Comparative Law 56, https://doi.org/10.1007/978-3-030-83090-8_8

entertainment, land excursions in the different ports of call, medical care. It should also be borne in mind that the more services offered, the more crew members will be needed, generating an important source of work. In turn, the increase in activity causes an impact on the environment that must necessarily be considered.

What has been said leads us to consider the need for a specific law that covers the entire spectrum of legal relationships that a cruise ship implies and that Argentina does not currently have.

2 The Importance of Cruises

When asked to place Argentina in the international cruise market, we can say that Argentina has been a destination very often chosen by cruises in the last 20 years and their number has been growing significantly. Many passengers coming from Europe or the United States choose Buenos Aires as their final destination and as a sightseeing point. We should, nevertheless, mention that speaking in global terms, it is clear that our country is not top of the list in this respect. According to the information of the International Association of Cruises, South America in its totality is, in world-wide terms, with a participation of approximately 3%, actually at the bottom of the list among the chosen destination areas.

With still satisfying numbers despite the wide margin for growth, Argentina is already part of the cruise circuit. It offers mainly two local maritime routes. The first one between Buenos Aires and Patagonia, known as "The Maritime Circuit of Austral Cruises", includes the harbours of Buenos Aires, Mar del Plata, Puerto Madryn and Usuhuaia. The second one, "The Glaciers Maritime Circuit" joins the Island of Tierra del Fuego with the South American continent—harbour of Comodoro Rivadavia or Puerto Deseado- and/or the Antarctic continent in combination with the Falkland Islands. At an international level, at the same time, our country takes part in the two most important Southamerican itineraries of the area: the Brasilian coast and the southern coast. We can also add that the demand from national as well as foreign tourists for cruises to the Antarctic leaving from or having a stop at the port of Ushuaia has increased considerably lately. Due to its convenient geographical location, this port is a strategic point for the touristic development of this remote area of our planet.

Furthermore, during the first three months of 2018 the city of Mar del Plata has been included in the cruise itinerary by "Alteza Cruises" featuring different circuits throughout the whole year, not only during the season, and with some short ones of 3 to 5 days between Buenos Aires and Mar del Plata.

Statistics on the evolution of the number of cruises and cruise passengers arriving, of passengers disembarking and of their nationalities, and of the money they spend on land do exist but not at national level. They are carried out by tourist boards of those places that count with a port of call, mainly Buenos Aires and Ushuaia.

In other words, we do not count with statistics on the performance of the Argentine harbour system as a whole, as is the case of other countries such as Brasil or Spain. Inspite of this, we can make some estimations resorting to the partial data collection published by some ports and the processing of other pieces of regional information.

The autonomous city of Buenos Aires carries out through the "General Directorate of Market Intelligence and Observatory of the Tourism Entity", under the Ministry of Modernization, Innovation and Technology, a detailed annual report on the statistics used in the area. This report analyzes various factors, such as the amount of arriving cruises, quantity of national and international passengers, demographic data and characteristics of the foreign tourists, type of travel, lodging, purchases done, etc.

There are indeed statistics at local level that reveal the importance of this business in our country. Due to the vastness of the Argentine territory many areas though mediterranean play no role in the cruise itinerary. For this reason surveys and reports are only carried out by tourist boards directly affected by the cruise tourism, as mentioned above. Based on this information, the current National Board of Tourism carries out various pertinent surveys to project the future plans in this field.

In this sense we can also say that since the year 2003 up to now the activity of cruises in the harbour of Buenos Aires has increased considerably, reaching with 160 landfalls and 510,815 cruise passengers its highest peak during the season 2012/2013. The last 3 years have nevertheless shown a decline. The season 2016/2017 finished with 82 moorings and 295,271 cruise passengers. An upturn of the activity in the next season is however expected based on the measures adopted to encourage it.

There are in fact policies meant to foster the cruise business, for example the Strategic Federal Plan of Sustainable Tourism of 2014, extending to the year 2015. This plan is included in the "Maritime Circuit of Cruises" featuring the sea roads mentioned above. On the other hand, the improvement of port terminals, as the cruise specific "Benito Quinquela Martín" in Buenos Aires as well as the inclusion of the port of Mar del Plata as a cruise destination.

In addition, the project to promote the river cruises, specially through the Paraguay-Paraná Waterway is a strong commitment. The project consists in building five river terminal stops in Corrientes, Entre Rios, Misiones and Santa Fe. The plan aims at encouraging the cruises with service on board and it also includes catamarans and coastal development.

Finally, we can mention some of the already in force measures to recover from the fall in this field in the last years, namely:

1. VAT return to inbound tourists.
2. Simplification of visa application procedure to potential tourists from countries with strong demand in the field.
3. Integration of a regional tourism proposal.

4. Reduction of migration fees: USD 14 per vessel itinerary, not per landfall in a port, as well as a special fee of USD 7 during low season to encourage the extension of the cruise season.
5. Electronic money order requests 4 years in advance.
6. Limit of 12,000 passengers a day to ensure a better service at the cruise terminals.
7. The Health Ministry has decided to require vaccination against yellow fever in the whole territory of Argentina.
8. New service for passengers and improvement of the facilities in the vicinity of the terminals.
9. Gradual reduction of terminal fees (season 2017–2018)
10. Differential fees for vessels with landfall and itinerary in MDQ (season 2017–2018).
11. Commitment of the private sector to promote the Port of Buenos- Aires and Argentina.
12. Activities of "Responsabilidad Social Empresarial" (RSE) (Corporate Social Liability) with cruise companies, the predisposition of the union sector, among others, to encourage a significant growth expectation in the long and medium term.

The service offered by the main ports is considered of good quality. Our country has the cruise terminal "Benito Quinquela Martín" in the port of Buenos Aires, which was opened up in March 2011 and which has become one of the largest and most modern in South America.

The supply in the ports of the national cruise road is also of good quality. As an example we can mention Puerto Madryn, which offers different services to vessels provided by the port administration itself as well as by third parties. These services include the supply of drinking water (the port has a network of pipelines with a potential of 15 to 20 m^3 per station for the provisioning of ships), the electric power supply (it has sockets for electromotive force of 380/220 v), solid waste collection and emergency health care, among others.

Despite the drop of the activity mentioned above the cruise industry has started to recover in 2016 thanks to the measures already stated. As a consequence of this we can note an upward trend in the number of landfalls, expected passengers, money spent by these and number of nights booked in the port of Buenos Aires. This trend can also be observed in other common cruise destinations in the country, such as Puerto Madryn and Ushuaia, the emergence of new destinations such as Mar del Plata and the ones that will soon be reached by the river cruises. From the point of view of the labour market the growth in the branch implies recovering as well as the creation of jobs, which had also been declining together with the business since 2012 and till the indicated turning point of the trend in 2016.

Although we cannot claim that the cruise business is among the main ones in the national labour market, we cannot deny either that the growth observed in the last 20 years has boosted its development. This impact can be appreciated mainly in the cruise landfall places. Thus, the wider the itinerary offers, the larger their scope will be. Currently the principal destinations are the ones that benefit most from the branch, directly as well as indirectly, and in relation to tourism (lodging, gastronomy and entertainment).

In general terms, i.e. not focusing on cruisers only, the industry and ship management turns out to be extremely significant for Argentina since the country has an extensive maritime coastline and a navigable fluvial waterway flanked by numerous port facilities. The activity here is mainly based on international trade, among others the exports of agricultural products rag out because of their volume. Also the exports and imports of diverse cargo transported in containers are specially significant due to their volume and value.

We consider, nevertheless, that the cruise business, as mentioned above, has had a remarkable increase in the recent years. This, together with the projects that aim at reinforcing it, makes the managing of vessels of these characteristics a stimulating economic factor, significant for the areas they navigate through.

Our country has a large number of shipyards equipped to deal with different sizes of cruisers. According to information supplied by the National Ministry of Tourism and, as an example, we can mention that one of the companies that aims at operating in the project Paraguay-Parana Waterway (Quasar), will do so using a Greek vessel, which will be renewed in national shipyards while awaiting the construction of a new ship.

3 General and Specific Rules Applicable to Cruises

Our legislation has no specific regulations on cruises. The regulations applicable to cruises are general, namely: at national level, the National Constitution, the Navigation Act No 20094, REGINAVE, the decreet No 4516/73 and Travel Agents Law No 18829. The Navigation Act deals, among other issues, with the carriage of people by water. At international level, the Athens Agreement on carriage of passengers and their luggage by sea of 1974 and its amending protocole of 1976, and the "Tratado de Montevideo de Derecho de Navegación Comercial Internacional" of 1940. The Navigation Act deals, among other issues, with the carriage of people by water.

Law No 24240 on Consumer Defence is in force. This regulation has expressly excluded the carriage by air, but does not specify anything on carriage by water. We understand it is applicable to it and so has the Court, which shows in several of its decisions.

We can mention for example G.M.I. vs. Los Cipreses S. A. -Damages and "Cardinal Zully Cristina vs. Los Cipreses S.A and y otro -/Injury and/or Death of passenger maritime transport", both relating to the limitation period in which it is resolved to give prevalence to the one incorporated by the Consumer Defense Act. On the other hand, the decision Unilever of Argentina S.A vs. DNCI -Consumer Defense, which confirms the application of the fine by the National Directorate of International Trade to an international cruise company for not indicating its legal domicile in the country when advertising an offer.

Law 24240 contains general rules that must be applied to these contracts, for example, the provisions of article 4, which provides that those who produce, distribute or commercialize goods or offer services, must provide consumers or users, truthful, detailed, effective and sufficient information about the essential characteristics of them in a certain and objective way; also, regarding offers and publicity, as stated in the articles 7, 8 and 10a, which refer to the breach of the offer or the contract and favours the consumer in the possibility of electing forced compliance, accepting another equivalent service or of terminating the contract with restitution of the paid, without prejudice to actions for damages. Other applicable provisions are without doubt those contained in chapter IX, those on the abusive terms and ineffective clauses, those which are considered unagreed clauses, those which distort the obligations, limit the liability, imply waiver or a restriction to the consumer's rights or those containing clauses imposing the inversion of the burden of proof to the detriment of the consumer ("Empresas de Turismo y Derecho del Consumidor", Mónica Canteros, *in http://eco.unne.edu.ar/revista/03/01.pdf*).

4 Labour Rules on Cruises' Workers

The Argentine legal system does not contain specific regulations on cruise workers, but on maritime workers. These are national and international regulations. In the absence of specific rules on cruise workers, general rules like The Navigation Act considers in its articles 631 to 674, the regulations referred to the contract related to workers on board of a ship. At international level art. 20–24 of the "Tratado de Montevideo de Derecho de Navegación Comercial Internacional" of 1940 are also applicable.

There are also no specific regulations on combined trips. In that case the responsibility of the travel agent, if there is one, should be stated according to what the Travel Agents Law specifies in Article 18829. The responsibility of the carrier is in turn also defined depending on where the damage was caused, water, air or ground.

In the first case the Navigation Law and the agreements mentioned above are referred to; in the second, the Aeronautic Code and the Montreal Agreement of 1999 and in the third, the common right by means of the application of the National Civil and Commercial Code and the various pertinent specific rules. In this sense, we can mention the following as the most relevant ones. In Vehicular Transport: Transit Law No 24449; Urban Transport decree 656/94; Inter-city Transport decree 958/92; International Passenger Transport resolution S.T. No 202/) and rule S.T. No 263/90; finally, the Penalty System decree 253/95. In Railway transport: General Railway Law No 2873 and the Railway General Regulation decree No 90.325/36 and its amendments. These regulations are both national and international.

5 Rules on Ports That Are Relevant Regarding Cruises

As we have already stated above the port regulations are not specific for cruises, but they are applied to these in a general way. In this case we have the Navigation Law No 20094, the Port Law No 20093 and its regulatory decree 769/93. The only regulation that could be considered specific on cruises is the regulation on cruisers entering the port of Buenos Aires, stated in regulation 052/16 of the General Port Administration S. E.

We should also mention that each port issues its own regulation, which should be taken into account, together with the aforementioned rules. Please note that these rules are valid at national level only.

The tax and fee system is a negative issue in our country though. In the first place, it is difficult to specify a system since each port has determined its own and therefore there are differences among them.

On the other hand, from a general point of view, the panorama is also not good. Compared to other destinations, the itineraries including our country are dearer. For example, leaving the port of Santos in the north the cost is less than half as high compared to that in the south.

Furthermore, if we differentiate between a cargo vessel and a cruiser, the difference is also considerable. For vessels with similar characteristics, for example a cargo ship (total length: 336 mts, width: 45,60 mts and total net registered tonnage: 57,577) pays for the the right to use the port of Buenos Aires USD 20,700 while a passenger vessel (total length: 333 mts, width: 38 mts and total net registered tonnage: 115,165) pays USD 41,500.

6 Rules on Environmental Impact of Cruises

Regarding environmental impact of cruises there are various national rules which, although not cruise-specific, apply to vessels, cruisers included:

- General Environmental Law No 25675 and complementary rules.
- Law No 25916 Management of Household Waste.
- Law No 24051 Hazardous Waste Management and supplementary rules.
- Law No 25670 Management of PCBs.
- Resolution of SRNyAH No 315/05 -"Protocolo Particular Adicional al Convenio de Cooperación Mutua" in force between the SAyDS and the PNA - Annex Hazardous Wastes.
- Provision No 431/12 of Sub-Secretariat of Ports and Waterways on operations to unload waste from ships.
- Resolution No 714/10 of SENASA (National Service of Health and Agri-food Quality) on the "Plan Nacional de Prevención de Ingreso y Transmision de Plagas y Enfermedades a través de Residuos Regulados.
- Decree No 674/89; Decree No 776/92 of industrial effluents.

- Resolution No 1102/04; Resolution No. 785/05 of the Department of Energy on fuels, and other applicable legislation.
- Law No 22190 Legal System for the Prevention of Water Pollution.
- Law No 24089 approves the International Convention for the Prevention of Pollution by Ships, 1973.
- REGINAVE Ruling on Maritime, Fluvial and Lake Navigation
- Ordinance No 8/98 (DPAM)—Volume 6—of the Argentine Naval Prefecture on the "Sistema Nacional de Preparación y Lucha contra la Contaminación por Hidrocarburos y otras Sustancias Nocivas y Sustancias Potencialmente Peligrosas".
- Ordinance No 2/14—Volume 6—of the Argentine Naval Prefecture on floating barriers during the loading or unloading of persistent hydrocarbons, of mineral or organic origin, in ports, terminals, platforms and monobuoys.

7 Jurisdiction and Arbitration

The rules relating to jurisdiction and arbitration are again not specific to cruises. The ones applied to these are referred to the carriage of people by water.

In this sense, the first thing we should therefore mention is that in our country the issues related to navigation are competence of the federal government. This has been established by the National Constitution in its article 116, which reads: "It is the duty of the Supreme Court and the Lower Courts of the Nation, to have the knowledge and decision on all causes that deal with points ruled by the Constitution, and by the national laws, with the reservation made in subsection 12, article 75 and by the treaties with foreign countries: . . .of the legal cases of admiralty and maritime jurisdiction: . . ."

In relation to the competent courts, the Navigation Act regulates, in its article 621, the extension of the jurisdiction: "given a fact generating a cause the knowledge of which corresponds to the national courts, residents in the country may agree, after that, to submit it to the judgment of arbitrators or foreign courts, if appropriate."

Once we have clarified this point, we must say that the Argentine Republic is part of the Convention on Carriage of Passengers and their baggage by sea, held in Athens on 13 December 1974. The agreement was approved by Law No 22718, the instrument of ratification was deposited on 26/05/1983 and it is in force in our country since 28/04/1987. The Convention currently has 25 member States.

The jurisdiction is ruled by article 17 of the Convention:

ARTICLE 17- Competent jurisdiction

1. The actions which may be invoked under this convention shall be tabled, at the election of the plaintiff, to one of the courts listed below, provided that the tribunal is a member state of the convention, namely:

   a) the Court of the habitual place of residence or that of the defendant's commercial headquarters;

b) the Court of the starting point or point of destination indicated in the transport contract;
c) a court of the state in which the claimant's domicile or habitual residence is located, if the defendant has a commercial establishment in this state and is subject to its jurisdiction, or
d) a court of the state in which the contract of carriage was concluded if the defendant has a commercial establishment in this state and is subject to its jurisdiction.

2. After the event causing the damage, the parties may agree that the litigation is subject to the jurisdiction of any one of the aforementioned courts or to arbitration.

ARTICLE 18- Nullity of contractual stipulations

Subject to the provisions in paragraph 4 of article 8, any contractual stipulation agreed upon before the incident that caused the death or bodily injury of a passenger or the loss or damage of his/her baggage shall be considered null and void if it intends to exempt the carrier from his responsibility regarding the passenger or to set a limit of liability lower than that laid down by this convention and so shall any stipulation whose object is to displace the burden of proof that rests on the carrier or limit the possibility of election mentioned in paragraph 1 of article 17. The nullity of such stipulations shall nevertheless not void the contract of carriage itself, which will be subject to the provisions of this convention.

The "Tratado de Montevideo de Derecho Comercial Internacional" of 1889 regulates the affreightment contract and not the transport, although, as Aguirre Ramírez explains, the term "affreightment" was used before indistinctly to refer both to the affreightment leasing of ships and to the transport itself. It is governed by article 14 according to "the laws and tribunals of the country in which the shipping agency with which the charterer has concluded the contract is domiciled". The following subsection, which states that "the affreightment intended to carry goods or passengers between ports of the same state, shall be governed by the laws thereof", ratifies that the rule refers to the contract of carriage.

The "Tratado de Montevideo de Derecho de la Navegación Comercial" of 1940 provides in its article 27 that they are competent to know in the respective litigations the courts of the place of execution without prejudice to the alternative of resorting "at the option of the plaintiff" to the Courts "of the defendant's domicile, being null and void any clause that establishes otherwise".

As Aguirre Ramírez explains, this double rule (that on the law and Court of the place of destination and that on the prohibition of the autonomy of the will in the matter) responds to the best defense of the regional interests and also to the best Argentine-Uruguayan tradition. This solution of the treaties of Montevideo is known internationally as the "Regla de Buenos Aires" since it was the solution advocated by the Argentine delegation at the International Law Association Conference held in Buenos Aires in 1922. This was consecrated by the historical sentence of the Argentine National Supreme Court of Justice in the famous case "Compte vs. Ybarra" (1936).

In cases where the aforementioned treaties are not applied, the Argentine internal source-law No. 20094 of navigation includes the principles of the sentence "Compte vs. Ybarra" and expressly declares the nullity of any clause that attempts to exclude the competence of the Argentine Courts (art. 614). Apart from this, the

Argentine Courts are besides competent according to the art. 612 in all cases in which the ship may be seized (forum Arresti).

The new national Civil and Commercial Code regulates in its article 2654 the jurisdiction in the contracts of consumption: the demands that deal with the consumer relations can be filed, at the choice of the consumer, before the judges of the place the contract is concluded, the fulfilment of the provision of the service, the delivery of goods, the fulfilment of the warranty obligations, the domicile of the defendant or the place where the consumer performs acts necessary to make the contract.

Also competent are the judges of the state where the defendant has a branch, agency or any form of commercial representation, when these have intervened in the conclusion of the contract or when the defendant has mentioned them for the purposes of the fulfilment of a contractual warranty.

The action tabled against the consumer by the other contracting party may only be filed before the judges of the state of the domicile of the consumer.

The forum election agreement is not supported in this area.

Bearing in mind that carriage contracts used by transport companies are a kind of pre-designed "form", it is not surprising that these clauses are inserted in them. However, for to their validity, please refer to the paragraphs above.

8 Choice of Law

Our legal system does not envisage specific rules on the election of the law on cruises either, nor does it in respect to passenger carriage by water.

In this sense, the new national Civil and Commercial Code regulates the applicable law in its article 2655: Consumer contracts are governed by the legal system of the state of the consumer's domicile in the following cases:

a) if the conclusion of the contract was preceded by an offer or publicity or activity carried out in the state of the consumer's domicile and it has fulfilled in it the necessary acts for the conclusion of the contract;
b) if the supplier has received the order in the state of the consumer's domicile;
c) if the consumer was induced by his supplier to travel to a foreign state in order to make his order;
d) if travel contracts include for a global price combined transportation and accommodation service.

Otherwise, consumer contracts are governed by the law of the country of the place of fulfilment. Should it be impossible to determine the place of fulfilment, the contract will be governed by the law of the place it was concluded.

On the other hand, article 2651 broadly regulates the autonomy of the will in international contracts and provides, in its last part, that this does not apply to consumer contracts.

As noted in the case law indicated below, in cases such as GMI vs. Los Cipreses, the Courts have considered that in the face of the conflict that may arise from the application of the Navigation Act and the Consumer Protection Act (in the particular case of a prescription issue) they have favoured the implementation of the CDA. "... *the art. 50 of the Consumer Defense Act 24240, text pursuant to Law 26361, states that: "The judicial, administrative and punitive actions arising from this law shall prescribe within THREE (3) years. Should other general or special laws set limitation periods other than those established above, the court will be more favorable to the consumer or user...".*"*...the "legal link" that binds the transporter or carrier, as a service provider, with the passenger as user or consumer of it, constitutes a typical consumer relationship, with adjustment to the first paragraph of art. 3 of Law 24240, reformed by Law 26361. This law is clearly framed, without a doubt, within the regulation of the mentioned "Consumer Defense ACT", which "aims precisely at defending the consumer or user. Hereby we mean any natural or legal person who acquires or uses goods or services for free or onerously as a final recipient, for his own benefit or his family's or social group's benefit"– art. 1° of this law – (cfr. Trigo Represas, Felix A., "La Prescripción en el Transporte de Personas y el Consumidor", LA LEY 12/12/2011, 1- LA LEY 2011-F, 1202).*

Under these conditions, and in order to ponder the relationship between the two competing norms – Law No 20094 and Law No 24240 –, the provisions of the third paragraph of art. 3° of the Consumer Protection Act must be taken into account. This stipulates that the consumer relations are ruled by the dispositions established in this law and its regulations. The supplier can, nevertheless, depending on his activity, be also subject to another specific regulation. Therefore, the regime established by the Navigation Act must yield to that of the consumer, which enjoys preeminence over any other regulation that may also be applicable to the same assumptions it regulates.

It only remains for me to add that this law has a constitutional character – as envisaged in the art. 42 of the National Constitution of 1994, which incorporated the consumer protection as a "fundamental right" – and which has public character. (art. 65 thereof)".

9 Legal Scholarship and Legal Education

For reference on private international law on cruises in our legal system please refer to Fernandez Gustavo N. Cruise Agreement: Prevalence of the Consumer Protection Act on the Navigation Act. Comment to the judgement "Meraviglia C. Costa Cruises".

We supply here a list in chronological order of the relevant case law concerning cruises:

- S.C.V de V vs. "Costa Cruceros" (8 September 2005)
- Casinhghino Horacio Daniel y otro vs. BUQUEBUS s/sumarísimo (6 November 2009)
- MSC Cruceros S.A vs. DNCI-Disp. 604/06 (19 April 2010)
- Q.T.S vs. Los Cipreses S.A. -Damages (1 September 2010)

- López, Néstor Nahuel vs. Los Cipreses S.A. -Loss/damage of baggage. (15 August 2012)
- Abella, Verónica vs. Los Cipreses S.A. -Injury and/or death of passenger maritime transport. (11 June 2013)
- Acuña Cabral, Sonia Raquel y otro vs. Belt S.A. y otro -Injury and/or death of passenger maritime transport. (27 June 2013)
- G.M.I. vs. Los Cipreses (Buquebus) S.A. -Damages. (18 February 2014)
- Unilever of Argentina SA vs. DNCI -Consumer defense (18 September 2015)
- Trunzo Alejandra Verónica y otro vs. Costa Cruceros S.A. -Ordinaria Buenos Aires (15 September 2016)
- Meraviglia, Graciela R. vs. Costa Cruceros SA -Injury and/or death of passenger (30 May 2017)

The Education programmes in Argentina are only partially related to the legal aspects of cruises. Not all Faculties of Law in the Argentine Republic teach Navigation Law. Those which do, teach the legal aspects of the contract for the transportation of people by water. In the case of the National University of Cordoba, there is though an optional subject, "Tourism Law", that deals thoroughly with the legal problems of cruises.

10 Conclusions

As we have said above, the Argentine Republic does not have specific legislation on cruises, which is an important flaw. The rules on the contract for the transport of people by water apply, but reality shows us that it is insufficient since the cruise involves much more than a simple transfer of a person from one port to another on board a ship.

It is an activity that involves hospitality, entertainment, gastronomy, which results in a variety of legal relationships that require special attention from the States in order to provide clarity in the face of the various situations that may arise.

The geographical location of Argentina presents disadvantages for not being on the main world cruise circuit, but also advantages such as having the port of access to Antarctica.

The cruise industry is growing and that is why actions must be taken such as issuing specific regulations that cover the entire spectrum of relationships that a cruise ship implies, that provide legal protection and security to travelers, consider the rights, obligations and qualification of the personnel affected by cruise ships, preserve the environment, and implement a rate policy that is attractive to shipping companies, among others.

U.S. Law and Policy for the Cruise Industry

Ved P. Nanda

Abstract The United States is a major player in the cruise industry. However, very few ocean-going cruise ships sail under the U.S. flag, as ship owners register ships under flags of convenience, that is, flags of countries with lax safety and labor regulations and weak enforcement policies. Notwithstanding the constraints caused by the use of flags of convenience because a flag state has exclusive jurisdiction over its flagged vessel on the high seas, the U.S. has a robust legislative framework regulating major aspects of cruises. This includes vessel design requirements, safety requirements, civil and criminal liability regimes, labor regulations, and environmental protection.

This chapter discusses the U.S. law and policy for the cruise industry, and the ongoing efforts to further strengthen the pertinent laws and regulations to fill the gaps still remaining.

1 Introduction

During the last decade, the global cruise industry has experienced massive growth, with the number of cruise passengers rising from 17.8 million in 2009 to 24.7 million in 2016, an estimated 25.8 million in 2017, and a projection of 27.2 million in 2018.[1] With over a million full-time employees, the cruise industry's impact on the global economy is impressive, indeed—$126 billion in total output and $41.1 billion in wages and salaries.[2] 17 new cruise ships joined the industry in 2017 and 16 more are

The author extends his gratitude to Kyle Ames, J.D. 2018, and Katharine Nanda, J.D. 1982, for their excellent assistance and support.

[1] Cruise Lines International Association, Inc. (CLIA), *2018 Cruise Industry Outlook*, Dec. 2017, at 7, http://cruising.org/docs/default-source/research/clia-2018-state-of-the-industry.pdf?sfvrsn=2.
[2] *Id.* at 13.

V. P. Nanda (✉)
The University of Denver, Denver, CO, USA
e-mail: vnanda@law.du.edu

C. Fresnedo de Aguirre (ed.), *Legal Aspects of Cruises*, Ius Comparatum - Global Studies in Comparative Law 56, https://doi.org/10.1007/978-3-030-83090-8_9

expected in 2018.[3] Notwithstanding the severe setback resulting from COVID-19, the cruise industry expects a rebound. Section 2 narrates the importance of cruises. Section 3 reviews general and specific rules applicable to cruises; Sect. 4 discusses the role of cruise passengers as consumers and consumer protection laws; Sect. 5 addresses labor rules on cruise workers, jurisdiction, arbitration, and choice of law; Sect. 6 covers rules on environmental impact of cruises; Sect. 7 enumerates the sources of law applicable to cruises, which precedes the final section, Sect. 8, the Conclusion.

2 The Importance of Cruises

The United States is a major player in the cruise industry. To illustrate, more than 50% of all cruise passengers are from the U.S.,[4] and one in five Americans has taken an ocean cruise.[5] The revenue from the cruise industry in the U.S. was $37.85 billion in 2016,[6] and big cruise lines, such as Norwegian Cruise Lines, Royal Caribbean International, and the world's largest, Carnival Corporation, are all headquartered in the United States. Cruise industry jobs in the U.S. number 314,000.[7] And 21 ports service cruise ships in the continental U.S. and three in the territorial/non-continental U.S.[8] The state of Alaska is also a popular global destination for cruises, receiving 4.1% of the global cruise capacity in 2016 (measured by available lower berth day).[9]

River cruises, too, have exploded in popularity, with 184 ships operating on rivers globally in 2015, and 13 more river cruise ships on order in 2017 to meet increased

[3] Cruise Industry News, *2018 Biggest Year for New Cruise Ships since 2001*, Jan. 4, 2018, https://www.cruiseindustrynews.com/cruise-news/18321-2018-biggest-year-for-new-ships-since-2001.html.

[4] CLIA, *Global Demand for Cruising Surpasses 22 Million Passengers, Increasing 68 Percent in Ten Years*, Oct. 19, 2015, www.cruising.org/about-the-industry/press%2D%2Droom/press-releases/global-demand-for-cruising-surpasses-22-million-passengers-increasing-68-percent-in-ten-years.

[5] Statistic Brain. *Cruise Ship Industry Statistics.* March 3, 2017, https://www.statisticbrain.com/cruise-ship-industry-statistics/ [hereinafter Cruise Ship Industry Statistics]. The percentage of Americans who have taken a cruise is 19.9%. *Id.*

[6] *Id.*

[7] Minister Responsible for Maritime Affairs, Merchant Shipping Act (Amendment to First Schedule), Notice, 2012, https://www.bahamasmaritime.com/wp-content/uploads/2015/08/MS-Maritime-Labour-Convention-Regulations-2012.pdf.

[8] All things cruise, *Cruise Departure Ports,* https://allthingscruise.com/cruise-research/cruise-departure-ports/.

[9] Florida-Caribbean Cruise Association, *Cruise Industry Overview, 2017,* http://www.f-cca.com/downloads/2017-Cruise-Industry-Overview-Cruise-Line-Statistics.pdf. *See also* CLIA, *2016 Cruise Industry Outlook,* at 8 https://www.cruising.org/docs/default-source/research/2016_clia_sotci.pdf.

demand.[10] The U.S. has several excellent locations for river cruises. For example, American Cruise Lines offers trips on the Mississippi River and in New England, Pacific Northwest, Alaska, and the Southeast.[11]

3 General and Specific Rules Applicable to Cruises

3.1 General

Despite the large number of American cruise travelers, very few ocean-going cruise ships sail under the U.S. flag. The tradition of flags of convenience, a fundamental principle of maritime law, is at the same time the crux of the most difficult challenges in this industry—for the governments that attempt to regulate personal and environmental safety and frustrated by their inability to raise tax revenues, for the public consumers of passenger ships, and for the industry itself, which continues to suffer crises endemic to its own nature and criticism over its resistance to regulation.[12]

Most cruise lines register ships under flags of convenience, which means that ship owners register a ship in a country other than their own, in order to evade their country's tax laws and to take advantage of the registry country's lax safety and labor regulations and weak enforcement policies. Only one big cruise ship built in the last 50 years—Pride of America, which is operated by Norwegian Cruise Lines and was launched in 2005—is currently registered in the U.S. and thus is U.S. flagged.[13]

Panama, which does not tax corporations for foreign source income, is the most popular flag of convenience, accounting for 22.6% of the entire global maritime fleet.[14] Next is Liberia and, in the third place, Bahama, which is the most popular registry for cruise ships[15] Fourteen cruise lines have ships registered in the Bahamas, including Carnival, Disney Cruise Line, Norwegian Cruise Line, and Royal Caribbean. In total, 88 cruise ships, or nearly 28% of the entire global cruise fleet, is

[10] CLIA, *2017 Cruise Industry Outlook* 14, https://www.cruising.org/docs/default-source/research/clia-2017-state-of-the-industry.pdf?sfvrsn=0.

[11] American Cruise Lines, *Cruises: Destinations*, https://www.americancruiselines.com/?utm_source=google&utm_medium=cpc&utm_campaign=us%20cruises&gclid=Cj0KCQiAyZLSBRDpARIsAH66VQKFNIvOBWc7wi7POordiVVcbId1kXlvsP3HPFYCU66KfffjKFXDBa8aAhItEALw_wcB.

[12] See, e.g., *How the cruise ship industry sails under the radar*, Jan. 24, 2012, reuters.com/article/uk-italy-ship-regulation/how-the-cruise-ship-industry-sails-under-the-radar-idUSLINEBON02M0120124.

[13] Pride of America, https://www.ncl.com/cruise-ship/pride-of-america.

[14] Cruise Mapper, *Cruise Ship Registry, Flags of Convenience,* http://www.cruisemapper.com/wiki/758-cruise-ship-registry-flags-of-convenience-flag-state-control.

[15] *Id.*

registered in the Bahamas.[16] Ships registered in these states do not have to comply with U.S. safety and labor regulations.

The time-honored right of every state to register ships under its flag and to determine the conditions for this right is authorized by the International Maritime Organization (IMO) and the United Nations Convention on the High Seas.[17] The United States Supreme Court stated the U.S. position on the law of the flag in *Lauritzen v. Larsen*:[18]

> Perhaps the most venerable and universal rule of maritime law relevant to our problem is that which gives cardinal importance to the law of the flag. Each state under international law may determine for itself the conditions on which it will grant its nationality to a merchant ship, thereby accepting responsibility for it and acquiring authority over it. Nationality is evidenced to the world by the ship's papers and its flag, The United States has firmly and successfully maintained that the regularity and validity of a registration can be questioned only by the registering state.[19]

Because a flag state has exclusive jurisdiction over its flagged vessel on the high seas, this compounds issues of jurisdiction and represents a unique challenge of the cruise industry. As this is a common practice for merchant vessels, injured passengers are often under the jurisdiction of nations with underdeveloped civil and criminal liability regimes, and may be forced to adjudicate their disputes in inconvenient foreign fora, under foreign laws, with no real connection to their case.

Notwithstanding the constraints caused by use of flags of convenience, the U.S. has a robust legislative framework regulating major aspects of cruises, including vessel design requirements, safety requirements, civil and criminal liability regimes, labor regulations, and environmental protection. Most of the legislative measures that apply to cruises are maritime laws applying to maritime vessels in general, although a few U.S. laws specifically apply to cruise vessels.

Cruises raise complex legal issues, presenting immense challenges; and the use of flags of convenience exacerbates this complexity. Major challenges include cruise vessel and passenger safety; civil and criminal liability; and environmental protection. The findings made by Congress as it enacted the Cruise Vessel Security and Safety Act of 2010 (CVSSA)[20] include disappearances from vessels on the high seas and other serious crimes that have occurred during cruises, such as sexual assault and physical assaults, both by passengers and crew members on other passengers and crew members, and the difficulty of obtaining reliable crime-related cruise data, because of involvement of multiple countries such as the flag country for the vessel,

---

[16] *Id.* See also CLIA, *2016 Cruise Industry Outlook* 15, https://www.cruising.org/docs/default-source/research/2016_clia_sotci.pdf.

[17] See IMO.org; United Nations Convention on the High Seas, 29 Apr. 1958, entered into force 30 September 1962, 450 U.N.T.S. 11, 82, http://www.gc.nowa.gov/documents/8_1_1958_high_seas.pdf.

[18] *Lauritzen v. Larsen*, 345 U.S. 571 (1953).

[19] *Id.* at 584.

[20] Cruise Vessel Security and Safety Act of 2010, Pub. L. 111-207, 124 Stat. 2243, et seq., Jul. 27, 2010, enacted at 46 U.S.C. §3507.

the nationality of particular passengers, and countries that have special or maritime jurisdiction.[21]

For cruise lines and other maritime companies owned by Americans the decision to fly the flag of another chosen state is made for legal as well as economic reasons.[22] A 2011 study by the U.S. Department of Transportation Maritime Administration found significant savings in operating costs for foreign flagged vessels. On average, vessels flagged in the U.S. spent 68% of operating costs on crew, whereas foreign flagged vessels spent only 35% of their total operating costs on crew.[23] Average daily operating costs for U.S. vessels in 2010 was $20,053, while foreign-flagged vessels expended only $7454.[24] The report's conclusion was that "the total average cost of operating a U.S.-flag vessel in foreign trade is estimated to be 2.7 times higher, on average, than foreign flag equivalents."[25]

Another financial issue that U.S. lawmakers are concerned with are the costs to the government for maintaining the ports used by cruises and to the Coast Guard, which is responsible for all prevention activities associated with the safe operation of vessels and facilities,[26] and thus for search and rescue operations. However, the cruise line industry pays very little in income taxes. To recover those costs, in August 2013, U.S. Senator Jay Rockefeller (D-W.Va.) proposed two bills, the Cruise Income Tax Loophole Repeal bill (S. 1449) and the Excise Tax on Cruise Income bill (S. 1450),[27] aimed at closing the tax loophole and forcing the cruise industry to pay their fair share of taxes. The Excise Tax bill would have levied a 5% excise tax on gross income for cruises that embark or disembark from the United States; and the proceeds of this proposed bill would have been earmarked for improving transportation infrastructure. At a July hearing before the Senate Commerce, Science and Transportation Committee, which he chaired, Rockefeller spoke about the proposed bills. As he addressed the presidents of Carnival Cruise Lines and Royal Caribbean, he noted that these companies paid an effective tax rate of 1.3%.[28] He chided them, saying:

---

[21] Pub. L. 111-207, 124 Stat. 2243, §2. Findings.

[22] There is voluminous literature on the topic. See, e.g., Negret (2016), p. 1.

[23] U.S. Department of Transportation Maritime Administration, *Comparison of U.S. and Foreign-Flag Operating Costs,* September 2011 at 6, https://www.marad.dot.gov/wp-content/uploads/pdf/Comparison_of_US_and_Foreign_Flag_Operating_Costs.pdf.

[24] *Id.* at 4.

[25] *Id.* at 11.

[26] *See* United States Coast Guard, homepage, http://www.uscg.mil/.

[27] *Cruise Lines Would Face Higher Federal Taxes Under Rockefeller Legislation*, Aug. 7, 2013, Wolters Kluwer Tax and Accounting, http://news.cchgroup.com/2013/08/07/cruise-lines-would-face-higher-federal-taxes-under-rockefeller-legislation/. See also Bill Poling, *Proposed Bills Could Raise Nearly $1 Billion in Cruise Taxes*, Travel Weekly, Aug. 11, 2013, www.travelweekly.com/Cruise-Travel/Proposed-bills-could-raise-nearly-a-billion-in-cruise-taxes.

[28] Remarks of Sen. John D. Rockefeller, IV, Chair, Senate Committee on Commerce, Science, and Transportation, 113th Congress, Hearing: Cruise Industry Oversight: Recent Incidents Show Need for Stronger Focus on Consumer Protection, July 24, 2013.

> Your companies are headquartered in the United States, most of your passengers are U.S. citizens. You use our ports, our courts and the services of the Coast Guard and many other government agencies, ... But because you flag your ships in other countries and maintain the fiction that you earn most of your income outside of U.S. territory, you do not pay your fair share of taxes in this country.[29]

As expected, the industry lobbied hard in opposition to these bills and they were not enacted; another effort was made in November 2017 in the proposed Tax Reform legislation in the U.S. Congress.[30] Ultimately, however, the cruise tax provisions were deleted from the text of the Tax Cuts and Jobs Act of 2017 that Congress finally adopted in December 2017.[31]

The majority of U.S. laws that apply to cruise lines are laws of general application, applicable to all maritime vessels. A few of those are summarized here:

3.2 The U.S. Constitution

It is appropriate to begin with the Constitution of the United States, which authorizes federal courts to adjudicate "all Cases of admiralty and maritime Jurisdiction."[32] Subsequently, Congress adopted the Judiciary Act of 1789[33] and authorized this grant of original jurisdiction. Although state courts have concurrent general maritime jurisdiction, as the Florida Supreme Court stated in the 2007 case of *Carnival Corp. v. Carlisle*: "Federal maritime law is an amalgamation of federal legislation, federal common law, and state maritime law."[34] *Carlisle* was a maritime case where the court had to decide the issue of a shipowner's vicarious liability toward passengers for the action of the shipboard director. The court observed that if an issue can be resolved by federal maritime law, state courts must apply such law,[35] but if there is no federal law on the issue, "maritime law may be supplemented or modified by the states where the supplement or modification does not conflict with an essential feature of exclusive federal jurisdiction." In applying maritime law, the court stated that it "must adhere to the federal principles of harmony and uniformity when applying federal maritime law."[36]

---

[29] *Id.*

[30] See Tom Stieghorst, *Senate bill would tax cruise line income*, Travel Weekly, Nov. 13, 2017, http://news.cchgroup.com/2013/08/07/cruise-lines-would-face-higher-federal-taxes-under-rockefeller-legislation/.

[31] Marex, *Tax reform passed, cruise tax deleted*, Dec. 2, 2017, www.maritime-executive.com/article/tax-reform-passed-cruise-tax-deleted.

[32] U.S. Const., art. III, § 2, cl. 1.

[33] 28 U.S.C. § 3033(1).

[34] *Carnival Corp. v. Carlisle*, 953 So.2d 461, 464 (Fl. 2007).

[35] *Id.*

[36] *Id.*

3.3 The Passenger Vessel Services Act of 1886

President Grover Cleveland signed the Passenger Vessel Services Act of 1886 (PVSA),[37] which was aimed at protecting the American shipping industry and American jobs. The Act restricts the coastwise transportation of people between U.S. points, reserving it for U.S. built, owned, and documented vessels. Thus, the Act prohibits commercial vessels such as cruise ships from allowing passengers to board at one U.S. port and disembark at another U.S. port, unless they meet the PVSA's nationality requirement. The applicable regulation for penalties in violation of the PVSA provides: "The penalty imposed for the unlawful transportation of passengers between coastwise points is $300 for each passenger so transported and landed . . . ."[38] The PVSA continues to face criticism that instead of protecting American jobs it has cost American jobs.[39]

3.4 The Jones Act

In June 1920, in the aftermath of the First World War, Congress adopted the Merchant Marine Act, also known as the Jones Act, which was aimed at supporting the U.S. Merchant Marine to provide for national defense. The Act was subsequently amended several times, most recently in 2006, and recodified.[40] The Jones Act also gives a cause of action to injured sailors to seek damages from their employers for the negligence of the ship owner.

The Act states:

> A seaman injured in the course of employment or, if the seaman dies from the injury, the personal representative of the seaman may elect to bring a civil action at law, with the right of trial by jury, against the employer. Laws of the United States regulating recovery for personal injury to, or death of, a railway employee apply to an action under this section.

If the ship owner is found negligent and the vessel is considered unseaworthy, a seaman can claim and may be able to recover compensation for injuries, pain and suffering, lost wages, and/or other related damage. The U.S. Supreme Court in a 1995 case, *Chandris, Inc. v. Latsis*,[41] held that in order to qualify under the Act, a seaman must spend 30% or more of his / her time working on a vessel on navigable waters. There are provisions for arbitration under special circumstances.

---

[37] Passenger Vessel Services Act, 46 U.S.C. § 55103(b).

[38] 19 C.F.R. § 4.80(b)(2).

[39] See, e.g., Buchholz and Buchholz (2017); Kasperkevic (2017); Mak et al. (2009).

[40] Jones Act, 46 U.S.C. §30104. The critics considered it to be protectionist and failing to serve the U.S. national interest. See generally Kashian et al. (2017), www.grassrootinstitute.org/2017/04/the-jones-act-in-perspective/.

[41] *Chandris, Inc. v. Latsis*, 515 U.S. 347 (1995).

It should be noted that for seamen the negligence action through the Jones Act is available only when the person has suffered an injury, the reason being that the Jones Act incorporated by reference the Federal Employers' Liability Act (FELA). According to the U.S. Supreme Court, "The Jones Act adopts 'the entire judicially developed doctrine of liability' under the Federal Employers' Liability Act,"[42] and the Court has also stated that the negligence principles that govern FELA cases should also apply to Jones Act cases.[43] In a 2012 case, the Eastern District of Pennsylvania ruled that because FELA requires a plaintiff to prove physical impairment or manifestation to claim a cognizable injury, it should be the same requirement for the Jones Act.[44]

3.5 Death on the High Seas Act

The Death on the High Seas Act (DOHSA)[45] is a U.S. admiralty law that established a cause of action for damages against the "person or vessel" responsible for a wrongful death in international waters—beyond 3 nautical miles from the shore of the United States—resulting from negligence. Only the decedent's family are permitted to recover,[46] and the Act bars recovery of emotional damages, including pain and suffering, and mental anguish. It has faced continuous criticism. Under the proposed Cruise Passenger Protection Act (CPPA), which will be discussed later, if enacted, families would be able to receive non-pecuniary compensation, as well.

3.6 Liability for Injury or Death

Under U.S. law, liability of a cruise ship for personal injury or death is clearly defined.[47] A special duty of care owed to passengers by cruise lines was set out in the Shipping Act of 1984, which deems cruise ships as common carriers.[48] Thus, the cruise lines have a duty to protect passengers from physical harm, including from negligence, and also attacks and other criminal behavior on board.

[42] *Am. Dredging Co. v. Miller*, 510 U.S. 443, 456 (1994).

[43] *Kernan v. Am. Dredging Co.*, 355 U.S. 426, 439 (1958).

[44] *In re Asbestos Products Liab. Litig.*, 2012 WL 3242420 * 7, 10 (E.D. Pa., Aug. 7, 2012).

[45] Death on the High Seas Act 46 U.S.C. app. §§ 761–768 (1920) (DOHSA), codified at 46 U.S.C. 303, et seq., US House of Representatives, Office of the Law Revision Council, *United States Code. Chapter 303 Death on the High Seas*, http://uscode.house.gov/view.xhtml?path=/prelim@title46/subtitle3/chapter303&edition=prelim.

[46] *Id.* § 30302.

[47] 46 U.S.C.A. § 30509 (Oct 6, 2006).

[48] Shipping Act of 1984, 46 U.S.C. §1702.

Generally, it is prohibited for a ship transporting passengers within the United States or between the U.S. and a foreign country to limit in the passenger's ticket or contract the liability of the owner, master, or agent for personal injury or death caused by the negligence or fault of the owner or the owner's employees or agents; or the right of a claimant for personal injury or death to a trial by court of competent jurisdiction. Any attempt to limit such liability is void.

Liability may be limited for emotional distress, mental suffering, and psychological injury, unless this injury is the result of physical injury caused by the ship or personnel, or caused by being at risk of such injury, or if the injury was intentional by the ship or personnel.

The liability of the owner, master, manager, agent, operator, or crewmember may not be limited in a case of sexual harassment, assault, or rape.

3.7 Crimes/Criminal Lability

Protection of a state's own nationals while abroad, gives rise to the Passive Personality principle, which allows a nation to exercise jurisdiction over individuals accused of criminal wrongdoing against its national, under customary international law.

Criminal liability is an underdeveloped area of cruise law. Only 16% of murders and 7% of rapes reported resulted in plea bargains or convictions.[49] Congress responded to growing concern about crimes committed against U.S. nationals on cruises, and held a series of hearings from 2005 to 2009, ultimately resulting the in the Cruise Vessel Security and Safety Act: "The bottom line is we are suspicious, candidly, that there's some huge problem in the cruise industry," said Rep. Chris Shays (R-Conn). "We think that people are not aware of some of the challenges and some of the potential problems they encounter."[50]

It should be noted that the CVSSA applies extraterritorially in accordance with another U.S. law, 18 U.S.C. § 7, Special Maritime Jurisdiction of the United States Defined.[51] Under its provisions, the U.S. can exercise extraterritorial maritime jurisdiction when: the vessels is owned in whole or part by U.S. nationals, the offense was committed by or against a U.S. national on the high seas, the incident occurs in a territorial sea of the U.S., or the incident was by or against a U.S. person during a voyage to or from a U.S. port.[52]

[49] Eric Weiner, Cruise, National Public Radio, https://www.npr.org/templates/story/story.php?storyId=5251675.

[50] ABC News, *Congress Eyes Cruise Ship Dangers*, Dec. 13, 2005, http://abcnews.go.com/GMA/story?id=1400466.

[51] Government Publishing Office. *18 U.S.C. § 7. Special maritime and territorial jurisdiction of the United States defined.*

[52] *Id.*, https://www.gpo.gov/fdsys/pkg/USCODE-2010-title18/pdf/USCODE-2010-title18-partI-chap1-sec7.pdf.

Table 1 U.S. Department of Transportation, cruise incidents for 2016 and 2017

	2016	2017 (Quarters 1–3)
Homicide	0	1
Death (suspicious)	4	1
Missing U.S. National	6	3
Kidnapping	0	2
Assault w/ serious bodily injury	14	10
Firing or tampering with vessel	0	0
Theft > $10,000	6	8
Sexual assault	62	60
Total major crimes reported	92	85

Prior to the CVSSA, cruise lines were under no obligation to report crimes committed against U.S. nationals to U.S. law enforcement agencies. As a consequence, there are no comprehensive crime statistics before the CVSSA went into effect.

Requiring cruise lines to report crimes is a positive step in providing safer cruise experiences. Eight "major" crimes must be reported: homicide, suspicious deaths, missing U.S. Nationals, kidnappings, firing or tampering with vessel, thefts over $10,000, and sexual assaults. Incidents are reported to the FBI and compiled by the U.S. Department of Transportation.[53] The department publishes crime reports quarterly, and sorts the data by the cruise line. This allows consumers to be aware of which cruise lines have the most criminal incidents and may provide an incentive to cruise lines to further reduce such incidents.

The numbers for 2016 and the first three quarters of 2017 follow in Table 1.

The reports of criminal activity to the FBI, however, suffer from several shortcomings:

The reporting agency changed a year into the data set from the Coast Guard to the Department of Transportation. According to sources citing to the FBI, the number of incidents of "major" crimes on cruise ships reported to the FBI does not match the published incident reports by the Coast Guard.[54]

Second, until the first quarter of 2016, there was a requirement that crimes reported as no longer under investigation by the FBI would not be included in the data set.[55] When comparing trends in the data, it is not possible to distinguish

[53] U.S. Dep't of Transp., Cruise Line Incident Reports, 2016 and 2017, https://www.transportation.gov/mission/safety/cruise-line-incident-reports [hereinafter DOT Incident Reports].

[54] Mike M. Alhers. *Passengers lack public info on cruise ship crime.* July 25, 2013. CNN. http://www.cnn.com/2013/07/24/travel/cruise-ship-crime/index.html.

[55] See DOT Incident Reports, *supra* note 53, original "not under investigation" restriction, which is appended to each quarter's data from January of 2010, to December of 2015: "The number of matters "no longer under investigation" provided on this Internet site is necessarily different than the aggregate number of matters required to be reported to the FBI per the above. A matter may be reported but not opened as a full investigation if, for example, there is insufficient evidence of a federal crime within FBI jurisdiction or prosecution is declined. The "matters no longer under

whether that is the reason for the threefold increase in major crimes between 2015 and 2016. It is also not clear whether the previous years requirement lead to systemic under-reporting of major crimes.

Finally, the categories of crimes that must be reported seems unnecessarily restrictive. Assaults without serious bodily injury and thefts under $10,000 are not reported or tracked, despite being the two most likely crimes that a cruise passenger may face. Since data on these incidents are not recorded and publicly available, cruise passengers, law enforcement, and the cruise lines themselves cannot know the extent of "non-major" crimes or see trends in their occurrence.

3.8 U.S. Applies International Maritime Organization (IMO) Standards and Regulations

The global shipping industry, including cruise ships, is subject to international legal regulation by the International Maritime Organization (IMO), the United Nations specialized agency that establishes standards for all kinds of shipping in order to promote the safe use of the seas and to protect the seas from the polluting effects of transport. Most relevant to the cruise industry are the IMO's International Convention for the Prevention of Pollution from Ships (MARPOL),[56] the first comprehensive anti-pollution convention, whose provisions cover pollution from both operational and accidental causes, and the Convention for the Safety of Life at Sea (SOLAS),[57] the primary treaty covering maritime safety, with regulations that must be observed by all shipping nations.

---

investigation" provided herein do not include: 1) open investigations or pending prosecutions; 2) reported matters other than homicide, suspicious death, a missing United States national, kidnapping, assault with serious bodily injury, sexual assault, firing or tampering with a vessel, or theft of money and property in excess of $10,000; 3) any matters that were reported that did not result in open investigations, investigations, e.g., lack of federal jurisdiction."

[56] International Maritime Organization. *International Convention for the Prevention of Pollution from Ships (MARPOL).* Adoption: 1973 (Convention), 1978 (1978 Protocol), 1997 (Protocol - Annex VI); Entry into force: 2 October 1983 (Annexes I and II) http://www.imo.org/en/about/conventions/listofconventions/pages/international-convention-for-the-prevention-of-pollution-from-ships-(marpol).aspx [hereinafter MARPOL].

[57] IMO, International Convention for the Safety of Life at Sea (SOLAS), 1974, www.imo.org/en/About/Conventions/ListOfConventions/Pages/International-Convention-for-the-Safety-of-Life-at-Sea-(SOLAS),-1974.aspx [hereinafter SOLAS]. "The Convention in force today is sometimes referred to as SOLAS, 1974, as amended," as new amendments enter into force under a "tacit acceptance procedure" contained in the 1974 version that requires express objections from an agreed number of States Parties to prevent it.

The IMO, whose 173 state members[58] account for 99% of the world's shipping, aims to maintain a regulatory framework that is

> fair and effective, universally adopted and universally implemented. . . . In other words, its role is to create a level playing-field so that ship operators cannot address their financial issues by simply cutting corners and compromising on safety, security and environmental performance. This approach also encourages innovation and efficiency.[59]

The agency was originally established in 1948 under the Convention on the International Maritime Organization[60] for maritime safety and navigation. As oil spillage became more clearly an urgent problem, and with the accidental Torrey Canyon disaster in the United Kingdom in 1967, the IMO undertook to prevent marine pollution, including liability and compensation resulting from such incidents.[61] In 1973, the International Convention for the Prevention of Pollution from Ships—MARPOL—was established to prevent oil spillage from ships. Subsequently, through a series of five annexes, it soon covered also pollution from noxious liquid substances in bulk, harmful substances carried by sea in packaged form, sewage, garbage, (1983–1988) and air pollution (in 2005). A section on limitation of greenhouse gas emissions was added in 2011.[62]

Under its Annex VI charge, MARPOL is presently tackling the problem of the marine industry's relying on heavy fuel oil. It passed a regulation creating an air

---

[58] As at Jan. 23, 2018. United Nations Treaty Collection, International Maritime Organization, https://treaties.un.org/Pages/ViewDetails.aspx?src=TREATY&mtdsg_no=XII-1&chapter=12&clang=_en.

[59] International Maritime Organization, Introduction to IMO, 2017, www.imo.org/en/About/Pages/Default.aspx.

[60] Convention on the International Maritime Organization, Geneva, 289 U.N.T.S. 3 (6 Mar. 1948), entry into force 17 Mar. 1958.

[61] The IMO also functions as Secretariat for the The Convention to Prevent Marine Pollution by Dumping Wastes and Other Matter of 1972, the "London Convention," and its 1996 Protocol, whose purpose is to "promote the effective control of all sources of marine pollution and to take all practicable steps to prevent pollution of the sea by dumping of wastes and other matter." http://www.imo.org/en/OurWork/Environment/Pages/Default.aspx.

[62] MARPOL Convention, annexes I-VI. The relevant Annexes are:

Annex I Regulations for the Prevention of Pollution by Oil (entered into force 2 October 1983); Annex II Regulations for the Control of Pollution by Noxious Liquid Substances in Bulk (entered into force 2 October 1983): "In any case, no discharge of residues containing noxious substances is permitted within 12 miles of the nearest land"; Annex IV Prevention of Pollution by Sewage from Ships (entered into force 27 September 2003): "[S]ewage which is not comminuted or disinfected has to be discharged at a distance of more than 12 nautical miles from the nearest land"; Annex V Prevention of Pollution by Garbage from Ships (entered into force 31 December 1988): "the most important feature of the Annex is the complete ban imposed on the disposal into the sea of all forms of plastics"; Annex VI Prevention of Air Pollution from Ships (entered into force 19 May 2005): "Sets limits on sulphur oxide and nitrogen oxide emissions from ship exhausts and prohibits deliberate emissions of ozone depleting substances; designated emission control areas set more stringent standards for SOx, NOx and particulate matter. A chapter adopted in 2011 covers mandatory technical and operational energy efficiency measures aimed at reducing greenhouse gas emissions from ships."

pollution buffer around the U.S. and Canada by requiring cruise ships, tankers, and cargo ships to switch to low-sulfur fuel when operating within 230 miles of the U.S. and Canada.[63] And it has undertaken a study into the availability of low sulfur content fuel. While today, fuel oil must have a maximum sulfur concentration of 3.5% m/m (mass by mass), MARPOL is implementing a .5% m/m sulfur limit by January 1, 2020 or 2025, pending the results of the availability study.[64]

In October 2017, the determination was made that 2020 would be the target. The move was called "a landmark decision" by one commentator, which would "reduce [] the contribution of shipping to the world's air pollution impact from about 5 percent down to 1.5 percent and . . . save millions of lives in the coming decades." It was also acknowledged that "[t]he refineries will need to run in a way they have never run before" as the shipping industry, a major consumer of lower-quality sulfur fuel, makes the adjustment. The director of policy and external relations of the International Chamber of Shipping association "welcomed what [his organization] said was the clear decision by IMO member states on the 2020 date."[65]

To comply with IMO's requirements, one major line, the Norwegian Cruise Line, already retrofitted three ships with "exhaust gas cleaning system technology" capable of reducing the emissions of sulfur by 99%. Other ships will also have to comply with the IMO regulations to reduce the sulfur content in the fuel from the current limit of 3.5% to .5% or less within a few years' time.[66]

Among MARPOL's important duties of special relevance to cruises is the regulation of shipping in a number of areas, defined in its Annexes I, II, and V, that are in need of extra protection from environmental damage. They are designated as either "Special Areas" and given appropriate regulatory protection,[67] or "Particularly

---

[63] See Jim Walker, *Over Cruise Industry's Objection, IMO Creates Air Pollution Buffer Around U.S. and Canada* http://www.cruiselawnews.com/2010/03/articles/pollution-1/over-cruise-industrys-objection-imo-creates-air-pollution-buffer-around-us-and-canada/.

[64] International Maritime Organization, *IMO regulations to reduce air pollution from ships and the review of fuel oil availability,* http://www.imo.org/en/MediaCentre/HotTopics/GHG/Documents/sulphur%20limits%20FAQ_20-09-2016.pdf. See, e.g., Jonathan Saul, *IMO Sets Regulations to Cut Sulphur Emissions by Ships from 2020*, Oct. 27, 2016, www.gcaptain.com/imo-sets-regulations-cut-sulphur-emissions-smips-2020/.

[65] *Id.*

[66] See Rittenhouse (2017), https://www.thestreet.com/story/13945339/1/regulators-force-cruise-lines-to-sail-green.html.

[67] Special areas means "a sea area where for recognized technical reasons in relation to its oceanographical and ecological conditions and to the particular character of its traffic, the adoption of special mandatory methods for the prevention of sea pollution by oil, noxious liquid substances, or garbage, as applicable, is required." IMO, Guidelines for the Designation of Special Areas under MARPOL 73/78 and Guidelines for the Identification and Designation of Particularly Sensitive Sea Areas, para. 2 [superseded], Resolution A.927(22), Adopted on 29 Nov. 2001, A/22/Res.927, 15 Jan. 2002, http://www.gc.noaa.gov/documents/gcil_sad_imo_927.pdf [hereinafter 2002 Guidelines].

In its Annexes I, IV, and V, MARPOL defines "special area" as areas "which, for technical reasons relating to their oceanographical and ecological condition and to their sea traffic, the adoption of special mandatory methods for the prevention of sea pollution is required. Under the

Sensitive Sea Areas" (PSSAs). These areas were listed under the 2002 MARPOL *Guidelines for the Identification and Designation of Particularly Sensitive Sea Areas*,[68] a list that was subsequently expanded prior to a 2005 revision of the *Guidelines*.[69] "A PSSA is an area that needs special protection through action by IMO because of its significance for recognized ecological, socio-economic, or scientific attributes where such attributes may be vulnerable to damage by international shipping activities."[70] Often the most effective means of preventing such damage is simply by mandating appropriate routing of ships:

> A PSSA can be protected by ships routing measures – such as an area to be avoided: an area within defined limits in which either navigation is particularly hazardous or it is exceptionally important to avoid casualties and which should be avoided by all ships, or by certain classes of ships. The IMO Publication Ships' Routeing includes general provisions on ships' routeing, first adopted by IMO in 1973, and subsequently amended over the years, which are aimed at standardizing the design, development, charted presentation and use of routeing measures adopted by IMO.[71]

The list of PSSAs includes 16 very vulnerable—"particularly sensitive"—areas from Papua, New Guinea, to the Cuban Archipelago (two of the 16 are extensions of a third, the Great Barrier Reef PSSA).[72]

It would serve to cite the purposes for two examples for which the PSSA process has been used, in order to illustrate the tremendous interest in the natural heritage that is protected by this regime:

Convention, these special areas are provided with a higher level of protection than other areas of the sea." Special Areas under MARPOL, 2018, http://www.imo.org/en/OurWork/Environment/SpecialAreasUnderMARPOL/Pages/Default.aspx.

[68] 2002 Guidelines, *supra* note 67.

[69] IMO, MARPOL 78/78, Guidelines for the Identification and Designation of Particularly Sensitive Sea Areas (PSSAs), Resolution A.982(24), adopted 1 Dec. 2005, A 24/Res.982, 6 Feb. 2006, http://www.imo.org/en/OurWork/Environment/PSSAs/Documents/A24-Res.982.pdf [hereinafter 2006 Guidelines].

[70] 2002 Guidelines, *supra* note 67, Annex at 16, 19.

[71] Routing measures (24).

[72] They are the Great Barrier Reef, Australia (designated a PSSA in 1990); The Sabana-Camagüey Archipelago in Cuba (1997); Malpelo Island, Colombia (2002); the sea around the Florida Keys, United States (2002); the Wadden Sea, Denmark, Germany, Netherlands (2002); Paracas National Reserve, Peru (2003); Western European Waters (2004); Extension of the existing Great Barrier Reef PSSA to include the Torres Strait (proposed by Australia and Papua New Guinea) (2005); Canary Islands, Spain (2005); the Galapagos Archipelago, Ecuador (2005); the Baltic Sea area, Denmark, Estonia, Finland, Germany, Latvia, Lithuania, Poland and Sweden (2005); the Papahānaumokuākea Marine National Monument, United States (2007); the Strait of Bonifacio, France and Italy (2011); the Saba Bank, in the North-eastern Caribbean area of the Kingdom of the Netherlands (2012); Extension of Great Barrier Reef and Torres Strait to encompass the south-west part of the Coral Sea (2015); the Jomard Entrance, Papua New Guinea (2016); and Tubbataha Reefs Natural Park, the Sulu Sea, Philippines (2017), http://www.imo.org/en/OurWork/Environment/PSSAs/Pages/Default.aspx. They can be seen at www.pssa.imo.org.

(1) The Great Barrier Reef, Australia, "the largest system of corals and associated life forms anywhere in the world."[73] Deserving of special protection as an "outstanding example of a biotic structured ecosystem of high diversity dependent on the structuring organisms," as "the most diverse ecosystem known to man,"[74] and as "particularly important in the history and culture of the indigenous Aboriginal groups of the coastal areas of north-east Australia,"[75] the area is extremely fragile and vulnerable. Accordingly, the Guidelines call for observance of Australia's compulsory pilotage rules to protect the Reef.[76]

(2) The Archipelago of Sabana-Camaguey, Cuba—designated as a PSSA in September 1997.[77] It comprises more than 2515 islands and small keys. Special protection is due to the coral reef bordering the archipelago, because of its unique, "highly significant features, particularly in terms of its biotic resources, on account of which it has been categorized as an independent and clearly defined bio-geographical, ecological and scenic unit."[78] According to the *Guidelines*,

> Within this area almost all the habitats, ecosystems and biocenosis found in the different Caribbean islands are represented. The particular ecological sensitivity of this territory lies in his high degree of interdependency, both internal and external. Internally, there is a high degree of interaction and interdependence between the coastal and marine ecosystems, especially in the sequence of coastal lagoons/ dune systems/ beaches/ algae/ coral reefs; and similarly in the combination of mangrove swamps; coastal lagoons/ algae/ coral reefs, which occurs most often and most extensively in the island group.[79]

The *Guidelines* prohibit any discharges in the inland and territorial waters of this area of oil, oily mixtures, noxious liquid substances, garbage or harmful substances from vessels of any type or size, as well as dumping of any types of garbage or discharging ballast water in these areas.[80]

It should be noted that the U.S. is a signatory to most but not all of the pertinent conventions. One such convention is the IMO Ballast Water Management (BWM) Convention, which entered into force on September 8, 2017.[81] While parties to the Convention must certify that they "ensure that the ship shall not discharge ballast water ... without presenting a threat of harm to the environment, human health,

---

[73] *Id.*, Appendix at 1.

[74] *Id.*

[75] *Id.*

[76] *Id.*

[77] Archipelago of Sabana-Camaguey, Cuba (MEPC.74(40)).

[78] *Id.* Appendix at 2.

[79] *Id.*

[80] *Id.*

[81] See Marinelog.com, USCG issues guidance on compliance with IMO BWM Convention, Sept. 8, 2017, http://www.marinelog.com/index.php?option=com_k2&view=item&id=27067:uscg-issues-guidance-on-compliance-with-imo-bwm-conventiom&Itemid=227&tmpl=component&print=1, with link to the USCG policy letter and the IMO BWM Convention documents.

property or resources,"[82] neither U.S. flagged ships nor ships of other nations operating in U.S. waters can be required to do so as the United States has not ratified the BWM convention. Accordingly, the Coast Guard issued "Guidelines for Voluntary Compliance" when the BWM entered into force on September 8, 2017, as U.S. ships abroad are expected to comply with port state authorities of nations that are members.

As a member state, the United States has put the force of law behind MARPOL. In December 2016, the Carnival Corporation's Princess Cruise Line pled guilty to seven felony charges for intentional pollution at sea—dumping of oil-contaminated waste from the Caribbean Princess cruise ship—and for covering up the offense. Under their settlement, Princess is required to pay a $40 million penalty and implement remedial measures on all their vessels.[83]

The case was based on the MARPOL treaty commitment of the United States as codified in U.S. Code § 33 and CFR § 33, the Act to Prevent Pollution from Ships, and enforced by the U.S. Coast Guard.

The Caribbean Princess was charged with having illegally dumped contaminated waste for at least eight years—2005–2013. The incident that triggered the investigation occurred off the coast of the United Kingdom and was reported by a whistle-blower. The investigation grew to include numerous other violations in a number of locations and at least four more of the Princess cruise ships, the Star Princess, Coral Princess, Grand Princess, and Golden Princess. Not only were there extremely serious violations of the anti-pollution laws, there were egregious incidents of lying and covering up of the offenses by the crew members involved.[84]

The U.S. also implements the Safety of Life at Sea Convention, which was first adopted before the First World War in 1914, after the 1912 Titanic disaster resulted in the deaths of more than 1500 passengers. In its most recent form it came into force in 1980, and currently has 162 member states.

> The main objective of the SOLAS Convention is to specify minimum standards for the construction, equipment and operation of ships, compatible with their safety. Flag States are responsible for ensuring that ships under their flag comply with its requirements, and a number of certificates are prescribed in the Convention as proof that this has been done. Control provisions also allow Contracting Governments to inspect ships of other Contracting States if there are clear grounds for believing that the ship and its equipment do not

[82] IMO Ballast Water Management Convention, Sept. 8, 2017, part 7, http://www.imo.org/en/About/Conventions/ListOfConventions/Pages/International-Convention-for-the-Control-and-Management-of-Ships'-Ballast-Water-and-Sediments-(BWM).aspx.

[83] See Reuters, Princess Cruise Lines to Pay Largest-Ever Criminal Penalty for Deliberate Vessel Pollution, Dec. 1, 2016, https://www.reuters.com/article/us-carnival-usa-pollution/carnival-princess-to-pay-record-40-million-for-pollution-cover-up-idUSKBN13Q4YB.

[84] U.S. Dept. of Justice, Office of Public Affairs, *Princess Cruise Lines to Pay Largest-Ever Criminal Penalty for Deliberate Vessel Pollution,* Dec. 1, 2016, including links to the criminal information, joint factual statement, and plea agreement, https://www.justice.gov/opa/pr/princess-cruise-lines-pay-largest-ever-criminal-penalty-deliberate-vessel-pollution.

substantially comply with the requirements of the Convention – this procedure is known as port State control.[85]

The Convention's provisions cover: construction of ships; fire protection; life-saving appliances; radio communications; safety of navigation; carriage of cargoes; carriage of dangerous goods; nuclear ships; management for safe operation of ships; safety measures for high-speed craft; special measures to enhance maritime safety; and special measures to enhance maritime security.[86]

The United States is represented at the IMO by the U.S. Coast Guard (USCG), which is responsible for enforcement of the IMO's regulations, for all policy development, and for addressing international maritime issues. For example, it proposed new rules on cruise ship security following the passage of the CVSSA, to implement the provisions of the Act. These proposed rules included height of deck rails and security guides, systems to detect or record falls overboard, crime prevention and criminal evidence-gathering, and response to and treatment of sexual assaults.[87] The Coast Guard requires cruise ships that take on passengers at U.S. ports to meet the SOLAS and other international regulations related to crew competency, fire protection, firefighting and lifesaving equipment, navigation safety, water craft integrity and stability, vessel control, safety management, and environmental protection.[88] For example, a new safety amendment addresses a passenger ship's capability to stabilize and remain afloat if it is flooded after a collision.[89]

3.8.1 U.S. Cruise-Specific Laws for Safety1. The Cruise Vessel Security and Safety Act (CVSSA) of 2010

In July 2010, Congress took a highly significant step in U.S. cruise specific legislation by passing the Cruise Vessel Security and Safety Act (CVSSA).[90] The CVSSA was in response to the widespread perception that U.S. passengers were not adequately protected from crime when cruising, especially on foreign flagged ships. The bill received bipartisan support and was signed into law by President Barack Obama in 2010. Congressman Ted Poe (R-Texas) explained the necessity of the new bill:

[85] IMO.org, About: International Convention for the Safety of Life at Sea (SOLAS), 1974, Adoption 1 Nov. 1974; Entry into force 25 May 1980, http://www.imo.org/en/About/Conventions/ListOfConventions/Pages/International-Convention-for-the-Safety-of-Life-at-Sea-(SOLAS),-1974.aspx.

[86] *Id.*

[87] See the website of U.S. Coast Guard, www.uscg.mil. See also David A. Tyler, *Coast Guard Proposes new rule on cruise ship security*, Professional Mariner, Apr. 29, 2015, http://www.professionalmariner.com/May-2015/Coast-Guard-proposes-new-rule-on-cruise-ship-security/.

[88] See USCG, www.uscg.mil.

[89] IMO, IMO Adopts Safety Amendments for Passenger Ships, June 16, 2017, https://worldmaritimenews.com/archives/222904/imo-adopts-safety-amendments-for-passenger-ships/.

[90] Cruise Vessel Security and Safety Act, Government Publishing Office, https://www.gpo.gov/fdsys/pkg/BILLS-111hr3360enr/pdf/BILLS-111hr3360enr.pdf [hereinafter CVSSA].

> Every year cruise line companies carry over 10 million Americans to and from American ports. The cruise lines promise Americans safety, security, fun, and relaxation aboard the ships. But as we have seen, safety is not something the cruise lines are always prepared to guarantee. . . .[91]

The CVSSA was designed to give cruise passengers additional protection both while onboard the ship and during onshore visits. Thus, its focus was on cruise vessel and passenger security and safety and requirements covered vessel design, equipment construction and retrofitting, videorecording, safety information provided to passengers, response to sexual assaults and confidentiality of sexual assault reporting, crew access to passenger staterooms, reporting requirements, and crime scene preservation training for crewmembers.[92]

More specifically, for passenger security and safety, CVSSA requires all passenger vessels to be fitted with railings not less than 42 inches tall, and peep holes or other visual identification devices on cabin doors.[93]

For vessels whose keel was laid down after enactment of the Act, it requires security latches, and time-sensitive key technology. Also, "the vessel shall integrate technology that can be used for capturing images of passengers or detecting passengers who have fallen overboard, to the extent that such technology is available." The owner of the vessel is required to provide a video surveillance system and access for law enforcement officials to video records.[94] The passengers are to be provided "security guides" which includes description of medical and security personnel and law enforcement processes.[95]

Related to sexual assault, which remains a major challenge, owners of cruise vessels are required to maintain on the vessel "adequate, in-date supplies of anti-retroviral medications and other medications designed to prevent sexually transmitted diseases after a sexual assault" and "equipment and materials for performing a medical examination in sexual assault cases to evaluate the patient for trauma, provide medical care, and preserve relevant medical evidence."[96] The owner is also required to make available medical personnel who are trained and licensed.[97]

In addition, the owner of the vessel is required to provide passengers "a private telephone line and Internet-accessible computer terminal by which [they] may confidentially access law enforcement officials, an attorney, and the information and support services available through the [hotline services]."[98] The CVSSA also

---

[91] U.S. Congressman Ted Poe, *Press Release, Cruise Vessel Security and Safety Act Becomes Law*, July 27, 2010, https://poe.house.gov/press-releases?ID=51809220-DB31-4890-9A6A-D475FF729F68.

[92] CVSSA, *supra* note 90.

[93] *Id.* § 3507(a).

[94] *Id.* § 3507(b).

[95] *Id.* § 3507(c).

[96] *Id.* § 3507(d) (1)-(2).

[97] *Id.* § 3507(d) (3).

[98] *Id.* § 3507(d)(5)(B).

provides for confidentially of sexual assault examination and support information.[99] Crew access to passenger staterooms is to be limited to certain crew and to certain times.[100]

To remedy the lack of adequate reporting of crime by cruise vessels, the owner of the vessel is required "record in a log book, either electronically, or otherwise, in a central location readily accessible to law enforcement personnel, a report" on all complaints of crimes and theft of property valued in excess of $1000, and to make such log-book available to the FBI, the Coast Guard, and law enforcement officials.[101] The owner is also required to report crimes to the FBI.[102] Other requirements include those related to crime scene preservation training for the crew and budgetary matters.[103]

In 2012, the cruise line industry's image was shaken by the disaster on the Costa Concordia cruise ship off the west coast of Italy, where the ship was sailed too close to the coast in order to make an impression on those on shore but ran aground, killing at least 16 people.[104] But in the aftermath, while certain efforts were taken to rectify the industry's public face, the issue appeared even more serious, as the existing regime was seen to be clearly insufficient to record and advise the marketplace of accidents that were not mandated to be reported.

Similarly, the Carnival Line's *Triumph*, which sailed in February 2013, was shown to have been in violation of numerous safety measures under SOLAS, which resulted in catastrophic failure of a large diesel engine that had not been maintained and for which records were inadequately kept by the flag and port states. This sailing ended with a fire in the engine room and near total shutdown of the ship's power, stranding the 4000-plus passengers for eight days at sea without fresh water, food, or facilities.[105]

Once the passengers had brought their several lawsuits, however, it was apparent that there would be no significant relief against the cruise line, as the customary limitation of liability based on the warranties of seaworthiness, would not render an award at law where there was no actual injury as a result. At the same time, negligence claims, which were allowed to go forward, required a showing of actual injury, which was for the most part, absent from the evidence for most of the plaintiffs.[106]

---

[99] *Id.* § 3507(e).

[100] *Id.* § 3507(f).

[101] *Id.* § 3507(g).

[102] *Id.* § 3507(g)(3).

[103] *Id.* § 3508.

[104] *See* Paul Hoskins, et al., *How the cruise ship industry sails under the radar*, Jan. 24, 2012, https://www.reuters.com/article/uk-italy-ship-regulation/how-the-cruise-ship-industry-sails-under-the-radar-idUSLNE80N02M20120124 [hereinafter Hoskins].

[105] *See* Walker (2013), https://www.cruiselawnews.com/2013/12/articles/flags-of-convenience/poop-cruise-reveals-shortcomings-of-port-and-flag-state-inspections/.

[106] *See, e.g., Terry v. Carnival Corp.*, Order on Motions for Summary Judgment, 3 F.Supp.3d 1363 (D. S.D. FL.).

The IMO's procedure, dating back to its 1974 origins, called for just the minimum reporting ("pertinent findings") and kept confidential the identity and nationality of involved ships. This process was revised over the years but never mandated information being released to the public, even up to 2008.

That year, the IMO's Maritime Safety Committee (MSC) met and agreed a new "Harmonized reporting procedure, amalgamating and harmonizing the procedures for reporting casualties to the Organization." Under the new procedures, following SOLAS regulation I/21 and MARPOL articles 8 and 12, "each Administration [*i.e.*, flag state] [undertook] to conduct an investigation into any casualty occurring to ships under its flag subject to those conventions and to supply the Organization with pertinent information concerning the findings of such investigations." The circular's language continues with "requested," "urged," "encouraged," and "invited," throughout: for example, "Administrations are requested to submit data for all 'very serious casualties' [those which involve total loss of the ship, loss of life, or severe pollution] and 'serious casualties.'"[107] Not surprisingly, even the IMO's database of information on Marine Casualties and Incidents is called "incomplete."[108]

Building on the CSVVA but motivated by the continuing sad state of regulation, the United States Senate held hearings in 2013 to update the oversight regime under the title "*Cruise Industry Oversight: Recent Incidents Show Need for Stronger Focus on Consumer Protection*."[109] Professor Ross A. Klein of Memorial University of Newfoundland, Canada, an international expert on the cruise industry, testified to the Committee:

> The cruise industry has received considerable attention in the media in recent years. In 2013 alone, the media has reported for cruise ships: three running aground; five with fires; two collisions; 19 mechanical problems, including power loss, propulsion problems, and generator problems; 10 canceled port calls and/or changes in itinerary; 16 cruises with delayed embarkation and/or debarkation; two cruises where passengers have been bumped; and eight ships that have failed U.S. health inspection.[110]

In his prepared statement, Professor Klein noted:

> [B]ased on data provided by the FBI in response to a Freedom of Information request by the International Cruise Victims Association[, b]etween October 1, 2007 and September 30, 2008, the data reveals there were 115 simple assaults, 16 assaults with serious bodily

---

[107] *See id.* Annex 6 at 33: *Data for Very Serious and Serious Casualties – Fire Casualty Record*, "In addition to supplying the information requested in this annex, Administrations [flag states] are urged to also supply the information listed in other relevant annexes . . .in particular the information contained in annex 1" (ship identification and particulars).

[108] Hoskins, supra note 104.

[109] Cruise Industry Oversight: *Recent Incidents Show Need for Stronger Focus on Consumer Protection*: Hearings before the S. Comm. on Commerce, Science, and Transportation, 113 Cong. 2013, Jul. 23, 2013, https://www.gpo.gov/fdsys/pkg/CHRG-113shrg94526/pdf/CHRG-113shrg94526.pdf.

[110] *Id.* at 45. See also Klein (2011), pp. 67–80.

injury, 89 thefts less than $10,000, 12 thefts more than $10,000, 154 sex related incidents, 7 people overboard, and 3 drug arrests.

3.8.2 The Proposed Cruise Passenger Protection Act (CPPA)

In another attempt to more effectively strengthen passenger safety on cruise ships, on April 26, 2017, Senator Richard Blumenthal (D-CT) and U.S. Representative Jim Himes (D-Ct) introduced the Cruise Passenger Protection Act (CPPA).[111] Senator Blumenthal commented: "Many cruise ships are the size of small towns – but with few emergency services and no law enforcement, these vessels are more Wild West than Atlantis," adding, "And when something goes wrong on a cruise ship, a dream vacation can quickly turn into a nightmare. Our legislation will ensure that consumers know the risks associated with cruise ship travel before they buy a ticket; and if their rights are violated, this bill will help ensure that they have a place to seek recourse."[112]

Representative Himes said, "Cruise ship safety strikes close to home in Connecticut's Fourth District," adding, "in 2005, a young man from Greenwich – George Smith IV – went missing while on his honeymoon cruise in the Mediterranean Sea. Since George disappeared, his family has fought tirelessly to improve safety on cruise ships and to protect cruise ship passengers. The fight continues today with the Cruise Passenger Protection Act. This bill bolsters current law with tighter crime reporting, expanded video surveillance equipment, and record-keeping requirements, and streamlined tracking and public reporting of alleged crimes on cruise ships. Safety improvements like these will help prevent more avoidable tragedies."[113]

Senator Edward J. Markey (D-MA) said: "With various safety and health incidents continuing to occur on cruise ships every year, we need to put measures in place to protect passengers who need medical services or become victims of crime."[114]

The proposed CPPA would apply to vessels "other than a vessel of the United States operated by the Federal Government or a vessel owned and operated by a State" that (1) carry at least 250 passengers; (2) have sleeping facilities for each passenger; (3) are on a voyage that embarks or disembarks passengers in the United States; and (4) are not engaged in a coastwise voyage.[115]

---

[111] Cruise Passenger Protection Act, S.965, 115th Cong. (2017–2018); https://www.congress.gov/bill/115th-congress/senate-bill/965; H.R. 2173, 115th Cong. (2017–2018); https://www.congress.gov/bill/115th-congress/house-bill/2173 [hereinafter CPPA].

[112] *Blumenthal and Himes Introduce Bicameral Legislation to Strengthen Cruise Passenger Safety Laws*, Apr. 26, 2017, https://www.blumenthal.senate.gov/newsroom/press/release/blumenthal-and-himes-introduce-bicameral-legislation-to-strengthen-cruise-passenger-safety-laws.

[113] *Id.*

[114] *Id.*

[115] CPPA, supra note 111, § 3525, SEC. 11.

The Act would the Secretary of Transportation to assess whether any of the rights enumerated in the International Cruise Line Passenger Bill of Rights are enforceable under federal law.[116] It would also direct a cruise vessel owner to notify the FBI within four hours of an alleged incident.[117] It would further mandate that the owner of the vessel or his designee notifies the FBI of an alleged incident if it occurs while the vessel is in a U.S. port, before it leaves the port.[118] Vessel owners would be required to report an alleged offense to the U.S. Consulate in the next port of call if the alleged offense is by or against a U.S. national.[119]

Video surveillance provisions in the CVSSA would be strengthened by clarifying that vessels must have equipment in all passenger common areas, and other areas where there is no expectation of privacy[120] and individuals must have access to video surveillance records, which are to be kept for 30 days after completion of the voyage, for civil action purposes.[121] The CPPA would also mandate that the Internet website of alleged crimes on cruise ships indicate whether the alleged crime victim is a minor.[122] It would direct the Department of Transportation in coordination with other agencies to study the feasibility of having an individual charged with victim support services on board each passenger vessel.[123] The Coast Guard would be directed to promulgate final standards within one year detailing requirements for the retention of video surveillance records.[124]

The CPPA would require a peephole or other means of visual identification to be in the entry door of a passenger stateroom or crew cabin to provide an unobstructed view of the area outside the stateroom or crew cabin.[125] It would also require that a qualified physician and sufficient medical staff be onboard at all times to treat passengers and that crew members receive basic life support training and important emergency medical and safety information.[126] And it would make additional compensation recoverable for non-pecuniary damages for deaths resulting from a passenger cruise ship accident that occurs beyond the territorial waters of the United States.[127]

Finally, the Department of Homeland Security would be enabled to withhold or revoke the clearance of, and the Secretary of the Department in which the Coast Guard is operating may deny entry into the United States to, any owner of a vessel

[116] *Id.* § 3522, SEC. 5.

[117] *Id.* SEC. 6.

[118] *Id.*

[119] *Id.*

[120] *Id.* SEC. 7.

[121] *Id.*

[122] *Id.*

[123] *Id.*

[124] *Id.*

[125] *Id.* SEC. 8.

[126] *Id.*

[127] *Id.* SEC. 11.

that: (1) commits an act or omission for which a penalty is imposed under the Act, or (2) fails to pay the penalty.[128]

3.9 Alaska

The State of Alaska takes great care to protect its uniquely fragile environment from the effects of its status as an immensely popular cruise destination, so its situation provides a good case in point. In 2017, the state expected more than one million visitors via visiting cruise ships.[129]

Under the Commercial Passenger Vessel Environmental Compliance Program,[130] ships must be registered and agree to follow discharge regulations.[131] The law "bars discharge of treated sewage, greywater, or other waste water without a permit" and requires the shipper to comply with very strict standards maintained to prevent the vessel traffic from unduly harming the local sea.[132] In 2015 the state's Department of Environmental Conservation (DEC) issued 19 violation notices covering 44 incidents that occurred between 2010 and 2014, apparently in the expectation that new lower-sulfur fuels would have an impact on the emissions coming from cruise ships.[133] On a related topic, the state's environmental protection monitoring system was facing budget cutbacks due to revenue deficits. However, as a result of the vigorous cruising industry, the proposed cuts were abated in favor of maintaining an environmentally healthy destination.[134]

---

[128] *Id.* SEC. 9.

[129] See, e.g., AP News, Alaska pollution regulators gear up for cruise ship season, May 3, 2017, https://www.apnews.com/d26c8908b52b41b1bbd579bd28427f85/Alaska-pollution-regulators-gear-up-for-cruise-ship-season.

[130] Alaska Commercial Passenger Vessel Environmental Compliance Program, http://www.legis.state.ak.us/basis/statutes.asp#46.03.462.

[131] *Id.* Para. 2.

[132] *See, e.g.,* Alaska Dept of Environmental Conservation [DEC], Division of Water, Frequently Asked Questions – Cruise Ship Wastewater Discharge Regulation and HB 80, Dec. 5, 2017, http://dec.alaska.gov/water/cruise_ships/faq.htm. See also Graywater Regulations 33-CFR Part 150, Marine Exchange of Alaska, pt. 159.3, et seq., sec. 1(a)(4), Pub. L. 106-554, 114 Stat. 2763; https://www.gpo.gov/fdsys/pkg/CFR-2017-title33-vol2/xml/CFR-2017-title33-vol2-part159.xml.

[133] See Pat Forgey, State didn't issue cruise ship pollution citations for years despite repeated violations, Aug. 13, 2015, https://www.adn.com/alaska-news/article/state-mum-years-cruise-ship-air-violations/2015/08/13/.

[134] See Rashah McChesney, State's cruise ship monitoring program shielded from budget cuts by tourists, Alaska Public Media, Jul. 26, 2017, https://www.alaskapublic.org/2017/07/26/states-cruise-ship-monitoring-program-shielded-from-budget-cuts-by-tourists/.

4 Cruise Passengers as Consumers: Consumer Protection

The U.S. has some consumer protection laws in place for cruise passengers, but has yet to enact strong regulations or laws for most aspects of cruises. The Federal Maritime Commission is an independent regulatory agency that oversees cruise industry financial responsibility issues by requiring cruise lines which embark passengers from U.S. ports and have berth accommodations for 50 or more passengers to have secured financial coverage to reimburse passengers in the event of nonperformance of transportation and to provide compensation when a passenger suffers death or injury on the high seas."[135]

The Commission's Office of Consumer Affairs & Dispute Resolution Services reviews any problems and inquiries from passengers and will contact a cruise line on the passenger's behalf. The office's role is to ensure a quick and fair consideration of the issues involved, but the final resolution of such complaints or inquiries remains between the cruise line and the individual: the consumer has to initiate action on her/his own behalf against the cruise line. It should be noted, further, that most forum selection clauses in cruise ticket agreements do not allow cruise passengers to utilize this service and hence the process is not very effective.

The FMC "does not have formal authority over cruise line service issues" other than its bonding requirement. In fact, there is no Federal Agency that regulates any aspect of cruise line service issues, from cancellations, to changes in itinerary, to special accommodations.

Tickets for travel on cruise ships often contain contractual agreements that contain specific provisions on a variety of issues, including clauses binding the passenger to a forum chosen in advance by the issuing company, the so-called "Forum Selection" or "Choice of Forum" clause. The U.S. Supreme Court's 1991 decision in *Carnival Cruise Lines v. Shute* is the definitive ruling on this issue, where the Court held that forum selection clauses in passenger contracts are enforceable if they are fair and reasonable. As the Georgia District Court said in the 2010 case of *Artistic Stone Crafters, Inc. v. Safeco Insurance Company*, "Forum selection clauses are presumptively valid and enforceable, with the party opposing the clause's application having the burden to show, under the circumstances, that enforcing the clause would be unfair, unreasonable, or sufficiently inconvenient to justify retention of the suit."[136]

[135] Federal Maritime Commission, *Cruise Vacations: Know Before You Go,* https://www.fmc.gov/assets/1/Page/PVO2014-508.pdf.

[136] *Artistic Stone Crafters, Inc. v. Safeco Ins. Company of America*, 2010 WL 317472 (S.D. Ga. 2010), *citing Carnival Cruise Lines, Inc. v. Shute*, 499 U.S. 585, 593-95 (1991), legislatively overruled on other grounds, by 46 U.S.C § 30509.

5 Labor Rules on Cruise Workers, Jurisdiction and Arbitration, and Choice of Law

When a crewmember signs an employment agreement with a cruise ship line, s/he is usually required, before beginning work, to sign the Seafarer's Employment Agreement, which mandates arbitration to settle claims. The place designated may be Panama or the Bahamas, and the choice of law will be that of either country.

The U.S. courts have traditionally upheld these agreements in accordance with the mandate of the Federal Arbitration Act (FAA)[137] and the United Nations Convention on the Recognition and Enforcement of Arbitral Awards (the New York Convention), enacted as legislation by Congress and codified under the "Convention Act."[138] The FAA applies in both federal and state courts within the U.S. and requires that instead of adjudicating their claims in court, parties must arbitrate once they have agreed to do so by accepting employment.[139]

In *Bautista v. Star Cruises*,[140] plaintiffs, who were employees or spouses of deceased employees of Norwegian Cruise Lines, brought claims against the company for negligence and unseaworthiness under the Jones Act, alleging failure to provide maintenance and cure and raising claims for unearned wages under the general maritime law of the U.S. These were all Filipino citizens who had previously signed employment contracts containing arbitration agreements with the cruise line. While the defendant employer's ship was at port in Miami, a steam boiler exploded, killing six crew members and injuring four.

The court had to consider this issue as of first impression. It noted that the Convention Act precluded application of the FAA's exemption of seamen from its provisions and thus it could exercise jurisdiction to determine the arbitration issue.[141] It then applied a four-part test to decide whether to enforce an arbitration agreement under the Convention Act: (1) whether there is a written agreement; (2) if the agreement calls for arbitration in the territory of a Convention party; (3) if the agreement arises out of a commercial relationship; and (4) if a party is not a U.S. citizen.[142] The court determined that the case would go forward in arbitration as it met all the elements of the test.[143]

---

[137] Federal Arbitration Act, 9 U.S.C. § 1 [hereinafter FAA].

[138] Convention on the Recognition and Enforcement of Foreign Arbitral Awards, 9 U.S.C. 201 (2012). See, e.g., *Quiroz v. MSC Mediterranean Shipping*, 522 Fed. App'x 655, 661 (11th Cir. 2013).

[139] FAA, *supra* note 137, at § 2.

[140] *Bautista v. Star Cruises*, 396 F.3d 1289 (11th Cir. 2005).

[141] *Id.* at 1295-97.

[142] *Id.* at 1294.

[143] *Id.* at 1303. See Anderson (2015), p. 335.

U.S. courts have continued to follow the four-part test from *Bautista*, as, for example, in the 2012–13 case of *Yuzwa v. M/V Oosterdam.*[144]

6 Rules on the Environmental Impact of Cruises

Cruise ships are often called "floating cities." Like their less mobile counterparts, cruise ships produce pollution from the day-to-day operations of the ship and its inhabitants. While cruise ships represent only one of the many sources of pollution of the maritime and littoral environments, they contribute a significant portion of pollution, especially in at-risk natural areas. The following discussion is focused on the federal efforts to address this problem with an example of one state's efforts, by briefly noting Alaska's initiatives in this area.

6.1 Water Pollution

The U.S. Environmental Protection Agency estimates that a single 3000-person cruise ship produces 150,000 gallons of sewage per week, and that the cruise ship industry can produce more than one billion gallons of sewage per year.[145] Untreated human waste can cause a host of environmental problems, such as nitrogen and phosphorus in sewage, causing algae blooms, which can deplete oxygen and suffocate sea-life; human waste transmits harmful bacteria and viruses, including Hepatitis A, Norovirus, and E. Coli,[146] and human pathogens emitted near coastlines can infect swimmers and bathers, or infect shellfish and later be consumed by humans.

6.2 Air Pollution

Cruise ship exhaust contains greenhouse gasses, sulfur oxides, nitrogen oxides, and particulate matter. According to a 2017 undercover study, a single cruise ship

[144] *Yuzwa v. M/V Oosterdam*, 2012 U.S. Dist. LEXIS 181458 (C.D. Cal. 2012). See also generally the extensive discussion in *Suazo v. NCL (Bahamas), Ltd.*, 822 F.3d 543 (11th Cir. 2016).

[145] Friends of the Earth, *2016 Cruise Ship Report Card*, https://1bps6437gg8c169i0y1drtgz-wpengine.netdna-ssl.com/wp-content/uploads/wpallimport/files/archive/Cruise_Report_2016.pdf.

[146] Centers for Disease Control and Prevention, National Center for Environmental Health Vessel Sanitation Program, *Health Practices on Cruise Ships: Training for Employees*, Transcript. https://www.cdc.gov/nceh/vsp/training/videos/transcripts/water.pdf.

produces more ultra-fine particulate matter (PM) per day than one million cars.[147] Researchers recorded PM concentrations as high as 226,000 particles per cubic centimeter near the exhaust stacks on deck, and concentrations of 84,000 particles per square centimeter downwind from the exhaust.[148] Cruise vacationers are exposed to air quality worse than many major metropolitan areas; the research team recorded PM concentrations of 38,400 in central London's congested Piccadilly Circus.[149]

Exposure to particulate matter can have serious health consequences. According to the Environmental Protection Agency, small particulate matter is the most harmful, as it may be small enough to enter the blood stream.[150] PM can have both acute and chronic health effects, including "respiratory and cardiovascular morbidity, such as aggravation of asthma, respiratory symptoms and an increase in hospital admissions; mortality from cardiovascular and respiratory diseases and from lung cancer."[151] PM exposure may also cause or worsen: "premature death in people with heart or lung disease, nonfatal heart attacks, irregular heartbeat . . .decreased lung function, increased respiratory symptoms, such as irritation of the airways, coughing or difficulty breathing."[152] The effects of PM exposure are greatest on the elderly, children, and those with cardiovascular and lung disease.[153] But particulate matter is not the only dangerous pollutant emitted. By one estimate, large cruise ships per day emit the equivalent of 83,678 cars' worth of CO2, 421,153 cars worth of NOx, and 376 million cars worth of sulfur dioxide.[154]

Pollution is not a problem unique to cruise lines. The global maritime fleet relies greatly on heavy fuel oil (marine fuel/heavy oil) as its primary fuel. Heavy fuel oil is a by-product of oil refinement that produces gasoline. Heavy fuel oil is much more "dirty" than other fuels, including diesel, as it contains 3500 times more sulfur than diesel.[155]

---

[147] Chloe Farand, *Air quality on cruise ship deck 'worse than world's most polluted cities,' investigation finds*. Independent, July 3, 2017, http://www.independent.co.uk/news/world/pollution-cruise-ships-po-oceana-higher-piccadilly-circus-channel-4-dispatches-a7821911.html.

[148] Id.

[149] Id.

[150] Environmental Protection Agency, *Health and Environmental Effects of Particulate Matter (PM)*. https://www.epa.gov/pm-pollution/health-and-environmental-effects-particulate-matter-pm.

[151] World Health Organization, Regional Office for Europe, *Health effects of particulate matter Policy implications for countries in eastern Europe, Caucasus and central Asia*. 2013, p. 6. http://www.euro.who.int/__data/assets/pdf_file/0006/189051/Health-effects-of-particulate-matter-final-Eng.pdf.

[152] Environmental Protection Agency, *Health and Environmental Effects of Particulate Matter (PM)*. https://www.epa.gov/pm-pollution/health-and-environmental-effects-particulate-matter-pm.

[153] Ib.

[154] John Vidal, *The world's largest cruise ship and its supersized pollution problem,* The Guardian, May 21, 2016. https://www.theguardian.com/environment/2016/may/21/the-worlds-largest-cruise-ship-and-its-supersized-pollution-problem.

[155] NABU, *This stinks! - Clean up cruise ships! NABU's campaign for a cleaner cruise industry,* https://en.nabu.de/issues/traffic/cruiseships.html.

Regulation of cruise ship pollution is complicated. Both the U.S. Environmental Protection Agency and the U.S. Coast Guard can set regulations for cruise ship pollution under different legislative acts. The EPA has the greatest authority over cruise ship pollution under the Clean Water Act, and the Clean Air Act. However, national environmental protections on their own would not be sufficient because of the limited jurisdictional reach of any national act. As a result, while the U.S. applies certain environmental standards to ships which fall under its extraterritorial maritime jurisdiction (which are a limited number of vessels), Congress has incorporated international standards set by the International Maritime Organization into U.S. law.

The Marine Protection, Research, and Sanctuaries Act (MPRSA, also known as the Ocean Dumping Act)[156] "prohibits (1) transportation of material from the United States for the purpose of ocean dumping; (2) transportation of material from anywhere for the purpose of ocean dumping by U.S. agencies or U.S.-flagged vessels; and (3) dumping of material transported from outside the United States into the U.S. territorial sea. A permit is required to deviate from these prohibitions."[157]

The two most important pieces of environmental legislation in the United States are the Clean Water Act (CWA) and the Clean Air Act (CAA). In general terms, the CAA regulates air pollution from stationary and mobile sources, while the CWA regulates pollution into the waters of the United States from point sources.

The Clean Water Act[158] set the lofty goal that "the discharge of pollutants into the navigable waters be eliminated by 1985."[159] While meeting this goal remains far off, the CWA remains the most important regulation for entities that discharge into navigable waters, including cruise ships that wish to discharge into the territorial water of the U.S. CWA §301 in no uncertain terms bars all pollution of "Navigable waters" of the United States from point sources. Discharges are only allowed under the National Pollution Discharge Elimination Program (NPDES), which creates a system for state and federal environmental agencies to issue discharge permits.

The Clean Water Act addresses the issue of marine sewage discharge: the administrator of the EPA "shall promulgate Federal standards of performance for marine sanitation devices (hereafter in this section referred to as "standards") which shall be designed to prevent the discharge of untreated or inadequately treated sewage into or upon the navigable waters from new vessels and existing vessels, except vessels not equipped with installed toilet facilities."[160] However, the Act only applies to "vessels owned and operated by the United States."

---

[156] Marine Protection, Research, and Sanctuaries Act (16 U.S.C. § 1431 and 33 U.S.C. § 1401).

[157] Environmental Protection Agency. *Laws and Regulations, Summary of the Marine Protection, Research, and Sanctuaries Act.* https://www.epa.gov/laws-regulations/summary-marine-protection-research-and-sanctuaries-act.

[158] 33 U.S.C. § 1251.

[159] Clean Water Act. §101, 33 U.S.C. § 1251 (a)(1).

[160] Environmental Protection Agency. *Clean Water Act*, CWA § 312 33 U.S.C. 1332 (b)(1), https://www3.epa.gov/npdes/pubs/cwatxt.txt.

U.S. national legislation was insufficient to control maritime pollution. The Act to Prevent Pollution from Ships[161] implements MARPOL and its annexes, and applies to all U.S. flagged ships and all ships in navigable waters of the United States or at port in the U.S. Recent efforts are underway in the cruising industry to meet the MARPOL targets of reducing sulfur in fuel from the current 3.5% to .5% by 2020,[162] other new IMO regulations are also responsible for developments in wastewater discharge levels of nitrogen and phosphorous,[163] and the industry is also cognizant of the Polar Code promulgated by the IMO, but not especially enthusiastic about its prospects for a good result.[164]

7 Sources of Law Applicable to Cruises

As mentioned above, the majority of U.S. laws that apply to cruise lines are laws of general application, applicable to all maritime vessels. These include:

- The United States Constitution, U.S. Const., Art. III, § 2, cl. 1.
- The Passenger Vessel Service Act of 1886, 46 U.S.C. § 55103 (b).
- The Jones Act, 46 U.S.C. § 30104.
- Death on the High Seas Act, 46 U.S.C. § 303, *et seq.*
- Liability of a Cruise Ship for Personal Injury or Death, 46 U.S.C. § 30509.
- Shipping Act of 1984, 46 U.S.C. §1702.
- Special Maritime and Territorial Jurisdiction of the United States Defined, 18 U.S.C. § 7.
- The Cruise Vessel Security and Safety Act (CVSSA) of 2010 (Public Law 111-207).
- Cruise Passenger Protection Act, S.965 115 (2017–2018).
- Alaska Commercial Passenger Vessel Environmental Compliance Program, AS 46.03.460 (2019–2020).
- Federal Arbitration Act., 9 U.S.C. § 1.
- Clean Water Act, 33 U.S.C. § 1251.
- Clean Air Act, 42 U.S.C. (1963).
- Marine Protection, Research, and Sanctuaries Act, 16 U.S.C. § 1431 and 33 U.S.C. § 3401.
- Coast Guard Regulations
- Federal Maritime Commission Regulations
- Maritime Administration Regulations
- Shipping Laws and Shipping Codes of Federal Regulations

[161] 33 U.S.C. §§1905-1915.

[162] See Bennett (2017), https://maritime-executive.com/magazine/cruisings-environmental-impact#gs.eOzkd98 [hereinafter Mar-Ex].

[163] *Id.* See IMO Marine Environment Protection Committee (MEPC) Resolution 227(64).

[164] Mar-Ex, *supra* note 235.

- International Maritime Organization Conventions.
- 2010 International Convention on Liability and Compensation for Damage in Connection with the Carriage of Hazardous and Noxious Substances by Sea.

8 Conclusion

The number of American cruise passengers continues to rise and despite various efforts to ensure passenger and vessel safety, the problem of crimes onboard cruise vessels, especially sexual assaults, has yet to be solved. Flags of convenience exacerbate the problems because with multiple nationalities and jurisdictions involved, most passengers are often at a loss as they lack clear guidance on where and how to enforce their claims.

Also, notwithstanding the ongoing efforts by the cruise line industry to inculcate a strong safety culture, the U.S. Congress strives to enact new legislation to undertake measures to strengthen vessel safety. And USCG findings still show several cruise ship deficiencies.

Marine pollution caused by cruise ships is also a continuing challenge with lax enforcement by the state of the flag and lack of implementation of many IMO measures. In a nutshell, much work still remains to be done to ensure security and safety onboard a cruise vessel and to protect the marine environment from cruise ships.

References

Constitution and U.S. Statutes

U.S. Const., art. III, § 2, cl. 1

Clean Water Act. §101, 33 U.S.C. § 1251 (a)(1)

Convention on the Recognition and Enforcement of Foreign Arbitral Awards, 9 U.S.C. 201 (2012)

Cruise Vessel Security and Safety Act of 2010, Pub. L. 111-207, 124 Stat. 2243, et seq., Jul. 27, 2010, enacted at 46 U.S.C. §3507

Death on the High Seas Act 46 U.S.C. app. §§ 761–768 (1920) (DOHSA), codified at 46 U.S.C. 303, et seq., US House of Representatives, Office of the Law Revision Council, *United States Code. Chapter 303 Death on the High Seas*, http://uscode.house.gov/view.xhtml?path=/prelim@title46/subtitle3/chapter303&edition=prelim

Federal Arbitration Act, 9 U.S.C. § 1

Government Publishing Office. *18 U.S.C. § 7. Special maritime and territorial jurisdiction of the United States defined*

Jones Act, 46 U.S.C. §30104

Marine Protection, Research, and Sanctuaries Act (16 U.S.C. § 1431 and 33 U.S.C. § 1401)

Passenger Vessel Services Act, 46 U.S.C. § 55103(b)

Shipping Act of 1984, 46 U.S.C. §1702

Cases

Am. Dredging Co. v. Miller, 510 U.S. 443, 456 (1994)
Artistic Stone Crafters, Inc. v. Safeco Ins. Company of America, 2010 WL 317472 (S.D. Ga. 2010)
Bautista v. Star Cruises, 396 F.3d 1289 (11th Cir. 2005)
Carnival Corp. v. Carlisle, 953 So.2d 461, 464 (Fl. 2007)
Chandris, Inc. v. Latsis, 515 U.S. 347 (1995)
Kernan v. Am. Dredging Co., 355 U.S. 426, 439 (1958)
Lauritzen v. Larsen, 345 U.S. 571 (1953)
Quiroz v. MSC Mediterranean Shipping, 522 Fed. App'x 655, 661 (11th Cir. 2013)
Suazo v. NCL (Bahamas), Ltd., 822 F.3d 543 (11th Cir. 2016)
Terry v. Carnival Corp., Order on Motions for Summary Judgment, 3 F.Supp.3d 1363 (D. S.D. FL.)
Yuzwa v. M/V Oosterdam, 2012 U.S. Dist. LEXIS 181458 (C.D. Cal. 2012)

Everything Else

Alaska Commercial Passenger Vessel Environmental Compliance Program, http://www.legis.state.ak.us/basis/statutes.asp#46.03.462

Alaska Dept of Environmental Conservation [DEC], Division of Water, Frequently Asked Questions – Cruise Ship Wastewater Discharge Regulation and HB 80, Dec. 5, 2017., http://dec.alaska.gov/water/cruise_ships/faq.htm

All things cruise, *Cruise Departure Ports,* https://allthingscruise.com/cruise-research/cruise-departure-ports/

American Cruise Lines, *Cruises: Destinations,* https://www.americancruiselines.com/?utm_source=google&utm_medium=cpc&utm_campaign=us%20cruises&gclid=Cj0KCQiAyZLSBRDpARIsAH66VQKFNIvOBWc7wi7POordiVVcbId1kXlvsP3HPFYCU66KfffjKFXDBa8aAhItEALw_wcB

Anderson LM (2015) Mandatory arbitration within cruise ship employment agreements: without global change, the disparity of power continues to expand. Loy Mar Law J 14:335

In re Asbestos Products Liab. Litig., 2012 WL 3242420 * 7, 10 (E.D. Pa., Aug. 7, 2012)

Bennett M (2017) Cruising's Environmental Impact: "The industry strives to go green and atone for past missteps," Jan.–Feb. 2017, https://maritime-executive.com/magazine/cruisings-environmental-impact#gs.eOzkd98

Buchholz VJ, Buchholz TG (2017) How Grover Cleveland ruined American cruises. L.A. Times, Aug. 3, 2017

Centers for Disease Control and Prevention, National Center for Environmental Health Vessel Sanitation Program, *Health Practices on Cruise Ships: Training for Employees*, Transcript. https://www.cdc.gov/nceh/vsp/training/videos/transcripts/water.pdf

Convention on the International Maritime Organization, Geneva, 289 U.N.T.S. 3 (6 Mar. 1948), entry into force 17 Mar. 1958

Cruise Industry Oversight: *Recent Incidents Show Need for Stronger Focus on Consumer Protection*: Hearings before the S. Comm. on Commerce, Science, and Transportation, 113 Cong. 2013, Jul. 23, 2013, https://www.gpo.gov/fdsys/pkg/CHRG-113shrg94526/pdf/CHRG-113shrg94526.pdf

Cruise Lines International Association, Inc. (CLIA), *2018 Cruise Industry Outlook*, Dec. 2017, at 7, http://cruising

Cruise Mapper, *Cruise Ship Registry, Flags of Convenience,* http://www.cruisemapper.com/wiki/758-cruise-ship-registry-flags-of-convenience-flag-state-control

Cruise Passenger Protection Act, S.965, 115th Cong. (2017-2018.); https://www.congress.gov/bill/115th-congress/senate-bill/965; H.R. 2173, 115th Cong. (2017-2018); https://www.congress.gov/bill/115th-congress/house-bill/2173

Cruise Vessel Security and Safety Act, Government Publishing Office, https://www.gpo.gov/fdsys/pkg/BILLS-111hr3360enr/pdf/BILLS-111hr3360enr.pdf

Environmental Protection Agency. *Laws and Regulations, Summary of the Marine Protection, Research, and Sanctuaries Act.* https://www.epa.gov/laws-regulations/summary-marine-protection-research-and-sanctuaries-act

Environmental Protection Agency. *Health and Environmental Effects of Particulate Matter (PM).* https://www.epa.gov/pm-pollution/health-and-environmental-effects-particulate-matter-pm

Florida-Caribbean Cruise Association, *Cruise Industry Overview, 2017,* http://www.f-cca.com/downloads/2017-Cruise-Industry-Overview-Cruise-Line-Statistics.pdf. *See also* CLIA, *2016 Cruise Industry Outlook,* at 8 https://www.cruising.org/docs/default-source/research/2016_clia_sotci.pdf

Graywater Regulations 33-CFR Part 150, Marine Exchange of Alaska, pt. 159.3, et seq., sec. 1(a)(4), Pub. L. 106-554, 114 Stat. 2763; https://www.gpo.gov/fdsys/pkg/CFR-2017-title33-vol2/xml/CFR-2017-title33-vol2-part159.xml

IMO.org, About: International Convention for the Safety of Life at Sea (SOLAS), 1974, Adoption 1 Nov. 1974; Entry into force 25 May 1980, http://www.imo.org/en/About/Conventions/ListOfConventions/Pages/International-Convention-for-the-Safety-of-Life-at-Sea-(SOLAS),-1974.aspx

International Maritime Organization. *International Convention for the Prevention of Pollution from Ships (MARPOL).* Adoption: 1973 (Convention), 1978 (1978 Protocol), 1997 (Protocol - Annex VI); Entry into force: 2 October 1983 (Annexes I and II), http://www.imo.org/en/about/conventions/listofconventions/pages/international-convention-for-the-prevention-of-pollution-from-ships-(marpol).aspx [hereinafter MARPOL]

IMO, Guidelines for the Designation of Special Areas under MARPOL 73/78 and Guidelines for the Identification and Designation of Particularly Sensitive Sea Areas, para. 2 [superseded], Resolution A.927(22), Adopted on 29 Nov. 2001, A/22/Res.927, 15 Jan. 2002., http://www.gc.noaa.gov/documents/gcil_sad_imo_927.pdf [hereinafter 2002 Guidelines]

IMO, IMO Adopts Safety Amendments for Passenger Ships, June 16, 2017., https://worldmaritimenews.com/archives/222904/imo-adopts-safety-amendments-for-passenger-ships/

IMO, Ballast Water Management Convention, Sept. 8, 2017, part 7, http://www.imo.org/en/About/Conventions/ListOfConventions/Pages/International-Convention-for-the-Control-and-Management-of-Ships'-Ballast-Water-and-Sediments-(BWM).aspx

International Maritime Organization, IMO regulations to reduce air pollution from ships and the review of fuel oil availability, http://www.imo.org/en/MediaCentre/HotTopics/GHG/Documents/sulphur%20limits%20FAQ_20-09-2016.pdf

IMO, International Convention for the Safety of Life at Sea (SOLAS), 1974., www.imo.org/en/About/Conventions/ListOfConventions/Pages/International-Convention-for-the-Safety-of-Life-at-Sea-(SOLAS),-1974.aspx

IMO.org; United Nations Convention on the High Seas, 29 Apr. 1958, entered into force 30 September 1962, 450 U.N.T.S. 11, 82, http://www.gc.nowa.gov/documents/8_1_1958_high_seas.pdf

Kashian R et al (2017) The Jones Act in perspective: a survey of the costs and effects of the 1920 Merchant Marine Act. Grassroot Institute of Hawaii, Apr. 9, 2017, www.grassrootinstitute.org/2017/04/the-jones-act-in-perspective/

Kasperkevic J (2017) Why there is only one cruise ship in the world with an all-American crew, marketplace.org, Sept. 29, 2017

Klein RA (2011) Sex at sea: sexual crimes aboard cruise ships. J Tour Mar Environ 7(2):67–80

Mak J et al (2009) The passenger vessel services act and America's cruise tourism industry. Univ. of Hawaii Economic Research Organization Working Paper, Jan. 22, 2009

Marinelog.com, USCG issues guidance on compliance with IMO BWM Convention, Sept. 8, 2017., http://www.marinelog.com/index.php?option=com_k2&view=item&id=27067:uscg-issues-guidance-on-compliance-with-imo-bwm-conventiom&Itemid=227&tmpl=component&print=1, with link to the USCG policy letter and the IMO BWM Convention documents

MARPOL Convention, annexes I-VI

NABU, *This stinks! - Clean up cruise ships! NABU's campaign for a cleaner cruise industry,* https://en.nabu.de/issues/traffic/cruiseships.html

Negret CFL (2016) Pretending to be Liberian and Panamanian; flags of convenience and the weakening of the nation state on the high seas. J Mar Law Com 47:1

Rittenhouse L (2017) The Government is Forcing Cruise Lines to Help Save the Environment . . . Or Else, Jan. 6, 2017, https://www.thestreet.com/story/13945339/1/regulators-force-cruise-lines-to-sail-green.html

Statistic Brain. *Cruise Ship Industry Statistics.* March 3, 2017., https://www.statisticbrain.com/cruise-ship-industry-statistics/ [hereinafter Cruise Ship Industry Statistics]..org/docs/default-source/research/clia-2018-state-of-the-industry.pdf?sfvrsn=2

U.S. Dept. of Justice, Office of Public Affairs, *Princess Cruise Lines to Pay Largest-Ever Criminal Penalty for Deliberate Vessel Pollution,* Dec. 1, 2016., https://www.justice.gov/opa/pr/princess-cruise-lines-pay-largest-ever-criminal-penalty-deliberate-vessel-pollution

U.S. Department of Transportation Maritime Administration, *Comparison of U.S. and Foreign-Flag Operating Costs,* September 2011 at 6, https://www.marad.dot.gov/wp-content/uploads/pdf/Comparison_of_US_and_Foreign_Flag_Operating_Costs.pdf

United States Coast Guard, homepage, http://www.uscg.mil/

Walker J (2013) Poop Cruise reveals shortcomings of port and flag state inspections. Cruise Law News, Dec. 22, 2013, https://www.cruiselawnews.com/2013/12/articles/flags-of-convenience/poop-cruise-reveals-shortcomings-of-port-and-flag-state-inspections/

World Health Organization, Regional Office for Europe, *Health effects of particulate matter Policy implications for countries in eastern Europe, Caucasus and central Asia.* 2013, p 6, http://www.euro.who.int/__data/assets/pdf_file/0006/189051/Health-effects-of-particulate-matter-final-Eng.pdf

Legal Aspects of Cruises on the Uruguayan Legal System

Victoria Zorrilla and Horacio Rau

Abstract The purpose of this article is to make a description of the existing regulation at the date of the cruise activity. Paradoxically, although the activity of these ships has a role that has been gaining importance in its impact on the activity of the country's tour operators, the Uruguayan legal order still lacks regulations that specifically regulate the activity of these vessels, although they are applicable general labor and environmental standards.

1 Introduction

Uruguay, like the rest of the countries of Latin America, has a legal system of continental tradition, and therefore, a fundamental role is granted to the laws. Although "jurisprudencia" (i.e., the decision of cases by judges) is of great importance, its impact is reduced to specific cases, not recognizing a role of formal source of law, so the sentences lack force of precedent. It could be considered that the maritime activity has had uneven legal development of its different areas: it was regulated through commercial laws, such as Book III of the Commercial Code (dating from the nineteenth century) and the activity of commercial cabotage through Law No. 12.091 of January 5, 1954, and through rules of public international law such as the United Nations Convention on the Law of the Sea of 1981, and the conventions adopted by the International Maritime Organization (SOLAS, MARPOL, etc.). A sector that has not been developed by specific maritime regulations is the labor law. It is expected that, through the importance that the operation of cruises has developed in the Uruguayan ports (basically, in the Port of Montevideo and in the Port of Punta del Este), and the impact that this has for local tour operators,

V. Zorrilla (✉)
Law School of University of the Republic, Institute of International Private Law, Montevideo, Uruguay

H. Rau
Law School of University of the Republic, Institute of Philosophy and Theory of Law, Montevideo, Uruguay

C. Fresnedo de Aguirre (ed.), *Legal Aspects of Cruises*, Ius Comparatum - Global Studies in Comparative Law 56, https://doi.org/10.1007/978-3-030-83090-8_10

Table 1 Number of cruises arrived and passengers disembarked, as well as amounts of money spent in the 2012 to 2017 season

	Season 2012–2013	Season 2013–2014	Season 2014–2015	Season 2015–2016	Season 2016–2017	Season 2016–2017
Cruisers arrived	223	237	172	161	150	140
Passengers arrived	411,370	409,370	332,118	317,205	260,704	242,466
Money spend (USD)	18,612,467	18,855,505	10,943,470	11,141,587	9,798,264	7,692,437

begin to project and adopt specific labor regulations for this important sector of maritime activity.

2 Importance of Cruises

According to the information published by the Ministry of Tourism (Ministerio de Turismo 2017), the cruise season takes place between the months of October and April, when around 200 cruises arrive in ports of Montevideo and Punta del Este with passengers of multiple nationalities. Since 2014 Uruguay is the embarkation and disembarkation point for passengers and crew of the Costa group, which allows tourists to remain in the country in the days close to the arrival of these cruises, increasing revenues from traditional tourism and boosting air connectivity of the country.

During 2006–2015, the number of cruises that arrived in Uruguay grew 24%. When analyzing the evolution, it can be observed that the arrival of cruises grew strongly, going from 130 in 2006 to 237 cruises in 2013—record year in arrivals. In the last two seasons, there were falls that represented 32% fewer arrivals than 2013, which represents 76 fewer cruises. However, the negative impact was cushioned by a larger size of the arriving vessels.

Regarding the number of cruise passengers, a 113% growth was observed in the last decade, which went from 149,000 tourists in the 2006–2007 season to 317,000 tourists in 2015–2016. This meant an annual increase of 8% average. In the last two seasons the number of tourists descended had a fall of 22%, this was matched with the lower arrival of cruises.

Statistics are publish by the Ministry of Tourism (Ministerio de Turismo 2019) and compile and compare many relevant data. For illustrative purposes, mention may be made of (see Table 1):

Since 2009 the Ministry of Tourism has made a detailed statistics of the relevant aspects of the activity of tourist cruises, analyzing not only categories such as the number of cruises and their passengers who have visited our ports, but also the survey of aspects such as the level of expenditure made by passengers according to their nationalities, the proportion of visitors according to their gender and age range, what they liked most about the Uruguayan ports and what they least liked, etc. Such work shows that the country is focused on promoting this type of tourist activity.

Although general policies to stimulate tourism at the national level have been designed through the Ministry of Tourism, the existence of specific policies for the stimulation of cruise ship activity has not been made public. However, in recent years the Uruguayan authorities have initiated some measures to encourage the arrival of tourist cruise ships. An example of this is the meeting held in 2016 in the city of Buenos Aires (Argentina) between Uruguayan and Argentine authorities for the purpose of planning bilateral cooperation plans that promote the arrival of cruise ships on both sides of the Río de la Plata (Ministerio de Transporte y Obras Públicas 2016).

In Montevideo Port the Administración Nacional de Puertos (National Ports Administration) offers all the necessary services for this type of vessels: dock for docking cruisers, waste treatment, sewage and black waters discharge, re-provisioning, tourist services for passengers, etc.

In Punta del Este Port the Dirección Nacional de Hidrografía (National Direction of Hydrography), because cruises must be anchored in Maldonado Bay, the offer of services is more limited: berths for cruise ship tenders and tourist services for passengers.

The statistics published correspond to the impact of tourism in general on the national labor market: tourism generates 1 out of every 15 jobs in the economy. Unfortunately, within the categories of work sources studied (accommodation, restaurants, bars and canteens, transport, etc.), the workforce related to cruises is not evaluated (Ministerio de Turismo 2017).

The management of ships in Uruguay is maintained at the level of a cabotage fleet, consisting mainly of fishing vessels, passenger traffic of minor and medium sized and some medium-sized tanks and cargo ships. There are not published statistics about the economic importance of such activities in the Uruguayan economy.

The dike with greater capacity of the country is the TSAKOS floating dock, located in the harbor of Montevideo, and whose characteristics are: length 200 m, inner breath of 31.5 m, a lifting capacity of 15,000 tons and two cranes of 10 and 15 tons.

3 Rules Applicable to Cruises

The Uruguayan legal system does not provide for specific rules on cruises neither on consumer protection applicable to passengers in cruises, but contain general legal rules that are applicable to them, both of national and international origin, such as:

a) Articles 1282 to 1289 of the Commercial Code that regulates carriage of passengers by sea,
b) the Law No. 17.250 about consumer relations,
c) several IMO Convention concerning safety, security, environmental and traffic facilitation aspects.[1]

According to afore mentioned rules, the main obligation of the carrier is to transport the person from one place to another. There are accessory obligations, such as provide accommodation and food to the passenger as well as to take care of their safety and health.

On the other hand, the main obligation of the passenger is to pay the price: to travel without paying is a criminal misconduct provided for in the Penal Code (Article 366) and the captain has the privilege over the baggage (Article 1289 Commercial Code). Obviously there are other accessory obligations: the day and time designated for the departure the passenger must be presented on board (Article 1283 *ejusdem*). The omission of compliance with this obligation is sanctioned with the obligation to pay the price, even if he miss the vessel and does not make the trip. The passenger also has the obligation to obey the captain (Article 1286 *ejusdem*) who has disciplinary power to keep order on board and even criminal investigation powers in case of crime (Article 1075 *ejusdem*) can arrest a passenger, handing it over to the authorities of the first port of arrival.

If the voyage is not take place because of the fault of the carrier, he owes damages according to the general rules on breach of contract.

According to art. 1285.1 *ejusdem* if the voyage is terminated by force majeure at the port of departure the contract is terminated, without any right to compensation.

If the suspension of the voyage by force majeure occurs "in another port of call or arrival, only the price corresponding to the part of the trip that has been made is owed": that is, the passenger owes a part of the price although the full voyage has not been completed.

As was mentioned before, the obligation to transport imply the obligation of security: the passenger must arrive safely at destination. This obligation is of public order and cannot be repealed by clauses of irresponsibility.

In this respect the Act. 17.250 of consumer relations is very clear. There can be no doubt that the passenger is a "final recipient" of the service and the passenger contract is an adhesion contract that refers to "general contracting conditions" imposed unilaterally by the carrier. The Art. 31 prohibits abusive clauses in contracts of adhesion ("any clause that determines clear and unjustified imbalances between

[1] Such as: Convention for the Safety of Life at Sea (SOLAS'74/78/88) ratified by Law No. 14.879 of April 23, 1979 and Law No. 17.504 of June 18, 2002; Convention for the Suppression of Unlawful Acts Against the Safety of Maritime Navigation (SUA'88/2005) ratified by Law No. 17.341 of May 25, 2001 and Law No. 19.312 of February 4, 2015; Convention for the Prevention of Pollution from Ships, 1973 (MARPOL'73/78/97) ratified by Law No. 14.885 April 25, 1979 and Annex VI ratified by Law No. 19.204 of April 11, 2014; Convention on Facilitation of International Maritime Traffic (FAL'65) ratified by Law No. 16.246 April 8, 1992.

rights and obligations of contractors to the detriment of consumers, as well as any other that violates the obligation to act in good faith...”), listing as examples of abusive clauses: the limitation and exemption from liability unless a rule of law allows it, the waiver of consumer rights, the authorization to the supplier to unilaterally modify the terms of the contract, those that revers the burden of proof to the detriment of the consumer, among others (for further information Aguirre Ramírez and Fresnedo 2011).

The law on international contracts could also apply.

The general rules on consumer protection are applicable to passengers in cruises: as was mentioned before, the Law No. 17.250 regulates consumer relations.

Although it does not contain specific provisions on cruises, according to the definition that it gives of “consumer relations”,[2] “consumer”[3] and “supplier”,[4] they are applicable to cruise passengers.

4 Labour Rules on Cruises' Workers

There are no specific labor rules for cruise ship workers. The labor regulation in the Uruguayan legal system is not codified, but is distributed in legal texts (the constitution, laws, decrees, etc.), in case law and in collective agreements reached between workers and employers within the different activity sectors that are reached through the Salary Councils (created by Law No. 10.499). These are applicable merchant ships (including passenger ships) to uruguayan flag, and salary, license, etc. are regulated by the negotiations carried out in the Group No. 13 of Wages Council called “Transport and storage” Subgroup N ° 09 “Maritime transport” (Ministerio de Trabajo y Seguridad Social 2018). The regulations aforementioned have a national origin exclusively.

The uruguayan legal system does not contain specific rules on “combined trips” (those that include not only the cruise but also the airplane trip to and from the port of departure, the land excursions chosen by the tourist when the ship is in port, and eventually some hotel night) (Ariza Herrerías 2014, p. 13). Its regulation would be within two areas: the regulation of the “tourist agency contract” (which would be within the contractual obligations regulated by the Civil Code, approved by Law No. 16.603 of October 19, 1994), and by the regulations on consumer relations (Law

[2] According to its article 4, Consumer relationship is the link established between the supplier that, for consideration, provides a product or provides a service and who acquires or uses it does it as a final recipient.

[3] According to its article 2, Consumer is any individual or legal entity that acquires or uses products or services as a final recipient in a consumer relationship or as a function of it.

[4] According to its article 3, Supplier is any natural or legal person, national or foreign, private or public, which develops professionally activities of production, creation, construction, transformation, assembly, import, distribution and marketing of products or services in a consumer relationship.

No. 17.250 of August 18, 2000) (Scofienza Pérez 2013). It should be mentioned that there is administrative law regulation that regulates one of the contracting parties (the travel agency, regulated by Decree No. 268/2015 of October 5, 2015 and Law No. 19.253 of August 28, 2014).

5 Rules on Ports That Are Relevant Regarding Cruises

The Uruguayan legal system doesn't contain specific rules on ports that are relevant regarding cruises.

Regarding taxes and rates port, in addition to the costs that the port authorities charge to each vessel that uses a port (docking, fresh water supply, electricity supply, etc.), the Prefectura Nacional Naval (Coast Guard) collects a rate for the use of the navigation aids on uruguayan waters (call "rate for aid to maritime navigation", created by article 216 of Law No. 13.637 of December 21, 1967).

6 Rules on Environmental Impact of Cruises

Regarding the environmental impact of the operation of cruises, there are no regulations in the Uruguayan legal system that specifically regulates it. However, there are national, binational and international rules that does reach them in its general regulation:

a) The national regulation is the Law No. 16.688 of December 22, 1994 that establishes the prevention and surveillance regime for possible contamination of the waters of national jurisdiction or other elements of that medium, arising from pollutants coming from ships, aircraft and naval artifacts. In addition to providing for a repressive and preventive regime of pollution, it establishes the authorities in charge of such regime: within the port waters, the Administración Nacional de Puertos (National Administration of Ports), the Dirección Nacional de Hidrografía (National Direction of Hydrography) and the Prefectura Nacional Naval (Coast Guard). Outside such waters, it is exclusive to the Prefectura Nacional Naval.
b) The binational regulation is the Treaty of de la Plata River and its Maritime Front, signed between Uruguay and Argentina on November 19, 1973 (ratified in Uruguay by Law No. 14.145 of January 25, 1974); regulates the shared use of de la Plata River by Uruguay and Argentina. It establishes areas of exclusive jurisdiction on the part of each signatory State, and a large area of shared use, and assigning jurisdiction to each one of the States in certain subjects (pilotage, rescue, etc.), and one of these issues is the prevention of polluting actions;
c) The international regulations are the following:

a. International Convention for the Prevention of Pollution from Ships (MARPOL 73/78), ratified by Law No.14.885 of April 25, 1979;
b. International Convention on the Control of Harmful Anti-fouling Systems on Ships (AFS) 2001, ratified by Law No. 18.971 of September 21, 2012;
c. United Nations Convention on the Law of the Sea (UNCLOS), ratified by Law No. 16.287of July 29, 1992.

7 Jurisdiction and Arbitration

The Uruguayan legal system does not provide for specific provisions on jurisdiction on cruises, but contains general provisions on jurisdiction regarding international contracts, which are applicable to cruises cases:

a) the Protocol on International Jurisdiction in Contractual Matters,[5] known as the Buenos Aires Protocol, that regulates jurisdiction in international civil or commercial contracts between private parties, whether individuals or legal entities. The contracts in which a State or a State company is a party are not included in the scope of its application (Article 1); it is important to highlight that the Protocol does not apply to contracts of employment, sale to consumers, transport, insurance, or agreements concluded in respect of reorganization and bankruptcy, family and inheritance law, social security, real rights, or administrative contracts (art 2). Therefore, depending on the legal relationship subject to analysis regarding cruises, the aforementioned Protocol will be applicable or not.
b) The Montevideo Treaties of 1889[6] and 1940[7] regulate international jurisdiction that varies accordance with the legal relationship subject to such regulation; it is important to highlight that the Treaties of Montevideo of 1889 do not contain specific rules on the subject of transport of passenger by sea. The 1889 Montevideo Treaty of Civil Law regulate direct international jurisdiction in his Title XIV. The art. 56 includes the general rule that established the competent court to bring personal actions, based on the following connections:

   (a) The competent judge is the judge of the State whose law is competent to regulate the legal relationship in question; and
   (b) Domicile of the defendant: It functions as a concurrent forum.

The 1889 Montevideo Treaty of Commercial Law contains a significant number of special rules of jurisdiction, among which can be highlighted:

[5] Signed in Buenos Aires on August 5, 1994 (Dec. CMC 1/1994 - MERCOSUR) and ratified by Uruguay by Law No. 17,721 of December 24, 2003. This Protocol is in force, having also been ratified by Argentina, Brazil and Paraguay.

[6] Ratified by Uruguay, Argentina, Paraguay, Colombia, Bolivia and Peru.

[7] Ratified by Uruguay, Argentina and Paraguay.

(a) Place where the company acts: it functions as a forum concurrent as well as its domicile, to solve the conflicts that arise regarding the operations that the company carries out in another State (article 7).
(b) Address of the branches or agencies: the authorities of the place where they operate are competent to understand the operations that they practice there.

On the other hand, the Treaty of the International Law of Commercial Navigation of Montevideo of 1940 expressly provides for the transportation of passengers, regulating it in the same articles that govern the transport of cargo (articles 25 to 27). According to it, international transport by water (whether of cargo or passengers) is governed by the law of place of fulfilment, understood for it as the port of disembarkation of persons. And are competent, at the plaintiff's option, the courts of the place of performance of the contract or those of the domicile of the defendant (Aguirre Ramírez and Fresnedo 2011).

c) In our national law, the general rules regarding international jurisdiction in matters concerning maritime law are regulated in article 7 of the Law 19.246 of August 15, 2014. This article states that when there is no binding treaty that regulates the applicable law and the competent jurisdiction in matters of maritime law, these will be determined in accordance with the rules of the Treaty of International Commercial Navigation Law, signed in the city of Montevideo, on March 19, 1940. Also, provide the possibility of the post-litem extension. The final part of article 7 states that whatever the competent jurisdiction according to the above rules, after the litigious event has occurred, the parties may agree that the litigation be submitted to another jurisdiction, be it judicial or arbitration.

Regarding the protection on the passenger as a consumer, the Art. 2403 of the Civil Code states, in its first part that the rules of legislative and judicial competence determined in its Appendix cannot be modified by the will of the parties. But then he adds an exception to the general principle: "This can only act within the margin conferred by the competent law." Competent law refers to the legal order referred to by the conflict rule applied in the case.

It can be understood that if it is not possible to pact a choice of jurisdiction clause, the passenger will be protected of abusive jurisdictions due to cost, etc.

Regarding the recognition of the validity and effectiveness of forum selection clauses included in general conditions of carriage of passengers in cruises, the general principle is the non-recognition of clauses of choice of jurisdiction. According to art. 2403 of the Civil Code, the rules of legislative and judicial competence determined in the Appendix of this Code cannot be modified by the will of the parties. The autonomy of the will can only act within the margin conferred by the competent law. And "competent law" refers to the legal order referred to by the conflict rule applied in the case.

Within MERCOSUR, there is the Buenos Aires Protocol that applies with respect to agreements entered into between persons domiciled in different MERCOSUR States (Article 1.a). The Protocol also applies even if only one of the parties is domiciled in a MERCOSUR State, when the jurisdiction of a State Party of

MERCOSUR has been agreed and there is a reasonable connection according to the rules of jurisdiction of the Protocol (Article 1.b). For reasonable connection is understood the place of fulfillment of any of the obligations, the domicile of any of the contracting parties (article 7.b and c) and the place of execution of the contract by a legal persons whose head office is in another State Party (Article 11). But, article 2.7 expressly excludes transport contracts and consumer sales contracts, but does not exclude all consumer relationships.

The international jurisdiction between a party domiciled in MERCOSUR and another party domiciled in a third State, when the jurisdiction of a State that is not part of MERCOSUR, is therefore excluded from its scope of application. Nor does the Protocol apply to determine international jurisdiction in contractual matters between persons domiciled in MERCOSUR and persons domiciled in third States, when there is no agreement of jurisdiction (article 1).

The Protocol allows to agree on the courts that will understand in the litigations that arise from international contracts. The forum choice agreement must be made in writing, at the time of conclusion of the contract or subsequently; even after the litigation arose (articles 4 and 5).

Regarding arbitration, it has to be mentioned that in the Uruguayan legal system there is no specific regulation in respect of arbitration clauses included in general conditions of carriage of passengers in cruises, but there are general provisions of international origin.

Uruguay is a State Party to the New York Convention of 1958 on the Recognition and Enforcement of Foreign Arbitral Awards[8] and to the Inter-American Convention of 1975 on International Commercial Arbitration[9] and according to both arbitration clauses that are not signed or otherwise consented by the adherent party to the contract are not admitted.[10]

8 Choice of Law

The Uruguayan legal system does not provide for specific provisions on choice of law regarding cruises. The general principle is the non-recognition of clauses of choice of law. According to art. 2403 of the Civil Code, the rules of legislative competence determined in the Appendix of this Code cannot be modified by the will of the parties. The autonomy of the will can only act within the margin conferred by the competent law. And "competent law" refers to the legal order referred to by the conflict rule applied in the case.

[8] Ratified by Law No. 15.229 of December 11, 1981.

[9] Ratified by Law No. 14.534 of June 24, 1976.

[10] According to article II of the 1958 New York Convention and article 1 of the 1975 Inter-American Convention.

The "competent law" is the law of place of fulfilment, understood for it as the port of disembarkation of persons, and if it is a round trip ticket, the place of disembarking is that of the final destination, which, in turn, coincides with the place of departures. For further information please see (Aguirre Ramírez and Fresnedo 2011, p. 409) and (Fresnedo de Aguirre 2015).

Furthermore, regarding applicable law in matters concerning maritime law are regulated in article 7 of the Law 19.246 of August 15, 2014. This article states that when there is no binding treaty that regulates the applicable law in matters of maritime law, these will be determined in accordance with the rules of the Treaty of International Commercial Navigation Law, signed in the city of Montevideo, on March 19, 1940.

This Treaty states as applicable law the place of disembarking of the passenger as was states supra, and article 5 of the Additional Protocol of the 1940 Montevideo Treaties state that the applicable law cannot be modified by the will of the parties unless the applicable law admits it.

9 Responsibility

The Uruguayan legal system does not provide for specific provisions on liability regarding cruises, but contains general provisions on responsibility regarding maritime transport, which are applicable to cruises cases.

According to our legal system, the carrier in exchange for a price undertakes to transfer on a ship, a person and their luggage from one port to another, so the typical characterizing obligation is the to carry out the transport, in the time and conditions agreed or that were of use. The carrier also has a series of accessory obligations such as provide lodging and food to the passenger and take care of its safety and health (Aguirre Ramírez and Fresnedo 2011, p. 401).

In the characterizing obligation the carrier is forced to produce a result, an *opus*. There is a compromised result.

The contract is only considered fulfilled if the final result occurs. The time devoted to achieving compliance, no matter how much it has cost for the carrier, cannot be classified as compliance, nor does it result in retribution. Only the final result extinguishes the obligation committed (Aguirre Ramírez and Fresnedo 2011, pp. 49–50).

Being an obligation of result has as a consequence that the person obligated or responsible must prove that the breach is not attributable to him, for having configured any of the causes of exoneration established legally or contractually.

Thus, before an obligation of result, the fault would be presumed faced with the failure to obtain the promised *opus* and it will be the debtor who will have to demonstrate the existence of some cause of exoneration of his responsibility.

Summarizing, the responsibility of the carrier emerges from the typical obligation that has assumed that it consists of disembarking at the port of destination of the passenger in the same conditions in which he embarked. Failure to comply with that principal obligation generates the corresponding responsibility.

10 Limit of Liability

Article 6 of Law 19.246, gave new wording to Article 1050 of the Commercial Code which regulated the so-called "*abandono liberatorio*" (abandonment of ship and freights).

The liability may be limited by abandoning the value of the ship plus all of its belongings, and the freight and passages received or to be received in the voyage to which the facts of the captain refer and credits in their favour that were arisen during such voyage.

This system is similar to the US system, which it follows in part since it allows limiting the liability to the value of the ship (like the US system), but unlike it, the value of the ship is taken before the accident and not the value of it at the end of the voyage. Nor does it follow that system because it does not distinguish between material damages and personal injuries by establishing different limits in both cases.

Finally, there is a single exception applicable to the limitation regime and is given in terms of liability for pollution. This is due to Law No. 18.996, which in Article 84 established a generic exception when determining that Article 1050 of the Commercial Code will not apply in cases of pollution from ships (Zorrilla Ferrés 2015, p. 125).

11 Conclusions

In consideration of the economic importance that the cruise activity currently has at the national level, and the various legal aspects that are affected, it is of high relevance that Uruguay adopts internal regulations that expressly regulate its activity in labor aspects, consumer relations, environmental aspects, etc.

References

Aguirre Ramírez F, Fresnedo C (2011) Transporte marítimo Volum III. Fundación de Cultura Universitaria, Montevideo

Ariza Herrerías Á (2014) Análisis jurídico-económico del transporte marítimo en el sector turístico. Universidad de Málaga. Disponible en: https://riuma.uma.es/xmlui/bitstream/handle/10630/8729/TRABAJO FIN DE MÁSTER - def.pdf?sequence=1

Fresnedo de Aguirre C (2015) "Normas de Derecho Internacional Privado en las Leyes N° 18.803 y N° 19.246 de Derecho Marítim", en *Reforma del Derecho Marítimo uruguayo*. Montevideo: Fundación de Cultura Universitaria, Asociación Uruguaya de Derecho Marítimo, pp 127–168

Ministerio de Trabajo y Seguridad Social (2018) Consejos de Salarios - 9- Transporte Marí-timo - Ministerio de Trabajo. Disponible en: https://www.mtss.gub.uy/web/mtss/9-transporte-maritimo (Accedido: 7 de enero de 2019)
Ministerio de Transporte y Obras Públicas (2016) Autoridades de Uruguay y Argentina buscan potenciar la llegada de cruceros - Noticias - MTOP. Disponible en: http://www.mtop.gub.uy/-/autoridades-de-uruguay-y-argentina-buscan-potenciar-la-llegada-de-cruceros?redirect=http%3A%2F%2Fwww.mtop.gub.uy%2Fbusqueda%3Fp_p_id%3D3%26p_p_lifecycle (Accedido: 7 de enero de 2019)
Ministerio de Turismo (2017) Investment opportunities. Tourism. Disponible en: https://www.uruguayxxi.gub.uy/uploads/informacion/Tourism Report - Uruguay XXI - March 2017-6.pdf
Ministerio de Turismo (2019) Turismo de Cruceros. Disponible en: https://mintur.gub.uy/index.php/estadisticas/turismo-de-cruceros (Accedido: 7 de enero de 2019)
Scofienza Pérez R (2013) El contrato de "agencia turistica" en el derecho positivo uruguayo. Revista de la Facultad de Derecho, (22). Disponible en: http://revista.fder.edu.uy/index.php/rfd/article/view/199/221 (Accedido: 7 de enero de 2019)
Zorrilla Ferrés V (2015) "Abandono liberatorio en la Ley N° 19.246", en *Reforma del Derecho Marítimo uruguayo*. Montevideo: Fundación de Cultura Universitaria, Asociación Uruguaya de Derecho Marítimo, pp 111–126

Part IV
National Reports: Asia and Euro-Asia

Legal Aspects of Cruises from Chinese Perspective

Xiao-nian Li and Si-qi Sun

Abstract China's cruise industry has developed quickly since 2006, the new mode of tourism brings new legal issues. The market access limitations for foreign investors in China's tourism market have given rise to a cruise market dominated by a unique charter sale (Charter sale (包船模式) means the cruise line company sold all the tickets to the travel agency in a package price.) with a complex legal relationship that conjoins the cruise line companies, the passengers and the travel agencies. Chinese national legal system does not contain any specific legal rules on cruises yet, but there are national laws governing sea carriage of passengers, such as China Maritime Code, China Tourism Law. Also, there are many guidelines, local regulations on cruises, such as *Guideline for Shanghai Cruise Tourism Operation*. In addition, other general rules and guidelines are also applicable to cruises on transport, tourism, consumer protection, labor, ports, environmental protection, jurisdiction, arbitration and choice of law, however, scattered in China Legal System.

1 Introduction

After several year's consisting booming, "China saw a decline in oceangoing cruise tourism last year, with 13 domestic ports welcoming fewer cruise ships and visits than in 2018.The 13 ports saw 969 cruises and 4.9 million visits, falling 17.95 percent and 0.98 percent, respectively, from 2017",[1] according to research by the China Cruise and Yacht Industry Association and the China Ports Organization. COVID-19 is a severe challenge to Chinese cruise ports. During the period between January 20–29 (when the Chinese authorities started to take strict measures to

[1] China Economic Net, https://en.ce.cn/Business/topnews/201902/11/t20190211_31444746.shtml, July 16, 2020 visit.

X.-n. Li (✉)
Shanghai Academy of Social Sciences, Institute of the Applied Economics, Shanghai, China

S.-q. Sun
Shanghai Maritime University, School of Law, Shanghai, China

C. Fresnedo de Aguirre (ed.), *Legal Aspects of Cruises*, Ius Comparatum - Global Studies in Comparative Law 56, https://doi.org/10.1007/978-3-030-83090-8_11

control the spread), all cruises from the terminal were cancelled. In particular, there are greater losses for those cruise ports only for passengers. e.g., Shanghai Wusongkou Port, which is a commercial cruise port, though created "zero infection" records, suffered a great loss since the Cruise ship calls are the only income for the port operator. About 90 calls have been cancelled, nearly a third of 2020's bookings. The tidal wave of lawsuits brings more consideration about the legal aspects of cruises in China.

2 Importance of Cruise Tourism in China

China is both a main cruise destination and outbound resources country in Asia, and China is also a main cruise departing country. Cruise tourism is booming in China since 2006, in particular, Shanghai of China. Shanghai Wusongkou International Cruise Terminal is now one of the largest cruise terminals in the world.[2] The People's Republic of China,[3] lying in the East Asia, is the third largest country in the world in terms of territorial area. It covers a land area of 9.6 million square kilometers and an area of inner and territorial sea of about 3 million square kilometers in the Yellow Sea, East China Sea and South China Sea from north to south. It has proximately 18,000 kilometers of coastline and 22,000 kilometers of land frontiers.[4] Both central government and local government lay great emphasis on the development of tourism industry. Motivated by both the government and the market, China Cruise Tourism is striking toward a bigger cruise market with global influences.[5] China's cruise industry has developed quickly over the last decade. Further developments are also anticipated with the implementation of the Belt and Road Initiative, which seeks to push forward more cooperation under the framework of 21st-century Maritime Silk Road. Shanghai aims to ride the waves of the cruise tourism economy by further tapping the potential as the city is set to welcome nearly 26 million cruise passengers by 2022, said a report released today by the Shanghai Academy of Social Sciences.

Shanghai has made great progress in the past decade in developing the cruise economy, bucking the global trend when this relatively new type of tourism was hit by the economic downturn. Ranked as the biggest cruise port in Asia and the fourth largest in the world, Shanghai saw 512 cruise ships depart or dock at the city's three ports in 2018, receiving 2.97 million visitors. The volume accounted for 43.3% of China's total. The city is expected to handle 25.7 million people on cruises by 2022. Global cruise giants including Carnival Corp, Royal Caribbean and MSC Cruises

[2]Wang (2017), p. 62.

[3]In this chapter, "the People's Republic of China" or "China" refers to the Mainland China unless otherwise expressly indicated.

[4]Hu (2015), p. 35.

[5]Wang (2017), p. 1.

have made Shanghai their port of call. Shanghai set up a joint venture in 2018 between China State Shipbuilding Corp Ltd and Italy's Fincantieri to build China's first cruise ship in 2023. The development of cruise economy has been laid great emphasis by different levels of governments in China.

3 General and Specific Rules Applicable to Cruises

3.1 General Rules Applicable to Cruises

The general legal rules that are applicable to cruises in Chinese legal system can be mainly divided into three parts: transport law, tourism law and consumer protection law.

3.1.1 Transport Aspect

3.1.1.1 Civil Law

In Chinese legal system, the following laws, regulations and provisions deal with special civil matters of maritime transport or relating to vessels:

- *Chinese Maritime Code*, adopted and promulgated on 7 November 1992, and was effective as of 1 July 1993. Chapter V "Contract of Carriage of Passengers by Sea" of *Chinese Maritime Code*, a reproduction of *Athens Convention Relating to the Carriage of Passengers and Their Luggage by Sea 1974* as amended by its SDR Protocol of 1976, deals with carriage of passengers by sea, either international or domestic.[6] Article 107 provides that: "A contract of carriage of passengers by sea is a contract whereby the carrier undertakes to carry passengers and their luggage by sea from one port to another by ships suitable for that purpose against payment of fare by the passengers."
- *Rules on Waterway Passenger Transport*, promulgated by the Ministry of Transport on 12 December 1995, came into force as of 1 June 1996, revised for the first time on 26 August 1997, and revised for the second time on 2 January 2014.

On 10 September 2018, the Standing Committee of the Thirteenth National People's Congress released its legislation working plan for the next five years including 116 pieces of legislation in 3 categories. Category I includes 69 legislative drafts which are relatively mature and planned for submission for deliberation. Category II includes 47 pieces of legislative drafts which need to be prepared without delay and are to be submitted for deliberation when becoming mature. Category III includes the legislative projects which do not have complete legislative

[6] Hu (2015), p. 305.

conditions and need to be further demonstrated. The revision of *Chinese Maritime Code* is included in category II, which means the revision may be submitted for deliberation when becoming mature before March 2023.

China has acceded to *Athens Convention Relating to the Carriage of Passengers and Their Luggage by Sea 1974* as amended by its SDR Protocol of 1976. Reservation was made on its application of the carrier's limitation of liability for loss of or personal injury to passengers and loss or damage to luggage to the carriage by sea between the Chinese ports. China has not ratified Protocol of 1990 or Protocol of 2002.

Besides, Section 2 of Chapter XVII "Transportation Contracts" of the *Contract Law of the People's Republic of China* (hereinafter referred to as "*Chinese Contract Law*") is "Passenger Transportation Contracts". *Chinese Contract Law* is the basic law of contract in China. China adheres to the principle that, where both special law and basic law contain provision concerning a certain matter, the special law has priority over the basic law to the extent of repugnancy. However, where special law contains no provision, the basic law shall apply.[7] Subject to this principle, *Chinese Contract Law* is a very important source of transport law in China. Moreover, China will finish the compilation of civil code in March 2020, and the rules on transportation contract including passenger transportation contract will be an important part of *Chinese Civil Code.*

3.1.1.2 Administrative Law

The following regulations and provisions deal with special administrative matters of maritime transport or relating to vessels:

- *Regulations of the People's Republic of China on International Ocean Shipping*, promulgated by the State Council on 11 December 2001, came into force on 1 January 2002, revised for the first time on 8 July 2013, and revised for the second time on 6 February 2016. Paragraph 1 of Article 2 provides that: "These Regulations shall be applicable to the business operations of international ocean shipping inward and outward from the ports of the People's Republic of China and the auxiliary business operations related to international ocean shipping." Paragraph 2 provides that: "The 'auxiliary business operations related to international ocean shipping' as used in the preceding paragraph include international ship agencies, international ship management, port handling of international ocean shipping, the storage of goods related to international ocean shipping, container stations and stacking of international ocean shipping, and other operations."
- *Regulation on the Administration of Domestic Water Transport*, promulgated by the State Council on 13 November 2012, came into force as of 1 January 2013,

[7] Hu (2015), p. 69.

revised for the first time on 6 February 2016, and revised for the second time on 1 March 2017. Paragraph 1 of Article 2 provides that: "The operation of domestic water transport and ancillary business shall be subject to this Regulation." Paragraph 2 provides that: "The term 'domestic water transport' (hereinafter referred to as 'water transport') as mentioned in this Regulation refers to the commercial transport of passengers and cargos in navigable waters, where the departure port, the calling port, and the destination port are all within the jurisdiction of the People's Republic of China." Paragraph 3 provides that: "The term 'ancillary water transport business' as mentioned in this Regulation refers to the business operations that are directly provided for water transport, such as vessel management, vessel agency, agency for water transport of passengers, and agency for water transport of cargos."

– *Provisions on the Administration of Domestic Water Transport*, promulgated by the Ministry of Transport on 3 January 2014, came into force on 1 March 2014, amended for the first time on 12 May 2015, and amended for the second time on December 2016. Paragraph 1 of Article 2 provides that: "These Provisions shall apply to the administration of domestic water transport." Paragraph 2 provides that: "For the purpose of these Provisions, the term 'water transport' refers to the commercial transport of passengers and cargo by vessels in navigable waters, where the departure port, the calling port, and the destination port are all within the jurisdiction of the People's Republic of China."

3.1.2 Tourism Aspect

In Chinese legal system, the following laws, regulations and provisions deal with special matters of tourism:

– *Chinese Tourism Law*, adopted on 25 April 2013, came into force as of 1 October 2013, firstly amended on 7 November 2016, and secondly amended 26 October 2018. *Chinese Tourism Law* deals with the following subjects: tourists, tourism planning and promotion, tourism operation, tourism service contracts, tourism safety, tourism supervision and administration, handling of tourism disputes and legal liabilities. Chapter V of *Chinese Tourism Law* is "Tourism Service Contracts", also referred to as organized travel contract, and Subparagraph 3 of Article 111 provides that: "Organized travel contract means a contract under which a travel agency arranges the tour in advance, provides, by itself or through a performance supporter, two or more items of tourism services of transportation, accommodation, catering, sightseeing, tour guide or tour leader, etc., and the tourist pays the tourism fees at an inclusive price."
– *Regulation on Travel Agencies*, issued by the State Council on 20 February 2009, came into force on 1 May 2009, amended for the first time on 6 February 2016, and amended for the second time on 1 March 2017. Paragraph 1 of Article 2 provides that: "This Regulation shall apply to the establishment and business activities of travel agencies within the People's Republic of China." Paragraph

2 provides that: "The term 'travel agencies' as mentioned in this Regulation shall refer to enterprise legal persons that engage in such activities as soliciting, organizing and receiving tourists, provide tourists with relevant tourism services, and conduct domestic tourism business, inbound tourism business, or outbound tourism business." More specifically, *Regulation on Travel Agencies* deals with the following subjects: establishment of travel agencies, foreign-invested travel agencies, operation of travel agencies, supervision and inspection and legal liabilities.
- *Provisions of the Supreme People's Court on Several Issues Concerning the Application of Law in the Trial of Cases about Tour Disputes*, promulgated by the Supreme People's Court on 26 October 2010 and was effective as of 1 November 2010. Paragraph 1 of Article 1 provides that: "A 'tour dispute' as mentioned in these Provisions refers to a contractual dispute or a tort arising from a tour between a tourist and the tour operator or any tour assistant."

3.2 Specific Policies

As something new to the traditional tourism, the cruise tourism has developed as a wind vane for the industrial transformation and development in coastal areas due to its rapid development, and plays a significant role in regional economic development with the supports of the governments at all levels.[8] There are many specific policies in China to favor the cruise business and to attract cruises to Chinese ports since 2008 as follows:

- *Opinions on Promoting the Development of Cruise Economy in China*, promulgated by the Ministry of Transport, National Development and Reform Commission, Ministry of Industry and Information Technology, Ministry of Public Security, Ministry of Finance, Ministry of Commerce, Ministry of Culture and Tourism, General Administration of Customs, State Taxation Administration and National Immigration Administration on 17 September 2018.
- *Opinions on Promoting the Development of Chinese Cruise Industry*, promulgated by the National Development and Reform Commission on 26 June 2008.
- *Opinions on Promoting the Sustainable Development of Cruise Transport Service in China*, promulgated by the Ministry of Transport on 18 March 2014.
- *Plans for Cruise Tourism Development in China*, promulgated by the National Tourism Administration in 2014.
- *Scheme for Layout Planning for National Coastal Cruise Ports*, promulgated by the Ministry of Transport on 10 April of 2015.
- *The 13th five-year Plan for Tourism Development*, by the Bureau of Tourism on October of 2016.

[8] Wang (2016), p. 7.

- *Opinions to promote the transport industry and tourism industry,* jointly promulgated by 6 ministries and bureaus in March of 2017.
- *Opinions to promote cruise industry* by ten central ministries and bureaus in September of 2018.

3.3 Specific Rules on Cruises

Chinese national legal system does not contain any specific legal rules on cruises yet. In national level, *Tourism Law, Maritime Code, International Shipping Ordinance* are applicable on cruise tourism in different aspects. Locally, there are many regulations on cruises. e.g., *Shanghai International Shipping Centre Construction Ordinance* have some general principles to promote cruise industry e.g., Enact the deployment plan and policies to develop cruise industry; make more innovation measures in FTZ to China Cruise Development Experimental Zone; Make more rules on sales of ticket, port service; implement more facilitation on entry-out of territory through cruise terminals; set in-out board free tax shopping store; encourage more foreign cruise line register and operate in Shanghai. In addition, Shanghai set the model contract for cruise tourism in 2015, made the experiment on using the cruise ticket in Shanghai. All these measures assist to have a better legal environment for health and sustainable development for cruise industry in Shanghai. Among which, *Shanghai Cruise Tourism Operation Rules* may be the most important one, being the first industry standard for cruise tourism in China.

Shanghai Cruise Tourism Operation Rules was promulgated by the Shanghai Municipal Administration of Tourism and Shanghai Municipal Transportation Commission on 6 March 2016. It aims to normalize the cruise tourism business of such subjects as cruise lines, travel agencies, international shipping agencies and cruise terminals in Shanghai that take Shanghai Port as home port. The rules mainly normalize cruise tourism from cruise tourism concept, management departments, industry associations, facilities and service standards, tour guides, business qualification, insurance, ticket sales, tourism service contract, cruise voyage change, special disclosure obligation, dispute settlement and credit management etc.[9]

As a local regulation on cruises of Shanghai, article 3 "Scope of Application" of *Shanghai Cruise Tourism Operation Rules* provides that the scope of application of the rules: cruise lines, travel agencies, international shipping agencies and cruise terminals in Shanghai that take Shanghai Port as home port. The rules address the issues on voyage change, the special disclosure obligation of cruise lines, travel agencies, international shipping agencies and cruise terminals, *however, it* does not contain specific rules on consumer protection applicable to passengers in cruises.

As *Shanghai Cruise Tourism Operation Rules* has only been implemented for a short time, and local regulation cannot be directly adopted in the judgment, there is

[9] Wang (2016), p. 48.

no specific problems regarding the implementation of *Shanghai Cruise Tourism Operation Rules*. Furthermore, Shanghai Administration for Industry & Commerce and Shanghai Municipal Administration of Tourism issued *Shanghai Cruise Tourism Contract Model Text (2015 Edition)*, the first cruise contract model text in the cruise market in China.

4 Cruise Passengers as Consumers

4.1 Law of the People's Republic of China on the Protection of Consumer Rights and Interests

Law of the People's Republic of China on the Protection of Consumer Rights and Interests (hereinafter referred to as "Chinese Consumer Protection Law") was adopted on 31 October 1993, came into force on 1 January 1994, amended for the first time on 27 August 2009, and amended for the second time on 25 October 2013.

Tourist is a very important kind of consumers in China. Article 2 of *Chinese Consumer Protection Law* provides that: "The rights and interests of consumers purchasing and using commodities or receiving services for daily consumption shall be protected by this Law; or be protected by other applicable laws and regulations if this Law is silent." Article 3 provides that: "In providing commodities produced or sold by them or services to consumers, business operators shall comply with this Law; or comply with other relevant laws and regulations if this law is silent."

Specifically speaking, *Chinese Consumer Protection Law* deals with the following subjects: rights of consumers, obligations of business operators, protection of lawful rights and interests of consumers by the state, consumer organizations, settlement of disputes and legal liabilities.

4.2 China's Unique Mode of Cruise Charter Sale by Travel Agency

In the traditional business mode of the foreign cruise markets, the travel agency is only the sales agency of the cruise line (as opposed to the operator of the package cruise tour products) and it is not therefore deeply involved in cruise tourism activities. Although the contractual relationship in this mode may involve on-board accommodation, catering, entertainment and services other than the carriage of passengers by sea, the overall legal relationship involved in cruise tourism in this mode is relatively simple, and mainly demarcates a contractual relationship between the passenger and cruise line. Because of limitations of tourism business on foreign travel agencies and cruise line companies in China, a unique chartered mode was formed under these circumstance.

4.2.1 Access Limitation of China's Tourism Market

At present, cruise lines in China's cruise market are mainly foreign-invested while outbound tourism accounts for the largest proportion of cruise tourism. Article 23 of the *Regulations on Travel Agencies* stipulates that: "No foreign-invested travel agency may operate the business in Chinese mainland residents' traveling to other countries and to Hong Kong Special Administrative Region, Macao Special Administrative Region and Taiwan region, unless it is otherwise decided by the State Council, or in the free trade agreements signed by China and by the arrangements on establishing closer economic partnership between Mainland and Hong Kong/ Macao (CEPA)."

According to the regulation mentioned above, even if the foreign-invested cruise lines have been granted the qualification of a travel agency, they are not allowed to run the outbound tourism business for Chinese mainland residents. However, Chinese tourists still consider the "destination" more important than "the cruise ship" itself, and lack the consciousness that "the cruise ship is the destination of trip". Most of Chinese tourists believe that the cruise ship is nothing but a more luxury and comfortable means of traffic.[10] Chinese passengers have higher expectation on onshore sightseeing, in particular, the overseas shopping. But cruise lines fail to provide outbound tourism that includes onshore sightseeing as they can only sell tickets separately.

The *Framework Plan for China (Shanghai) Pilot Free Trade Zone* allows qualified foreign-invested travel agencies that are registered in the Pilot Free Trade Zone (hereinafter referred to as "FTZ") to engage in outbound tourism services, with the exception of Taiwan District.[11] The *Decision of the State Council to Temporarily Adjust the Provisions of Relevant Administrative Regulations, Documents of the State Council, and Departmental Rules Approved by the State Council in Pilot Free Trade Zones*, which were published on 25 December 2017, also announced that the implementation of Article 23 of the *Regulations on Travel Agencies* in the FTZ would henceforth be suspended. Despite these change, only a few cruise lines, including MSC Cruises and Royal Caribbean International, have registered or established travel agencies in the FTZ. In other words, the positive impacts of the aforementioned special regulations of the FTZ have yet to be observed.

This is perhaps attributable to the market access limitations, which reinforce the reliance of cruise lines on travel agencies, whom they depend upon to sell package tour products. This results in a unique business mode that is based on the exclusive sales of cruise tickets by travel agencies, which can only be found in China. In contrast, the cruise tickets are sold by the cruise line company directly or in a retail mode instead of "wholesale mode". The alleged exclusive sale of cruise tickets by travel agencies entails an arrangement where the travel agencies negotiate booking

[10] Wang (2017), p. 34.

[11] Section 10 of Part III of the *Measures for the Expansion of Opening-Up of the Service Industry in China (Shanghai) Pilot Free Trade Zone*.

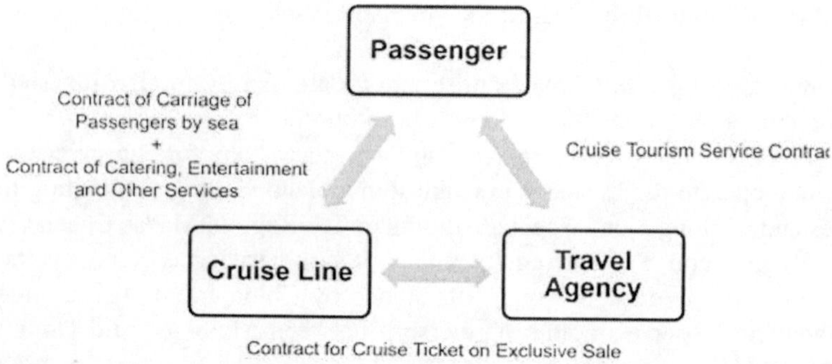

Fig. 1 Tripartite legal relationship under the buyout mode

prices with cruise lines before the sale of cruise tickets begins; they then pay a deposit to book all or some of the cruise cabins provided by the cruise line. Once the cabins are booked, the travel agency will design and price the package cruise tour products in accordance with market demand and its own resources. The cruise ticket is usually packaged and sold along with travel services such as onshore sightseeing that are provided by the travel agency, as well as the group tour guides and visa services. The travel agency's profits mainly originate from the price difference between the purchase of cruise tickets and the sale of package cruise tour products, including the commission obtained through onshore sightseeing, especially the shopping section. This arrangement—often referred to as the "bought deal mode"—changed the relationship between the ship owner and the traditional travel agency, therefore incurring more complicated liability issues relating to cruise disputes.

Statistics obtained from Shanghai Maritime Court in 2017 suggest that the proportion of ticket sales that are purchased by travel agencies (through rights of exclusive sale) and then resold to passengers account for almost all (98%) of total sales. Article 30 of the *Regulations on Travel Agencies (Revised Draft for Review)*, which was published in 2016, still retains the current market access limitation and this lends further credence to the proposition that the "bough deal mode" will persist and predominate in the future.

4.2.2 Tripartite Legal Relationship Under the Buyout Mode

China's unique buyout sale mode establishes a complex legal relationship that conjoins the cruise line, the passenger and the travel agency (see Fig. 1). In the first instance, the passenger signs the cruise tourism service contract with the travel agency. This contract is a kind of the tourism service contract that is set out in Chapter V 'Tourism Service Contracts' of the *Tourism Law of the People's Republic of China* (hereinafter referred to as "*Chinese Tourism Law*").

In the second, the buyout mode reduces the cruise ticket to a component of the package tour product, and it is therefore no longer a product that can be directly sold in the traditional mode. Article 110 of the *Maritime Law of the People's Republic of China* (hereinafter referred to as "*Chinese Maritime Code*") provides that: "The passage ticket serves as evidence that a contract of carriage of passengers by sea has been entered into." Therefore, the cruise ticket provides evidence of the contract of carriage of passengers by sea that has been established between the passenger and the cruise line. Passengers' rights and obligations vis-à-vis the carrier are of a contractual nature with the contract evidenced by the issuance of the ticket.[12] In any dispute between a passenger and the contractual carrier, the law of contract and the terms of the contract of carriage between the parties will determine their rights and liabilities, subject only to applicable statutory interventions.[13] This contractual relationship can be adjusted within the provisions established by Chapter V "Contract of Carriage of Passengers by Sea" of the *Chinese Maritime Code* and the *Athens Convention Relating to the Carriage of Passengers and Their Luggage by Sea.* Moreover, other service contract relationships such as accommodation, catering and entertainment may also exist.

In the last instance, the cruise line signs a contract with the travel agency on cruise tickets in the buyout sale mode, in which some specific details such as booking prices, cabins, itineraries and passenger numbers are included.

5 Combined Trips, Package Travels, Package Tours or Package Holidays

5.1 Confusion in Practice Caused by the Deficiency in Law

As above-mentioned in Sect. 4.2.2, it is not so difficult to differentiate the liability issues between the cruise line company and the travelling agency since the latter has the unique eligibility to enter into tour contract with the tourists, including combined trips, package travels, package tours or package holidays. Therefore the main issue still focuses on who is the organizer, who is the local travel agency and their different liabilities.

Let's analyze from a case as follows: Beijing Huangcheng Travel Service purchases round trip air tickets for Beijing to Kunming, and signs a contract with Kunming A Travel Service to entrust Kunming A Travel Service to provide local reception services. Based on the above operation, the products of "Yunnan 7 Day Tour" are formed. Beijing Didu Travel Agency sells tourism products of the Imperial City Travel Agency, and tourists and Didu Travel Agency signed a "domestic group

[12] Baatz (2018), p. 217.
[13] Lewins (2016), p. 33.

tour contract" to buy "Yunnan 7 day tour products". The question is: in the above cases, who is the group tour agency?

The answer is simple and the reasons are not complicated. Article 111 of the Tourism Law stipulates the definition of "group agency": "group agency refers to the travel agency that enters into a package tour contract with tourists". In the case, the travel agency that enters into a package tour contract with tourists is the Di du travel agency, so the Di du travel agency is the group agency.

There is no definition in the laws, regulations or national standards or industry standards of the term "group agency", which is commonly used in the industry, before the law defines the group agency. In a newly revised version on national standard, i.e., "Terminology of Tourism in 2017 (GB/T 16766-2017旅游业基础术语)", there is no definition of "group agency", but only "group business" and "outbound tour group agency". The definition of "group business" is "to sell tourism products to tourists through tourism retailers, and to provide tourists with satisfactory tourism experience together with tourism reception service providers, so as to obtain the business operation of enterprise profits". From this definition, it is more in line with the travel agency industry understanding.

But its definition of "outbound tour group" is somewhat rough, only defined as "travel agency that obtains the qualification of outbound travel business according to law", this definition is more like to explain: "outbound travel agency", but does not explain the keyword "group". In addition, in this standard, only the definition of "outbound tourism group" appears, there is no definition of "outbound tourism group", there is no definition of "domestic tourism group", it seems to express the meaning that "outbound travel group" only exists in the field of outbound business, obviously incomplete. In the new edition of the basic terms of tourism, there is no definition of "group agency" or "group business".

Because there is no authoritative definition, it leads to cognitive confusion in the actual operation, which will affect the legitimate rights and interests of tourists: when the rights and interests of tourists are violated, tourists bring claims to the travel agency that signed the contract, and the contracted travel agency often argues that it is not the travel agency that actually operates the product, is not its own "group", all the problems are caused by "group travel agency", thus shirking responsibility. And when the tourists find the "group travel agency", the tourists are told that the tourists should find the travel agency with which they sign the contract, so the tourists are kicked around.

During the drafting of the Law on Tourism, some key terms were defined and the principles prevailing in the industry were defined. Through the definition of these terms, strengthen the contractual obligations of contracted travel agencies. To require "group agencies" to assume the responsibility of product package tour producers complies the legal logic to protect the rights and interests of tourists.

In the Law on Tourism, the definition of "group agency" is followed by the definition of "local agency" which refers to the travel agency entrusted by the group agency to receive tourists at the destination. Then the problem arises.

Above cases, from the business relationship, the local agency is Kunming A travel agency. But from the above analysis, the group agency is Didu travel agency, and Kunming A travel agency is not commissioned by Didu travel agency. Huangcheng travel agency is not a package tour contract with guests. As a result, it is clear that Kunming A travel agency should not be a local agency as defined in the Tourism Act. If the Kunming A travel agency is recognized as a local agency, then according to the definition of the local agency, the Didu travel agency should be recognized as a group agency, the logic is confused. What's the problem?

Under normal circumstances, if the travel agency independently purchases resources, operates the route to form the self-owned product, sells by itself, signs the contract with the tourist, then "the travel law" in the group agency, the ground connection agency concept is appropriate. But this "normal situation" is no longer normal, travel agencies have established a zero-approval system, and travel agencies each other entrusted to sell tourism products is very common. Article 60 of the Tourism Law stipulates: "Where a travel agency entrusts other travel agencies to sell package-price tourism products and conclude a package-price tourism contract with tourists, the basic information of the agency and agency shall be stated in the package-price tourism contract." According to this regulation, the imperial city and the imperial capital travel agency constitute the principal-agent relationship, the imperial city travel agency is the "entrustment agency", the imperial capital travel agency is the "agency agency". In accordance with the provisions of the Tourism Law, the Tidu Travel Service shall specify in the travel contract that it is entrusted by the Huangcheng Travel Service to sell the tourism product.

The following questions need to be discussed separately: Did the Tidu Travel Agency disclose the actual entrustment agency? This is not only the issue of whether Tidu travel agency violates the provisions of Article 60 of the Tourism Law, but also involves the contract relationship between the imperial city, the imperial capital and the tourists. This problem can not be simply analyzed according to the Tourism Law, and the relevant provisions of the Contract Law need to be introduced.

The Contract Law regards "entrustment contract" as a special chapter of a famous contract, in which Article 402 stipulates that "a contract concluded by a trustee in his own name with a third party within the scope of the principal's authorization, if the third party knows the agency relationship between the trustee and the principal at the time of the conclusion of the contract, the contract directly binds the principal and the third party, provided that there is firm evidence that the contract is binding only the trustee and the third party".

The following can be understood in combination with the case: the imperial city travel agency is the principal, the imperial city travel agency is the trustee, and the tourist is the third person. If the Tidu travel agency discloses in the contract that the client of the product is the Huangcheng travel agency, or the tourist also knows that the Huangcheng travel agency is the actual product provider, then the travel contract signed by the tourist and the Tidu travel agency directly binds the Huangcheng travel agency and the tourist. However, if there is conclusive evidence that the travel contract only binds Tidu Travel Agency and tourists. For example, Tidu travel agency for promotion, in the contract promise to give tourists luggage, the promise is only valid between tourists and Tidu travel agency.

In fact, this is the contract law in the "explicit agent" and "anonymous agent" problem. If the Didu travel agency disclosed the imperial city travel agency, it constitutes a "prominent agent", the Didu travel agency is only an agent, its contract with tourists, the equivalent of the contract signed between the imperial city travel agency and tourists. In this case, according to the definition of group agency in the Tourism Law, Huangcheng travel agency should be a group agency. There is no logical confusion in defining the group and the local community. However, based on the uneven legal literacy of travel agency practitioners and tourists, not all can recognize this legal relationship. It may be limited to the Didu travel agency, which believes that it is a group agency, and does not consider the issue of "prominent agent".

But if Didu travel agency does not disclose to tourists, it constitutes a "anonymous agent", then the travel contract only binds Didu travel agency and tourists, Didu travel agency is defined by the "Tourism Law" group agency, so as to define the premise of this case of "local contact", there will be logical confusion.

It is reasonable for the Tourism Law to define the "group agency" according to the criteria of "concluding the package tour contract with tourists". But it should also be recognized that the concept of "group" emphasizes "group", which is the word "jargon" precipitated over the years, and emphasizes the meaning of "tourism team organization", which is applicable in the case of "integrated production and marketing" of travel agencies. Concepts are gradually alienated in the development of the industry, and the law defines one of the meanings, which leads to cognitive differences.

5.2 *Possible Solution on Amendment to Tourism Act*

A seemingly reasonable legal or academic definition, when considered in reality and linked to other concepts, exposes problems.

The solution is simple to say, but it is difficult to do so, with a comprehensive combing and careful definition of concepts and definitions.

First of all, it is necessary to conduct a comprehensive investigation of the current situation of industry operation, especially to carefully distinguish the established "jargon" in the industry, which cannot be easily denied or changed. To learn from market experience and the consensus formed by practitioners, this consensus generally has its profound market background and historical origin. The term that can pass down in the industry for a long time, certainly have its existence value and reason.

Secondly, it is necessary to make academic induction and legal definition of the concepts that exist in the industry after market and time test, to remove the factors that do not adapt to reality, to straighten out the logic between concepts, and to define them carefully.

Thirdly, legal definitions should be carefully defined for concepts that have not yet formed a unified understanding. Because the law has the force, also has the very strong stability, once determined will be very difficult to modify, easily modifies, will cause the bigger cognition confusion.

For industry terminology, more consideration should be given to defining in recommended industry or national standards that are not mandatory. At the same time, practitioners should be fully consulted on the drafting of these industry and national standards. Especially for the concepts often used by market operators, it is not only the scholars behind closed doors or only in the text logic.

Therefore, the author suggests that we should analyze the popular understanding of the concept of "group agency" in the industry, and if we can form a unified understanding, we should unify the definition. If there was no uniform understanding, the definition of the concept in law should be removed.

In order to solve the problem of contract relationship, the first is to define "agency" by legal logic, and the second is to add the concept of "provider of tourism products" and "seller of tourism products" by business thinking.

Respect industry operation habits, improve and sublate jargon terms; at the same time, distinguish legal concepts and business terms, follow legal theory, clarify contractual relationships, and define business logic. Only in this way can we clarify the relationship between the various parties involved in the travel agency industry, and let more than 20,000 travel agencies in the country at different business levels and stages, in the group agency, local contact agency, agency, wholesaler, retailer, product provider or seller in many concepts, to find out what they are a "society."

6 Labour Rules on Cruises' Workers

Chinese legal system does not contain specific legal rules on cruises' workers. In the absence of specific rules, some general rules or relating laws such as *Chinese labor law, Chinese Social Security Laws, Chinese Master and Crew Laws* will be applicable.

6.1 Labor Law and Social Security Law

In Chinese legal system, the following laws, regulations and provisions deal with special matters of labor and social security:

- *Labor Law of the People's Republic of China* (hereinafter referred to as "*Chinese Labor Law*"), adopted on 5 July 1994, came into force on 1 January 1995, amended for the first time on 27 August 2009, and amended for the second time on 29 December 2018. Paragraph 1 of Article 2 stipulates that: "This Law applies to enterprises, individually-owned economic organizations (hereinafter referred to as the employer) and laborers who form a labor relationship with them within the boundary of the People's Republic of China." Paragraph 2 provides that: "State departments, institutional organizations and social groups and laborers who form a labor relationship with them shall follow this Law." Concretely speaking, *Chinese Labor Law* deals with the following subjects: promotion of employment, labor contracts and collective contracts, working hours and rests, wages, labor safety and sanitation, special protection for female staff and workers and juvenile workers, professional training, social insurance and welfare treatment, labor disputes, supervision and inspection and legal liabilities.

- *Labor Contract Law of the People's Republic of China* (hereinafter referred to as "*Chinese Labor Contract Law*"), adopted on 29 June 2007, came into force on 1 January 2008, amended on 28 December 2012. Paragraph 1 of Article 2 provides that: "This Law shall apply to the establishment of employment relationship between employees and enterprises, individual economic organizations, private non-enterprise entities, or other organizations (hereafter referred to as employers), and to the formation, fulfillment, change, dissolution, or termination of labor contracts." Paragraph 2 provides that: "The state organs, public institutions, social organizations, and their employees among them there is an employment relationship shall observe this Law in the formation, fulfillment, change, dissolution, or termination of their labor contracts." More specifically, *Chinese Labor Contract Law* deals with the following subjects: formation of labor contracts, fulfillment and change of labor contracts, dissolution and termination of labor contracts, collective contract, worker dispatch, part-time employment, supervision and inspection and legal liabilities.
- *Social Insurance Law of the People's Republic of China*, adopted on 28 October 2010, came into force 1 July 2011, and amended on 29 December 2018, deals with the following subjects: basic endowment insurance, basic medical insurance, employment injury insurance, unemployment insurance, maternity insurance, collection and payment of social insurance premiums, social insurance funds, social insurance agencies, social insurance supervision and legal liabilities.
- *Labor Dispute Mediation and Arbitration Law of the People's Republic of China*, adopted on 29 December 2007, and came into force as of 1 May 2008. Article 2 provides that: "This Law shall apply to the following labor disputes arising between an employer and an employee within the territories of the People's Republic of China: (1) A dispute arising from the confirmation of a labor relationship; (2) A dispute arising from the conclusion, performance, modification, rescission or termination of a labor contract; (3) A dispute arising from the removal or layoff of an employee or the resignation or retirement of an employee; (4) A dispute arising from the work hours, breaks, vacations, social insurance, benefits, training, or labor safety; (5) A dispute arising from the labor remunerations, medical expenses for a work-related injury, economic indemnity, compensation, etc.; or (6) Any other labor dispute as provided for by a law or administrative regulation."
- *Regulation on the Implementation of the Employment Contract Law of the People's Republic of China*, promulgated by the State Council on 3 September 2008 and came into force as of 18 September 2008, deals with the following

subjects: conclusion, dissolution and termination of employment contract, special provisions on labor dispatch and legal liabilities.

- *Interim Provisions on Labor Dispatch*, promulgated by the Ministry of Human Resources and Social Security on 24 January 2014 and came into force on 1 March 2014. Paragraph 1 of Article 2 provides that: "These Provisions shall apply to the provision of labor dispatch services by labor dispatch entities and to the employment of dispatched workers by enterprises (hereinafter referred to as the 'employers')." Specifically speaking, *Interim Provisions on Labor Dispatch* deals with the following subjects: scope and proportion of employment, conclusion and performance of labor contracts and labor dispatch agreements, rescission and termination of labor contracts, social insurance with respect to cross-regional labor dispatch and legal liabilities.
- *Interpretation of the Supreme People's Court on Several Issues about the Application of Laws for the Trial of Labor Dispute Cases*, promulgated by the Supreme People's Court on 16 April 2001, came into force on 30 April 2001, and amended on 16 December 2008.
- *Interpretation (II) of the Supreme People's Court on Several Issues about the Application of Laws for the Trial of Labor Dispute Cases*, promulgated by the Supreme People's Court on 14 August 2006 and came into force as of 1 October 2010.
- *Interpretation (III) of the Supreme People's Court on Several Issues about the Application of Laws for the Trial of Labor Dispute Cases*, promulgated by the Supreme People's Court on 13 September 2010 and came into force on 14 September 2010.
- *Interpretation (IV) of the Supreme People's Court on Several Issues about the Application of Laws for the Trial of Labor Dispute Cases*, promulgated by the Supreme People's Court on 18 January 2013 and came into force as of 1 February 2013.

6.2 Master and Crew Law

Under *Chinese Maritime Code* or other Chinese Law, the word "crew" includes the master and other crewmembers. Traditionally, however, the master is different from other crewmembers in international treaties to his unique position.[14] As a service personal on cruise, a cruise ship steward, also known as marine steward, should hold a Seafarer's Passport of the People's Republic of China and a Seafarer's Record Book. Therefore, cruise ship steward is a kind of crew, and the crew law is applicable to cruise ship stewards. In Chinese legal system, the following laws, regulations and provisions deal with special matters of master and crew:

[14] Hu (2015), p. 115.

- Chapter III "Crew" of *Chinese Maritime Code*, including basic principles and functions and powers of the master.
- *Regulation of the People's Republic of China on Seamen* (hereinafter referred to as "*Chinese Regulation on Seamen*"), promulgated by the State Council on 14 April 2007, came into force on 1 September 2007, revised for the first time on 18 July 2013, revised for the second time on 7 December 2013, revised for the third time on 29 July 2014, and revised for the fourth time on 1 March 2017. Article 2 provides that: "This Regulation applies to the registration, assumption of office, training and professional security of seamen and the provision of seaman service within the border of the People's Republic of China." More specifically, *Chinese Regulation on Seamen* deals with the following subjects: registration and qualifications of seamen, duties of seamen, professional safeguard for seamen, seaman training and service, supervision and inspection and legal liabilities.
- *Administrative Provisions of the People's Republic of China on Seaman Service*, promulgated by the Ministry of Transport on 22 July 2008, came into force as of 1 October 2008, amended on 31 August 2013, deals with the following subjects: qualification of seaman service agencies, rights and obligations of seaman service agencies, supervision and inspection, and legal liabilities.
- *Provisions of the People's Republic of China on the Administration of Overseas Assignment of Seamen*, promulgated by the Ministry of Transport on 7 March 2011, came into force on 1 July 2011, amended on 11 April 2016, deals with the following subjects: qualifications of institutions engaged in overseas assignment of seamen, responsibilities and obligations of the institutions engaged in overseas assignment of seamen, disposal of emergencies, supervision and inspection and legal liabilities.

In addition, the *Maritime Labour Convention 2006* was ratified by China on 29 August 2015 and came into force in China as of 12 November 2016. *Maritime Labour Convention 2006* adopted by the International Labour Organization in 2007 is deemed as one of the four pillar conventions among the international maritime conventions. China has taken and is taking measures to comply with the *Maritime Labour Convention 2006*.

7 Rules on Ports That Are Relevant Regarding Cruises

Chinese legal system does not contain specific rules on ports that are relevant regarding cruises. *Law of the People's Republic of China on Ports* (hereinafter referred to as "*Chinese Port Law*") was adopted on 28 June 2003, came into force on 1 January 2004, amended for the first time on 24 April 2015, amended for the second time on 4 November 2017, and amended for the third time on 29 December 2018. Article 2 provides that: "Whoever engages in port planning, construction, maintenance, business operation, management and the related activities shall be governed by the present Law." Paragraph 1 of Article 3 provides that: "Port mentioned in the present Law means an area composed of a certain scope of water area and land area, which has the functions for vessels to enter and exit, to berth, to anchor, for passengers to embark and disembark, and for goods to be loaded and unloaded, lightered, stored, etc., and which has the corresponding wharf facilities." More concretely, *Chinese Port Law* deals with the following subjects: port planning and construction, business operation of ports, port safety and supervision and legal liabilities.

From a policy point of view, as early as in 2006, the *China National Coastal Ports Arrangement Planning* was introduced by the Ministry of Transport and the National Development and Reform Commission, stipulating the overall layout for the infrastructure construction of cruise industry based on the space distribution of cruises ports in China. In 2015, with the rapid and sound development of Chinese cruise industry, the Ministry of Transport introduced the *Scheme for Layout Planning for National Coastal Cruise Ports*, stipulating the establishment of two or three cruise home port clusters in the coastal areas in China and the promotion of China to rank among the world's top three cruise transport markets before 2030.[15]

8 Rules on Environmental Impact of Cruises

Environmental protection is one of the state's fundamental policies in the developing China, following which China emphasizes the legislation and implementation of laws in the area of environmental protection, especially in the area of marine environmental protection.[16] There is no specific rule on environmental impact of cruises in Chinese legal system, and the following laws, regulations and provisions deal with matters of marine pollution, especially caused by ships:

– *Environmental Protection Law of the People's Republic of China* (hereinafter referred to as "*Chinese Environmental Protection Law*"), adopted on 26 December 1989, came into force as of 26 December 1989, and revised on 24 April 2014. Article 2 provides that: "For the purposes of this Law, 'environment' means the entirety of all natural elements and artificially transformed natural elements that affect the survival and development of human beings, including but not limited to air, water, seas, land, minerals, forests, grasslands, wetland, wildlife, natural and cultural relics, nature reserves, scenic spots, historical sites, and urban and rural areas." Article 3 provides that: "This Law shall apply to the territory of the People's Republic of China, and other sea areas under the jurisdiction of the People's Republic of China." Concretely speaking, *Chinese Environmental Protection Law* deals with the following subjects: environmental

[15] Wang (2016), p. 34.
[16] Hu (2015), pp. 268–269.

protection and improvement, prevention and control of pollution and other public nuisances, information disclosure and public engagement and legal Liabilities.

- *Marine Environmental Protection Law of the People's Republic of China* (hereinafter referred to as "*Chinese Marine Environmental Protection Law*"), adopted on 23 August 1982, revised on 25 December 1999, came into force on 1 March 1983, amended on 28 December 2013, amended for the second time on 7 November 2016, and amended for the third time on 4 November 2017. Paragraph 1 of Article 2 provides that: "This Law shall apply to the internal waters, territorial seas, contiguous zones, exclusive economic zones and continental shelves of the People's Republic of China and all other sea areas under the jurisdiction of the People's Republic of China." Paragraph 2 provides that: "All units and individuals engaged in navigation, exploration, exploitation, production, tourism, scientific research or other operations in the sea areas under the jurisdiction of the People's Republic of China, or engaged in operations in the coastal land areas which have impact on the marine environment shall comply with this Law." Specifically speaking, *Chinese Marine Environmental Protection Law* deals with the following subjects: supervision and control over the marine environment, marine ecological protection, prevention and control of pollution damage to the marine environment caused by land-based pollutants, coastal construction projects, marine construction projects, dumping of wastes, vessels and their related operations and legal liabilities.
- *Water Pollution Prevention and Control Law of the People's Republic of China*, adopted on 11 May 1984, came into force as of 1 November 1984, amended for the first time on 15 May 1996, revised on 28 February 2008, and amended for the second time on 27 June 2017. Paragraph 1 of Article 2 provides that: "This Law applies to the prevention and control of pollution of rivers, lakes, canals, irrigation channels, reservoirs and other surface waters and ground waters within the territory of the People's Republic of China." Paragraph 2 provides that: "The prevention and control of marine pollution shall be governed by the Marine Environmental Protection Law of the People's Republic of China." Section 5 of Chapter IV is "Prevention and Control of Water Pollution from Vessels".
- Paragraph 3 of Article 26 of *Chinese Port Law* provides that: "The business operator of port shall, in accordance with the relevant laws and regulations on environmental protection, take effective measures to prevent and control the pollution and harmfulness to the environment."
- *Regulation on the Prevention and Control of Vessel-induced Pollution to the Marine Environment*, promulgated by the State Council on 9 September 2009, came into force on 1 March 2010, revised for the first time on 18 July 2013, revised for the second time on 7 December 2013, revised for the third time on 29 July 2014, revised for the fourth time on 6 February 2016; revised for the fifth time on 1 March 2017, and amended on 19 March 2018, deals with the following subjects: general provisions on the prevention and control of the pollution caused by vessels and the relevant operations to the marine environment, discharge and reception of vessel pollutants, prevention and control of the pollution caused by vessels and the relevant operations, emergency response of vessel-induced

pollution accidents, investigation and handling of vessel-induced pollution accidents, compensation for damages caused by vessel-induced pollution accidents and legal liabilities.

- *Administrative Provisions of the People's Republic of China on the Prevention and Control of Marine Environmental Pollution by Vessels and Their Operations*, promulgated by the Ministry of Transport on 16 November 2010, came into force on 1 February 2011, amended for the first time on 31 August 2013, amended for the second time on 24 December 2013, amended for the third time on 13 December 2016, and amended for the fourth time on 23 may 2017, deals with the following subjects: discharge and receiving of vessel-induced pollutants, carrying cargos with hazardous pollutants and other relevant operations through vessels, dismantlement, salvage, repair and building of vessels and other above-water and underwater construction operations relating to vessels and legal liabilities.
- *Administrative Provisions of the People's Republic of China on the Prevention and Control of Vessel-Induced Pollution to the Inland Water Environment*, promulgated by the Ministry of Transport on 31 December 2015, and came into force as of 1 May 2016, deals with the following subjects: discharge and reception of vessel pollutants, pollution prevention and control for vessel-related operations, emergency response to vessel-induced pollution accidents, investigation and handling of vessel-induced pollution accidents and legal liabilities.

Besides, China has ratified or acceded to the following international treaties in the area of prevention and civil liability of marine pollution:

- *International Convention for the Prevention of Pollution from Ships*, signed in London on 2 November 1973 as amended by its Protocol of 1978, and its Amendments.
- *Convention on the Prevention of Marine Pollution by Dumping of Wastes and Other Matters*, signed in London on 13 November 1972, and its Amendments.
- *International Convention on Civil Liability for Bunker Oil Pollution Damage*, signed in London on 23 March 2001.
- *International Convention relating to Intervention on the High Seas in Cases oil Pollution Casualties*, sign in Brussels on 29 November 1969, its Protocol of 1973 and *Amendment of 1991*.

9 Jurisdiction and Arbitration

9.1 Jurisdiction

In China, disputes regarding cruise tourism fall mainly into two categories, the first of which is alteration of itinerary or so called voyage change. It is normally the case that passengers will sue the travel agencies while invoking the cruise tourism service contract, and this constitutes the dispute over the tourism contract specified in the

Provisions on Causes of Action in Civil Cases that has been released by the Supreme People's Court.[17] The second category is personal injury to the passenger. The passenger will file a lawsuit regarding the tort liability against the cruise line, and this constitutes the dispute over tort liability at the sea that is specified in the *Provisions on Causes of Action in Civil Cases.*[18]

There are eleven maritime courts as special people's courts in China, including Dalian Maritime Court, Tianjin Maritime Court, Qingdao Maritime Court, Shanghai Maritime Court, Ningbo Maritime Court, Xiamen Maritime Court, Guangzhou Maritime Court, Haikou Maritime Court, Beihai Maritime Court, Wuhan Maritime Court and Nanjing Maritime Court. Some of them have their branches in the neighboring cities. Each maritime court has its statutory basic jurisdiction area. That is, a maritime court shall have jurisdiction as court of first instance over maritime cases occurring in a certain geographical area.[19]

9.1.1 Legal Provisions

Chinese legal system does not contain specific provisions on jurisdiction of cruises cases, and *Civil Procedure Law of the People's Republic of China* (hereinafter referred to as "*Chinese Civil Procedure Law*"), *Special Maritime Procedure Law of the People's Republic of China* (hereinafter referred to as "*Chinese Maritime Procedure Law*") and *Provisions of the Supreme People's Court on the Scope of Cases to be Accepted by Maritime Courts* deal with matters of jurisdiction of civil cases but do not give special protection to cruise passengers or even ordinary tourists as consumers.

Chinese Civil Procedure Law was adopted on 9 April 1991, came into force on 9 April 1991, amended for the first time on 28 October 2007, amended for the second time on 31 August 2012, and amended for the third time on 27 June 2017. The following provisions of *Chinese Civil Procedure Law* are applicable to the jurisdiction of cruises cases:

- As regards the jurisdiction of contract disputes, Article 23 provides that: "An action instituted for a contract dispute shall be under the jurisdiction of the people's court at the place of domicile of the defendant or at the place where the contract is performed."
- As for the jurisdiction of transportation contract disputes, Article 27 provides that: "An action instituted for a dispute arising from a railway, road, water, air, or multi-mode transportation contract shall be under the jurisdiction of the people's court at the place of departure or destination of transportation or at the place of domicile of the defendant."

[17] Subparagraph 5 of Article 120 of the *Provisions on Causes of Action in Civil Cases.*
[18] Article 180 of the *Provisions on Causes of Action in Civil Cases.*
[19] Hu (2015), p. 72.

- With respect to the jurisdiction of tort disputes, Article 28 provides that: "An action instituted for a tort shall be under the jurisdiction of the people's court at the place where the tort occurs or at the place of domicile of the defendant."
- As regards the jurisdiction of transportation accident disputes, Article 29 provides that: "An action instituted for damages for a railway, road, water or air transportation accident shall be under the jurisdiction of the people's court at the place where the accident occurs, where the vehicle or vessel first arrives or where the aircraft first lands or at the place of domicile of the defendant."
- With respect to the autonomy of will on jurisdiction, Article 34 provides that: "Parties to a dispute over a contract or any other right or interest in property may, by a written agreement, choose the people's court at the place of domicile of the defendant, at the place where the contract is performed or signed, at the place of domicile of the plaintiff, at the place where the subject matter is located or at any other place actually connected to the dispute to have jurisdiction over the dispute, but the provisions of this Law regarding hierarchical jurisdiction and exclusive jurisdiction shall not be violated."
- As for the foreign-related civil relationships, Article 265 of Part Four "Special Provisions on Foreign-Related Civil Procedures" provides that: "Where an action is instituted against a defendant which has no domicile within the territory of the People's Republic of China for a contract dispute or any other property right or interest dispute, if the contract is signed or performed within the territory of the People's Republic of China, the subject matter of action is located within the territory of the People's Republic of China, the defendant has any impoundable property within the territory of the People's Republic of China, or the defendant has any representative office within the territory of the People's Republic of China, the people's court at the place where the contract is signed or performed, where the subject matter of action is located, where the impoundable property is located, where the tort occurs or where the domicile of the representative office is located may have jurisdiction over the action."

Chinese Maritime Procedure Law was adopted on 15 December 1999 and came into force on 1 July 2000, and the following provisions are applicable to the jurisdiction of cruises cases:

- Subparagraph 1 of Paragraph 2 of Article 6 provides that: "A lawsuit brought on maritime tortious may be, in addition to the provisions of Articles 19 to 31 of the Civil Procedure Law of the People's Republic of China, under jurisdiction of the maritime court of the place of its port of registry;"
- As for the jurisdiction of maritime transportation contract disputes, Subparagraph 2 of Paragraph 2 of Article 6 provides that: "A lawsuit brought on maritime transportation contract may be, in addition to the provisions of Articles 82 of the Civil Procedure Law of the People's Republic of China, under jurisdiction of the maritime court of the place of its port of re-transportation;"
- Article 8 provides that: "Where the parties to a maritime dispute are foreign nationals, stateless persons, foreign enterprises or organizations and the parties, through written agreement, choose the maritime court of the People's Republic of

China to exercise jurisdiction, even if the place which has practical connections with the dispute is not within the territory of the People's Republic of China, the maritime court of the People's Republic of China shall also have jurisdiction over the dispute."

Provisions of the Supreme People's Court on the Scope of Cases to be Accepted by Maritime Courts was promulgated by the Supreme People's Court on 1 March 2016 and came into force as of 1 March 2016, and the following types of cases related to cruises should be accepted by maritime courts:

- Cases concerning disputes over liability for infringement upon other persons' rights and interests arising from the navigation, service, and operation of vessels and other activities.
- Cases concerning disputes over contracts on carriage of passengers or luggage at sea or in water areas leading to the sea.

9.1.2 Conditions of Carriage

Conditions of carriage, also known as the passage terms, passage contact, passenger ticket contract or guest ticket contract, is the document published by the cruise line to specify the rights and obligations of the cruise line and passenger. It is also the main content of the contract of carriage of passengers by sea. Conditions of carriage are generally drafted to benefit the carrier/cruise line and often feature in disputes. Some of the jurisdiction clauses contained in the conditions of carriage in China are as follows:

- Clause 9 of the *Guest Ticket Contract* of Royal Caribbean International stipulates that: "For personal injury, illness or death of a passenger, it is agreed by and between passenger and carrier that all disputes and matters whatsoever arising under, in connection with or incident to this agreement, passenger's cruise, cruise tour, land tour or transport, shall be litigated, if at all, in and before a competent Chinese court in Shanghai. Passenger hereby consents to jurisdiction and waives any venue or other objection that he may have to any such action or proceeding being brought in the applicable court located in Shanghai."
- The *Booking Terms and Conditions* of MSC Cruises stipulate that: "All claims against the Carrier shall be brought in and be subject to the exclusive jurisdiction of the Courts of Naples, Italy.
- Article 25 of the *Terms and Conditions* of Costa Crociere stipulates that: "The Court of Genoa has exclusive jurisdiction for any controversies which may arise regarding this contract."
- Article 21 of the *Passage Terms* of Star Cruises stipulates that: "This Passage Contract shall be interpreted, construed and governed by the laws of Hong Kong Special Administrative Region and all claims by the Guest against the Carrier must only be brought in the Courts of Hong Kong Special Administrative Region to the exclusive of other courts."

There is no legal precedent that establishes how the validity of the conditions of carriage is regarded by Chinese courts. Article 39 of the *Chinese Contract Law* provides that: "Standard terms are clauses that are prepared in advance for general and repeated use by one party, and which are not negotiated with the other party when the contract is concluded." Paragraph 1 of Article 26 of *Chinese Consumer Protection Law* also provides that: "Business operators which use standard terms and conditions in business activities shall, in a conspicuous manner, remind consumers to pay attention to the quality, quantity, and prices or fees of commodities or services, duration and manner of performance, safety precautions and risk warnings, after-sales service, civil liability, and other terms and conditions vital to the interests of consumers, and provide explanations as required by consumers."

In the buyout mode, a passenger directly signs a contract with the travel agency, and there is no process of negotiation with the cruise line for the contract of carriage of passengers by sea. Most cruise lines directly list the conditions of carriage on their website. Therefore, the conditions of carriage constitute the standard terms stipulated by Chinese law and should be regulated by the mandatory provisions of the law. It is currently the case that the conditions of carriage issued by the cruise lines in China's market are generally directly adopted from versions issued in the European and American markets. These have not all been fully localized, and accordingly some regulations may jeopardize the interests of Chinese passengers. In addition, the content of some of the conditions of carriage obviously conflicts with the regulations of Chinese law. The *Guest Ticket Contract* published by the Norwegian Cruise Line being a case-in-point. It states that any guest under 21 years of age is considered a minor. However, Chinese law stipulates that a natural person attaining the age of eighteen is an adult.[20]

In the judicial practice of China, cases about disputes over liability for alteration of itinerary are usually accepted by local courts, and cases about disputes over liability for personal injury of tourists are often accepted by maritime courts.

9.2 Arbitration

Arbitration is not an important alternative dispute resolution besides litigation for the settlement of cruise disputes between tourists and cruise lines or travel agencies in China at present, and arbitration clauses are not often included in the conditions of carriage of passengers in cruises celebrated in China. Some of the arbitration clauses are as follows:

- Clause 9 of the *Guest Ticket Contract* of Royal Caribbean International stipulates that: "Arbitration of all other claims: any and all other disputes, claims, or

[20] Article 17 of the *General Provisions of the Civil Law of the People's Republic of China* provides that: "A natural person attaining the age of eighteen is an adult. A natural person under the age of eighteen is a minor."

controversies whatsoever, except for personal injury, illness or death of a passenger, whether based on contract, tort, statutory, constitutional or other legal rights, including but not limited to alleged violation of civil rights, discrimination, consumer or privacy laws, or for any losses, damages or expenses, relating to or in any way arising out of or connected with this contract or passenger's cruise, no matter how described, pleaded or styled, shall be referred to and resolved exclusively by the China International Economic and Trade Arbitration Commission ("CIETAC") in accordance with CIETAC's arbitration rules in effect at the time of applying for arbitration (the "rules"), which rules are deemed to be incorporated by reference into this clause and may be amended by the rest of this clause."

- Article 15 of the *Passage Contract* of Princess Cruises stipulates that: "Forum and Jurisdiction for Legal Action: Any dispute against Carnival plc arising out of or in connection with this Passage Contract or, transportation and/or services provided or to be provided by Carnival plc shall be litigated against Carnival plc only before China International Economic and Trade Arbitration Commission for arbitration in Shanghai."

Besides, Article 11 of *Shanghai Cruise Tourism Contract Model Text (2015 Edition)* chooses Shanghai Arbitration Commission as the arbitration commission of cruise tourism disputes.

10 Choice of Law

10.1 Legal Provisions

Chinese legal system does not contain specific provisions on choice of law to cruise cases, and *Law of the People's Republic of China on Choice of Law for Foreign-related Civil Relationships* (hereinafter referred to as "*Chinese Private International Law*") and *Chinese Maritime Code* deal with matters of choices of law regarding cruises cases but do not give special protection to cruise passengers or even ordinary tourists as consumers. Only Article 42 of *Chinese Private International Law* empower consumers to unilaterally choose the applicable laws at the locality of the provision of goods or services.

Chinese Private International Law was adopted on 28 October 2010 and came into force on 1 April 2011. There is only specific rule on choice of law of consumer contracts but not tourism contract. The following provisions of *Chinese Private International Law* are applicable to the choices of law regarding cruises cases:

- As for the application law of contracts, Article 41 provides that: "The parties concerned may choose the laws applicable to contracts by agreement. If the parties do not choose, the laws at the habitual residence of the party whose fulfillment of obligations can best reflect the characteristics of this contract or other laws which have the closest relation with this contract shall apply."

- As regards the application law of consumer contracts, Article 42 provides that: "The laws at the habitual residence of consumers shall apply to consumer contracts; If a consumer chooses the applicable laws at the locality of the provision of goods or services or an operator has no relevant business operations at the habitual residence of the consumer, the laws at the locality of the provision of goods or services shall apply."
- As for the application law of tort, Article 44 provides that: "The laws at the place of tort shall apply to liabilities for tort, but if the parties have a mutual habitual residence, the laws at the mutual habitual residence shall apply. If the parties choose the applicable laws by agreement after any tort takes place, the agreement shall prevail."
- Besides, Paragraph 2 of Article 2 provides that: "If there are no provisions in this Law or other laws on the application of any laws concerning foreign-related civil relations, the laws which have the closest relation with this foreign-related civil relation shall apply."

Chapter XIV of *Chinese Maritime Code* is "Application of Law in Relating to Foreign-related Matters", but there is no specific rule on choice of law of cruises or even contracts of carriage of passengers by sea. Article 269 stipulates that: "The parties to a contract may choose the law applicable to such contract, unless the law provides otherwise. Where the parties to a contract have not made a choice, the law of the country having the closest connection with the contract shall apply." Moreover, *Chinese Maritime Code* does not contain general rule on choice of law of liabilities for tort but only specific rule on collision of ships.[21]

10.2 Conditions of Carriage

Applicable law clauses are always included in the conditions of carriage of passengers in cruises celebrated in China, and usually the applicable law is Italian Law or American Law but rarely Chinese Law. Some of the Applicable law clauses are as follows:

- Clause 19 of the latest edition of the *Guest Ticket Contract* of Royal Caribbean International stipulates that: "This Guest Ticket Contract shall be governed by and construed in accordance with the laws of the People's Republic of China." According to the edition before 2019, the applicable law was the laws of the State of Florida, United States.
- Article 15 of the *Passage Contract* of Princess Cruises stipulates that: "Governing Law: All claims arising out of or related to the Passage Contract or Your Cruise shall be governed by English law. If a court or tribunal applies any law other than English law, Carrier shall (in respect of all exclusions and

[21] Article 273 of *Chinese Maritime Code*.

limitations of liability) be entitled to the maximum protection allowed by that law including statutory protection of limitation as to the amount of damages recoverable."

- The *Booking Terms and Conditions* of MSC Cruises stipulate that: "The applicable law for these Conditions of Carriage shall be Italian law."
- Article 25 of the *Terms and Conditions* of Costa Crociere stipulates that: "This contract and the general terms and conditions are governed by Italian law."
- Article 21 of the *Passage Terms* of Star Cruises stipulates that: "This Passage Contract shall be interpreted, construed and governed by the laws of Hong Kong Special Administrative Region and all claims by the Guest against the Carrier must only be brought in the Courts of Hong Kong Special Administrative Region to the exclusive of other courts."

The legal regulation of standard terms therefore focuses on limiting and ultimately invalidating the conditions of carriage. In cruise tourism disputes it is however sometimes the case that ensuring the validity of the conditions of carriage can more effectively protect passengers' rights and interests. One example is the *Sapphire Princess* case that was concluded by the Shanghai Maritime Court in April 2018, which is frequently referred to as the first case relating to the personal injury of Chinese cruise passengers on the high seas.[22] Article 15 of the *Passage Contract* published by the Princess Cruises chose English law as the Governing Law. While the passenger may not be aware of the *Passage Contract* and accordingly did not present the *Passage Contract* as evidence when she filed the lawsuit or advocate the application of English law (on the grounds that the *Sapphire Princess* is a British vessel), the cruise line still deemed it necessary to explicitly advocate the application of Chinese law. *Chinese Private International Law* permits parties to select the law that is applicable to the tort liability. In this circumstance, the purpose of protecting the passengers' rights and interests could be better implemented. If it was agreed that the passenger and the cruise line had, in accordance with the applicable law clause of the *Passage Contract*, mutually assented to the legal application of the tort liability, it would also be consistent with the passenger's own legal choice interests. But because Chinese law was, in accordance with the principle of the most closely linked, finally applied in this case, the applicable law clause of the *Passage Contract* was not considered.

[22] Yang Shu-ying v. Carnival Corporation & plc, China Travel Service Zhejiang Group Co., Ltd. (case about disputes over liability for personal injury at sea or in water areas leading to the sea).

11 General Conditions Used by Companies Offering Cruse Services

There are various kinds of companies offering cruise services. No national special law on the companies offering cruise services, however, a set of rules for cruise business operation were enacted in Shanghai in 2017. The full name of the rules is "Shanghai Cruise Tourism Management Standards". Its scope of application is for cruise companies, travel agencies, international shipping agencies, cruise terminals and other business entities engaged in cruise-related tourism operations within the administrative area of Shanghai City, and Shanghai Tourism Bureau is responsible for the supervision and management of cruise services operated by travel agencies, and Shanghai Transportation Commission is responsible for the maintenance of cruise terminal order, the cruise companies operating cruise transportation business, and the supervision and management of cruise ship ticketing by international shipping agency companies. The district government where the cruise terminal is located is responsible for emergency handling of cruise tourism emergencies within its administrative area, and formulates emergency handling plans for cruise tourism in this district. The relevant administrative departments such as the maritime affairs, public security, and joint inspection units at the port shall do well in the service and management of cruise tourism operations in accordance with their respective responsibilities. The standards include the rules for industry association, the facilities and service standards for cruise tourism and the operational qualification for those who operate outbound packaged cruise tourism business or sell packaged packaged cruise tourism products as agents shall obtain a travel agency's permission to operate outbound tourism business. Agents selling cruise ship tickets shall obtain the qualification of international shipping agents. Foreign-funded enterprises should obtain the "Registration Certificate of International Shipping Agency Business Qualification", and domestic-funded enterprises should go through the relevant filing procedures with China Shipping Agency and NVOCC. There are also other provisions on the obligations of the tour leader, the cruise insurance, the sale of cruise tickets. The shipping companies established by cruise companies in China can directly sell cruise tickets, or they can entrust qualified travel agencies and international shipping agencies to sell cruise tickets. The cruise company shall publish the guide price for ticket sales. However, as above mentioned, there are still restrictions on foreign invested cruise shipping companies to sell the cruise tickets by themselves.

The unique feature in the standards is to address "cruise ticket", which requires many contract details relating to sea carriage of passengers contracts such as the carrier's name, ship's name, voyage, departure port, approach port, return port, cabin class, boarding date, sailing time, embarkation location (dock) and other basic information, and should inform the safety of cruise travel Matters needing attention, risk warnings, etiquette regulations, civil responsibilities and obligations, voyage changes due to force majeure, risk sharing standards after cancellation, exemptions, complaint calls, legal aid channels, etc. and the number of service items on board, height, weight, Restrictive requirements such as age. The cruise company shall publish the above information through various forms such as a boarding manual, bulletin board, and website notification. Article 12 regulates "Cruise Ticket Sales and Agency Contracts" while Article 13 regulates Cruise Tourism Service Contract in which it shall include 10 clauses such as basic information, dispute settlements and compensation standards etc. Article 14 sets the Special obligation to inform for cruise companies, travel agencies, and international shipping agency companies who sell cruise tickets to tourists. Article 16&17 regulates the normal issue on the change of destination or schedule. Finally, article 18&19 regulates the dispute settlement and credit management. All in all, it is a rather comprehensive standard for different kinds of companies offering cruises service.

12 Sources of Law Applicable to Cruises

12.1 National Laws, Industry Plans and Policy

There is no special law on cruise tourism in China, the following laws are applicable to cruises: The Tourism Law of the People's Republic of China, the Port Law of the People's Republic of China, the Maritime Law of the People's Republic of China, the Regulations of the People's Republic of China on International Maritime Transport, and the Ministry of Transport on the Promotion of China's Cruise Industry Guiding Opinions on Sustainable and Healthy Development. Recently, the amendment of Chapter five, which is regulating the sea carriage of passengers in China Maritime Code is in hot discussion.

There are many special plans, policies and guidelines relating to cruise tourism at national level or rules enacted by national government authorities. In September 2018, ten departments including the Ministry of Transport, the Development and Reform Commission, the Ministry of Industry and Information Technology, the Ministry of Public Security, the Ministry of Finance, the Ministry of Commerce, the Ministry of Culture and Tourism, the General Administration of Customs, the State Administration of Taxation, and the Immigration Bureau jointly issued the document named as "Opinions Regarding Promotion the Development of China's Cruise Economy" (referred to as "Opinions"), the purpose is to promote the upgrading and development of China's cruise economy.

12.2 Local Legislation

Most of the local regulations come from Shanghai, the biggest cruise port city in China. "Shanghai International Shipping Center Construction Act" (上海国际航运中心建设条例) regulates four aspects on cruise tourism as follows: the implementation of transit and entry-exit visa-free policies within a specific time limit at cruise ports, the establishment of two-way convenient duty-free shopping stores for both inbound and outbound cruise tourists, to promote the facilitation of cruise ship supply services and accelerate the development of cruise-related service trade. The other legal resources in local lever includes "Shanghai Tourism Act", "Shanghai Standard for Cruise Operators", "Notice on Shanghai Pilot Cruise Ticket System" jointly issued by Shanghai Municipal Transportation Commission, Shanghai Tourism Administration Bureau and Shanghai Immigration Bureau (Shanghai Jiaohang (2017)1464)" etc. Now the local innovation of cruise ticket rules is upgraded to national rules and applicable in the whole country.

Also, in other cruise port cities and provinces such as Qingdao, Shenzhen, Guangzhou, Xiamen and Dalian, there are many industry policies to promote the development of cruise economy.

12.3 Regulations or Guide Lines by Different Government Authorities

Several national ministries enacted legal documents to promote cruise development. In 2009, the former National Tourism Administration Bureau (now the China Ministry of Culture and Tourism) adopted yachts and cruises as an important carrier for the development of water tourism in the "Twelfth Five-Year" development plan. The National Development and Reform Commission also included cruise ships, yachts and other related equipments into the country's catalog of industries encouraged to develop. Especially since 2012, the former National Tourism Administration Bureau has successively approved the establishment of Shanghai, Tianjin, Guangdong, Shenzhen Qingdao, Fuzhou as "China Cruise Tourism Development Experimental Zones", with the purpose to promote the rapid development of China's cruise tourism industry. In March 2017, the Ministry of Transport, the National Tourism Administration and other six departments jointly issued the "Several Opinions on Promoting the Integrated Development of Transportation and Tourism", once again proposing the development of cruise tourism. National Tourism Bureau is working with the National Development and Reform Commission, the Ministry of Finance, the Ministry of Transportation, and the National Bureau of Immigration to formulate the "National Cruise Tourism Development Master Plan." On October 10, 2019, the China (Shanghai) Cruise Tourism Development Demonstration Zone was officially inaugurated. Shanghai has become a city model for the innovative development of China's cruise tourism and will lead China and the Asia-Pacific cruise market into a stage of high-quality development.

13 Conclusions

To sum up, the legal rules in China relating to cruise are fragmented, no special law on cruises, most of rules are industry policies. Recently there is the trend to reform China Maritime Code and China Tourism Law to adapt to the new development of cruise industry. Innovation of cruise industry brings new legal issues in China. Some local rules, in particular, enacted by Shanghai and other main cruise port cities can be the legal safeguards for cruises in China.

References

Baatz (ed) (2018) Maritime law, 2018th edn. Informa law from Routledge

Hu (2015) Transport law in China, 2015th edn. Kluwer Law International

Lewins K (2016) Cruise ship operators, their passengers, Australian consumer law and state civil liability acts (Part II). Aust N Z Maritime Law J 30

Yuan Zhenmin's translation: International Travel Contract Convention. Law Translation Series 1992, third issue

Wang (ed) (2016) Annual report on China's cruise industry (2017), 2016th edn. Social Sciences Academic Press (China)

Wang (ed) (2017) Annual report on China's cruise industry (2017), 2017th edn. Social Sciences Academic Press (China)

Xiao-nian Li Ph.D of Law in Kyushu University, Japan. Senior Research Fellow, Director of 21st Century Maritime Silk Road Institute, Faculty of the Applied Economics. Visiting Scholar and of UNIDROIT, Guest Profess of UBC, Canada. She has already published more than 10 books, 30 academic reports, more than 50 academic papers on Maritime Law and Cruise Tourism. Academic affiliation: Institute of Maritime Silk Road, Shanghai Academy of Social Sciences. Address: 7 Huaihai Middle Road 622, Shanghai, China. Telephone number: +86 18916261180. email: lxn2017@sass.org.cn.

Si-qi Sun Ph.D of Shanghai Maritime University, now is a lecturer in the university. He has already published more than 50 papers on Maritime Law. His first book, Elements of Cruise Tourism Law, was published by Law Press China in November 2018. He is also a member of working group of the revision of Chinese Maritime Code. Academic affiliation: Law School, Shanghai Maritime University. Address: 1550 Haigang Ave, Shanghai, P.R. China 201306. Telephone number: 86 13681642003. email: sqsun@shmtu.edu.cn.

Japan National Report: Cruise Industry in Japan and Applicable Laws and Regulations

Fumiko Masuda, Shinichi Takano, and Takashi Hakoi

Abstract This report aims to give an overview of Japanese law relating to cruises. No legislation specifically designed for cruises exists under the Japanese legal system. Therefore, cruises are generally subject to regulations and private laws on marine transport, ports, environment, carriage of passengers, travel agencies, consumer contracts, international contracts and so on. The government initiative to encourage cruise businesses is also taken within the existing regulatory framework.

1 General

The Japanese legal system belongs to the civil law family and has a clear distinction between public law and private law.[1] Cruise operators may be subject to relevant public regulations relating to marine transport, seafarers, port authorities or the environment. Travel companies selling, for example, package holidays, including cruises, are also subject to administrative regulations. The application of these rules is territorially limited (see Sects. 3.1, 3.2.1, 3.2.2, 3.5, and 3.6). While there are no public regulations specifically addressed to the cruise industry, the government is willing to accommodate cruise operators' demands within the existing regulatory

[1] However, it should be noted that the Japanese judicial system is unitary and centralised under the Supreme Court of Japan: There are no special courts dealing with constitutional or administrative issues.

F. Masuda (✉)
Okayama University, Okayama, Japan
e-mail: fumiko.masuda@okayama-u.ac.jp

S. Takano
Amemiya Law Office, Tokyo, Japan
e-mail: takano@maritimelaw.jp

T. Hakoi
Waseda University, Tokyo, Japan
e-mail: htaka@waseda.jp

C. Fresnedo de Aguirre (ed.), *Legal Aspects of Cruises*, Ius Comparatum - Global Studies in Comparative Law 56, https://doi.org/10.1007/978-3-030-83090-8_12

framework, considering the growing importance of tourism and the cruise industry (see Sect. 2).

Contracts and torts are generally governed by the general rules in the Civil Code along with some special rules in the Commercial Code (see Sects. 3.1, 3.2.4, and 3.3), and these rules will be applicable to international civil or commercial disputes through conflict of law rules (see Sect. 4.1). Consumers are protected by special legislation (see Sect. 3.2). The Japanese legislature has never enacted specific rules for cruise contracts and civil liability of cruise operators, and therefore, the general and special rules above apply to these matters. This report is based on the law and facts before the COVID-19 crisis.

2 The Cruise Industry in Japan

2.1 Background

The cruise industry did not attract much public attention until the mid-2010s in Japan. In 1989, some major Japanese shipping companies launched leisure cruise services with luxurious ships, and in 2013, the global cruise lines under Carnival Corporation & plc started to offer regular cruise services departing from and returning to Japanese ports. Both attempts failed to boost consumer demands for cruises in Japan at that time. It was only after a considerable number of Chinese tourists began to visit Japan by cruise ship that the Japanese government recognised the potential economic impact of the cruise industry and inbound tourism (Ikeda 2019). The government now actively tries to promote cruise travel (see Sect. 2.2).

2.2 Government Initiatives to Promote Cruise Businesses (Question 4)

The Ministerial Council on the Promotion of Japan as a Tourism-Oriented Country has set out annual action programmes to promote inbound tourism since 2013 based on the Basic Act on the Promotion of Japan as a Tourism-Oriented Country (Act No. 117 of 2006).[2] Supporting inbound cruise businesses is one of the core policies in the programmes. The action programmes contain various plans to respond to increasing demands for accessible cruise ports and smooth immigration clearance for cruise passengers.

In accordance with the policy strategy, access to Japanese ports has improved. For example, some berths for cargo vessels are made available for cruise ships; the

[2]The programmes can be accessed at the Tourism Agency's website (see References), but only in Japanese.

Ministry of Land, Infrastructure, Transport and Tourism (MLIT) started to provide a single contact point for all enquiries relating to cruises to pass them on to relevant administrative authorities and to give their responses back to the enquirers in 2013. The portal website of cruise ports and nearby tourism attractions was opened in 2014 by the Japan Tourism Agency;[3] since 2016, the MLIT has implemented a subsidy programme for local governments or private entities that intend to improve and modernise port facilities to safely and efficiently accommodate cruise passengers.[4] In addition, the Port and Harbour Act was amended in 2017 to enable local port authorities to solicit investment in the passenger terminal facilities from global cruise lines.[5]

2.3 *Statistics (Questions 1–3)*

The Statistics Bureau of Japan regularly produces key statistics, and the MLIT generates statistics on transport and tourism.[6] In addition, the MLIT has published statistics on cruises every year since 2016 and delivers a monthly report on the number of cruise ship calls at Japanese ports on its website. The MLIT annual statistics include the number of Japanese passengers who travel by cruise ship domestically or internationally, their purposes of cruise trips, the length of their voyages, their destinations, the approximate number of foreign visitors by cruise ship and the number of cruise ship calls at Japanese ports. Statistical information on travel in general is available on the website of the Japan Tourism Agency. The international visitor survey covers the consumption behaviour of cruise ship tourists

[3] The Japan Tourism Agency is an administrative agency affiliated with the MLIT, which was established in 2008.

[4] In the 2019 fiscal year, 712 036 000 yen was granted to the projects at 19 ports for measures including renovation of passenger terminals, construction of roofed passages or installation of a mobile boarding bridge, which cost 2 136 110 000 yen in the aggregate.

[5] Act to amend a part of the Port and Harbour Act (Act No. 55 of 2017). Under the amended Port and Harbour Act, the MLIT may designate any international port suitable for accommodating large cruise ships as a 'Kokusai-ryokyakusen-kyoten-keisei-kowan' (prospective international hub port for passenger ships). The port authority of the designated port is to develop a construction plan for the port facilities; it is then expected to make an agreement with the relevant private partner, that is, the investing cruise company. The cruise company has preferential access to the port facilities, including the berthing facilities, but the access to the passenger terminal constructed under the plan must be open to other operators when the investing cruise company does not need to use the facilities. Currently, the following nine ports are designated as the potential hub ports: Yokohama Port, Shimizu Port, Sasebo Port, Yatsushiro Port, Motobu Port, Hirara Port, Kagoshima Port, Shimonoseki Port and Naha Port.

[6] Some of the data are also available in English at the website 'e-Stat: The portal site of official statistics of Japan'. The MLIT statistics include those on volume of transport on a mode-by-mode basis, the number of ships calling at Japanese ports and so on. Statistics on the wages of seafarers working on board Japanese ships are also available in Japanese at the portal website, but these do not distinguish cruise workers from other seafarers working on general passenger ships.

departing from Hakata Port in Fukuoka, Nagasaki Port and Naha Port in Okinawa. Port cities, such as Yokohama or Kobe, also collect statistical data relating to the ports located in the cities.[7]

The statistics show that the cruise industry has recently been growing in its importance.[8] The number of calls at Japanese ports nearly tripled, increasing from 1001 (628 by foreign operators and 373 by Japanese operators) in 2013 to 2930 (1913 by foreign operators and 1017 by Japanese operators) in 2018. The number of foreign visitors by cruise ship in 2018 was 14 times bigger than that in 2013, growing to 2451 thousand from 174 thousand. Meanwhile, the number of Japanese cruise passengers rose to 321.1 thousand in 2018 from 238.2 thousand in 2013. Hakata Port, Naha Port and Nagasaki Port are three major cruise ports that had more than 200 calls in 2018. Yokohama Port ranks fourth, with 168 calls. Cruise tourists to Japan mainly come from China.

2.4 *Impact of Cruises on Employment (Question 6)*

It is sometimes argued that cruise ship calling at Japanese ports contributes to local tourism business, but it has yet to be analysed how much employment the cruise business generates. In terms of employment of seafarers, the impact of cruise business remains small. There are several institutions devoted to education and training for prospective seafarers, but the Japanese shipping industry chronically suffers from a shortage of seafarers and relies on foreign nationals in international shipping. The operation of cruise ships is no exception.

2.5 *Cruise-Related Services (Questions 5, 7 and 8)*

It is said that the services offered to cruises in Japanese ports are of good quality. Some shipbuilding companies, such as Mitsubishi Heavy Industries, Ltd (MHI) or Japan Marine United Cooperation (JMU), have a good reputation for building large

[7] Yokohama City estimates that the economic effect attributable to cruise travel per cruise ship call in Yokohama amounts to 246 million yen in the case of world cruises by 50 000 GT Japanese ship, 62 million yen in the case of domestic cruise by 50 000 GT Japanese ship and 120 million yen in the case of Asia cruise by 110,000 GT foreign ship (City of Yokohama 2017). The estimation is said to be based on the amount of port charges, fuel and water supply to the ships, ship equipment, passengers' consumption and visitors' consumption, as well as interviews. The spending of cruise tourists in Japan was 39 710 yen per person in 2019 according to the international visitor survey.

[8] An analysis suggests that the nationwide economic impact of cruises in 2017, including direct effects and ripple effects, can be estimated at 215.9 billion yen (Sasaki et al. 2018). It is argued that the economic impacts and contribution to local economy vary depending on the roles of ports in cruise ship operation (Sakai and Yuguchi 2016).

passenger ships, although MHI announced withdrawal from large cruise ship building businesses in 2016. Several smaller shipyards also have the capacity to build small or medium-sized passenger ships.

3 Laws and Regulations Applicable to Cruises

3.1 General (Questions 9–16, 20, 22, 27, 31, 45 and 46)

No special legislation exclusively for cruise business exists in Japanese law.[9] Therefore, cruise operators are subject to relevant general regulations as follows: the Marine Transport Act (Act No. 187 of 1959); the Act on Prevention of Collisions at Sea (Act No. 62 of 1977) implementing the Convention on the International Regulations for Preventing Collisions at Sea, 1972 (COLREGs); and the Port and Harbour Act (for Question 27); the Act on Prevention of Marine Pollution and Maritime Disaster (Act No. 136 of 1970) regarding Question 31 (see Sects. 3.5 and 3.6). As for Questions 20 and 22, the Seafarers Act (Act No. 100 of 1947) regulates conditions of employment of seafarers (see Sect. 3.4).

Japan is not a Contracting State of the Athens Convention relating to the Carriage of Passengers and their Luggage by Sea (PAL) 1974 or its 2002 Protocol. With respect to commercial or civil matters, the general law of obligations provided in the Civil Code (Act No. 89 of 1896) applies to cruise contracts and the civil liability of cruise operators. The Commercial Code (Act No. 48 of 1899) contains special rules on the liability of carriers for the damage sustained by passengers (see Sect. 3.3). It should be noted, however, that contracts for travel are subject to the regulations on contract terms under the Travel Agency Act (Act No. 239 of 1952), and that any contracts, as far as they fall within the definition of 'consumer contracts', are regulated by the Consumer Contract Act (Act No. 61 of 2000; see Sect. 3.2). As for Questions 14–16, 45 and 46, these general rules of national origin, which are not specifically designed for cruises, apply to cruise contracts and non-contracting obligations arising out of, or in connection with, cruise contracts when Japanese law applies, in cases of international contracts, through the choice of law rules described in Sect. 4.

3.2 Regulations on Contract (Question 18)

Consumer travellers or passengers are protected by a multi-layered legal regime under Japanese law, including regulatory acts on travel contracts (Sect. 3.2.1) and

[9] Therefore, the answer to Question 9 is 'No', and Questions 10–14 are not applicable.

transport contracts (Sect. 3.2.2), the Consumer Contract Act (Sect. 3.2.3) and relevant rules in the Civil Code (Sect. 3.2.4).

3.2.1 Travel Contracts

3.2.1.1 Regulatory Regime

Cruise passengers often conclude contracts including cruise services through travel companies. The Travel Agency Act seeks to protect the interests of travellers with administrative measures, violation of which will trigger administrative penalty. For instance, travel agencies must be registered by the commissioner of the Japan Tourism Agency before they start business (Articles 3–6-4); travel agencies are required to deposit a specified amount of money at competent legal affairs bureaus as financial security for their transactions with travellers in case the travel agencies become insolvent (Articles 7–9); the conditions for travel contracts must be approved by the commissioner of the Japan Tourism Agency beforehand (Article 12-2). To be approved by the commissioner, the conditions for travel contracts must satisfy the two following requirements: the conditions must not be detrimental to the legitimate interests of travellers, and the conditions must contain clear stipulations on receipt of fees and/or any other payments from travellers and their refunding, as well as the liability of the travel agency. The commissioners of the Japan Tourism Agency and the Consumer Affairs Agency[10] may lay down 'standard conditions for travel contracts' for the convenience of travel agencies,[11] and if a travel agency chooses to use the standard conditions as its conditions for travel contracts, its conditions are deemed to be approved by the commissioner of the Japan Tourism Agency. Travel agencies are also obliged to explain the fees, relevant travel services and their prices to the applicant travellers, and when the agencies have arranged travel, they must immediately give details of these matters in writing, or if the travellers agree, by electronic means.

3.2.1.2 Terms of Travel Contracts and Liability of Travel Agencies

The terms and conditions for travel contracts are standardised through administrative supervision as described above. As travel agencies provide a wide variety of services to (potential) travellers, the standard conditions for travel contracts are divided into five parts, which are as follows: (1) pre-fixed package travel, (2) custom-made package travel, (3) arrangement of travel services for travellers, (4) services relating

[10]The Consumer Affairs Agency is an administrative agency affiliated to the Cabinet Office; it was established in 2009.

[11]The standard conditions were promulgated by the Notice of Ministry of Transport in 1983 and have been amended several times since then.

to formalities of immigration clearance and (5) travel consultation. The current standard conditions do not contain specific provisions on package travel consisting of flights and cruises,[12] but the travel agencies selling this type of package holiday are supposed to draft appropriate conditions and obtain the approval required under the Travel Agency Act.

It is generally agreed that travel agencies providing travel services categorised as (1), (2) or (3) above undertake to arrange, rather than perform, safe and appropriate travel services, and they are not automatically responsible for any failure of the actual service providers, such as carriers, hotels or cruise lines. Therefore, it is when damage incurred by a traveller is caused by the travel agency's breach of obligations to arrange travel services or to give appropriate information to the traveller that the travel agency will be held liable for damages (Articles 415 and 416, Civil Code). However, under the standard conditions, travel agencies selling package holidays, (1) and (2) above, promise to pay a specified amount of compensation and/or consolation money in case travellers lose their lives, experience injury or lose their belongings during the package travel, irrespective of whether the relevant travel agencies are legally liable for the accidents (Miura 2018, pp. 163–167).[13] Travel agencies take out insurance to cover the agreed liability. In principle, travellers are also entitled to a specified amount of compensation when travel services are substantially changed.[14]

3.2.2 Contracts for Carriage of Passengers

While domestic public transport is subject to similar but not identical administrative regulations to those applicable to travel agencies, Japanese law imposes less rigorous regulations on cruise contracts as contracts for carriage of passengers. Under the Marine Transport Act, ship operators who intend to provide domestic non-liner services must obtain permission from the minister of Land, Infrastructure, Transport and Tourism, specifying the planned sea route (Article 21). Their conditions of

[12] The authors understand that 'combined trips' in Question 24 means this type of package travel.

[13] For example, in cases of overseas travel, if a traveller were to lose their life, the heir(s) would be entitled to 25 million yen; if a traveller were injured and admitted to hospital, 40–400 thousand would be paid to the traveller for consolation, depending on the number of days of hospitalisation; and if a traveller were to lose their personal belongings, actual value of the lost property will be compensated to the traveller, with an upper limit of 150 thousand. When a legally liable travel agency pays damages to the traveller or their heir, and if the amount of damages exceeds that of compensation, the damages paid will be deducted from the compensation and/or consolation money. Of course, there are some exceptions to this scheme.

[14] For instance, if a hotel described in the travel contract is changed to a different one after the contracted travel starts, the traveller can claim 2 per cent of the price for the package holiday. The rate is 1 per cent if the travel has not yet started. The standard conditions list nine events that give rise to such claims. Changes due to overbooking are covered by the scheme, while the scheme is disapplied where the travel agency is legally liable for the changes and the traveller has a claim for damages. There are also some exceptions to this scheme.

carriage must be submitted to and approved by the minister (Article 9). International non-liner services are not covered by such regulations.

Considering the lack of legal protection for travellers enjoying international cruises, the Japan Oceangoing Passenger Ship Association (JOPA) drew up a model contract for international cruises in 1991 (Shintani and Hachisuga 1991). Japanese cruise ship operators adopt the essence of this model contract.

3.2.3 Consumer Contracts

If a cruise contract is a 'consumer contract', that is, a contract concluded between a 'business operator' and a 'consumer' (Article 2 (3), Consumer Contract Act), then the passenger or traveller is protected by the Consumer Contract Act.[15] The Act defines a consumer as 'an individual natural person except when they become a party to a contract as or for their business' and a business operator as 'a legal person or any other form of associations, or an individual natural person when they become a party to a contract as or for their business' (Article 2 (1) and (2), Consumer Contract Act). The Act specifically invalidates any contract term that purports to exempt the business operator totally from any liability arising out of or in connection with the consumer contract, as well as any term limiting liability of the business operator for losses caused by an intentional act or gross negligence on the part of the business operator (Article 8 (1), Consumer Contract Act).[16] Conditions of contracts incorporating PAL will be invalidated by the Act as far as the conditions conflict with Article 8 (1).

The Act also renders the following contract terms null and void:[17] a term that deprives the consumer of the right to terminate the consumer contract (Article 8-2, Consumer Contract Act); a liquidated damages clause or penalty clause that obliges the consumer to pay damages exceeding the average amount of losses in case the consumer terminates the consumer contract (Article 9, Consumer Contract Act); or any contract term that restricts the rights of the consumer or imposes further obligations on the consumer in comparison with the default rules in law and damage

[15] The Consumer Contract Act also protects consumers from undue influence in concluding consumer contracts, giving the right to avoid the contracts more widely than the Civil Code does (Articles 4 and 5).

[16] Japanese law allows concurrence of claims. Article 8 (1) (i) and (ii) covers clauses exonerating business operators from contractual liability, and Article 8 (1) (iii) and (iv) deal with tort liability arising in connection with the performance of the consumer contracts. A claim arising from a contract shall be extinguished by prescription unless the claim is invoked within five years from the time the creditor has come to know that the claim is enforceable, or within ten years from the time the claim has become objectively enforceable (Article 166 (1), Civil Code). A tort claim shall be extinguished by prescription within three years from the time when the victim has come to know of the damage and the identity of the wrongdoer, or twenty years from the time when the tortious act has been committed (Article 742, Civil Code).

[17] The terms listed here are not exhaustive. Articles 8, 8-2 and 9 include the blacklist of invalid terms, and Article 10 is a catch-all clause.

the interests of the consumer so unilaterally that it is contrary to the fundamental principle of good faith declared in Article 1 (2) of the Civil Code (Article 10, Consumer Contract Act).

3.2.4 Other Relevant Rules in the Civil Code

Other aspects of contracts, such as formation or termination of contracts, and torts are governed by the Civil Code[18] except the special rules in the Commercial Code described in Sect. 3.3. The law of obligations was modernised by the Act to Revise a Part of the Civil Code (Act No. 44 of 2017), which came into force on 1 April 2020. The revised Civil Code has rules on incorporation of the general terms and conditions used for 'standardised transactions' (Articles 548-2–548-4).[19] As cruise contracts will usually fall under the definition of standardised transactions in the provision, in concluding cruise contracts, cruise operators need to clearly show the travellers their intent that they want to make the contracts based on their terms and conditions. They should also be aware that terms too onerous to the travellers will not be incorporated into the contracts under the rules. The rules apply irrespective of whether the contract in question is a 'consumer contract'.

3.3 Special Private Law Rules on Carriage of Passengers (Question 15)

3.3.1 Special Rules in the Commercial Code, Particularly on the Liability of Carriers

Some aspects of contracts for carriage of passengers are governed by Articles 589–594 of the Commercial Code. These provisions were modernised by the Act

[18] As the Japanese Civil Code follows the German Pandectist approach, the relevant rules in Book I: General Rules and Book III: The Law of Obligations govern contractual issues. Book III consists of the general rules and the rules on contracts, *negotiorum gestio*, unjust enrichment and torts.

[19] Article 548-2 provides that a party that agrees to enter into a 'standardised transaction' shall be deemed to agree to the respective clauses in the general terms and conditions for the transaction when the party agrees to incorporate the general terms and conditions into the contract ((1) (i)) or when the other party that has prepared the general terms and conditions declares its intent to incorporate them into the contract to the party before entering into the transaction ((1) (ii)). The party shall not be deemed to agree to such clauses in the general terms and conditions as restricting the rights of the party or imposing further obligations on the party and unilaterally damaging the interests of the party, contrary to the fundamental principle of good faith in light of how transactions are conducted, the realities of the transactions and common social sense in such transactions (Article 548-2 (2)). A 'standardised transaction' is defined as one of the transactions that the drafting party is expected to make with many and unspecified persons and in which it is reasonable to the both contracting parties that the terms of transactions are wholly or partly standardised. Regarding the revised Civil Code, see Tsutsui and Muramatsu (2018).

to Revise a Part of the Commercial Code and the International Carriage of Goods by Sea Act (Act No. 29 of 2018), which came into force on 1 April 2019.[20] The rules in the Commercial Code take precedence over those provided by the Civil Code (Article 1, Commercial Code), but they do not override the rules in the Consumer Contract Act (Article 11, Consumer Contract Act).

A contract for carriage of passengers is defined as a 'contract under which a carrier undertakes to carry a passenger, and the passenger promises to pay fare for the result' (Article 589). The carrier is liable for any damage sustained by the passenger due to the transport unless the carrier proves that it has exercised due care in carrying the passenger (Article 590). Article 591 invalidates any contract term that purports to exclude or reduce the liability of the carrier arising from the loss of life or personal injury of the passenger, with three exceptions. The exceptions are clauses excluding or reducing liability caused by delay in arrival; such clauses agreed under the circumstances where carriage takes place under the threat of massive fire such as volcano eruption, an earthquake or any other disaster; such clauses agreed when the carrier undertakes to carry a vulnerable person whose condition will be liable to deteriorate to a critical level because of the vibration or any other conditions normally associated with transport. Therefore, conditions of carriage limiting the liability of the cruise operator for the death of or personal injury to a passenger in accordance with the PAL will be void insofar as they reduce the liability of the cruise operator when the operator's fault has caused the death or injury.

The carrier is liable for the loss of, damage to or delay in arrival of the luggage the carrier takes delivery from the passenger unless the carrier proves that it has exercised due care as if it were a carrier undertaking carriage of goods (Article 592 (1)). Regarding cabin luggage and personal belongings, the carrier is liable for losses only when the passenger proves that the losses have been caused by an intentional act or negligence on the part of the carrier (Article 593 (1)). Contract terms limiting the liability for losses related to luggage and belongings will be valid under the Commercial Code.[21]

3.3.2 Special Rules on Global Limitation of Shipowners' Liability

Japan is a Contracting State to the 1996 Protocol of the Convention on Limitation of Liability for Maritime Claims (LLMC), and the Act on Limitation of Shipowner Liability (Act No. 94 of 1975) incorporates the rules of the Convention and sets down procedures for limitation of shipowners' liability. However, Japan chooses to

[20] Before the revision, the Commercial Code also contained special provisions for carriage of passengers by sea, but these provisions were deleted because many were too obsolete.

[21] The rules on liability of carriers who undertake carriage of goods (Articles 570–588, Commercial Code) are non-mandatory, and therefore, the contracting parties are free to agree on the liability of such carriers as far as the agreement is not against the public policy (Article 90, Civil Code), subject to the general restrictions described in Sects. 3.2.3 and 3.2.4.

exclude the claims for the loss of life or personal injury to the passenger of a ship from the global limitation scheme in accordance with Article 15 (3*bis*). Therefore, the carrier's liability for loss of life or personal injury to passengers is unlimited under Japanese law, not only in that contractual limitation is prohibited by the Commercial Code (see Sect. 3.3.1) but also in that the liability is not subject to the global limitation.

3.4 *Labour Rules for Cruise Workers (Questions 20–25)*

No special legislation for cruise workers exists in Japanese law.[22] The Seafarers Act is a special statute to the Labour Standard Act (Act No. 49 of 1947) to provide labour standards fitting for seafarers. The statute of national origin was revised by the Act to Revise a Part of the Seafarers Act (Act No. 87 of 2012) to implement the Maritime Labour Convention 2006, and it took on a clear international character. The International Convention on Standards of Training, Certification and Watchkeeping for Seafarers 1978 (STCW) is incorporated into Japanese law partly by the Seafarers Act and partly by the Act on Ship Officers and Boat Operators (Act No. 149 of 1951).

3.5 *Rules on Ports Relevant to Cruises (Questions 27–29)*

Apart from the policy-led scheme described in Sect. 2.2 under the Port and Harbour Act, no specific rules for cruises are provided by any acts relating to ports. Sea traffic in port areas is governed by the Act on Port Regulation (Act No. 174 of 1948), a special domestic legislation relating to the Act on Prevention of Collisions at Sea, which has international origin. The Port and Harbour Act and other acts relating to ports are of national origin.

Information on taxes or port charges is available on the website of each port. For example, as of 1 October 2019, for an oceangoing vessel for international voyage exceeding 700 GT to enter the Yokohama Port, 2.70 yen per gross tonne is to be paid. The wharfage is 10.5 yen per gross tonne for the mooring of less than 12 h, and an additional 6.7 yen per gross tonne must be paid for extra hours, levied every 12 h. Separate charges are imposed for the use of passenger facilities.

---

[22] This is also true for 'combined trips' in Question 24. Therefore, the answer to the first question in Question 24 is 'No', and Question 25 is not applicable.

3.6 Rules on Environmental Impact of Cruises (Questions 31 and 32)

The Act on Prevention of Marine Pollution and Maritime Disaster was originally enacted as a part of measures to grapple with environmental pollution at large in 1970. It is by this Act that the Protocols to the International Convention for the Prevention of Pollution from Ships (MARPOL) are implemented under Japanese law.

Japan became a State Party to the International Convention on Civil Liability for Bunker Oil Pollution Damage 2001 (BUNKER) and Nairobi International Convention on the Removal of Wrecks 2007 in 2020. Both Conventions are implemented by the Act on Liability for Oil Pollution Damage Caused by Ships (Act No. 95 of 1975), which was originally enacted to incorporate the International Convention on Civil Liability for Oil Pollution Damage 1969 (CLC) and the International Convention on the Establishment of an International Fund for Compensation for Oil Pollution Damage 1971 (FUND); it has been amended several times to reflect amendments or developments relating to the Conventions. Other relevant acts on environmental protection, which are either of national or international origin, will apply to cruise operators accordingly.

3.7 Case Law on Cruises (Questions 19, 26, 30 and 33)

There are unreported cases where cruise passengers brought action against the company, which was the travel agency selling, and the time charterer of the vessel employed for, around-the-world cruise travel.[23] In one case, the travellers sought damages for delay or changes in the itinerary and for degraded services due to malfunctioning interior facilities and engine troubles. In another case, the travellers claimed damages for long suspension of voyage and degraded services due to blackout leading to engine shutdown, first in the South China Sea and second in the waters off Somalia. The liability of the company was denied because it neither took responsibility as carrier nor warranted the quality of services to be provided by the carrier (see Sect. 3.2.1.2).[24] To the authors' knowledge, no other cases on cruises under Japanese law have been reported so far.

---

[23] The first case is the Judgement of Tokyo District Court, 28 May 2014, and the second case is Judgement of Tokyo District Court, 13 January 2017, approved by Judgement of Tokyo Hight Court, 29 June 2017. The defendant travel agency in the cases is the same.

[24] Compensation for substantial changes described in Sect. 3.2.1.2 was also denied in these cases because the list giving rise to the compensation claim in the standard conditions for travel contracts at that time did not cover this type of events. The list of events was revised later.

4 Private International Law Aspects

4.1 General (Questions 34, 35, 40 and 41)

Japanese law does not have any special rules for cruises regarding jurisdiction, arbitration or choice of laws. No special rules for carriage of passengers exist either.[25]

The Code of Civil Procedure (CCP; Act No. 109 of 1996) provides for when Japanese courts shall exercise jurisdiction over international civil or commercial disputes.[26] The Arbitration Act (Act No. 138 of 2003), which is based on UNCITRAL Model Law on International Commercial Arbitration 1985 without the amendments adopted in 2006, lays down the requirements for valid arbitration agreements. The validity of arbitration clauses at the stage of recognition and enforcement of arbitral awards is governed by the Convention on the Recognition and Enforcement of Foreign Arbitral Awards 1958 (New York Convention), to which Japan became a Contracting State in 1961. The Act on General Rules for Application of Laws (AGRAL; Act No. 78 of 2006), which sets out principles of choice of laws, contains rules to determine which law is applicable to an international contract. All the rules contain special provisions for consumer contracts. As for Questions 34, 35, 40 and 41, general rules on jurisdiction, arbitration and choice of laws apply to international disputes arising from or in connection with cruise contracts, and consumer travellers will enjoy protection under each regime.

4.2 Jurisdiction (Questions 35, 36 and 39)

Because of the provisions on consumer protection, whether a Japanese court has jurisdiction over disputes relating to a cruise contract will depend on which party to the contract intends to bring an action before the Japanese court.

[25] The only exception is the carriage by air governed by the Montreal Convention 1999 or other air law conventions.

[26] Until 2011, the CCP did not contain express provisions on jurisdiction over international disputes. Japanese courts analogously applied the rules on territorial jurisdiction over domestic disputes to international disputes, and necessarily, there was no express provision to protect consumers in international contracts. The CCP was amended by the Act to revise a part of the CCP and the Civil Provisional Remedies Act (Act No. 36 of 2011), which came into force on 1 April 2012, to lay down express rules on international jurisdiction. The revised Code contains provisions designed to protect a contracting party in a weaker position than a counter party, that is, consumers and employees. See Sato and Kobayashi (2012) in general.

4.2.1 When a Consumer Traveller Sues the Cruise Operator

In accordance with general rules on international jurisdiction, a cruise passenger as a contracting party to the cruise contract will have access to Japanese courts in the following cases:

- When the defendant cruise company has its principal office in Japan (or when its representative or any other principal person in charge of its business is domiciled in Japan in case the company has no office or the location of its office is unknown; Article 3-2 (3), CCP).[27]
- When the place of performance of the obligation in question, as specified in the contract or determined by the governing law chosen by the parties, is located in Japan under the cruise contract (Article 3-3 (i), CCP).
- When the cruise operator has an office or a place of business in Japan and the passenger's claim is related to the activities carried out by the office or the place of business (Article 3-3 (iv), CCP).
- When the cruise operator engages in business in Japan, irrespective of whether it has an office or a place of business in Japan, and the passenger's claim is related to the operator's business in Japan (Article 3-3 (v), CCP).
- Where the passenger is a 'consumer' under the Article 3-4 of the CCP, that is, an individual natural person except when they become a party to a contract as or for their business, when their domicile[28] is located in Japan either at the time of bringing an action against the cruise operator or at the time of concluding the consumer cruise contract (Article 3-4 (1), CCP).

A cruise passenger could also bring an action in tort for damages, in which case, Japanese courts shall in principle have jurisdiction when the tort occurred in Japan, that is, when the harmful act is committed in Japan or when the direct result of such act is realised in Japan (Article 3-3 (viii), CCP).

The CCP also contains special rules for maritime claims. If the passenger's claim is secured by a maritime lien,[29] the passenger may bring an action before a Japanese court when the ship to which the lien is attached is located in Japan (Article 3-3 (vi), CCP). Regarding claims for damages arising from a collision of ships or any other accident at sea, Japanese courts shall have jurisdiction when the first place at which

---

[27] Theoretically, if a cruise operator is a natural person, which is unlikely in practice, Japanese courts, in principle, shall have jurisdiction over disputes against the person when they are domiciled in Japan (Article 3-2 (1)).

[28] The concept of domicile under Japanese law is not as strict as it is in common law jurisdictions. Article 22 of the Civil Code provides that the principal place wherein a person lives shall be their domicile.

[29] Article 842 of the Commercial Code gives maritime liens of the first rank to the claims for damages arising from loss of life or personal injury occurring on board or in direct connection with the operation of the ship.

the damaged ship has arrived is located in Japan (Article 3-3 (ix), CCP).[30] A consumer claimant may invoke any of the bases of jurisdiction provided by Articles 3-2, 3-3 and 3-4 of the CCP, as described above.

4.2.2 When the Cruise Operator Sues the Consumer Traveller

When a cruise operator attempts to sue a consumer passenger, the options listed in Article 3-3 of the CCP are not available (Article 3-4 (3), CCP). As a result, the operator can start proceedings before a Japanese court only when the consumer passenger is domiciled in Japan at the time of bringing an action (Articles 3-2 (1), 3-4 (1), CCP) or was domiciled in Japan at the time the consumer made the contract with the operator (Article 3-4 (1), CCP).

4.2.3 Rejection of Taking Jurisdiction

Japanese courts may dismiss the whole or part of the proceedings if special circumstances surrounding the case require them to do so in light of fairness between the parties and the proper and efficient conduct of a hearing (Article 3-9, CCP). The net effect of this rule is similar to that of *forum non-convenience*, which allows a court to discretionally dismiss or suspend a case.

4.2.4 How Consumers Are Protected Under the Rules (Question 36)

The provisions above protect the passenger as a consumer as follows:

- First, a consumer passenger living in Japan can usually bring an action against a cruise operator before a Japanese court. A consumer who lived in Japan at the time of contracting but has since moved to a different country can also sue the cruise operator in Japan if it is convenient for them.
- Second, such passengers will not be forced to appear before a foreign court by the cruise operator. Japanese courts cannot reach out to a consumer who is domiciled in Japan and sued before a foreign court, for example, by ordering the cruise operator to stop foreign proceedings. Nevertheless, if the consumer simply chooses not to respond to an action before the foreign court, the decision rendered by the foreign court will not be recognised and enforced in Japan on the grounds that the foreign court lacks jurisdiction under the Japanese jurisdiction rules (Article 118 (i), Article 3-4 (3), CCP). Thus, the CCP practically deprives the efficacy of foreign proceedings against consumers living in Japan.

[30] By the same token, Japanese courts shall have jurisdiction over an action relating to salvage when the salvage was performed in Japan or where the first place at which the salvaged ship arrived is located in Japan (Article 3-3 (x), CCP).

- Third, a consumer having no domicile in Japan will not be forced to appear before a Japanese court by the cruise operator, while they may bring an action before a Japanese court if the cruise operator has its principal place of business in Japan (Article 3-2 (3), CCP) or any of the options listed in Article 3-3 of the CCP are applicable, subject to the caveat of Article 3-9 of the CCP.

4.2.5 Validity of Forum Selection Clauses (Question 37)

Generally, Japanese courts have generously enforced choice-of-court agreements in international contracts in accordance with the requirements established by *The Cisadane* (Supreme Court Judgement on 28 November 1975, Minshu vol. 29 (10) 1554), which held that an exclusive jurisdiction clause in a bill of lading selecting a court at the principal place of business of the carrier was valid. Most of the requirements are now expressly provided in the CCP. Article 3-7 (1)–(3) roughly provides that a choice-of-court clause is valid on the conditions that the agreement satisfies a formal requirement (in writing or by electronic or magnetic means) and the agreement is concerned with an action arising from a certain legal relationship. The formal requirement is relaxed as a bill of lading containing a jurisdiction clause on the back proved sufficient, although it seems that much depends on the particular circumstances of each case. An exclusive jurisdiction clause designating a foreign court will be valid unless it is contrary to the public policy of the Japanese legal system. In case the designated court is legally or factually unable to exercise jurisdiction, the clause may not be invoked (Article 3-7 (4)).

The validity and effect of choice-of-court agreements in consumer contracts are significantly curtailed by Article 3-7 (5) (i) of the CCP. It is only when a choice-of-court agreement designates a court of the consumer's domicile at the time of contracting that such agreement made before disputes arising between a cruise operator and a consumer passenger will be held valid and effective. Even if a clause is intended to be an exclusive jurisdiction clause, the clause shall not have a derogative effect and be interpreted as just giving a consumer another option on where to sue. For example, a clause stating that a passenger shall bring an action exclusively before a court of the country where the cruise operator has its principal place of business will not be given an intended effect: The clause will be valid only when the counter party, a consumer, happens to be domiciled in the same country as the operator's principal place of business at the time they have concluded a contract, and it will not prevent the consumer from bringing an action before any other courts competent under the statutory jurisdiction rules.

Despite the restriction of party autonomy above, if a consumer passenger commences proceedings in the chosen court based on the jurisdiction clause or mounts a defence by invoking the jurisdiction clause before any other court where the cruise operator brings an action against the consumer, the jurisdiction clause shall take effect (Article 3-7 (5) (ii), CCP). Moreover, a cruise operator can enter into a jurisdiction agreement with a consumer after disputes arise between them, and such agreement will be valid and effective because the special rule under Article

3-7 (5) (i) of the CCP does not cover jurisdiction agreements made after disputes arise.

4.2.6 Possible Problems and Case Law (Question 39)

It is suggested that the rules could lead to tough consequences for businesses that restrict their scope of business to domestic transactions (Takahashi 2011, p. 168).[31] For example, if a foreign small business doing business solely in its country makes a contract with a consumer domiciled in Japan, the foreign business can be sued in Japan by the consumer and it cannot protect itself by a choice-of-court clause, although Japanese courts may deny its jurisdiction over such disputes under Article 3-9 of the CCP. As Article 3-9 may not be useful for cruise liners operating ships globally, such cruise liners should be prepared for legal proceedings in the domiciles of consumers.

Potentially, as in cases of carriage of goods by sea, there may be difficulty in terms of how courts interpret 'the place of performance' of contractual obligations (Article 3-3 (i), CCP) or whether 'a tort occurred in Japan' (Article 3-3 (viii), CCP). However, the authors think these issues are rather trivial in consumer contracts because a consumer would prefer to bring an action in their domicile while a business operator is practically bound to sue before the court of the consumer's domicile.

4.3 Arbitration Clause (Questions 38 and 39)

The requirement for the validity of arbitration is provided by Article 13 of the Arbitration Act, which is very similar to Option I in Article 7 of the UNCITRAL Model Law. In principle, Japanese law is friendly to arbitration. However, regarding consumer contracts, Article 3 of the Schedule to the Act allows a consumer to rescind an arbitration agreement with a business operator at any time unless the consumer initiates arbitration proceedings. An arbitration agreement in a consumer contract merely gives an option for the consumer to file for an arbitration and does not have the effect of limiting possibilities of the operator being sued before otherwise competent courts.

Japanese cruise operators stipulate no arbitration clause in their conditions of carriage, while the conditions of a foreign cruise operator require the passengers to settle disputes relating to any other claims than those for personal injury or death before an arbitral tribunal in Tokyo. The effect of this clause will be restricted by

[31] The discussions leading to the current provisions are explained, for example, in Dogauchi (2010, pp. 196–198).

Article 3 of the Schedule accordingly. No relevant cases have been reported so far on the validity or effect of arbitration agreements in cruise contracts.

4.4 *Choice of Law (Questions 41–44)*

4.4.1 Governing Law of Contract (Question 41)

In principle, the parties to a contract may choose the law applicable to a contract (Article 7, AGRAL). In the absence of choice, the law of the place with which a contract is most closely connected governs the contract (Article 8 (1), AGRAL). If only one of the parties is to provide the characteristic performance under the contract, the law of the habitual residence of the party providing the characteristic performance (or when such party has a place of business connected with the contract, the law of the place of business, or when such party has more than two places of business connected with the contract located in different jurisdictions, the law of the principal place of business) is presumed to be the law of the place with which the contract is most closely connected (Article 8 (2), AGRAL). The parties may change the law applicable to a contract after they enter into the contract, although they may not invoke the fresh choice against a third party whose rights would otherwise be prejudiced by the change of the governing law (Article 9, AGRAL). Formalities are satisfied if the parties comply with the requirements provided either by the law applicable to the formation of the contract or the law of the place where the parties conclude the contract[32] (Article 10 (1) (2), AGRAL).

4.4.2 Special Rules for Consumer Contracts (Questions 41 and 42)

Consumer contracts are subject to special rules in Article 11 of the AGRAL. A consumer contract is defined as a contract between a consumer, that is, an individual natural person except when they become a party to a contract as or for their business on the one hand, and a business operator, that is, a legal person or any other form of association or foundation, or an individual natural person when they become a party to a contract as or for their business on the other, a contract of employment being excluded.

[32]For a general account of the AGRAL, see Koide (2014). In addition to the two provisions in the text above and a special rule for rights *in rem* (Article 10 (5)), Article 10 of the AGRAL provides that, where a declaration of intent has been made to a person in a place where a different law applies, the place from which the notice of the declaration has been despatched shall be deemed as the place of the contract in Article 10 (2) (Article10 (3)). Where a contract is concluded between persons in different jurisdictions, the formalities for a contract that comply with either the law of the place from which the notice of offer has been dispatched or the law of the place from which the notice of acceptance has been dispatched shall be valid (Article 10 (4)).

The parties to a consumer contract may choose a law applicable to a contract in accordance with Article 7 of the AGRAL, and they may also change the chosen law pursuant to Article 9 of the AGRAL. However, despite such a choice, the consumer may invoke any specific provisions that would otherwise be mandatorily applicable to the consumer contract under the law of the place where the consumer has habitual residence (Article 11 (1), AGRAL), in addition to the chosen law.

A similar but slightly different rule is set out for the formalities (Article 11 (3), AGRAL): The consumer may invoke any mandatory provisions prescribing formalities in the law of its habitual residence, and in such a case, formalities are solely subject to the mandatory provisions in the law of the habitual residence; in contrast, if the consumer does not do so, formalities will be satisfied when requirements either under the law governing the formation of the contract or under the law of the place where the contract is concluded are met (Article 10 (1) (2), AGRAL). When the law chosen in accordance with Article 7 of the AGRAL is the law of the place where the consumer has its habitual residence, and the consumer declares their intent to make the same law exclusively applicable to the formalities, the formalities are subject to the law of the consumer's habitual residence (Article 11 (4), AGRAL).

If the parties to a consumer contract do not choose a law applicable to the contract, the contract shall be governed by the law of the place where the consumer has its habitual residence (Article 11 (2), AGRAL), the application of Article 8 being excluded. The law of the consumer's habitual residence also governs formalities (Article 11 (5)).

The special rules above do not apply where a consumer, without preceding inducement by a business operator, travels to a place where a law that is the same as the law of the relevant business operator's place of business connected with the contract and different from the law of the consumer's habitual residence applies, and the consumer concludes a contract in that place, or receives or is supposed to receive the whole of the performance under the contract in that place (Article 11 (6) (i) (ii), AGRAL). The same is true where a business operator has not known the place of residence of the consumer with good reason or a business operator mistakenly takes a consumer as not being a consumer with good reason (Article 11 (6) (iii) (iv), AGRAL).

4.4.3 Overriding Mandatory Provisions of the Forum (Questions 41 and 42)

In addition to the special rules in the AGRAL above, it is generally understood that consumers will enjoy protection under overriding mandatory provisions of the forum. It is not clear, however, which provisions of what acts should be characterised as having such an overriding nature.

4.4.4 How Consumers Are Protected Under the Rules (Questions 42 and 43)

The rules on choice of law above protect the passenger as a consumer as follows:

- In most cases, a consumer can appeal to consumer protection provided by the law of their habitual residence, unless the consumer has voluntarily and actively chosen to contract with a business operator in a place where a law differs from the law of its habitual residence applies.
- As for the validity of choice of law clauses included in the general conditions of carriage of passengers in cruises, the AGRAL does not set out different rules for adhesive terms and conditions. Therefore, consumers will enjoy the consumer protection described in Sects. 4.4.2 and 4.4.3, whether contracts are documented in general terms and conditions or not. The limitation of party autonomy is also explained in the same sections.

4.4.5 Possible Problem and Case Law (Question 44)

Article 11 of the Act is criticised because of its complexity for consumers (Nomura 2016, p. 1477). From a practical perspective, it is not necessarily clear in what cases advertising on the Internet will qualify as 'inducement' in Article 11 (6) (i) (ii) of the AGRAL, with the effect that a business operator is exempted from the application of the law of a consumer's habitual residence.

In a case mentioned in Sect. 3.7, the cruise passengers tried to hold the defendant company as the charterer of the vessel liable for the alleged damages with the doctrine of piercing the corporate veil under Japanese law. The claimant invoked Article 11 (1) of the AGRAL in doing so, but the attempt failed.[33]

[33] Judgement of Tokyo District Court, 13 January 2017, approved by Judgement of Tokyo Hight Court, 29 June 2017. Under the conditions of carriage, English law was chosen as the governing law of the contract, and the court denied the application of the doctrine on the ground that whether the doctrine was to apply should be determined by English law. As the governing law of the contract for passengers in this case was English law, strictly speaking, a part of the court holding referred in Sect. 3.7 is not about Japanese law, whereas the court decision substantially seems to be based on Japanese law rather than English law.

5 Legal Scholarship and Legal Education

5.1 *Bibliography of Private Law Aspects of Cruises (Question 47)*

To the authors' knowledge, there are no books or articles that specifically address private law aspects of cruises. Hakoi (2003), Matsui and Oono (2018) and Shintani and Hachisuga (1991) in the references provide materials relating to legal aspects of carriage of passengers, and Miura (2018) discusses travel contracts.

5.2 *List of Cases (Question 48)*

There have only been a few cases on cruises so far, and the following cases are not published in any case reports:

- Judgement of Tokyo District Court, 28 May 2014;
- Judgement of Tokyo District Court, 13 January 2017; and
- Judgement of Tokyo Hight Court, 29 June 2017.

See Sects. 3.7 and 4.4.5 for details.

5.3 *Educational Programme (Question 49)*

To the authors' knowledge, no institutions in Japan provide educational programmes specifically devoted to legal aspects of cruises.

6 Concluding Remarks

It is only recently that Japanese society has come to consider the impact of cruises. Reflecting these circumstances, the legal aspects of cruises have not been well examined so far in Japan. It has yet to be thoroughly analysed whether there are any legal issues unique to cruises under Japanese law, and if there are, how these issues should be addressed.

References

Books and Articles

Dogauchi M (2010) Nihon-no-atarashii-kokusai-saiban-kankatu-rippou-ni-tuite (Forthcoming rules on international jurisdiction). Kokusai-shiho-nenpo (Jpn Yearb Priv Int Law) 12:186–211

Hakoi T (2003) Kaijo-ryokyaku-unso-keiyaku (Contracts for carriage of passengers by sea). In: Ochiai S, Egashira K (eds) Kaiho-taikei (Systematic theory of maritime law). Shojihomu, Tokyo, pp 397–421

Ikeda Y (2019) Kuruzu-gannen-to-sonogo-no-wagakuni-no-kuruzu-sijo (The first year of the Japanese cruise era and the market development process). Unyu-to-keizai (Transp Econ) 79 (4):28–32

Koide K (2014) Chikujo-kaisetsu Ho-no-tekiyou-ni-kansuru-tsusokuho (Commentary on the act on general rules for application of laws), expanded edn. Shojihomu, Tokyo

Matsui N, Oono A (2018) Ichimon-itto-heisei-30nen-syoho-kaisei (Questions and answers for the revision of the Commercial Code in 2018). Shojihomu, Tokyo

Miura M (2018) Hyojun-rokogyo-yakkann-kaisetsu (Commentary on standard conditions for travel contracts), 2nd edn. Jiyu-kokumin-sya, Tokyo

Nomura Y (2016) Syohisya-keiyaku-no-junkyoho: tsuusokuho11jo-hihan (The Japanese conflict-law rules for a consumer contract: causes and remedies of their complexity). Hos0-jiho (Lawyers Assoc J) 68(6):1453–1480

Sakai H, Yuguchi K (2016) Gaiko-kuruzu-kyakusen-yuchi-katudo-ni-okeru-genjo-to-kadai (Current state and problems in activities for attraction of foreign cruise ships in Japan). Kaiun-keizai-kenkyu (J Logist Shipp Econ) 50:31–40

Sasaki T, Akakura Y, Sugita T (2018) Wagakuni-ni-kiko-suru-kuruzu-no-juyodoko-to-sono-koka-ni-kansuru-bunseki (Trend analysis and impact estimation of cruise ships calling at ports in Japan). Technical Note of National Institute for Land and Infrastructure Management (NILIM) No. 1401. http://www.ysk.nilim.go.jp/kenkyuseika/pdf/ks1041.pdf. Accessed 8 Aug 2020

Sato T, Kobayashi Y (2012) Ichimon-itto-heisei-23nen-minjisosyoho-kaisei (Questions and answers for the revision of the Code of Civil Procedure in 2011). Shojihomu, Tokyo

Shintani K, Hachisuga M (1991) Nihon-gaiko-ryokyakusen-kyokai-seitei 'hyojun-ryokyaku-unnso-yakkann-ni-tsuite (On standard carriage conditions established by JOPA). Kaiun 770:53–59

Takahashi K (2011) Japan's newly enacted rules on international jurisdiction: with a reflection on some issues of interpretation. Kokusai-shiho-nenpo (Jpn Yearb Priv Int Law) 13:146–170

Tsutsui T, Muramatsu H (2018) Ichimon-itto-minpo-saiken-kankei-kaisei (Questions and answers for the revision of the Civil Code (the law of obligations)). Shojihomu, Tokyo

Websites and Online Resources

Academic Society for Cruise & Ferry, Japan. http://cruise-ferry.main.jp/. Accessed 7 Aug 2020

City of Yokohama (2017) The economic effect of Port of Yokohama. https://www.city.yokohama.lg.jp/kanko-bunka/minato/taikan/manabu/chiikikeizai.files/0003_20180817.pdf. Accessed 7 Aug 2020

Cruise port guide of Japan. https://www.mlit.go.jp/kankocho/cruise/. Accessed 7 Aug 2020

e-Stat: Portal site of official statistics of Japan. https://www.e-stat.go.jp/en. Accessed 7 Aug 2020

Japan Oceangoing Passenger Ship Association (JOPA). http://www.jopa.or.jp/. Accessed 7 Aug 2020

Japan Society of Transportation Economics. https://koutsu-gakkai.jp/index.html. Accessed 7 Aug 2020

Japan Tourism Agency: Statistical information. https://www.mlit.go.jp/kankocho/en/siryou/toukei/index.html. Accessed 7 Aug 2020

Japan Tourism Agency: Seisaku-ni-tsuite (About government policies). https://www.mlit.go.jp/kankocho/shisaku/index.html. Accessed 7 Aug 2020

Ministry of Land, Infrastructure, Transport and Tourism (MLIT): Kuruzu-shinkou (Promotion of cruises). https://www.mlit.go.jp/kowan/kowan_tk4_000019.html. Accessed 7 Aug 2020

Statistics Bureau of Japan. http://www.stat.go.jp/english/index.html. Accessed 6 Aug 2020

Statistics Bureau of Japan (2019) Statistical handbook 2019. https://www.stat.go.jp/english/data/handbook/index.html (2019). Accessed 7 Aug 2020

Legal Rules Applicable to Cruise Ships Under Turkish Law

Melisa Konfidan

Abstract Turkey is a popular destination for international cruise ships with its developing cruise tourism and new cruise ports. Most of the cruises sail to the ports not only in Istanbul, but also in Kuşadası, İzmir, Bodrum, Marmaris, Alanya, Antalya and Çanakkale where the frequent visitors are mostly from Germany, United Kingdom, United States of America and Italy. Despite having lower expectations due to current pandemic, Turkey aims to be prepared for the future of the cruise tourism. This report lays out the legal rules applicable to cruise ships under Turkish law generally.

1 Introduction

Turkey is a cruise destination. Most of the cruises sail to the ports not only in Istanbul, but also in Kuşadası, İzmir, Bodrum, Marmaris, Alanya, Antalya and Çanakkale. In 2015, 44% of the cruises came to Kuşadası, followed by Istanbul (11%) and Marmaris (8%) whereas in 2013, 30% of the cruises came to Istanbul, followed by Kuşadası (26%) and Izmir (22%).[1]

Statistics show the evolution of the number of cruises and cruise passengers arriving in Turkey. In 2016, 1296 cruises came to Turkey carrying 1,889,000

This report was prepared in February 2017 for the XXth International Congress of Comparative Law and amendments were made in November 2020. Please kindly note that the following aspects of the subject are not covered in this report: Cruise passengers as consumers; Combined trips, package travels, package tours or package holidays; Jurisdiction and arbitration; Choice of law.

---

[1] See http://tobb.org.tr/Documents/yayinlar/2015/TURIZM16/index.html#2/z. http://atlantis.udhb.gov.tr/istatistik/istatistik_kruvaziyer.aspx. https://yigm.ktb.gov.tr/TR-9854/sinir-giris-cikis-istatistikleri.html.

M. Konfidan (✉)
Piri Reis University, Faculty of Law, Department of Maritime Law, Istanbul, Turkey
e-mail: mkonfidan@pirireis.edu.tr

C. Fresnedo de Aguirre (ed.), *Legal Aspects of Cruises*, Ius Comparatum - Global Studies in Comparative Law 56, https://doi.org/10.1007/978-3-030-83090-8_13

passengers.[2] In 2013, 1572 cruises came to Turkey carrying 2,240,000 passengers whereas the number was 1587 cruises and 2,095,673 passengers in 2012.[3]

The nationalities of the passengers, according to sea border statistics of 2015 are as follows: The most frequent visitors were from Germany with a number of 350,000 passengers, followed by 330,000 English passengers, 268,000 American passengers, and 170,000 Italian passengers. Also in 2013, the average spending by a cruise passenger was approximately USD 150 daily.[4]

2 Maritime Law Rules in General That Are Applicable to Cruise Ships

2.1 Carriage of Passengers and Their Baggages by Sea

Rules in respect of carriage of passengers and their baggage by sea can be found under the Turkish Commercial Code[5] ("TCC"), Fifth Book Maritime Law, Fifth Chapter Contract of Carriage of Passengers by Sea, Articles 1247–1271. These rules are applicable for ships. TCC enacted these rules from 2002 Athens Convention[6] in order to govern the liability from the death and personal injury of the passengers and the liability from the loss and/or damage to the baggage of the passengers. The most important feature of the rules is that the liabilities are limited within certain amounts depending on the different types. Those rules are enacted from the 2002 Athens Convention.[7] Thus, Turkey commenced the paperwork[8] in order to become a party to the 2002 Athens and expected to become soon.

[2] 2016 Sector Council Report of The Union of Chambers and Commodity Exchanges of Turkey and the statistic received from the Ministry of Transportation, Maritime Affairs and Communications, Directorate of Sea Commerce (current name: Ministry of Transport and Infrastructure).

[3] See Association of Turkey Travel Agency's (TURSAB) report of 2013 and 2012.

[4] See http://www.tursab.org.tr/dosya/12193/tursab-kruvaziyer-turizmi-raporu107153521118_12193_5644498.pdf.

[5] *Türk Ticaret Kanunu* (Turkish Commercial Code, number 6102, Official Gazette: 14.02.2011/27846).

[6] Athens Convention relating to the Carriage of Passengers and Their Luggages by Sea, 2002 is Consolidated Text of 1974 Athens Convention relating to the Carriage of Passengers by Sea amended by 2002 Protocol. The Turkish translation of the Convention is available at: Sürücü et al. (2013), pp. 263–332.

[7] Hereinafter referred to in the rext as "2002 Athens". For more information on this subject, see Algantürk Light (2003), pp. 581–588; Can (2001); Taşkın (2016); Damar (2016), pp. 153–180; Atamer (2017), p. 176 and 427–443; Işıklar (2018), p. 121; Yazıcıoğlu (2020), p. 431.

[8] 09.03.2017 dated and 6990 numbered Code on Approval of Becoming Party to 2002 Protocol of the Athens (Official Gazette: 03.04.2017/30027). Thus, both English and Turkish versions of the Convention was published in the appendix of 18.09.2020 dated Presidential Decree number 1580 (Official Gazette: 19.09.2019/30893, 1bis). It is expected that the certificate of deposit shall be submitted to IMO General Secretariat soon. Demir (2020), p. 33; https://wwwcdn.imo.org/localresources/en/About/Conventions/StatusOfConventions/Status%20-%202020.pdf.

The most important part of the rules enacted from 2002 Athens Convention is the compulsory insurance. Article 4bis of the 2002 Athens Convention was enacted into Article 1259(2) and in this regard, carriers need to maintain insurance[9] for ships carrying more than twelve passengers. Such insurance shall cover liability in respect of the death of and personal injury to passengers and the limit of the compulsory insurance shall not be less than 250,000 Special Drawing Right[10] per passenger on each distinct occasion. This rule is also applicable to cruise ships.

2.2 Environmental Law

Maritime law's rules in respect to environmental issues are designed to apply to the incidents arising from ships. The biggest concern is the pollution from ships. Again, there are no rules specifically for pollution from the cruises. However there are general rules for the ships. Maritime environmental rules are complicated in terms of application and a list[11] is as follows:

- Code no. 5312[12] [*Deniz Çevresinin Petrol ve Diğer Zararli Maddelerle Kirlenmesinde Acil Durumlarda Mudahale Ve Zararlarin Tazmini Esaslarina Dair Kanun*]
- Environmental Code[13] [*Çevre Kanunu*]
- International Convention on Civil Liability for Bunker Oil Pollution Damage, 2001[14] (BUNKER)
- International Convention on Civil Liability for Oil Pollution Damage, 1992[15] (1992 CLC)
- Civil Liability Fund Convention, 1992[16] (1992 CLC FUND)

[9] P&I insurance covers this liability. P&I insurance, H&M insurance and cargo insurance are the main three marine insurance types. For detailed info please see: Hazelwood and Semark (2014); Şeker Öğüz (2001), p. 1; Yazıcıoğlu (2003), p. 13; Algantürk Light (2006), p. 3–15; Konfidan (2020), p. 1.

[10] See https://www.imf.org/en/About/Factsheets/Sheets/2016/08/01/14/51/Special-Drawing-Right-SDR.

[11] For the list of the Conventions see Atamer (2016), p. 206, 207.

[12] Code number 5312, 03.03.2005; Official Gazette: 11.03.2005/25752.

[13] Code number 2872, 09.08.1983; Official Gazette: 11.08.1983/18132.

[14] Turkey became party to 2001 BUNKER by acceptance of Code number 6439, 26.02.2013 (Official Gazette: 27.07.2013/28720).

[15] Turkey became party to 1992 CLC by acceptance of Code number 4507, 27.01.2000 (Official Gazette: 29.01.2000/23948).

[16] Turkey became party to 1992 CLC Fund by acceptance of Code number 4508, 27.01.2000 (Official Gazette: 29.01.2000/23948).

- International Convention on Liability and Compensation for Damage in Connection with the Carriage of Hazardous and Noxious Substances by Sea, 2010[17] (2010 HNS Convention)

Apart from BUNKER, the other international agreements are not likely to be applied to cruise ships due to their nature of usage. For example a cruise, falls outside the definition of ship in the 1992 CLC (Article 1(1)).

The most important aspect of the international agreements in respect of maritime disputes of the environmental law is that the above mentioned international agreements require the ship having a relevant insurance protection[18] in case of an incident. In terms of a cruise ship, BUNKER may be applicable. Article 7(1) of BUNKER requires compulsory insurance for the ships more than 1000 gross tonnage. P&I insurance[19] covers this liability.

2.3 *Labour Law*

Turkish legal system does not contain any specific labour rules on cruise workers. In general, Maritime Labour Code [*Deniz İş Kanunu*][20] applies to the crewmembers of the Turkish flagged ships carrying a cargo of 100 gross tonnage and above and working under a contract (Article 1 of the Maritime Labour Code). In case the cruise is Turkish flagged, the applicable labour rules are Maritime Labour Code and in case of any reference, Labour Code [*İş Kanunu*][21] would also be applicable. A crewmember is defined as master,[22] officers, crewmen and others who are working in a ship under a contract (Article 2/B of the Maritime Labour Code).

Important set of rules for marine labour law are also included in the 2006 Maritime Labour Convention. 2014 amendments of the 2006 Maritime Labour

[17]Code number 6949 on Approval of Becoming Party to 2010 Protocol of the HNS (which was accepted on 08.03.2017) Official Gazette: 03.04.2017/30027. The 2010 HNS Protocol will enter into force 18 months after the date on which it is ratified by at least twelve States, including four States each with not less than 2 million units of gross tonnage, and having received during the preceding calendar year a total quantity of at least 40 million tonnes of cargo that would be contributing to the general account. The Protocol was open for signature at the headquarters of the IMO between 1 November 2010 and 31 October 2011. It now remains open for accession. See https://www.hnsconvention.org/status/.

[18]See Kender (2004), pp. 583–597.

[19]See fn. 9.

[20]Code number 854, 20.04.1967 (Official Gazette: 29.04.1967/12586). More information on this Code can be found in Bedük (2012), pp. 39–41.

[21]Code number 4857, 22.05.2003 (Official Gazette: 10.06.2003/25134).

[22]Detailed comments on Maritime Labour Code can be found in: Süzel (2016), p. 101; Süzel (2009), p. 436, 437.

Convention's most important feature is its requirement of compulsory financial security (Standard A.2.5.2).[23]

3 Legal Rules Specifically Related with Cruise Ships

In addition to maritime law's general rules listed above, other legal rules including the wording of "cruise" (in Turkish, *kruvaziyer*) or related with cruise tourism are also listed below in three categories.

3.1 Tourism

- Tourism Incentive Code[24] [*Turizmi Teşvik Kanunu*]

The cruise ship has been listed in the group of "sea tourism vehicles" under Article 3 (i) of Tourism Code. Article 3(i)(2) defines what a cruise ship is. It is a seaworthy pleasure ship on a prescheduled route having a swimming pool and luxury cabins and able to sail in international waters with a high passenger capacity. Thus, Article 8(A)(1)(g) of sets out rules governing condemnation of an area in order to be provided for cruises (i.e. cruise ports). Also cruise casinos should be shut down in case the cruise is in Turkish waters under Article 28.

- Council of Ministers' Frame Decision on Tourism Incentive[25] [*Turizmi Teşvik Çerçeve Kararı*]

  Article 2(j) provides that the cruise tourism will be supported by the government.

- Official Statement on Implementation of Bylaw of Sea Tourism[26] [*Deniz Turizmi Yönetmeliği Uygulama Tebliği*]

[23] Turkey is not yet party to MLC but commenced the proceedings in this respect. Code no. 6898 on Approval of Becoming Party to 2006 MLC (Accepted on 02.03.2017, Official Gazette: 25.03.2017/30018). However the process of Turkey, becoming party to 2006 MLC shall by Council Ministers' approval of 2006 MLC who has the authority to enforce the Code number 6898 by Article 4 of the same Code. Also, Council of Ministry has an authority to approve amendments of the Rules, Code and the Appendixes by Article of the same Code. See http://www.ilo.org/dyn/normlex/en/f?p=NORMLEXPUB:11310:0::NO::P11310_INSTRUMENT_ID:312331.

[24] Tourism Incentive Code (Code number 2634/12.03.1982; Official Gazette: 16.03.1982/17635).

Code on Amendment of Tourism Incentive Code [*Turizmi Teşvik Kanununda Değişiklik Yapılmasına Dair Kanun*] Code number 5761/07.05.2008; Official Gazette: 15.05.2008/26877. Recently, Articles of the Tourism Incentive Code was amended by Code number 7334 (Official Gazette: 28.07.2021).

[25] Council of Ministers' Frame Decision on Tourism Incentive (20.06.1980/8/1135; Official Gazette: 27.06.1980/17030).

[26] Official Gazette: 28.04.2010/27565.

Article 14(1) stipulates that the conditions mentioned in the ByLaw on the Documentation and Quality of the Tourism Facilities[27] [*Turizm Tesislerinin Belgelendirilmesi ve Niteliklerine İlişkin Yönetmelik]* shall be taken into account during the set-up of the food and the accommodation services of a port of cruise ships.

- Currently, there is an ongoing construction project in İstanbul, Salıpazarı named "Galataport" between Karaköy Berth and Fındıklı Campus of University of Mimar Sinan including a construction of a cruise port.[28] There was a cruise port called Karaköy Pier in the same area previously. This project is still ongoing.

3.2 Coasts

- Code on Coasts[29] [*Kıyı Kanunu*]

Article 6(4)(c) stipulates that it is permitted to build a cruise port on a coast.

- Bylaw on Implementation of Code on Coasts[30] [*Kıyı Kanununun Uygulanmasına Dair Yönetmelik*]

  The cruise port is defined under Article 4.[31]

- Bylaw on Obtainment of License for Operation of Coast Facilities[32] [*Kıyı Tesislerine İşletme İzni Verilmesine İlişkin Usul ve Esaslar Hakkında Yönetmelik*] set outs the requirements for the coast facilities in order to commence their operations at coasts.

---

[27] It was decided to accept this ByLaw by Council of Ministers' Decision (number 2005/8948, 10.05.2005; Official Gazette: 21.06.2005/25852).

[28] The project was initially included in the Council of Ministers' 2013 and 2014 year programmes. Please see 2003 year programme (*2003 yılı Programı*, number 2002/4810, 08.10.2002). This was an addendum for the Decision of Council of Ministers (Official Gazette: 25049 1bis/15.03.2003) and An Addendum to the Implementation, Coordination and Observation of 2004 Year Programme Decision of Council of Ministers published in Official Gazette (21.10.2003/25266, *2004 yılı Programı 21.10.2003 gün ve 25266 sayılı Resmi Gazete'de Yayımlanan 13.10.2003 gün ve 2003/6286 sayılı 2004 yılı Programının Uygulanmasi, Koordinasyonu ve İzlenmesine Dair Bakanlar Kurulu Kararı Ekidir* Official Gazette 28.10.2003/25273, 1bis). The aim was to complete the project in April 2020 however the plans were postponed. See https://www.reuters.com/article/turkey-tourism-galataport/istanbul-cruise-port-galataport-to-open-in-q2-2020-chairman-idUSL5N25M1JD.

[29] Code number 3621, 04.04.1990; Official Gazette: 17.04.1990/20495. However Article 6(4)(c) was added by Article 13 of the Code number 5398, 3.7.2005.

[30] Official Gazette: 03.08.1990/20594. This ByLaw was amended by Bylaw Amending the Bylaw of Implementation of Code on Coasts [*Kıyı Kanununun Uygulanmasına Dair Yönetmelikte Değişiklik Yapılması Hakkında Yönetmelik*] Official Gazette: 30.03.2004/25418.

[31] This provision corresponds to Article 1 of Bylaw Amending the Bylaw of Implementation of Code on Coasts mentioned in previous footnote.

[32] Official Gazette: 18.02.2007/26438.

- Bylaw on Ports[33] [*Limanlar Yönetmeliği*]

  The cruise port is listed as one of the coastal facilities under Article 4(1)(k).

- Bylaw Amending the Bylaw of Implementation of Code on Coasts [*Kıyı Kanununun Uygulanmasına Dair Yönetmelikte Değişiklik Yapılması Hakkında Yönetmelik*][34]

  The definition of cruise port is included in Article 4.

3.3 Other Subjects

- The Union of Chambers and Commodity Exchanges of Turkey and Code on Commodity Exchanges[35] [*Türkiye Odalar ve Borsalar Birliği ve Odalar ve Borsalar Kanunu*]

Article 5(1) gives permission for setting up a Chamber of Shipping for cruise tourism companies together with other companies dealing with other types of maritime affairs and Article 25 sets out condition for the payment of relevant fees of the cruise ships to the Chambers.

- Official Statement for Value Added Tax[36] [*Katma Değer Vergisi Genel Tebliği*]

  Works described under Article 1.3 which are related to cruise ports are exempted from value added tax.

- ByLaw on Administration of Property of the Treasury[37] [*Hazine Taşınmazlarının İdaresi Hakkında Yönetmelik*]

  Article 12(9) gives discretion to the Ministry of Finance to determine relevant amounts for the permission of construction of a cruise port.

- ByLaw on Regulation of Statistics of Sea Commerce[38] [*Deniz Ticareti İstatistiklerini Düzenleme Yönetmeliği*]

  Article 2(1)(d) states that the statistics of cruise ship and passengers had to be provided by managers, port managers and agents.

[33] Official Gazette: 31.10.2012/28453.

[34] Official Gazette: 03.08.1990/20594.

[35] Code number 5174, 18.05.2004; Official Gazette: 01.06.2004/25479.

[36] Official Announcement number: 93, Official Gazette: 19.01.2005/25705.

[37] Official Gazette: 19.06.2007 /26557.

[38] Official Gazette: 01.03.2013/28574.

It can easily be understood that the rules listed under the last heading are mostly added for administrative purposes (setting up a Chamber, tax payments) or as a result of a tourism policy of the country for the improvement of the cruise ports and cruise tourism.

4 Case Law

In 2006, the Constitutional Court[39] [*Anayasa Mahkemesi*] considered whether Article 6(4)(c) of Code on Coasts no. 3621 was in contrary with Article 43 of the Constitution.[40] In this matter, the claim was deletion of the Article 6(4)(c). This provision allows building cruise ports on the coasts. However on the other hand Article 43 of the Constitution explicitly states that *coasts are under the sovereignty and at the disposal of the State. In case of utilization of the coast, public interest shall be taken into consideration with priority.* This wording gives judges a wide discretion at which project is for public interest or not. On this matter, the Court rejected the claim.

In 2013, 6th Circuit of Council of State[41] [*Danıştay 6. Dairesi*] considered whether a government construction plan including a construction of a cruise port and a sports centre[42] should be cancelled or not. Relevant legislation was Articles 6 and 7 of the Code on Coasts and in the subject matter the plan was found in order with the legal rules and it was not cancelled. Similarly, in 2008, the Court considered whether the administrative court's decision should be reversed or not.[43] The decision of the administrative court was cancellation of the government construction plan of a cruise port. However 6th Circuit of Council of State, acting as a cassation court reversed the administration court's decision and ruled in favour of the plaintiffs. The reasonings behind both decisions were that the plan shall benefit the public interest.

[39] 05.01.2006 dated decision with a merit number of 2005/98 and decision number of 2006/3.

[40] Turkish Republic Constitution [*Türkiye Cumhuriyeti Anayasası*], number: 2709, 07.11.1982.

[41] 25.11.2013 dated decision with a merit number of 2010/13301 and decision number of 2013/7272.

[42] The subject matter was about the plan at Trabzon Akyazı Cruise Port. It was claimed that the plan is not in line with the environmental position of the area. However the Court held that, a cruise port is needed in that area and rejected the claim.

[43] 6th Circuit of Council of State, 22.10.2008 dated decision with a merit number of 2006/6449 and decision number of 2008/6992.

5 Conclusion

There are not any set of rules designed merely for cruise ships under Turkish law. Rules applicable to ships may also be applicable to cruise ships unless specified.

Being a significant and growing contributor to the Turkish economy, the cruise industry has taken financial losses due to the COVID-19. Travel restrictions[44] and fear of the spread of the disease is ongoing. Although there are few cruises commenced voyage[45] in Mediterranean recently, 2020 experience throughout the world shows that there is a strong decline in cruise tourism.[46] The ongoing crisis has seen many sailings cancelled for both 2020 and 2021.[47] Even if the pandemic is over,[48] the inevitable effects shall of course continue for Turkey, too.

References

Books and Articles

Algantürk Light D (2003) Yolcuların ve Bagajlarının Deniz Yolu ile Taşınması Hakkında 1974 Atina Konvansiyonu'na 2002 Protokolü ile Getirilen Temel Değişiklikler [Main changes of 2002 protocol of 1974 Athens convention relating to carriage of passengers and their luggage by sea]. Atatürk Üniversitesi Erzincan Hukuk Fakültesi Dergisi [Atatürk University Erzincan Law Faculty Magazine] 7(1–2):581–588

Algantürk Light D (2006) Deniz Sigorta Hukukunda Kulüp Sigortası [P&I Club Insurance in Marine Insurance Law]. Arıkan Basım Yayın.

Atamer K (2016) In: Atamer K, Damar D (eds) Marine pollution, transport law in Turkey, 2nd edn. Wolters-Kluwer, pp 206–210

Atamer K (2017) Deniz Ticareti Hukuku [Maritime law], Cilt 1. On İki Levha Yayıncılık

Bedük MN (2012) Deniz İş Sözleşmesi [Maritime labour contract] Ekin Basım Yayım Dağıtım

Can M (2001) Türk Hukuku'nda ve Milletlerarası Hukukta Deniz Yolu ile Yolcu Taşıma Sözleşmesi [Contract of carriage of passengers under Turkish and international law]. Imaj Yayıncılık

Damar D (2016) Carriers' liability for passengers, baggage and cargo. In: Atamer K, Damar D (eds) Transport law in Turkey, 2nd edn. Wolters-Kluwer, pp 153–180

[44] Travel restrictions are changing very frequently. However currently, Turkey is excluded from EU's coronavirus list of "safe countries" from which non-essential travel is allowed. See https://t24.com.tr/haber/avrupa-birligi-turkiye-ye-kapilarini-kapatti-seyahat-yasagi-31-agustos-ta-da-kalkmayabilir,897192.

[45] In 16 August 2020, around 2500 passengers braved the risk of the virus to return to the seas as the cruise ship "MSC Grandiosa" set sail from Genoa in Italy on a seven-day voyage, becoming the first major cruise ship to resume tours of the Mediterranean in the wake of the pandemic. See https://www.bbc.com/news/world-europe-53802045.

[46] See https://www.ft.com/content/d8ff5129-6817-4a19-af02-1316f8defe52.

[47] See https://www.weforum.org/agenda/2020/11/impact-coronavirus-pandemic-cruise-ships/.

[48] See https://www.independent.co.uk/life-style/health-and-families/coronavirus-when-will-it-end-date-outbreak-stop-a9414196.html.

Demir İ (2020) 2002 Atina Sözleşmesi Çerçevesinde Deniz Yoluyla Yolcu Taşıma [Carriage of passengers by sea under the 2002 Athens convention]. Yetkin Yayınları
Hazelwood SJ, Semark D (2014) P&I Clubs law and practice, informa law. Routledge, pp 1–8
Işıklar GK (2018) 2002 Atina Sözleşmesi Çerçevesinde Deniz Yolu ile Yolcu Taşımalarında Zorunlu Sorumluluk Sigortası [Compulsory liability insurance for carriage of passengers by sea under 2002 Athens convention]. On İki Levha Yayıncılık
Kender R (2004) Uluslararası Deniz Hukukunda Kirlenme Zararları İçin Zorunlu Sorumluluk Sigortası [Compulsory liability insurance for the losses from pollution under international maritime law]. Milletlerarası Hukuk Bülteni [Int Law Bulletin] 24(1–2):583–597
Konfidan M (2020) Deniz Araçları Sorumluluk Sigortası Sözleşmesi [Contract of sea vehicles' liability insurance], PhD Thesis, University of Istanbul, Social Sciences Institute, Istanbul
Sürücü M, Süzel C, Atamer K (2013) Deniz Yoluyla Yolcu ve Bagajlarının Taşınmasına İlişkin 2002 Atina Sözleşmesi'nin Tercümesi [Translation of the Athens convention relating to the carriage of passengers and their luggage by sea 2002]. In: Atamer K, Suzel C (eds) Yeni Deniz Ticaret Hukuku'nun Kaynakları [Sources of the new maritime law]. On İki Levha Yayınları, pp 263–332
Şeker Öğüz Z (2001) Deniz Yoluyla Yük Taşınmasında Sigorta Himayesinin Kapsamı [Scope of insurance cover for carriage of cargo by sea]. Beta Yayınları
Süzel C (2009) Deniz İş Kanunu Kapsamında Kaptan ve Kaptanın İş Sözleşmesi [Master and his employment contract under maritime labour code], Prof. Dr. Saim Üstündağ'a Armağan [Liber Amicorum to Prof. Dr. Saim Üstündağ], pp 433–463
Süzel C (2016) In: Atamer K, Damar D (eds) Master and seamen, transport law in Turkey, 2nd edn. Wolters-Kluwer, pp 96–110
Taşkın M (2016) Deniz Yolu ile Yolcu Taşıma Sözleşmesinde Taşıyanın Gemi Kazasından Doğan Sorumluluğu [Carrier's liability from collisions under contract of carriage of passengers]. On Iki Levha Yayıncılık
Yazıcıoğlu E (2003) Tekne Sigortası Sözleşmesi [Contract of hull and machinery insurance]. Beta Yayınları
Yazıcıoğlu E (2020) Kender/Çetingil Deniz Ticareti Hukuku [Kender/Çetingil Maritime Law], 15. bası, Filiz Kitabevi

Websites (All Accessed 30 November 2020)

BBC (British Broadcasting Corporation) News article available at: https://www.bbc.com/news/world-europe-53802045
Financial Times article, "Coronavirus: is this the end of the line for cruise ships?" Avaliable at: https://www.ft.com/content/d8ff5129-6817-4a19-af02-1316f8defe52
HNS Convention. https://www.hnsconvention.org/status/
ILO (International Labour Organization). http://www.ilo.org/dyn/normlex/en/f?p=NORMLEXPUB:11310:0::NO::P11310_INS TRUMENT_ID:312331
IMO (International Maritime Organisation). https://wwwcdn.imo.org/localresources/en/About/Conventions/StatusOfConventions/S tatus%20-%202020.pdf published on 24.11.2020
IMF (International Monetary Fund). https://www.imf.org/en/About/Factsheets/Sheets/2016/08/01/14/51/Special-Drawing- Right-SDR
Independent article, "If anyone tells you a date they're using a crystal ball: When can we really expect coronavirus to end?" https://www.independent.co.uk/life-style/health- and-families/coronavirus-when-will-it-end-date-outbreak-stop-a9414196.html
Ministry of Culture and Tourism. https://yigm.ktb.gov.tr/TR-9854/sinir-giris-cikis- istatistikleri.html
Reuters' article. https://www.reuters.com/article/turkey-tourism-galataport/istanbul-cruise- port-galataport-to-open-in-q2-2020-chairman-idUSL5N25M1JD

T24 (Independent Internet Newspaper) article "EU closed its doors to Turkey" [Avrupa Birliği Türkiye'ye kapılarını kapattı], https://t24.com.tr/haber/avrupa-birligi-turkiye- ye-kapilarini-kapatti-seyahat-yasagi-31-agustos-ta-da-kalkmayabilir,897192

TOBB (The Union of Chambers and Commodity Exchanges of Turkey). http://tobb.org.tr/Documents/yayinlar/2015/TURIZM16/index.html#2/z

TURSAB (Association of Turkish Travel Agencies). http://www.tursab.org.tr/dosya/12193/tursab-kruvaziyer-turizmi raporu107153521118_12193_5644498.pdf

Türkiye Cumhuriyeti Ulaştırma ve Altyapı Bakanlığı. (Turkish Republic Ministry of Transportation and Infrastructure) https://atlantis.udhb.gov.tr/istatistik/istatistik_kruvaziyer.aspx

World Economic Forum COVID Action Platform, "These startling pictures show the impact of COVID-19 on the cruise industry", Available at: https://www.weforum.org/agenda/2020/11/impact-coronavirus-pandemic-cruise-ships/

Melisa Konfidan is Assistant Professor of Maritime Law at Piri Reis University Faculty of Law. She obtained both her LL.B. and Ph.D. in private law from Istanbul University and her LL.M. degree in maritime law from University of Southampton. Her areas of interest are Maritime Law, Marine Insurance Law, Insurance Law.

Annex 1: Questionnaire on Legal Aspects of Cruises

I. Importance (or significance) of cruises in your country

1. Is your country a main cruise destiny?
2. Are there any statistics on the evolution of the number of cruises and cruise passengers arriving in your country, of passengers disembarking and of their nationalities, and of the money they spend on land?
3. Are there any statistics on the importance of the cruise business in your country?
4. Are there specific policies in your country to favour the cruise business and to attract cruises to your ports?
5. Are the services offered to cruises in your ports of good quality, for example regarding potable water supply, waste removal?
6. Is the cruise business relevant regarding the labour market in your country?
7. Is the ship management industry important in your country?
8. Are there good shipyards in your country to provide services to cruises?

II. Specific rules on cruises

9. Does your legal system contain specific legal rules on cruises?
10. Are those specific rules on cruises of international or supranational origin, of national origin or both? (Do not describe those provisions; just mention them with the information about their entry into force in your country).
11. What is the scope of application of those rules?
12. Are there specific rules on consumer protection applicable to passengers in cruises?
13. Are there any specific problems regarding the implementation of the aforementioned rules? Please indicate case-law, if any.

III. General rules applicable to cruises

14. Does your legal system contain general legal rules that are applicable to cruises?
15. Are those general provisions on carriage of passengers by sea, though not specifically on cruises?

C. Fresnedo de Aguirre (ed.), *Legal Aspects of Cruises*, Ius Comparatum - Global Studies in Comparative Law 56, https://doi.org/10.1007/978-3-030-83090-8

16. Are those provisions even more general, on international contracts, but applicable to cruises?
17. Are the provisions indicated in your response to questions 14-17 of international or supranational origin, of national origin or both?
18. Are there general rules on consumer protection applicable to passengers in cruises?
19. Are there any specific problems regarding the implementation of the aforementioned rules? Please indicate case-law, if any.

IV. Labour rules on cruises' workers

20. Does your legal system contain specific labour rules on cruises' workers?
21. Are those rules of international or supranational origin, or are they of national origin, or both?
22. Does your legal system contain general labour rules that are applicable to cruises' workers, in the absence of specific rules on the matter?
23. Are those rules of international or supranational origin, or are they of national origin, or both?
24. Does your legal system contain specific rules on combined trips[1] or, in the absence of such specific rules, general rules that are applicable to combined trips?
25. Are the provisions indicated in your response to question 24 of international or supranational origin, of national origin or both?
26. Are there any specific problems regarding the implementation of the aforementioned rules? Please indicate case-law, if any.

V. Rules on ports that are relevant regarding cruises

27. Does your legal system contain specific rules on ports that are relevant regarding cruises?
28. Are those rules of international or supranational origin, of national origin or both?
29. Specify, if possible, the system of taxes and rates that ports charge to cruises in your legal system.
30. Are there any specific problems regarding the implementation of the aforementioned rules? Please indicate case-law, if any.

VI. Rules on environmental impact of cruises

31. Does your legal system contain specific rules on **environmental impact** of cruises?

[1] Combined trips are those that include not only the cruise but also the airplane trip to and from the port of departure, the land excursions chosen by the tourist when the ship is in port, and eventually some hotel night (Álvaro Ariza Herrerías, "Análisis Jurídico-Económico del Transporte Marítimo en el Sector Turístico, Trabajo Fin de Máster", Universidad de Málaga, Facultad de Turismo, p. 13, http://riuma.uma.es/xmlui/bitstream/handle/10630/8729/TRABAJO%20FIN%20DE%20M%C3%81STER%20-%20def.pdf?sequence=1).

32. Are those rules of international or supranational origin, of national origin or both?
33. Are there any specific problems regarding the implementation of the aforementioned rules? Please indicate case-law, if any.

VII. Jurisdiction and arbitration

34. Does your legal system contain specific provisions on jurisdiction applicable to cruises that you have not mentioned in previous parts of your response?
35. In case it does not, does your legal system contain general provisions on jurisdiction regarding international contracts, which are applicable to cruises cases?
36. How do these specific or general provisions on jurisdiction protect the passenger as a consumer?
37. Are forum selection clauses included in general conditions of carriage of passengers in cruises recognised as a valid and effective choice of court agreement? Explain the limitations imposed on party autonomy in this sphere, if any.
38. Are arbitration clauses usually included in general conditions of carriage of passengers in cruises celebrated in your country?
39. Are there any specific problems regarding the implementation of the aforementioned rules? Please indicate case-law, if any.

VIII. Choice of law

40. Does your legal system contain specific provisions on choice of law regarding cruises that you have not mentioned in previous parts of your response?
41. In case it does not, does your legal system contain general provisions on choice of law regarding international contracts, which are applicable to cruises cases?
42. How do these specific or general provisions on choice of law protect the passenger as a consumer?
43. Are choice of law clauses included in general conditions of carriage of passengers in cruises considered to be valid and effective? Explain the limitations imposed on party autonomy in this sphere, if any.
44. Are there any specific problems regarding the implementation of the aforementioned rules? Please indicate case-law, if any.

IX. Responsibility

45. Does your legal system contain specific or general provisions on liability regarding cruises that you have not mentioned in previous parts of your response?
46. Are there any specific problems regarding the implementation of the aforementioned rules? Please indicate case-law, if any.

X. Legal scholarship and legal education

47. Please include a short bibliography of outputs concerning private international law on cruises in your legal system (listed by author in alphabetic order).
48. Please include a list of the relevant case law concerning cruises (listed by dates in chronological order).

49. Is there, in your country (or in your organization), any specific education program (in Universities or other institutions) totally or partially devoted to legal aspects of cruises?

Annex 2: Questionnaire sur les aspects légaux des croisières

I. Importance des croisières dans votre pays

1. Votre pays, est-il une destination principale de croisière?
2. Existe-t- il des statistiques sur l'évolution du nombre de croisières et de passagers de croisière qui arrivent dans votre pays, des passagers débarquant et de leurs nationalités, et de l'argent qu'ils dépensent à terre (ou quand ils débarquent)?
3. Existe-t- il des statistiques sur l'importance de l'activité des croisières dans votre pays?
4. Y a-t-il des politiques spécifiques ou particulières dans votre pays pour favoriser l'activité des croisières et pour attirer des croisières vers vos ports?
5. Les services offerts aux croisières dans vos ports, sont-ils de bonne qualité, par exemple en ce qui concerne l'approvisionnement en eau potable et l'élimination des déchets?
6. Dans votre pays, l'activité dans le secteur des croisières, est-elle remarquable en relation au marche de travail?
7. Dans votre pays, l'industrie des armateurs est-elle important?
8. Y a-t-il de bons chantiers navals dans votre pays pour fournir des services aux croisières?

II. Des règles spécifiques sur les croisières

9. Est-ce que votre système juridique contient des règles juridiques particulières sur les croisières?
10. Ces règles spécifiques sur les croisières, ¿sont-elles d'origine internationale ou supranationale, nationale ou les deux?
11. Quel est le champ d'application de ces règles ?
12. Y a-t-il des règles spécifiques sur la protection des consommateurs applicables aux passagers en croisières?
13. Y a-t-il des problèmes spécifiques en ce qui concerne la mise en œuvre des règles précitées? S'il vous plaît indiquer la jurisprudence, s'il y en a.

C. Fresnedo de Aguirre (ed.), *Legal Aspects of Cruises*, Ius Comparatum - Global Studies in Comparative Law 56, https://doi.org/10.1007/978-3-030-83090-8

III. Règles générales applicables aux croisières

14. Est-ce que votre système juridique contient des règles juridiques générales applicables aux croisières?
15. Ces dispositions générales, sont-elles relatives au transport de passagers par mer, bien qu'elles ne soient pas spécifiques des croisières?
16. Ces dispositions sont-elles encore plus générales, sur les contrats internationaux, mais applicable aux croisières?
17. Les dispositions renseignées dans votre réponse aux questions 5-7 sont-elles d'origine internationale ou supranationale, nationale ou les deux?
18. Y a-t-il des règles générales relatives à la protection des consommateurs applicables aux passagers en croisières ?
19. Y a-t-il des problèmes spécifiques en ce qui concerne la mise en œuvre des règles précitées? S'il vous plaît indiquer la jurisprudence, s'il y en a.

IV. Règles de travail relatives aux travailleurs de croisières

20. Votre système juridique contient des règles de travail spécifiques sur les travailleurs de croisières?
21. Ces dispositions, sont-elles d'origine internationale ou supranationale, nationale ou les deux?
22. Est-ce que votre système juridique contient des règles de travail générales applicables aux travailleurs de croisières?
23. Ces dispositions, sont-elles d'origine internationale ou supranationale, nationale ou les deux?
24. Votre système juridique contient des règles spécifiques sur les voyages combinés[2] ou, en absence de telles règles spécifiques, règles générales qui soient applicables aux voyages combinés?
25. Les dispositions renseignées dans votre réponse à la question 14, sont-elles d'origine internationale ou supranationale, nationale ou les deux?
26. Y a-t-il des problèmes spécifiques en ce qui concerne la mise en œuvre des règles précitées? S'il vous plaît indiquer la jurisprudence, le cas échéant.

V. Règles sur les ports qui sont importants en ce qui concerne les croisières

27. Est-ce que votre système juridique contient des règles juridiques particulières sur les ports qui son importants en ce qui concerne les croisières?
28. Ces dispositions, sont-elles d'origine internationale ou supranationale, nationale ou les deux?
29. Indiquez, si possible, le système de taxes et tarifs utilisé dans les ports aux croisières dans votre système juridique.

---

[2] Voyages combinés sont ceux qui comprennent non seulement la croisière mais aussi le trajet en avion vers et depuis le port de départ, les excursions terrestres choisies par le touriste lorsque le navire est dans le port, et, peut-être, une nuit d'hôtel (Álvaro Ariza Herrerías, "Análisis Jurídico-Económico del Transporte Marítimo en el Sector Turístico, Trabajo Fin de Máster", Universidad de Málaga, Facultad de Turismo, p. 13, http://riuma.uma.es/xmlui/bitstream/handle/10630/8729/TRABAJO%20FIN%20DE%20M%C3%81STER%20-%20def.pdf?sequence=1).

30. Y a-t-il des problèmes spécifiques en ce qui concerne la mise en œuvre des règles précitées? S'il vous plaît indiquer la jurisprudence, le cas échéant.

VI. Règles relatives à l'impact sur l'environnement des croisières

31. Est-ce que votre système juridique contient des règles juridiques spécifiques relatives à l'impact sur l'environnement des croisières?
32. Ces dispositions, sont-elles d'origine internationale ou supranationale, nationale ou les deux?
33. Y a-t-il des problèmes spécifiques en ce qui concerne la mise en œuvre des règles précitées? S'il vous plaît indiquer la jurisprudence, s'il y en a.

VII. Compétence et arbitrage

34. Est-ce que votre système juridique contient des règles juridiques spécifiques sur la compétence applicable aux croisières que vous n'avez pas renseignées dans vos réponses précédentes?
35. Si vous n'avez pas des règles juridiques particulières sur la compétence applicable aux croisières, est-ce que votre système juridique contient des règles juridiques générales sur la compétence relatives aux contrats internationaux qui soient applicables aux croisières?
36. Comment ces dispositions spécifiques ou générales relatives à la compétence protègent le passager en tant que consommateur? Expliquez les limitations imposées à l'autonomie des parties dans ce domaine, le cas échéant.
37. Les clauses de sélection du forum inclus dans les conditions générales du transport de passagers en croisières, ¿sont-elles reconnues comme un choix valable et efficace de l'accord de la cour?
38. Dans votre pays, les clauses d'arbitrage, sont-elles généralement inclus dans les conditions générales de transport de passagers en croisières?
39. Y a-t-il des problèmes spécifiques en ce qui concerne la mise en œuvre des règles précitées? S'il vous plaît indiquer la jurisprudence, s'il y en a.

VIII. Choix de la loi

40. Est-ce que votre système juridique contient des règles juridiques spécifiques sur le choix de la loi applicable aux croisières que vous n'avez pas renseigné dans vos réponses précédentes?
41. Si vous n'avez pas des règles juridiques spécifiques sur le choix de la loi applicable aux croisières, est-ce que votre système juridique possède des règles juridiques générales sur le choix de la loi relatives aux contrats internationaux qui soient applicables aux croisières?
42. Comment ces dispositions spécifiques ou générales relatives au choix de la loi protègent le passager en tant que consommateur?
43. Les clauses de choix de la loi inclus dans les conditions générales de transport de passagers en croisières, ¿sont-elles reconnues comme un choix valable et efficace? Expliquer les limitations imposées à l'autonomie des parties dans ce domaine, le cas échéant.
44. Y a-t-il des problèmes spécifiques en ce qui concerne la mise en œuvre des règles précitées? S'il vous plaît indiquer la jurisprudence, le cas échéant.

IX. Responsabilité

45. Est-ce que votre système juridique contient des règles juridiques spécifiques ou générales sur la responsabilité en ce qui concerne les croisières que vous n'avez pas renseigné dans les réponses précédentes?
46. Y a-t-il des problèmes spécifiques en ce qui concerne la mise en œuvre des règles précitées? S'il vous plaît indiquer la jurisprudence, le cas échéant.

X. Bourse d'études juridiques et la formation juridique

47. S'il vous plaît inclure une courte bibliographie des résultats en matière de droit international privé sur les croisières dans votre système juridique (énumérés par auteur dans un ordre alphabétique)
48. S'il vous plaît inclure une liste de la jurisprudence remarquable concernant les croisières (classées par dates dans un ordre chronologique).
49. Y a-t-il, dans votre pays (ou dans votre organisation), un programme de formation spécifique (dans les universités ou d'autres institutions) totalement ou partiellement consacré aux aspects juridiques des croisières?

Appendix: General Act on Private International Law

1. Last Minute Modification of the Uruguayan Legal System

On 17 November 2020 Uruguay adopted a new General Act on Private International Law—Act N° 19.920—(hereinafter, UGAPIL),[3] which entered into force on 16 March 2021 and repealed the Appendix of the Civil Code, dealt with throughout the General Report and the Uruguayan National Report in this book. The UGAPIL applies when there is no applicable international treaty (Article 1.1rst paragraph).

The following are the innovations that are relevant regarding the topics in this book.

2. International Contracts

2.1 General Rule on the Applicable Law

Under Article 45, the general rule is party autonomy, though only for "international" contracts, which are those where the parties have their habitual residence or establishment in different States or the contract has relevant objective relationships with more than one State. The contract cannot be "internationalized" by the mere will of the parties (Article 44). The will of both parties is required, excluding thus the validity of unilateral clauses "choosing" the applicable law by one party only.

[3] After a long process of negotiations, the UGAPIL was finally approved on November 17, 2020, published in the Official Newspaper N° 30.586 on December 16, 2020, into force since March 16, 2021. Accesible in Spanish at https://legislativo.parlamento.gub.uy/temporales/docu3891089075598.htm. There is no official English version.

C. Fresnedo de Aguirre (ed.), *Legal Aspects of Cruises*, Ius Comparatum - Global Studies in Comparative Law 56, https://doi.org/10.1007/978-3-030-83090-8

2.2 Special Rule on the Law Applicable to Consumer Contracts

Article 50 provides for a set of special rules regarding some contracts which, though international, are not governed by the previous provisions (Articles 45–49) but by this one. Among those we find contracts entered into in consumer relationships, like those between passengers and cruise lines or travel agencies. These contracts shall be governed by the law of the State where the goods are purchased or the services are used by the consumer; if the goods are purchased or the services used in more than one country or the above mentioned law cannot be determined for any other reason, those relationships are governed by the law of the consumer's domicile; regarding contracts entered into from a distance or those where the contract was preceded by specific offers or publicity at the consumers' domicile, the law of the consumers' domicile shall be applicable, as far as the consumer had consented in that State (Article 50.E).

2.3 Rules on Jurisdiction Regarding Contracts

The general rule on jurisdiction regarding contracts is party autonomy (Article 60, paragraph 1), but the contracts excluded from the possibility of choosing the applicable law in Article 50 are also excluded from the possibility of choosing jurisdiction (Article 60, paragraph 2). Consumer contracts are therefore excluded from the possibility of choosing jurisdiction by the parties.

Under Article 59.D, Uruguayan courts have jurisdiction regarding consumer relationships, when the consumer is the claimant, as far as the contract was made in Uruguay, or when the service was rendered or the good delivered within the jurisdiction.

This special solution is in addition to the general criteria in Article 57. Those criteria, attribute jurisdiction to the Uruguayan courts—under certain conditions—in the following situations: when the defendant's domicile or contractual domicile is within the jurisdiction; when the defendant has an establishment, agency, branch or any other kind of representation in Uruguayan territory, as far as the contract was made through it or it has intervened in the transaction/act that gives rise to the claim; when the issue that is the object of the claim is governed by Uruguayan law, under Uruguayan conflict-of-laws rules; in case of counterclaims, third party claims or third parties' intervention; and claims that are closely connected to another one with respect to which Uruguayan courts have jurisdiction. Article 57.G) admits *post litem* prorogation of jurisdiction in personal actions when the defendant accepts it.

Paragraph H) incorporates *forum necessitatis*, which is an innovation in Uruguayan PrIL. It requires that the following conditions are cumulatively fulfilled: that the entertainment by the Uruguayan court is necessary in order to prevent denial of justice; that it is impossible that the cause is adjudicated in another State or it is not reasonably possible to require that the claim is filed abroad; that the case has relevant links with Uruguay; that Uruguayan courts can guarantee due process and that the judgment to be issued can be enforced internationally.

3. Torts

3.1 Applicable Law

Regarding torts, the general rule is the *lex loci delicti* or the *lex loci damni*, at the claimant's option (Article 52.1). It can be said that it is a *favor laesi* solution. This solution is harmonic with the interpretation that Uruguayan courts have made of the former rules, stretching the *lex loci delicti* rule in some cases in order to allow the law of the place of the injury to apply. There are some statutory exceptions to the lex loci delicti or lex loci damni rule in the UGAPIL. Article 52.2 provides that "If the defendant and the claimant had their domicile in the same State, the law of that State should be applied."

Article 52.3 deals with a situation where the *lex loci delicti* rule cannot be applied: "If the fact that causes the injury occurs during navigation by air, sea, river or lake in an area which is not subject to the exclusive sovereignty of any State, it will be considered that it occurred in the State of the vessel's flag or of the plain's registry, without prejudice to what special rules may provide." This solution is based on Article 27 of the 1889 Montevideo Treaty on International Civil Law.

3.2 Jurisdiction

Regarding torts, the general criteria in Article 57, explained supra in this Appendix, apply.